James Halliday

Wine Atlas *of* Australia

James Halliday

Wine Atlas *of* Australia

UNIVERSITY OF CALIFORNIA PRESS

BERKELEY LOS ANGELES

Foreword

In the eight years since the forerunner of this book (*Wine Atlas of Australia and New Zealand*) was published, the Australian wine industry has changed beyond all recognition. The number of wineries has increased from 990 to over 2200; the national vineyards have increased from 98 500 hectares to over 164 000 hectares; wine production has risen from 737 to over 1500 million litres; dozens upon dozens of new grape varieties have come into commercial production (a total of over 80, and with more coming); and the number of officially registered wine regions (called Geographic Indications, or GIs for short) is now 56, with further GIs knocking on the door.

But the most dramatic change has been in the area of exports. In 1985 Australia imported more wine than it exported (measured in dollars), and its exports of $8.5 million didn't even register in international trade figures. Twenty years later, it was exporting 600 million litres worth $2.74 billion, in fourth place in world rankings, and closing fast on third-placed Spain.

This has led to a massive shift in the balance of wine trade from the Old World (or Western Europe) to the New World (chiefly Australia, New Zealand, South Africa, California, Chile and Argentina). In 1989 the Old World had 97 per cent of world exports; if you treat movements within the European Union as domestic trade (equivalent to state movements in Australia or the United States, for example) the Old World's share has now plunged to 69 per cent, with no sign yet of the trend lines flattening out.

By any measure, Australia ignited (and has sustained) this attack on Old World dominance, but its New World competitors are an increasingly important part of the mix, caring little whether they take market share from each other or from the Old World.

So far, at least, Australia has persuaded the wine consumers in its many overseas markets that, whether the price point is low or high, its wines over-deliver on quality compared to those of other countries.

Equally, if not more importantly, Australia produces an unequalled, rainbow-like, spectrum of wine styles.

'Wine style' in this context is used in the broadest possible sense, and it is here that this *Atlas* takes up the story. Style is determined by the grape variety (or varieties) chosen for the wine; by the climate in which they are grown, which in turn blends with the terroir (a concept discussed at some length in pages 1–7); and by the philosophy and techniques adopted by the winemaker in dealing with the grapes, thence the wine.

So it is that Australia is able to offer fine sparkling wine from Tasmania and the coolest parts of southern Victoria and the Adelaide Hills; elegant and piercingly pure Riesling from the Clare and Eden Valleys of South Australia, Great Southern of Western Australia, and Tasmania; unique unoaked long-lived Semillon from the Hunter Valley in New South Wales, and – more international – partially barrel-fermented Semillon Sauvignon Blanc blends from the Adelaide Hills and Margaret River; Chardonnay ranging from flinty, minerally Chablis-like wines from the coolest regions in southern Victoria and Tasmania moving through degrees of richness until the Montrachet-like wines of the best Margaret River producers; Pinot Noir from Tasmania, southern Victoria and (less consistently perhaps) the

[ABOVE] Chrismont Wines, King Valley, Victoria. [PREVIOUS] Seppelt Great Western Cellar, Grampians, Victoria. [OVERLEAF] Autumn in Lenswood, Adelaide Hills, South Australia.

Adelaide Hills, which is constantly and wrongly assumed to be inferior to that of New Zealand, Oregon and Burgundy; Shiraz in a magically enticing array of flavours, texture, weight, alcohol and tannins, with a startling ability to reflect the terroir from which it comes, ranging from the majestic power of the Barossa and Clare Valleys, and McLaren Vale in South Australia, to the equally majestic yet very different lusciousness of Central Victoria, with Heathcote in the vanguard; thence to the continental climates (cool nights, warm days) of the Great Southern, and the Central Ranges of New South Wales, where spice, pepper and liquorice start to come alongside the rich blackberry, plum, leather, dark chocolate and earth of the warmer, less continental climates; and finally to the coolest regions (other than Tasmania, simply too cool) where viognier fits seamlessly in a glove of intense black fruits, liquorice, black pepper and spice; Cabernet Sauvignon, while not quite such an inveterate and sophisticated traveller as Shiraz, flourishes in many places, none more than Coonawarra, with its Bordeaux climate replicate and – just to confuse things – a limestone-based soil similar to that of Burgundy and Champagne producing fluid, seamless, cassis, mulberry and blackcurrant wines; Great Southern's Cabernet Sauvignon with imposing dark berry fruit, great structure, but seldom rough or

tannic; the multi-faceted, extremely complex Cabernet of Margaret River, typically with some Merlot as a blend (or bed) mate; Langhorne Creek's supple, sotto voce wine in contrast to the masculine, sometimes macho, Cabernets of the Clare Valley, McLaren Vale and Barossa Valley (listed in descending order); the raw power and focus of Central Victoria contrasting with the finesse of regions such as the Yarra Valley. Finally, there are the unique, dazzlingly rich and complex fortified muscadelle (locally called Tokay) and Muscat (brown frontignac) of north-east Victoria, and the even richer and absolutely unique Para Liqueur of Seppelt in the Barossa Valley, kept in cask and released when it is 100 years old.

This breakneck gallop across Australia's wine scene leaves out many more varieties, regions and styles than it includes. The purpose of this *Atlas* is to give you a far more detailed insight, however constrained by the tyranny of word-length and space. The unifying thread is the sheer quality, in world standards, of the best marriages between variety, climate, terroir and technology. This *Atlas* very properly focuses on the first three legs, but do not for one moment believe that wine is made in the vineyard alone. A chef given the most perfect ingredients still has to create the dish which best expresses the quality of those ingredients; so it is with the winemaker.

The Wine Zones of Australia ❧

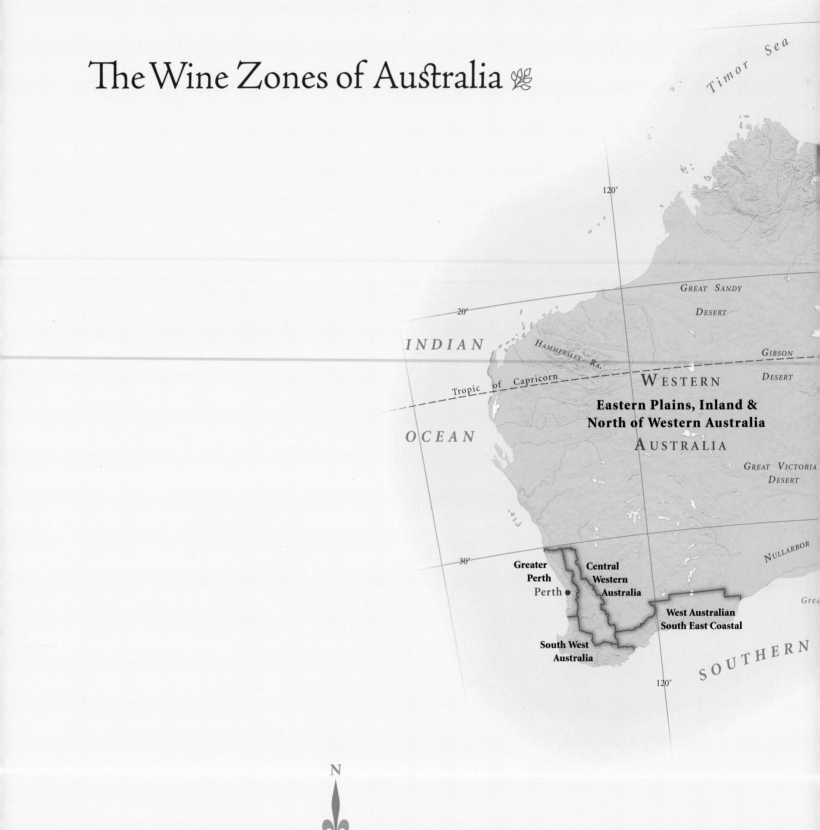

Timor Sea

INDIAN

OCEAN

GREAT SANDY

DESERT

HAMMERSLEY RA.

GIBSON

Tropic of Capricorn

WESTERN

DESERT

Eastern Plains, Inland & North of Western Australia

AUSTRALIA

GREAT VICTORIA

DESERT

120°

20°

30°

Greater Perth

Perth ●

Central Western Australia

NULLARBOR

West Australian South East Coastal

Gre

South West Australia

SOUTHERN

120°

N

0   500 km

Arafura Sea

●Darwin

Gulf of Carpentaria

Coral Sea

BARKLY TABLELAND

GREAT

NORTHERN

TERRITORY

Barrier

DIVIDING

Reef

QUEENSLAND

Tropic of Capricorn

McDONNELL RA.

ANAMI

ESERT

Simpson

Desert

RANGE

●Brisbane

Lake Eyre North

Far North

SOUTH AUSTRALIA

Lake Torrens

Northern
Slopes

Range

Northern Rivers

PLAIN

Western Plains

NEW

Lake Gairdner

SOUTH

Hunter
Valley

Darling

Central
Ranges

Mt Lofty
Ranges

ustralian Bight

The Peninsulas

WALES

Barossa

Lower
Murray

Big Rivers

Sydney

Tasman

OCEAN

Adelaide ●

North
West
Victoria

Southern

South Coast

Fleurieu

Murray R

NSW

A.C.T.

CANBERRA

Sea

**Limestone
Coast**

**Central
Victoria**

**North East
Victoria**

Dividing

**Western
Victoria**

● Melbourne

Gippsland

Great

**Port
Phillip**

VICTORIA

Bass Strait

TASMANIA

● Hobart

10°   140°   10°   150°   20°   30°   130°   40°   140°   40°   150°

Contents

Legend

Maps
● Winery with
   cellar door facilities

○ Winery without
   cellar door facilities

Locator Maps
▪ Wine region within state
▪ Wine subregion within region

Text
🍷 Winery with
   cellar door facilities

🚫 Winery with no
   cellar door facilities

🍴 Winery with restaurant

Note Where a winery is shown as having
a cellar door, this does not mean that
it is open every day, or even every
weekend. Before visiting, always check
that the cellar door will be open.

[above] Adelaide Hills in autumn,
South Australia.

Introduction ❧

While the following sections on climate, climate change, irrigation and terroir in the main discuss these topics separately, there are continuous cross-links, most obviously between climate and terroir.

The French do not speak of soil, but of 'terroir', one of those wonderful words which encapsulates many different things. In 1990 a French researcher, P. Laville, listed the components of terroir one by one, but did not disagree with the description given some years earlier by Bruno Prats, then the proprietor of Château Cos d'Estournel, in Bordeaux, which went thus:

'The very French notion of terroir looks at all the natural conditions which influence the biology of the vinestock and thus the composition of the grape itself. The terroir is the coming together of the climate, the soil and the landscape. It is the combination of an infinite number of factors: temperatures by night and by day, rainfall distribution, hours of sunlight, slope and drainage, to name but a few. All these factors react with each other to form, in each part of the vineyard, what French wine growers call a terroir.'

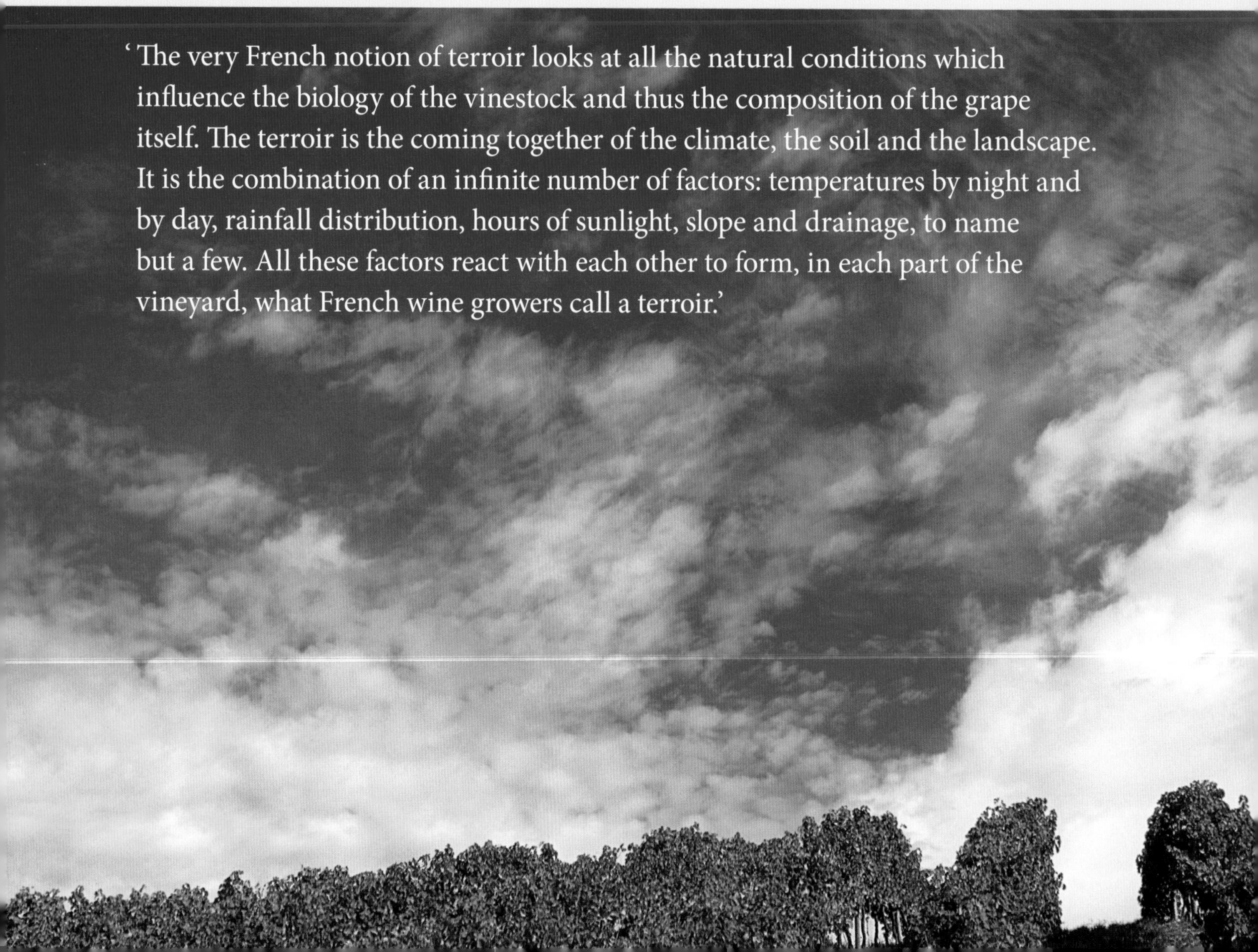

The two unspoken propositions are that each terroir, small or large, is unique and hence not duplicated anywhere else in the world; and that the terroir's soil, which Laville describes in terms of its geology and pedology (the basic physical and chemical characteristics of the soil, but also adding hydrology, or soil–water relations) is of paramount importance to its wines.

The New World, while consciously or unconsciously accepting all the various components of terroir as relevant to viticultural choice and practice, places primary importance on climate as the determinant of grape quality. Over the coming centuries, New and Old World views may coalesce. For the time being, terroir is of utmost importance to the Old World, for the financial and marketing reasons that terroir makes it impossible for New World wine-producing countries to duplicate the great wines of Bordeaux, Burgundy and so forth.

Conversely, the New World is currently on a helter-skelter search for new varieties and new regions, with no necessary link between the two. But the enduringly great wines of the New World of the future will only come from a precise correlation between terroir and variety, the latter coming from fully mature vines.

Climate

As a grapegrower and winemaker, I have come face to face with climate and with weather (the two are quite different, but more or less equally important) for 35 years. As a wine writer and author, I have had to try to come to grips with explaining the means of measuring climate for 25 years. But it is only in the last 15 years that I have come to some understanding of the precise ways that climate impacts on the way vines grow and the way they ripen their grapes.

My first mentor was Dr Richard Smart, arguably Australia's foremost consultant viticulturist, ironically recognised more internationally than he is domestically. The second was (and is) Dr John Gladstones, whose peerless work *Viticulture and Environment*[1] should be compulsory reading for anyone contemplating planting a vineyard, or trialling new varieties in an existing vineyard.

As a grapegrower, I quickly came to appreciate the difference between macro-climate (regional climate), meso-climate (site climate) and micro-climate (the climate within a grapevine canopy), the last a much-misused word. I wager that both Smart and Gladstones share the same misgivings as I do in ascribing data to any wine region, small or large, New World or Old World. So much depends on the topography of the region; if it is laser flat, the data may well be accepted at face value. But even there, the French notion of terroir comes into play: this encompasses both terrestrial and aerial factors. Thus Coonawarra has a homogenous climate, but vines growing on the terra rossa (red soil) produce vastly superior Cabernet Sauvignon and Shiraz than those on the sandy grey or (worse still) heavy black soils which, right or wrong, also fall within the official Coonawarra geographic area.

I have also come to appreciate just what an important factor wind is in determining the ability of a region, an individual site and/or a particular vintage to produce grapes of a predictable quality or style. The easiest example to comprehend (if one has visited it) is California's Salinas Valley, followed closely by California's Carneros. Both of these are relatively flat (Salinas particularly) and the winds blow virtually every day through the growing season for a predictable time each day and in an absolutely inevitable direction. They effectively turn what would be warm growing conditions in the absence of wind into cool conditions.

Now take an area like the Yarra Valley in Victoria, with multiple hills and sub-valleys facing variously every point of the compass. South-facing slopes are in principle the coolest, north-facing the warmest. The dominant wind, particularly when wind speed increases, is north or nor' west. In some circumstances a sheltered south-west-facing slope may creep up on an exposed north-east-facing slope in terms of ripening capacity.

Nonetheless, for Australia (exceptions such as Coonawarra to one side) climate is the most significant factor (outside vignerons' control) impinging on grape quality and wine style. As I have observed earlier, for the winemakers of France, terroir is of greater importance.

Indeed, if one looks at Bordeaux and Burgundy, France's two greatest wine districts, and then focuses the microscope on their principal subregions, climatic variation has little relevance and terroir becomes all-important in determining the character of the wines. For example, the macro-climate of Château Margaux is the same as that at Château Lafite Rothschild, in Pauillac 25 kilometres to the north, and abutting St Estèphe. Similarly, if you consider the Côte de Nuits, the macro-climate of Nuits-St-Georges at the southern end is identical to that of Gevrey-Chambertin at the northern end.

It is true that spring frosts and summer hailstorms may hit one spot and miss another, and no less true that one château or grower may be more successful than his neighbour in one year but not the next. Even more so is it true that climatic swings from one vintage to the next are of crucial importance in shaping the quality (and to a lesser degree the character) of the wines of each vintage.

There is a fundamental distinction between climate and weather, and by their very nature these swings or changes cannot usefully be individually recorded; one inevitably has to take long-term averages in

---

[1] Winetitles, Adelaide, 2002.

[OPPOSITE] ADELAIDE HILLS IN SUMMER, SOUTH AUSTRALIA.

ascribing temperature, rainfall, humidity, wind, frost and whatever other data one wishes to use in presenting an overall picture of the macro-climate of a region. So it is understandable that the French tend to take macro-climate for granted, and to look to the effect of terroir to explain and characterise their wines.

All of this in turn proceeds on patterns of classification and constraint which have been built up over many centuries, even if formal French codification did not start until the middle of the nineteenth century and only gained legislative teeth in the twentieth century.

How different the position of the New World. There are effectively no constraints on which grape varieties you can plant, how you prune them or how you use and blend the wine you make from the grapes. Almost every one of the regions discussed in this book is of much larger scale and of more diverse topography than most of the regions of France: Coonawarra, Padthaway, the Riverland in South Australia and Riverina in New South Wales are four topographic exceptions on the Australian front.

If this were not enough, the New World's experience in matching terroir, climate and grape varieties is typically less than a century old, and frequently less than 20 years old. Many classic Australian matches have appeared in this short time – Hunter Valley Semillon, Yarra Valley Pinot Noir, Coonawarra Cabernet Sauvignon, Clare Valley Riesling, Barossa Valley Shiraz, Margaret River Chardonnay – but each of these regions produces a multiplicity of other varieties, and none has an exclusivity on its core variety.

So with an impossibly complex matrix of grape variety, soil, aspect and topography within each Australasian region (and each subregion) we have had little option but to come back to climate as the most significant factor in determining wine character. In doing so the experts in Australasia and the United States have encountered great difficulties in providing climatic indices which are on the one hand sufficiently succinct to be understood and of practical use, and which on the other hand are meaningful and reasonably accurate.

Nonetheless, most attention has focussed on temperature as being the most important aspect of climate in determining wine style. In 1944 the distinguished American oenologists Amerine and Winkler introduced a classification system which traces its roots back to 1735, and thence to the mid-nineteenth century observation by de Candolle that there is little vegetative growth in the vine at temperatures below 10°C (50°F). Amerine and Winkler assumed a seven-month growing season (in Australasia, this means October to April) and calculated what is now called heat degree days, HDD, by taking the difference between 50°F (or 10°C) and the mean

[ABOVE] SANDALFORD, SWAN VALLEY, WESTERN AUSTRALIA.

temperature of the month, multiplying that difference by the number of days in the month, and then adding the resultant figures for each of the seven months. Having done that, they then divided California's wine regions into five, using 500 day degree increments (expressed in degrees Fahrenheit), starting with Region I (the coldest) at less than 2500 HDD.

The system has been refined, adapted and also roundly criticised, but remains the most widely used and understood system available for defining and comparing climates, and in the regional summaries which appear in boxes throughout this book I have given the HDD and Mean January Temperature (MJT) figures. (Dr Richard Smart and Peter Dry provided the first methodical and detailed statistics for Australia in *Viticulture* Volume 1. *Resources in Australia*.[2] As well as HDD and MJT, they covered annual rainfall, growing season rainfall, relative humidity and sunshine hours per day, among other measurements.

The major refinement has been that of Dr Gladstones. He introduced the concept of biologically effective heat degree days, principally by cutting off monthly average mean temperatures at 19°C, ignoring any excess in his calculations. This derives from the dual observations that the optimum temperature band for the ripening of grapes is between 20°C and 22°C, and for vine growth between 23°C and 25°C. The total span of 20–25°C is narrow enough, that for grape ripening is even less.

Quite obviously, there is no wine region in the world which precisely and regularly conforms to this ideal, but in John Gladstones' words,

'A general conclusion can be drawn. The narrower the range of variation about a given mean or average ripening temperature, the greater the grape flavour, aroma and pigmentation will be at a given time of ripening and sugar level. In cool climates the grapes will achieve full flavour ripeness even though sugar may remain low and acid high. In warm, sunny climates they will attain full flavour ripeness before sugar level and pH have become too high, and acid too low; or breakdown processes have started to predominate in the berries. In all cases the colour, flavour and desirable aroma qualities in the wine that can only come from fully ripe grapes are enhanced relative to potential alcoholic strength.'

Climate Change & the Greenhouse Effect

In recent years climate change has become a subject of worldwide attention, with the 2003 vintage in Europe adding spice to the sauce for wine lovers. (It was the hottest and earliest since 1929, 1893, 1540; pick the date you most like.) The first book I read on climate change was *Times of Feast, Times of Famine: A History of Climate Since the Year 1000* by Emmanuel Le Roy Ladurie, first published in Paris in 1967. It used as its databases three sources: the advance and retreat of the European glaciers;

[2] P. R. Dry and B. G. Coombe (eds), Australian Industrial Publishers, Adelaide, 1988, pp. 37–60.

the ring growths of California redwoods; and the starting dates of grape harvests recorded in French monasteries.

The first papers I read on the subject of global warming were those of Smart ('Climate Change and the New Zealand Wine Industry', 1989)[3] and Gladstones – the latter delivered in a lecture at the University of Western Australia in 1990. The most detailed and thought-provoking are chapters 25 and 26 in Gladstones' *Viticulture and Environment*.

Extreme and long-lasting changes in climate in the past 100 000 years produced environmental extremes far, far greater than those of the past thousand years or those predicted by the most passionate doomsayers of today – something I return to later. More recently, from the eighth century to the early fourteenth century, there was a prolonged warm period, with temperatures in Europe on average 1°C above those of the twentieth century.

Thereafter temperatures fluctuated wildly up and down. In 1540 the River Rhine stopped flowing in the heat and could be crossed by foot: even though the wine was was safer to drink (and presumably more enjoyable), it was cheaper than water. But between 1550 and 1830 there was a period known as 'The Little Ice Age'. Glaciers grew exponentially; the River Thames froze repeatedly; summer frosts killed the wheat crops across Europe causing widespread famine; between 1689 and 1693, Château Latour made no wine at all, and next to none in the three following years; and in 1709 the great freeze saw the temperature in Marseille drop to 17.5°C below zero, and many of the vineyards of France were destroyed and had to be replanted. Conditions then warmed until a final brief freeze from 1812 to 1820.

While there have been fluctuations since that time, they have been of a much lesser magnitude. Moreover, while there has been global warming since 1970, and while most of the predictions reported in the general press have been apocalyptic, attributing the warming to human activity, there is in fact much argument about both outcomes and causes.

It is a fascinating but very complex subject. Apart from greenhouse gas warming there are three influences on climatic warming and cooling: the Earth's orbit around the sun; sunspot activity; and volcanic eruptions.

The Milankovich model, mathematically analysing the Earth's orbital patterns, is generally accepted as explaining the causes of major swings in climate over the past million years (a blink of an eye in terms of the Earth's history). The model shows, first, that there are changes in the Earth's elliptical orbit around the sun varying over a 100 000-year cycle. This causes the heat received by the Earth to vary by up to 30 per cent in each year when the orbit is at its elliptical extreme, compared to the seven per cent for the present, more circular, orbit.

Next, there are pendulum-like swings in the tilt of the Earth's axis from the vertical of its plane of orbit around the sun, ranging between 21.8° and 24.4° (at present 23.4°) over a 40 000-year cycle, likewise affecting seasonal changes in temperature each year. The third is a wobble in the Earth's axis of spin, with a 22 000-year cycle, and this controls the timing of the equinoxes and solstices.

Thus the last ice age ended abruptly 12 000 years ago, with lowest temperatures on the equator 5°C cooler than today. The present interglacial period peaked 5000–7000 years ago, with equatorial temperatures 2°C warmer than today. Temperatures since then have fallen gradually but irregularly; thus it is not so long ago that the majority of climatologists, following the Milankovich model, were predicting the onset of another little ice age. However, since modern temperature measurements began in the mid nineteenth century, the eight warmest years on record have occurred since 1990.

The second major influence is sunspot activity, recorded regularly since 1600, more sketchily before then. The incidence varies in a 10–12-year cycle, but with longer-term fluctuations in peak intensities, which are more important. Thus the 'Maunder Minimum' of 1645–1715, when there was no recorded sunspot activity, corresponds well with one of the very cold periods of recent centuries. On the other hand, the warm eleventh to thirteenth centuries coincided with a prolonged period of intense sunspot activity, similar to that of the late twentieth century.

Finally, on the other side of the coin, is the role of volcanic dust circulating in the stratosphere, which cuts the amount of sunlight reaching the Earth's surface, and has a cooling effect.

So with future climatic warming – its extent, its duration and some of its causes – you pay your money and take your choice. Moreover, most experts agree the amount of warming will be greater for the northern hemisphere than for the southern. But on two related points, there is neither disagreement nor doubt.

First, chlorofluorocarbons (CFCs) are 100 per cent lethal in thinning the ozone layer and allowing a higher incidence of radiation to penetrate the atmosphere. Even here, however, the impact on grape composition and quality is uncertain, and not necessarily bad.[4]

The second is that carbon dioxide levels are on the march. They are 25 per cent in excess of pre-Industrial Revolution levels, but the present levels are projected to double by the end of this century. It is here that a number of paradoxes for viticulture and winemaking become apparent. Dr Gladstones points out that photosynthesis and growth by well-watered plants can be limited by any or all of three main environmental factors: temperature, light, and atmospheric carbon dioxide concentration.

---

[3] R. E. Smart, 'Climate change and the N.Z. wine industry. Prospects for the third millenium'. *Proc. Seminar Innovations in Viticulture and Oenology*, Masterton, N.Z. 1988. N.Z. Soc. for Viticulture and Oenology. pp. 25–36.

[4] Schultz, 'Climate change and viticulture: A European perspective on climatology, carbon dioxide and UV-B effects', *Australian Journal of Grape and Wine Research*, Vol. 6, No. 1, 2000.

Through a somewhat convoluted pathway, the optimum flavour of ripe grapes involves enzyme accumulation as well as simple sugar accumulation. Research with other fruits, both in glasshouses and outside, strongly suggests that extra carbon dioxide can raise the temperature at which sugar remains in surplus under any given canopy light regime. This surplus is the key to enzyme activity. Thus increased carbon dioxide in the atmosphere would not only raise the upper limit of optimum temperatures to produce optimum fruit quality, but may also have the potential to increase the absolute intensity of fruit flavour and colour at these higher optima.

The wholly unexpected consequence for the southern hemisphere, argues Dr Gladstones, is that global warming at the lower end of the scale (1°C) by the middle of the century would favour a shift to warmer climates; it is only if the forecasts of warming of 1.8°C to 4.5°C were to eventuate that there would be a shift of commercially optimum areas towards cooler-climate regions or a change in the varieties grown.

The bottom line of all this is no less unexpected: global warming may not be bad news for the southern hemisphere wine regions. First, the increased carbon dioxide levels may result in better wines. Second, there is no barrier, formal or informal, to changing the varietal mix planted in New World vineyards in response to clearly established changes in climate. How different the position is for France, with its Appellation Contrôlée System prescribing in absolute terms what varieties can be planted in certain areas and what can't. It is nigh on certain that any change to these French regulations will take place long after the horse has bolted.

Irrigation: Good or Bad?

Primarily in the Old World (centred on France), but also to a degree in the New World, irrigation is a dirty word in winegrowing. If you choose to irrigate your vines, the implication is that you are concerned only to increase yield, and at the expense of quality. Opponents of irrigation argue that if the rainfall occurs at the right time of year, the soil has the appropriate moisture-holding capacity and the vines are mature, then the amount of rainfall should be sufficient to allow the vine to ripen its grapes to the appropriate degree and the use of irrigation is needless and inappropriate.

Even at this point, however, there is a major caveat. There are drought years, there are wet years; there are cool years, there are hot years; the annual rainfall, and the growing season rainfall, even if of the right total amount, may come at the right time or the wrong time.

New World or Old, there is little the vignerons can do in years of consistently excessive rainfall, particularly given that such years are likely to be cooler rather than warmer. But in the dry years – axiomatically likely to be the hot years – there is one element of climate which can be controlled by the vigneron: the amount and timing of water made available to the vine.

And this needn't (and usually isn't) made available in the indiscriminate way of the heavens opening and the rain falling equally over a few square metres – or a few thousand or more square metres. Modern irrigation methods are precisely calibrated and targeted: regulated deficit irrigation (RDI) means that only enough water is applied to keep the vine functioning without harmful stress; partial root drying (PRD) means that by alternating water application between one side of the vine and the other, the vine can be tricked into believing it should focus its energy on ripening the grapes rather than growing more leaves. Both of these techniques are used not to increase yield but quality, by avoiding excessive stress on the vine leading to ripening achieved simply by dehydration and raisining.

As I have already noted, climate change (warming) is having – and is projected to continue to have – a greater impact on the northern hemisphere than the southern. Thoroughly alarmed, the European Union has increased the areas in which irrigation of vines is permitted, and is experimenting (using some Australian technology) in methods of establishing the levels to which irrigation can be used without impacting on quality. The EU – and France – is nothing if not pragmatic.

All of this said, irrigation can be and is used simply to increase yield, as is the case in the Riverina and Riverland regions. Here hot, low-humidity conditions, free-draining sandy soils and a flat landscape all allow highly mechanised, highly efficient grapegrowing. Costs (and hence prices) are low, quality is reliable, and in cool years (such as 2002) the wines can be remarkably good.

Soil and Terroir

Terroir expresses the coming together of climate, soil and landscape, thereby incorporating the influences of temperature, rainfall, sunlight; of soil depth, structure, pH, minerals and water-retention capacity; of slope, aspect and drainage. To the French in particular, terroir assumes almost mystical importance. Says the late Peter Sichel, former president of the Grand Crus de Bordeaux, 'Terroir determines the character of a wine, man its quality'.

It lies at the heart of the French appellation system, built up by a thousand years of practical experience and observation, which has led to a most precise and detailed delineation of quality, to the identification of a limited number of grape varieties considered to be especially suited to the

terroir (and the climate) in a particular area, and to the exclusion by force of law of all others. It has led to the prescription of pruning methods, the specification of maximum yields (but with such a dose of pragmatism as to render the restraints largely meaningless) and of minimum alcoholic strengths (again largely emasculated by the rampant use of chaptalisation – the addition of sugar to the ferme nting wine).

History shows that the vineyards of France were originally planted by default, in terroir which was too deficient to support other forms of horticulture or farming. In Bordeaux there is a saying 'If these soils were not the best in the world, they would be the worst'. But that in no way diminishes the validity of the subsequent matching of grape and soil, nor of the identification of those microscopic dots on the face of the earth which produce wines of the ineffable majesty of Château Pétrus (Bordeaux), Romanée-Conti and Le Montrachet (Burgundy) and their ilk.

Australian vignerons may be denied the extraordinary prestige and marketing power of the top French producers, but there are compensations: we are free of the rigidity and constraints of the appellation system, and can (and do) prove that fine wine can be made in a far wider range of circumstances than the French would ever admit.

It may well be that ignorance was bliss, but the average Australian vigneron of the recent past made little attempt to correlate specific soil types with particular grape varieties and, outside of certain broad parameters, made almost no attempt to link soil type and quality. (Such linkage as occurs is between climate, variety and quality.) Those broad parameters define an ideal soil as a sandy loam, preferably interspersed with gravel or small, fragmented rock. It should be deep, free draining and of low to moderate fertility. There should be no mineral element deficiencies and, while free draining, should have sufficient water-holding capacity to supply just enough moisture to the vines to prevent premature senescence and defoliation.

Conversely, the most frequently encountered problems in vineyards' soils are excess clay and excess acidity. Heavy clay drains poorly, holding too much water after rain or irrigation, and is frequently associated with dense and hard subsoils that roots cannot penetrate. Excessively acid subsoils are far more widespread in Australia than is commonly realised, and have a significant adverse impact on vine health and vigour. The vine's roots cannot tolerate the aluminium toxicity which is associated with high acidity (low pH), which forces them to remain in the shallow topsoils (usually less acid), making the vine much more susceptible to drought, even though the local rainfall may in theory appear adequate.

Correct moisture supply is all-important, and apart from anchorage and nutrients, is the principal function of soil in determining growth.

During early shoot growth up until flowering (early November to late December, depending on region and variety) vines should be well supplied with moisture. By the time the fruit starts to ripen (January to February) available water should tail off, causing vegetative growth to stabilise, and the vine to focus its attention on ripening the grapes by sugar accumulation. (The photosynthetic activity of the vine's leaves causes carbohydrates stored in the system to be converted to sugar in the grapes.)

Another problem for Australian winemakers is that a large proportion of grapes are grown by farmers who sell to the winemaker. That winemaker may have never visited the vineyard and thus lacks any intimate knowledge of variation in vine growth within its confines. By contrast, the French winemaker will typically know every vine, every tiny variation in soil. Moreover, that observation will have been repeated over many centuries and handed down through the generations, whereas in Australia experience in winemaking is typically confined to one or two generations. But such experience does exist in the small estate, and is very probably one of the reasons why the small Australian winery can produce top-quality wine to rank with the best the big winery can produce.

All observers are agreed that the future of Australian winemaking lies in the vineyard, and, as a consequence, attitudes and practices are changing significantly. Cutting-edge technology is being used: airborne sensing via electromagnetic radiation (EMR) directed at the soil, the EMR device measuring the amount of energy reflected back. Together the radio wave emissions, radar, and laser-imaging radar and near-infrared radiation data collected by the EMR device can provide detailed images of the soil structure (and vine growth and cropping levels) on areas of 100 metres by 100 metres.

The changes in attitude are also epitomised by the 'distinguished site' concept devised and promoted by Brian Croser. This can be applied both to existing vineyards and (equally importantly) to evaluating sites and soil suitability for intended plantings. The soil may be physically examined by excavation on a grid pattern as small as 5 metres. All of a sudden, a large company can acquire intimate knowledge of its plantings; Wynns Coonawarra Estate is one example of a large producer using these techniques to selectively harvest the crop and to make replanting decisions.

To summarise, the regulated supply of moisture – neither too much nor too little, made available at the right times – is crucial for quality grapes. If this can be achieved naturally, through the soil's moisture retention, so much the better. In France, it is provided by the alluvial gravel and clay mix of Bordeaux, and the limestone marl (a mix of limestone and

[ABOVE] IRRIGATION FROM FARM DAMS IS NECESSARY IN MANY VINEYARDS.

clay) of Burgundy. But in both Australia and France, identification of the best terroir (in the broadest sense of that term) is (or was) of paramount importance. In France, the search concluded centuries ago; in Australia, it has only just begun.

Geographic Indications: Appellation by Any Other Name

In December 1993 Australia took the last step in completing a statutory framework governing the labelling of wine in a manner consistent with the laws of the European Union, albeit with none of the prescriptive provisions governing viticultural and winemaking practices. It was a journey which began in 1963, when each of the states passed similar (though not identical) legislation under their respective Pure Foods Acts. The 1993 regulations covered myriad matters, ranging from wine additives (what is not specifically permitted is ipso facto illegal) to label claims concerning vintage, variety and region.

I will not follow the changes which have occurred over the past 30 years except to say that the laws are now federal, and effectively contained in the Commonwealth Food Standards Code, in the *Australian Wine and Brandy Corporation Act* or in regulations proclaimed under that act.

Moreover, the Australian wine regulations have been brought into line with European law. The cornerstone is what might be called the 85 per cent rule: if a label claims a single vintage, a single region and/or a single variety, 85 per cent of the wine must be from that vintage, region and/or variety. If more than one variety or region is specified, they must be listed in descending order of importance – but with some particularly complicated laws concerning varietal blends which I will pass by here. Legislative changes at the end of the 1980s instigated and funded by Australia's winemakers put in place an effective policing of all label claims, the so-called Label Integrity Programme. Briefly, this involves both specific and wide-ranging audit programs which really do guarantee truth in labelling.

However, there were some gaps, and some remain. The major continuing gap is, if you will, a sin of omission, and a deliberate one at that: winemakers are not obliged to make any claim about vintage (witness casks, which rarely specify the vintage), variety or region, unless they feel so inclined.

The gap occurs because many Australian wineries, and virtually all the larger ones, purchase or grow grapes in many regions, not just the region in which the winery is situated. If nothing is said on the label, the unwary may well assume the wine comes from the home region.

[ABOVE] Shadowfax, Geelong, Victoria.

Until October 1994 there was an additional problem: there was no mechanism for determining, nor any regulation of, regional boundaries. However, the *Australian Wine and Brandy Corporation Act* (and regulations gazetted under it) has now put that mechanism into place.

There is now a hierarchy of regional descriptions. The broadest is South Eastern Australia, which takes in the whole of New South Wales, Victoria and Tasmania, and those sectors of Queensland and South Australia in which grapes are (or may conceivably in the future) be grown.

Next come individual states, descriptions which need no explanation. Each state is then divided into zones; securing agreement on the names and boundaries of the zones (through the State Viticulture Associations) proved to be far more difficult than anyone had imagined, but was completed in 1996. The zones appear on the map on pages xiii–ix; the only anomalies are the Adelaide Super Zone, which encompasses the Mount Lofty Ranges, Fleurieu and Barossa Zones of South Australia and the Murray Darling Zone, which straddles New South Wales and Victoria. The regulations provide that a zone is simply an area of land, without any particular qualifying attributes.

Each zone can then be subdivided into regions, and each region into subregions. A region must be a single tract of land, comprising at least five independently owned wine grape vineyards of at least 5 hectares each, and usually producing at least 500 tonnes of wine grapes in a year. A region is required to be *measurably* discrete from adjoining regions and have *measurable* homogeneity in grape-growing attributes over its area.

A subregion must also be a single tract of land, comprising at least five independently owned wine grape vineyards of at least 5 hectares each, and usually producing at least 500 tonnes of wine grapes annually. However, a subregion is required to be *substantially* discrete within the region and have *substantial* homogeneity in grape-growing attributes over the area. As is obvious, the legislation is vague, and the difference between a region and a subregion of extreme subtlety.

A minor and little-known anomaly is that a region can extend across zonal boundaries. Thus the Peel region of Western Australia lies partly in the Greater Perth Zone and partly in the Central Western Australia Zone; and the Southern Flinders Ranges region of South Australia is mainly in the Far North Zone, its southern extremity extending into the Mount Lofty Ranges Zone. Indeed, close inspection of the state maps showing zones and regions will reveal a number of other minor instances of overlap.

All these zones, regions and subregions are called Geographic Indications, and the process of determination and ultimate registration of each Geographic Indication in the Register of Protected Names is the responsibility of the Geographical Indications Committee constituted under Sections 40N to 40Z of the *AW&BC Act*. Ugly bureaucratic terminology, much of it, and the procedures were and are inevitably tortuous and slow.

First, the application for registration (and the detailed supporting material) must come from the region's vignerons. This predicates the will, the ability and the mutual agreement of those vignerons; there have been prolonged internal disagreements about both names and boundary lines which have delayed applications. In other instances, no one has been prepared to undertake the unpaid work which is involved in preparing an application. Moreover, if regional boundaries abut, there has to be inter-regional agreement, as the Committee has decided that there cannot be regional overlap of the kind one finds under comparable legislation in the United States.

Then the Committee has to determine whether the application meets the statutory criteria; if it is so satisfied, it will publish an interim determination in the *Government Gazette*. It must then consider any objections, and, having done so, publish its final determination. However, that determination can be challenged by anyone with a demonstrable interest and who is not satisfied with it; the appeal is to the Administrative Appeals Tribunal, with the possibility of further appeal to the High Court.

The six-year battle over the boundaries of Coonawarra, costing many millions of dollars in legal and experts' fees, showed just how drawn out the process can be. Moreover, the outcome was neither advocated nor anticipated by any of the initial protagonists, the ultimately decided boundaries being wider than anyone imagined, yet still having illogical sections at various points along the way.

As the number of Australian wineries continues to increase, and their geographic spread likewise, the process of mapping will continue. The one limiting factor is the absence of any power of the Geographic Indications Committee to change either the name or boundaries of any registered Geographic Indication, presumably an oversight in drafting the regulations.

The process has been, and will continue to be, tortuous and bureaucratic, but this in no way diminishes its importance for the future.

Australia's success in storming the export markets of the world has, for better or worse, been primarily founded on cheap and cheerful, sunshine in a bottle, wines. From Jacob's Creek to yellowtail, from the UK to Japan to the United States, it has been a continuous story of success. These wines will continue to be the foot soldiers defending our market share. But over 95 per cent of the individual wines made in Australia have a specific regional base, and the industry has realised the next phase of its development hinges on taking its high quality, regional wines on to centre stage.

The primary focus of this *Atlas* is on those regions, their leading wine producers, and their wines. I hope it will assist you in finding your way around the vast viticultural canvas of this lucky country.

South Australia

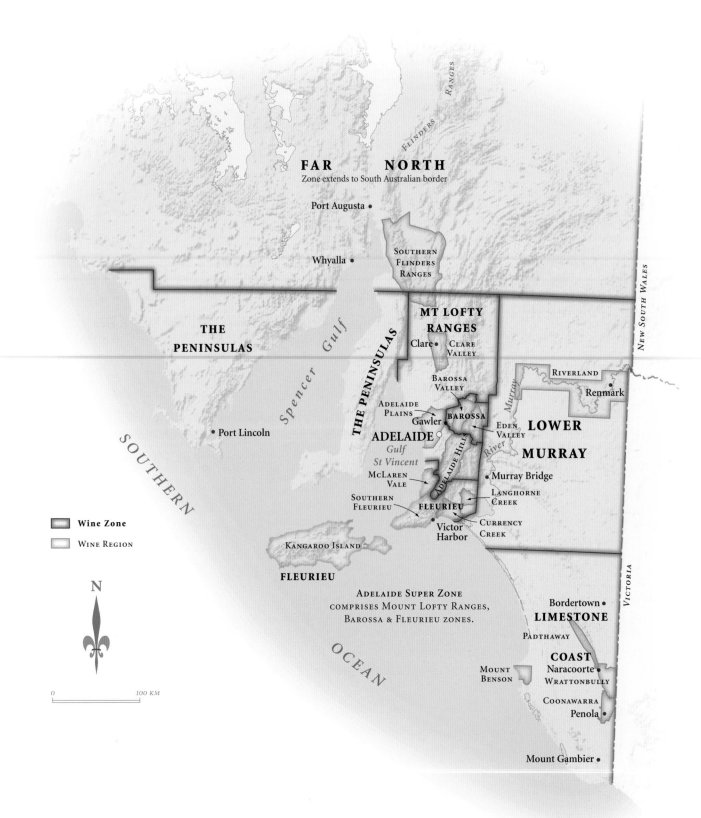

FAR NORTH
Zone extends to South Australian border

Port Augusta •

Whyalla •

SOUTHERN
FLINDERS
RANGES

FLINDERS RANGES

THE
PENINSULAS

THE PENINSULAS

MT LOFTY
RANGES
Clare • • CLARE
VALLEY

BAROSSA
VALLEY

ADELAIDE
PLAINS
Gawler • BAROSSA

ADELAIDE
Gulf
St Vincent

McLAREN
VALE

SOUTHERN
FLEURIEU

FLEURIEU

Victor
Harbor

RIVERLAND

Renmark •

EDEN
VALLEY

LOWER

MURRAY

• Murray Bridge

LANGHORNE
CREEK

CURRENCY
CREEK

NEW SOUTH WALES

VICTORIA

• Port Lincoln

Kangaroo Island

FLEURIEU

Wine Zone

WINE REGION

N

0   100 KM

ADELAIDE SUPER ZONE
COMPRISES MOUNT LOFTY RANGES,
BAROSSA & FLEURIEU ZONES.

SOUTHERN

OCEAN

Bordertown •

LIMESTONE

PADTHAWAY

MOUNT
BENSON

COAST
Naracoorte •
WRATTONBULLY

COONAWARRA
Penola •

Mount Gambier •

Introduction ❧

Victoria may have more wineries and regions, New South Wales more zones, and Western Australia may have the largest single zone, but South Australia still rightly calls itself the wine state. It has 42 per cent of the nation's vineyards, is responsible for 46 per cent of the annual crush, makes more than 50 per cent of the annual wine output (it is a nett buyer of grapes and bulk wine from the other states), and is headquarters for five of the six largest wine groups in Australia.

It was not always thus: in 1889, at the height of Victoria's production (before the onset of phylloxera), South Australia produced 2.29 million litres compared to Victoria's 7.1 million litres. Federation (which removed state duties) and the progressive opening of the Riverland areas along the Murray River led to an all-time high share of 80 per cent by South Australia in 1946. By the 1980s South Australia's contribution to the national make varied between 58 per cent and 65 per cent, according to the vagaries of vintage.

In 1991 it was responsible for 51 per cent of the crush, so it might seem there has been little change. In fact, in that year Australia made 394 million litres of wine; in 2004 the total was 1432 million litres. The size of the cake has grown exponentially, South Australia's production with it.

With the exception of the Far North Zone (and its single region, the Southern Flinders Ranges), all the viticultural activity huddles in the extreme south-eastern corner of the state. This may suggest a degree of homogeneity in varietal choice and wine style, when nothing could be further from the truth.

Altitude, latitude and land forms interact with, and in some instances determine, regional and/or site specific climate; widely different soil types then join to help create terroir. So it is that fine sparkling wines are made in the cooler parts of the Adelaide Hills, less than an hour's drive from the searingly hot Adelaide Plains, and only a little further from the home of Australia's unique, unctuously rich, almost treacly Para Liqueur Vintage Tawny, the 100-year-old fortified wine first released when it has reached its centenary birthday.

[PREVIOUS] NEPENTHE VINEYARDS, ADELAIDE HILLS. [ABOVE] COONAWARRA IN SUMMER. [BELOW] NEPENTHE VINEYARDS, ADELAIDE HILLS.

Adelaide Super Zone ❧

The Adelaide Super Zone exists on paper to encompass the Mount Lofty Ranges, Fleurieu and Barossa Zones. It enables the makers of blended wines from any of the regions (or zones) within its boundary to use a single geographic indication: Adelaide. In reality, this is not much used on wine labels; in more concrete terms it facilitates the grouping together of all South Australia's important fine-wine regions other than those of the Limestone Coast.

Nor, as the Mount Lofty Ranges Zone amply demonstrates, is there any requirement of climatic or geographic homogeneity. The Adelaide Plains is unambiguously hot and even more obviously laser-flat, with no stone buildings or charming towns, just light industrial factories on its perimeter.

The Adelaide Hills vineyards are a bare 25 minutes' drive from the Adelaide CBD, with hills and valleys criss-crossing in all directions, offering ever-changing vistas, the vivid display of yellow, gold and red deciduous trees in autumn pointing to a very cool climate with ample rainfall.

It is true the main geological structure of the Mount Lofty Ranges extends to the Clare Valley region, but the feel and atmosphere of the Adelaide Hills and the Clare Valley respectively are as different as chalk and cheese. The premier varieties of the Adelaide Hills are Sauvignon Blanc, Chardonnay and Pinot Noir (the latter two also used for fine sparkling wine); the Clare Valley's trio is Riesling, Shiraz and Cabernet Sauvignon.

But, as always, wineries of note can and do fall outside regional nets, and so it is here.

[OPPOSITE] PENFOLDS MAGILL ESTATE.

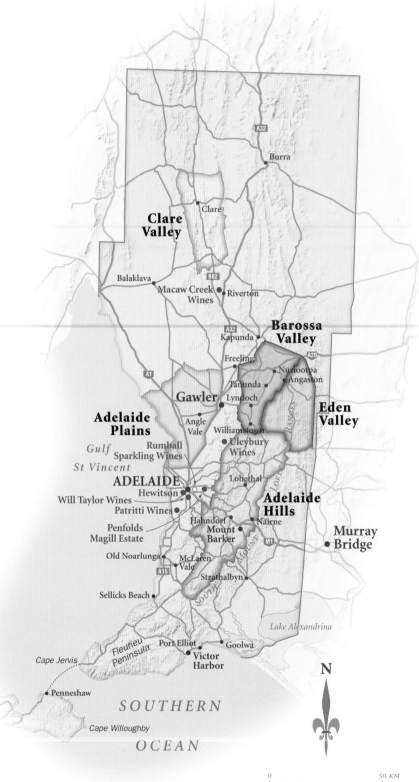

Wineries of the Adelaide Super Zone

Hewitson Est. 1996

The Old Dairy Cold Stores,
66 London Rd, Mile End 5031
www.hewitson.com.au

⚲ exports to UK, US

Dean Hewitson was a Petaluma winemaker for ten years, and during that time managed to do three vintages in France and one in Oregon as well as undertaking his Masters at UC Davis, California. The Hewitson wines are immaculately made from a technical viewpoint, but the exceptional quality of the wines is founded on old, low-yielding vines. He has secured long-term contracts for 30-year-old Riesling from the Eden Valley, 70-year-old Shiraz from McLaren Vale, 145-year-old Mourvèdre at Rowland Flat, and 60-year-old Shiraz and Grenache at Tanunda.

Signature wine: Old Garden Mourvèdre

Journeys End Vineyards

Est. 2001

248 Flinders St, Adelaide 5000 (postal)
www.journeysendvineyards.com.au

⚲ exports to UK, US

A highly successful business in the 'virtual winery' category which, while focused on McLaren Vale Shiraz, also has contracts for other varieties in the Adelaide Hills and Langhorne Creek. The very impressive Shiraz comes in four levels, and, for good measure, uses five different clones of Shiraz to amplify the complexity which comes from having contract grapegrowers in many different parts of McLaren Vale, drawing on contract winemaker Ben Riggs' contacts in the region, not to mention his considerable winemaking skills.

Signature wine: Arrival Shiraz

Macaw Creek Wines Est. 1992

Macaw Creek Rd, Riverton 5412
www.macawcreekwines.com.au

⚲ exports to US

The property on which Macaw Creek Wines is established has been owned by the Hooper family since the 1850s, but development of the estate vineyards did not begin until 1995; 10 ha have been planted since that time, with a further 20 ha planted in the winter/spring of 1999. Rodney and Miriam Hooper established the Macaw Creek brand previously (in 1992) with wines made from grapes from other regions, including the Preservative Free Yoolang Cabernet Shiraz. Rodney Hooper is a highly qualified and skilled winemaker with experience in many parts of Australia and in Germany, France and the US.

Signature wine: Yoolang Preservative Free Shiraz

Penfolds Magill Estate Est. 1844

78 Penfold Rd, Magill 5072
www.penfolds.com.au

⚲ ⊞ exports to UK, US

The birthplace of Penfolds, established by Dr Christopher Rawson Penfold in 1844, his house still part of the immaculately maintained property. It includes 6 ha of precious Shiraz used to make Magill Estate; the original and subsequent winery buildings, most still in operation or in museum condition; the Penfolds corporate headquarters; and the much-acclaimed Magill Restaurant, with panoramic views back to the city, a great wine list and fine dining. All this a 20-minute drive from Adelaide's CBD.

Signature wine: Magill Estate Shiraz

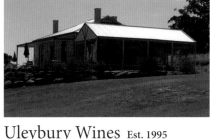

Uleybury Wines Est. 1995

Uley Rd, Uleybury 5114
www.uleybury.com

⚲ ⊞

The Pipicella family – headed by Italian-born Tony – has established nearly 45 ha of vineyard near the township of One Tree Hill in the Mount Lofty Ranges. Ten varieties have been planted, with more planned. Daughter Natalie Pipicella, who has completed the wine marketing course at the University of South Australia, was responsible for overseeing the design of labels, the promotion and advertising, and the creation of the website. The wines are made by Tony Pipicella, who seems able to invest them with great texture and mouthfeel. A cellar door opened in June 2002; an on-site winery followed in 2003.

Signature wine: AP Reserve Sangiovese

Will Taylor Wines Est. 1997

1B Victoria Ave, Unley Park 5061
suzanne@willtaylor.com.au

⚲ exports to US

Will Taylor (a partner in the leading Adelaide law firm Finlaysons, specialising in wine law) has established a classic negociant wine business, having wines contract-made to his specification. Moreover, he chooses what he considers to be the best regions across South East Australia for each variety, and his judgment is impeccable. Most of the high-quality wine is sold to restaurants, with small volumes sold to a select group of fine wine stores and mail order.

Signature wine: Clare Valley Riesling

Barossa Zone

Barossa Valley ❧

In the new millennium Australia prides itself as a multicultural society, yet by the 1850s the Barossa Valley was that and more. On the one hand came the British gentry, led by George Fife Angas (who gave his name to Angaston), Joseph Gilbert (Pewsey Vale, 1847), Samuel Smith (founder of Yalumba in 1849) and William Salter (Saltram, 1859). On the other side were the far more numerous and usually less wealthy Lutheran emigrants from Prussia, who left en masse in protest against a new Reformed Church prayer book proclaimed by Kaiser Friedrich Wilhelm III. These pioneers included Johann Gramp (1847), Joseph Seppelt (1851) and William Jacob (1854). Today family winemaker names include Basedow, Dutschke, Glaetzer, Jenke, Kaesler, Kalleske, Kies, Kurtz, Lehmann, Liebich, Roehr, Schilde and Schubert, among countless others content to grow and sell grapes.

The two cultural strands built in bluestone designed to stand for centuries, and went about building enterprises, small and large, for their descendants to inherit. The typical Barossa–Deutsch grapegrower would work six days a week from dawn to dusk, every week of the year. The Lutheran faith was (and is) fundamental, attendance at church on Sunday mandatory. Drought, floods and bushfires only strengthened their mutual resolve, more often than not expressed in the German dialect which persisted as a preferred spoken language until well into the twentieth century.

By the end of the nineteenth century a pattern had been established which was to continue until the middle of the next century. Shiraz, Grenache and Mataro (Mourvèdre) accounted for 70 per cent of total plantings, Pedro Ximenez and Frontignac another ten per cent or so. Most of these were used in the production of various forms of port and sherry, much destined for the UK market. A lesser – though significant – amount of full-bodied dry red wine was made, built around Shiraz.

One reminder of those days is the annual release of Seppelt's 100 Year Old Para Liqueur, the first in 1978 (of the 1878 vintage). In that year Benno Seppelt laid down a puncheon of his very best port, and followed up every year thereafter. Seppelt still has (much diminished) quantities of all of the nineteenth-century Paras (post release) and significant amounts of future annual releases. It is a true vintage wine, only topped up (by moving to smaller barrels) with the same wine, and is unrivalled (even by Madeiras of the same age) in its explosively luscious richness, intensity and complexity.

The Barossa Valley now has sixth-generation winegrowing families and blocks of vines over 150 years old. It has undergone periods of rapid expansion and painful contraction; seen second- and third-generation vignerons interned in the First World War and Kaiser Stuhl renamed Mount Kitchener; and seen wine fashion push varietal plantings first one way and then another.

There were periods of trouble in 1860 to 1880 (over-production) and in the early 1930s (the Great Depression), yet the Barossa's nadir came in the 1970s, when its very identity seemed threatened. The massive swing in popular tastes from red to white table wines, the remorseless contraction of the fortified wine market, the sale of many family-owned businesses to multinationals, the ignominy of the state-funded Vine Pull Scheme (a largely ineffective attempt to remove ancient low-yielding vines, then unwanted, now priceless), and the emergence of the new and trendy cool-climate wine regions all suggested the Valley was nearing its use-by date. It not only survived, but has emerged stronger than ever.

Since 1950 fortified winemaking has shrunk to a small volume of high-quality tawny style (no longer called port) and an even smaller amount of vintage style. The century-old plantings of Grenache and Mourvèdre, once solely used for fortified wine, are now an important part of the red table wine matrix. More than 75 per cent of the area planted (8800 hectares) is of red grapes, and the rate of planting reds exceeds that of white varieties, so there will be little change over the next decade or so.

A constant has been the scenery, the valley floor widening and narrowing, but only flat in small parts. Age-old eucalypts cover hillsides, occasionally standing sentry in the middle of a vineyard. Gnarled old vines run in erratic rows, younger plantings more military in their precision. In winter yellow soursobs carpet the rows between the bare vines; in summer the vines provide a verdant green contrast to golden paddocks; sunset suffuses the valley in a warm glow, turning to purple as the sun sets.

The Barossa Valley of today is a bustling place, full of confidence about its future, its history and culture proudly displayed wherever you look. Small high-quality wineries mix easily with the industry giants, all of which except Hardys are headquartered here. Excellent restaurants abound, and the accommodation ranges from luxurious hotel to micro-sized bed-and-breakfast operations out of century-plus stone houses. Unlike (say) the Napa Valley, traffic into and out of the Barossa is not a problem, even at weekends. Small wonder it is a Mecca for tourists of all kinds.

[OPPOSITE, BELOW & OVERLEAF] BAROSSA VALLEY.

Truro

Kalleske

Stockwell

HWY

STURT

Wolf Blass

Tim Smith
Wines

Gibson
The Willows Vineyard

Greenock

HWY

STURT

Nuriootpa

Kassebaum Wines

Schubert Estate

Elderton

A20

Gnadenfrei Estate

Torbreck
Vintners

Penfolds

Kaesler
Wines

Seppelt

Penrice

Barossa Cottage Wines

Seppeltsfield

Heritage
Wines

Viking
Wines

Two Hands Wines

Dorrien

Hamilton's
Ewell Vineyards

Saltram

Hare's Chase

Peter
Lehmann

Haan
Wines

Angaston

Langmeil
Winery

Richmond
Grove

Tanunda

Murdock Barossa

Teusner

Turkey Flat

Glaetzer Wines

B19

St Hallett

Bethany Wines

Rosedale

Grant Burge

Rockford

Charles Melton

Kabminye
Wines

Glen Eldon

BAROSSA

Yaldara Wines

Rowland
Flat

Orlando*

Charles
Cimicky

Jenke
Vineyards

Liebich Wien

N

Sandy
Creek

Kies Family Wines

Burge Family
Winemakers

Lyndoch

Sandy
Creek
Cons.
Park

Ross Estate Wines

Schild Estate Wines

Dutschke
Wines

B31

0   5 KM

Adelaide ●

Williamstown

Linfield Road Wines

Domain Day*

Hale CP

B31

B34

Warren CP

Cellar Doors

* Orlando at Jacob's Creek Visitor Centre, Barossa Valley Way.

** Domain Day by appointment only at 4 Queen St,
  Williamstown, 5351.*

BAROSSA VALLEY

Latitude **34°29'S**

Altitude **250–370 m**

Heat degree days **1710**

Growing season rainfall **160 mm**

Mean January temp. **21.4°C**

Harvest **End February to late April**

Chief viticultural hazard **Drought**

The Region

CLIMATE

Warm and dry, with low relative humidity and rainfall in the growing season. It is continental in nature, with cool to cold nights and hot summer daytime temperatures. Taken with long daily sunshine hours, the biologically effective temperature summation is (surprisingly) only slightly warmer than that of Bordeaux and the Margaret River. Harvest runs from the end of February to late April.

SOIL & TOPOGRAPHY

The complex system of transverse sub-valleys and twisting hills results in a multiplicity of varying slopes, aspects and sites. The soils vary widely, but fall in an overall family of relatively low-fertility clay loam through to more sandy soils, ranging through grey to brown to red. As in so much of south-east Australia, acidity increases in the subsoils, restricting root growth and vigour.

PRINCIPAL GRAPE VARIETIES

Overall, 68 per cent red, 32 per cent white.
In descending order:

SHIRAZ

CABERNET SAUVIGNON

SEMILLON

CHARDONNAY

GRENACHE

RIESLING

MERLOT

MOURVÈDRE.

[ABOVE] BAROSSA VALLEY.
[RIGHT] YALUMBA, BAROSSA ZONE.

WHITE WINE STYLES

Semillon, once a dark horse, is now a charging white stallion. Gone are the days of coarse and phenolic skin-contacted wine and American oak; in are earlier-picked, steel-fermented wines of real merit and clear varietal character.

Chardonnay has some parallels with Semillon; reduced skin contact and better oak (more French) now makes generous, if relatively quick-developing, styles.

Riesling. Here, too, generosity rather than finesse or elegance rules the day, with wines which develop far more quickly than their counterparts from the Eden or Clare Valleys. Most of the best Barossa-made Rieslings' grapes come from those sources.

RED WINE STYLES

Shiraz is, by a considerable distance, the best wine grown in the Barossa Valley. Traditional American oak maturation is in part yielding to some use of French oak, and the co-fermentation of ten per cent or less Viognier has proved highly successful. The wines are lush, velvety and mouthfilling, with flavours in the black cherry to blackberry spectrum, the tannins ripe and soft. A certain amount of controversy exists over the levels of extract and alcohol, which have excited much approval and high prices in the US.

Cabernet Sauvignon performs best on cooler sites and in moderately cool vintages. French oak is largely but not universally preferred to American, and the overall style is more restrained and firmer than that of Shiraz.

Merlot. The overwhelming urge to plant and make Merlot is as evident here as in most parts of Australia. The necessity for cool site selection is even more critical than for Cabernet Sauvignon, with which it is often blended.

Grenache and Mourvèdre. Grenache is often blended with Shiraz and Mourvèdre, but is also presented as a varietal in its own distinctive right – juicily sweet, almost jammy (the best examples stop short of this). The two and three varietal blends display a rich tapestry of flavours and textures.

Fortified. Tawny style is the most frequently encountered, albeit made in small quantities. Some old parcels have often been acquired by those persevering and form the base of a solera system. Fragrant and nutty, they enjoy a dedicated following. Seppelt 100 Year Old Para Liqueur (a vintage tawny style) is in a class of its own, as are the Seppelt sherry styles.

Wineries of the Barossa Valley

Charles Melton Est. 1984

Krondorf Rd, Tanunda 5352
www.charlesmeltonwines.com.au

🍷 exports to UK, US

Charlie Melton is one of the great characters of the Barossa Valley, part of a group which breathed life back into the Valley when he opened his then tiny wooden winery in 1984. It has grown since, though is still an owner-winemaker, hands-on operation. Rose of Virginia is one of Australia's best rosés, but his red wines are (if anything) even better: Shiraz, Cabernet Sauvignon, and the irreverent Nine Popes, the first Barossa Valley Shiraz Grenache Mourvèdre blend, and still its best.

Signature wine: Nine Popes

Haan Wines Est. 1993

Siegersdorf Rd, Tanunda 5352
www.haanwines.com.au

🍷 exports to UK, US

Hans and Fransien Haan established their business in 1993 when they acquired a 19 ha vineyard near Tanunda (since extended to 36.7 ha). The primary focus was on Merlot and in particular on the luxury Merlot Prestige, supported by Semillon, Viognier and Shiraz, all wines with great character.

Signature wine: Merlot Prestige

Kalleske Wines Est. 2000

Vinegrove Rd, Greenock 5360
www.kalleske.com

🍷

The Kalleske family has been growing and selling grapes on a mixed farming property at Greenock for over a century. Fifth-generation John and Lorraine Kalleske embarked on a trial vintage for a fraction of the grapes in 1999, an immediate success leading to the construction of a small winery with (son) Troy Kalleske as winemaker. The vineyards, with an average age of 50 years, see no chemical fertilisers or pesticides, and some blocks are certified fully organic. The density of the flavour of the Shiraz and Grenache is awesome.

Signature wine: Greenock Shiraz

Dutschke Wines Est. 1990

Lyndoch Valley Rd, Lyndoch 5351 (postal)
www.dutschkewines.com

🍷 exports to UK, US

Wayne Dutschke had 20 years of winemaking experience with major wine companies in all of the eastern states of Australia and had six Flying Winemaker stints in France, Spain and California before he came back home to establish Dutschke Wines with uncle Oscar Semmler, a leading grapegrower in the Barossa Valley and (now) Adelaide Hills. Most of the table wines are built around Shiraz; there is also a range of fortified wines.

Signature wine: Oscar Semmler Shiraz

Kaesler Wines Est. 1990

Barossa Valley Way, Nuriootpa 5355
www.kaesler.com.au

🍷 🍴 exports to US

Do not be misled by the establishment date: there is a real history here, starting with the arrival of the Kaesler family in 1845, and the vineyards in 1893. After the Kaesler family sold the vineyards in 1968 there were several changes of ownership; it is now in the hands of a Swiss banking family, with Flying Winemaker Reid Bosward in charge. His extensive experience of making wines in many different countries, regions and climates shows through in the wines made from 24 ha of 1893 Shiraz, Grenache and Mourvèdre, plus Grenache and Mourvèdre planted in the 1930s.

Signature wine: Old Vine Shiraz

Leo Buring Est. 1931

Tanunda Rd, Nuriootpa 5355
leoburing.australianwines.com.au

🍷 exports to UK

One of innumerable wineries in Australia which throw up challenges for wine atlases or regionally based books, for although the winery is situated in the Barossa Valley, it no longer sources grapes from there. It now only makes Riesling, for which it is famous, sourced from the Clare and Eden Valleys. John Vickery was its master winemaker through decades of Lindemans/Southcorp ownership, and although he has left, his tradition is now fiercely protected, the accent on quality, not price.

Signature wine: Leonay Riesling

[ABOVE LEFT] CHARLIE MELTON.
[BOTTOM LEFT] WAYNE, BRENDA AND DAUGHTER SAMANTHA DUTSCHKE. [ABOVE RIGHT] THREE GENERATIONS OF THE KALLESKE FAMILY FROM LEFT: CLARENCE, JOHN, TROY [FRONT].

Orlando Est. 1847
Jacob's Creek Visitor Centre,
Barossa Valley Way, Rowland Flat 5352
www.orlandowines.com

⬡ ⎙ exports to UK, US

Ownership by Pernod Ricard (of France) has in no way fettered the growth of Orlando; indeed, it has contributed to the global reach of Jacob's Creek, one of the largest-selling brands in the world. But, as with the other big Australians, Orlando has an Aladdin's cave of high-quality wines, identified by variety and region. The Reserve and Limited Release versions of Jacob's Creek (outstanding value) apart, the flagships are St Hugo Coonawarra Cabernet Sauvignon, Lawson's Padthaway Shiraz, St Helga Eden Valley Riesling and St Hilary Padthaway Chardonnay.

Signature wine: Centenary Hill Barossa Shiraz

Penfolds Est. 1844
Tanunda Rd, Nuriootpa 5355
www.penfolds.com.au

⬡ exports to UK, US

The roadside billboards used to read 'Penfolds 1844 to Evermore'; the billboards have gone, but the evermore is still true. It is one of the world's most recognised and highly regarded wine brands, with products at every price point and quality, from humble to great. Notwithstanding its successful efforts with super-premium Yattarna Chardonnay, it remains a red wine-focussed company, with a cavalcade of distinguished wines, most with a 30–50 year pedigree. The iconic Grange to one side, RWT Shiraz (100 per cent Barossa), Magill Estate Shiraz (100 per cent single vineyard), Bin 707 Cabernet Sauvignon and Bin 389 Cabernet Shiraz are key quality brands, Koonunga Hill and Rawson's Retreat supplying the volume.

Signature wine: Grange

Peter Lehmann Est. 1979
Para Rd, Tanunda 5352
www.peterlehmannwines.com

⬡ exports to UK, US

Peter ('Mudflat') Lehmann is the ultimate person-ification of the Barossa Valley, his craggy face (hence, Mudflat), slow smile and gravelly voice accurately telling all he is as tough as teak and absolutely passionate about his beloved Barossa grapegrowers. It was in their defence that he left Saltram to found his winery in 1979, and when Allied Domecq tried to storm the citadel in 2003, his tigerish response drove it away; control has passed to the Swiss/Californian Hess Group, his preferred outcome. All the Lehmann wines are as honest as the man, always reasonably priced. The top wines are The Mentor (a Bordeaux blend), Stonewell Shiraz and Eight Songs Shiraz, plus the Reserve Riesling, sold when five years old.

Signature wine: Eden Valley Reserve Riesling

Rockford Est. 1984
Krondorf Rd, Tanunda 5352
info@rockfordwines.com.au

⬡ exports to UK, US

The wines are sold through Adelaide retailers only (and cellar door) and are unknown to most eastern Australian wine-drinkers, which is a great pity because these are some of the most individual, spectacularly flavoured wines made in the Barossa today, with an emphasis on old, low-yielding dryland vineyards. This South Australian slur on the palates of Victoria and NSW is exacerbated by the fact that the wines are exported worldwide; it all goes to show we need proper authority to protect our living treasures.

Signature wine: Basket Press Shiraz

Seppelt Est. 1851
1 Seppeltsfield Rd, Seppeltsfield
via Nuriootpa 5355
www.seppelt.com.au

⬡ exports to UK, US

The most historic winery and greatest showpiece in the Barossa Valley, an absolute must-see for anyone making their first visit to the Barossa. It is now exclusively a fortified-wine producer, sustained by its unmatched reserves of old wines and the single-minded, zealous focus of its long-serving winemaker, James Godfrey. His skills range across the finest, freshest Manzanilla-type sherry, upwards through Oloroso style to the classic DP90 Tawny, the best of the true tawnys in Australia, and ultimately to the treasure trove of Para Liqueur, first released when it is 100 years old. He is also the custodian of superb Rutherglen Muscats and Tokays.

Signature wine: 100 Year Old Para Liqueur

Torbreck Vintners Est. 1994
Roennfeldt Rd, Marananga 5352
www.torbreck.com

⬡ exports to UK, US

Of all the Barossa Valley wineries to grab the headlines in the US, with demand pulling prices up to undreamt-of levels, Torbreck stands supreme. David Powell has not let success go to his head, nor subvert the individuality and sheer quality of his wines, all created around very old, dry-grown, bush-pruned vineyards. The top trio is led by The RunRig (Shiraz Viognier), then The Factor (Shiraz) and The Descendant (Shiraz Viognier); next The Struie (Shiraz) and The Steading (Grenache Shiraz). Notwithstanding the depth and richness of the wines, they have a remarkable degree of finesse.

Signature wine: The RunRig

Two Hands Wines Est. 2000

Neldner Rd, Marananga 5355
www.twohandswines.com

🍷 exports to UK, US

The two hands are those of South Australian businessmen Michael Twelftree and Richard Mintz, Twelftree having extensive experience in marketing Australian wine in the US (for other producers) and now turning that experience to his own account. On the principle that if big is good, bigger is better, and biggest is best, the style of the wines has been aimed fairly and squarely at the palate of Robert Parker Jnr. The individual wines are made in microscopic quantities (down to 50 dozen), the policy being (one assumes) to keep demand well in excess of supply.

Signature wine: Lily's Garden Shiraz

Wolf Blass Est. 1966

Bilyara Vineyards, Sturt Hwy, Nuriootpa
5355 www.wolfblass.com.au

🍷 exports to UK, US

It would come as no surprise if we were never to see the like of Wolf Blass again: after leaving his native Germany almost 45 years ago, his smile is as cheeky as ever, his bow ties as bright, and his mangling of English as complete. He has deservedly made money from the wine industry, and created a legend in his own time. A forward-looking, hugely capable and youthful team has taken over, seamlessly modernising wine style and quality. Whatever be the label colour (in ascending order red, yellow, gold, grey, black and platinum) the wine will over-deliver.

Signature wine: Black Label
Cabernet Sauvignon Shiraz

[OPPOSITE LEFT] EMMA DAL BROI, WINEMAKER. [OPPOSITE MIDDLE] TIM AND BASKET PRESS.
[OPPOSITE RIGHT] ARTHUR O'CONNOR, WINEMAKER. [THIS PAGE LEFT] PENFOLDS GRANGE.
[THIS PAGE ABOVE] WOLF BLASS VISITOR CENTRE.

Barossa Zone
Eden Valley 🌿

Captain Joseph Gilbert planted the first vines at his Pewsey Vale vineyard in 1847, the same year as Johann Gramp planted the first vines in the Barossa Valley at Rowland Flat. By 1862 Gilbert had established a substantial vineyard and cellar described in a series of articles published in the *Adelaide Advertiser* and ultimately collected in a book entitled *The Vineyards and Orchards of Australia* in 1862. Sixteen acres (6.5 hectares) of vines were in full bearing, and the two-storey winery was in the course of being doubled in size. He was producing Riesling, Shiraz and Carbonet (an odd spelling of Cabernet Sauvignon), with stocks going back to 1852, his first vintage, and including a then-famous 1854 Riesling. So the Eden Valley has an equally long history of viticulture, and (surprisingly) covers an area as large as the Barossa Valley proper, albeit less intensely developed.

High Eden is an officially registered subregion at the southern end of the Eden Valley. Its generally higher altitude (450–550 metres) results in a cooler climate and a later harvest time; wind, too, provides a constant challenge here, met either by protected site selection or windbreaks. Mountadam is the only winery in the subregion.

However, the Eden Valley proper is also windswept country; exposed hills with moderately steep gradients are commonplace. Slope, aspect and – in particular – a degree of protection from wind are as important as the correct match of site and variety. Because the topography is so varied, and the climate neatly balanced, the Eden Valley produces a range of excellent wines. It is justifiably famous for its Riesling, vying for supremacy with the Clare Valley, but is also home to renowned Shiraz vineyards.

In 1952 Cyril Henschke, whose family had been in the area since 1868, and who both grew grapes and made wine in bulk for sale to other wineries (and to customers with BYO containers for filling), decided to bottle and label the Mount Edelstone Shiraz. This pre-dated Hill of Grace by six years, first bottled in 1958 – both wines of extreme importance for Australia's international reputation.

The other event of lasting significance was a decision by Yalumba in 1961 (and running on through the 1970s). In what now seems like a perfectly obvious move, but which at the time took both courage and vision, it began to move the sources of all its all-important Riesling from the warmer floor of the Barossa Valley to the much cooler slopes of the Eden Valley. Pewsey Vale came first, its early Rieslings having immediate success, and encouraging Yalumba to follow up with Heggies (and its evocative label) in 1971.

Sauvignon Blanc, Cabernet Sauvignon and Merlot all do well in the Eden Valley, too; Irvine Wines was an early harbinger of the popular move to and interest in Merlot.

EDEN VALLEY

Latitude **34°35'S**

Altitude **380–550 m**

Heat degree days **1390**

Growing season rainfall **280 mm**

Mean January temp. **19.4°C**

Harvest **Mid March to early May**

Chief viticultural hazard **Autumn rain**

[OPPOSITE] Eden Valley.

Cellar Doors

* *Heggies, Hill Smith and Pewsey Vale at Yalumba, Eden Valley Rd, Angaston.*

* *Irvine Wines at Eden Vale Hotel, Eden Vale.*

The Region

CLIMATE

Altitude is all-important in determining meso-climate, although aspect and slope are also important in the varied, hilly terrain. Thus the Pewsey Vale and Heggies vineyards at an altitude of about 500 metres at the southern end of the Eden Valley are appreciably cooler than the Henschke vineyards around Keyneton at an elevation of 380–400 metres. Overall, of course, growing season temperatures are significantly lower than those of the Barossa Valley, and the final stages of ripening (and harvesting) take place in much cooler conditions.

SOIL & TOPOGRAPHY

As one might expect given the varied and hilly terrain, there are a number of soil types, but the most common range is grey to brown in colour and from loamy sand to clay loams, with subsoils deriving from weathered rock. Ironstone gravels, quartz gravels and rock fragments are present in both the surface and subsurface. Water resources are strictly limited, with dams (no larger than 5 megalitres) the main source.

PRINCIPAL GRAPE VARIETIES

Overall, 55 per cent red and 45 per cent white. In descending order:

SHIRAZ

RIESLING

CABERNET SAUVIGNON

CHARDONNAY

MERLOT

PINOT NOIR

SEMILLON

SAUVIGNON BLANC.

[ABOVE] LOUISA ROSE, WINEMAKER, PEWSEY VALE, EDEN VALLEY. [RIGHT] HILL OF GRACE, HENSCHKE, EDEN VALLEY. [OPPOSITE] PETER GAMBETTA.

WHITE WINE STYLES

Riesling is the most important white grape (and wine) of the region, developing strong lime juice aromas and flavours, and with great intensity of flavour on the palate, ultimately allied with touches of lightly browned toast as the wines age. Good Eden Valley Riesling made in traditional fashion will take ten years or more to reach its peak.

Chardonnay. The first commercial planting in South Australia was established at Mountadam in 1973. The variety has proved to be successful, with rich complex wines being produced, their flavours ranging through a classic array of melon, fig and cashew. The only problem (which also affects other varieties) is the low yield from vineyards insufficiently protected from the wind.

RED WINE STYLES

Shiraz. Contrary to expectations, the wines rarely show the spicy/peppery characters of cool-climate Shiraz from other parts of southern Australia (notably Victoria); rather, they tend to riper plum and black cherry fruit characters, sometimes associated with touches of liquorice, and more gamey/foresty characters. Structurally, the wines are very smooth, with ripe tannins well balanced and integrated, guaranteeing a long life. Henschke's Hill of Grace stands second only to Penfolds' Grange (drawing upon vines planted in the 1860s).

Cabernet Sauvignon. Site climate is of key importance; the wines produced from vineyards around the Eden Valley village are of the highest quality, with perfectly ripened cassis-accented fruit flavours, but those from higher, cooler sites display more elegant dark berry characters with green leaf undertones.

Merlot. James Irvine has invested considerable faith in the variety, using it to make both table and sparkling wines, with particular success in export markets.

Wineries of the Eden Valley

Eden Hall Est. 2002

8 Martin Ave, Fitzroy 5082 (postal)
www.edenhall.com.au

David and Mardi Hall purchased the historic Avon Brae property in 1996. The 120 ha property has now been planted to 32 ha of Cabernet Sauvignon (the lion's share), Shiraz, Merlot, Cabernet Franc, Riesling (over 9 ha) and Viognier. The majority of the production is contracted to Yalumba, St Hallett and McGuigan Simeon, with 10 per cent of the best grapes held back for winemaking by James and Joanne Irvine. The Riesling, Shiraz Viognier and Cabernet Sauvignon are all excellent, the red wines outstanding.

Signature wine: Shiraz Viognier

Heggies Vineyard Est. 1971

Heggies Range Rd, Eden Valley 5235
www.heggiesvineyard.com

(at Yalumba); exports to UK, US

Heggies was one of the trail-blazing high-altitude (570 m) vineyards established by S. Smith & Sons (Yalumba), with plantings on the 120 ha former grazing property commencing in 1973, now reaching 62 ha. The original focus on Riesling has grown to encompass Viognier, Chardonnay, Pinot Noir and Merlot as well. The Riesling (under screw-cap) flowers gloriously with five years' bottle age.

Signature wine: Museum Reserve Eden Valley Riesling

Henschke Est. 1868

Henschke Rd, Keyneton 5353
www.henschke.com.au

exports to UK, US

Rated as the leading medium-sized red wine producer in Australia, Henschke has gone from strength to strength over the past two decades under the guidance of Stephen and Prue Henschke. The red wines fully capitalise on the very old, low-yielding, high-quality vines lovingly cared for by Prue Henschke, and are superbly made with sensitive but positive use of new small oak: Hill of Grace (planted 1861–9) is second only to Penfolds' Grange as Australia's red wine icon.

Signature wine: Hill of Grace

Hill Smith Estate Est. 1979

Flaxmans Valley Rd, Eden Valley 5235
www.hillsmithestate.com

(at Yalumba); exports to UK, US

One of the few single-variety brands of note in Australia, its Sauvignon Blanc coming from 15 ha of 25-year-old estate plantings. As one might expect, the wine is at its best in cooler vintages, but can also perform unexpectedly well in the warmer years.

Signature wine: Sauvignon Blanc

Irvine Wines Est. 1980

PO Box 308, Angaston 5353
merlotbiz@irvinewines.com.au

(at Eden Valley Hotel); exports to UK, US

Industry veteran Jim Irvine, assisted by winemaker-daughter Joanne, has successfully guided the destiny of many South Australian wineries. He quietly introduced his own label in 1991, initially concentrating on export markets. The planting commenced in 1983 and is now a patchwork quilt of 12 ha of vines. While he produces an eclectic range of wines under both the Eden Crest and James Irvine labels, the heart of the business is successfully focussed on opulently flavoured Merlot.

Signature wine: Grand Merlot

Pewsey Vale Est. 1961

PO Box 10, Angaston 5353
www.pewseyvale.com

(at Yalumba); exports to UK, US

Pewsey Vale was a fêted vineyard established in 1847 by Joseph Gilbert, so it was appropriate that when Yalumba began the renaissance of the high Eden Valley plantings in 1961, it should purchase Pewsey Vale and establish 40 ha of Riesling and 2 ha each of Gewürztraminer and Pinot Gris. The Riesling has finally benefitted from being the first wine to be bottled with a screw-cap, back in 1977.

Signature wine: The Contours Riesling

Robert Johnson Vineyards Est. 1997

PO Box 6708, Halifax St, Adelaide 5000
rjv.wine@internode.on.net

The home base for Robert Johnson is a 12 ha vineyard and olive grove purchased in 1996, with a 0.4 ha planting of Merlot (previously sold to Irvine Wines) and 5 ha of olive trees. Over the ensuing years 2.1 ha of Shiraz planted, an additional 1.2 ha of Merlot and a small patch of Viognier likewise established. Wines from the estate-grown grapes are released under the Robert Johnson label. The second range of Alan & Veitch wines is made from grapes purchased from Sam Virgara's vineyard in the Adelaide Hills region.

Signature wine: Eden Valley Merlot

Wroxton Wines Est. 1995

Flaxman's Valley Rd, Angaston 5353
www.wroxton.com.au

Ian and Jo Zander are third-generation grape-growers on the 200 ha Wroxton Grange property established and named in 1845. The Zander family purchased the property in 1920, and planted their first vines; since 1973 the family has progressively established Riesling (15.4 ha), Shiraz (10.5 ha), Chardonnay (6.9 ha), Semillon (2.5 ha) and Traminer (2 ha). The vast majority of the grapes are sold, with limited amounts of high-quality wine contract-made.

Signature wine: Single Vineyard Eden Valley Riesling

Yalumba Est. 1849

Eden Valley Rd, Angaston 5353
www.yalumba.com

exports to UK, US

Family-owned and run by Robert Hill-Smith, the fifth-generation descendant of Samuel Smith (hence S. Smith & Sons Pty Limited), Yalumba has a proud history. The company survived the recession of the late 1980s and early 1990s, and thereafter flourished. The sale of the fortified wine business to Mildara and the 1990 launch of the Oxford Landing brand were turning points. Its wines are diverse, spanning Viognier through to the staples of Riesling, Shiraz and Cabernet Sauvignon.

Signature wine: Signature Cabernet Shiraz

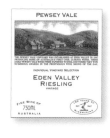

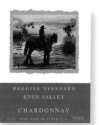

Mount Lofty Ranges Zone
Adelaide Hills ❦

Laws relating to the sale of alcohol have never been rational, and are unlikely to ever become so: there are too many competing forces – ranging from neo-prohibitionists to governments wishing to extract ever-increasing tax revenue. But Walter Duffield must stand as one of the great martyrs: in 1844 he sent a case of 'Echunga Hock' to Queen Victoria, and was promptly prosecuted for making wine without the requisite licence.

Notwithstanding this bizarre start, viticulture flourished in the Adelaide Hills, with over 530 hectares of vines in bearing in the 1870s. For the same reasons which bore down on other cool-climate regions across South Australia and Victoria, vines slowly but surely disappeared until the last were removed in the 1930s. When viticulture recommenced in 1971, it was in the warmest north-western corner of the region, courtesy of Leigh and Jan Verrall, but the arrival of Brian Croser to found Petaluma in 1976 marked the birth of the Adelaide Hills region as it is known today.

From the outset, the 400-metre contour line circumscribed the southern and eastern boundaries, and continues to do so. This might suggest a neat parcel of climate, soil and wine type, but in fact there is considerable climatic variation between the northern and central areas. In the northern vineyards spread around the hamlets of Paracombe, Birdwood and Gumeracha (and most notably those with a west-facing tilt) heat summations rise substantially, and full-bodied red wines are made. In the centre, Chardonnay, Sauvignon Blanc and Pinot Noir are dominant, producing fine table wine.

But even this constitutes a dangerous generalisation, for site selection is all-important: as Brian Croser has handsomely demonstrated at Petaluma, Chardonnay grown within the Piccadilly Valley subregion is profoundly influenced by the aspect of the vineyard, with north-, east- and west-facing slopes producing wines with markedly different aromas and flavours.

This subregion, and the adjacent Lenswood subregion, are particularly attractive. The roads twist and turn, rise and fall, offering cameo vistas with bewildering frequency. It is exceedingly beautiful in autumn, yet is still a largely undiscovered treasure. Although it is less than 30 minutes' drive from the centre of Adelaide, no one should venture into this country without a detailed road map, for it is impossible to navigate by simply using one's sense of direction.

Further south still is the Kuitpo area, not far from the escarpment leading down to McLaren Vale. Here are some of the largest vineyard developments – notably those of eminent viticulturist Geoff Hardy and that of Rosemount Estate – and the accent swings to Semillon, Shiraz, Merlot and Sauvignon Blanc. There is a distinct change in the character of the countryside, more akin to that of the north, and the wine style follows suit, even though ripening is very late.

The potential of the Adelaide Hills is limited only by the need to protect the water catchment by restricting development, and by alternative land use for intensive horticulture – market gardening, apple growing and so forth. It will be interesting to see how the competing interests are resolved in the long term, but it is certain that viticulture will claim a significant portion of the available resources. Proper control and disposal of winery effluent into such a sensitive water catchment area is the major concern, and only five winery licences have been granted since 1976.

However, regardless of the number of operating wineries, this is a truly outstanding region for a day trip from Adelaide. The historic and beautiful Bridgewater Mill and Mount Lofty House offer first-class restaurants for lunch (and Mount Lofty House luxurious accommodation and dinner). Particularly in spring and autumn, the patchwork quilt of little hills and valleys blazes with colour.

The sheer quality of the wines coming from the wineries is the icing on the cake. Petaluma, the wines of which are sold through Bridgewater Mill, needs no further praise, nor do the Henschke Lenswood wines, nor the TK (Knappstein) Lenswood Vineyards, nor Geoff Weaver's wonderful creations. But there are also the less well-known names, such as Ashton Hills, which make an equally valuable contribution to a great wine region.

[opposite & below] Nepenthe Vineyards, Adelaide Hills.

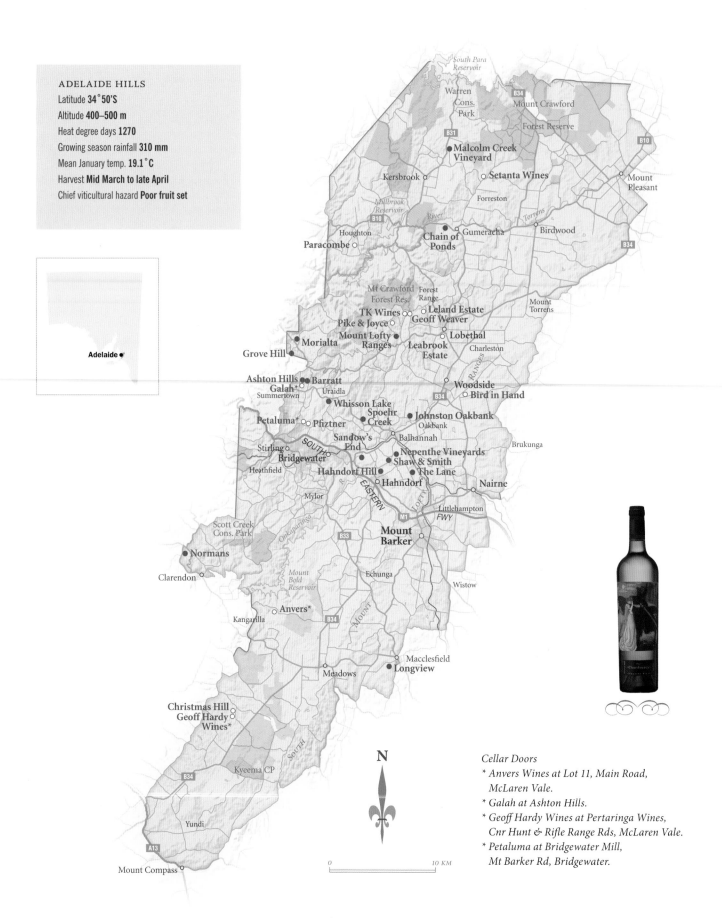

ADELAIDE HILLS
Latitude **34°50'S**
Altitude **400–500 m**
Heat degree days **1270**
Growing season rainfall **310 mm**
Mean January temp. **19.1°C**
Harvest **Mid March to late April**
Chief viticultural hazard **Poor fruit set**

Cellar Doors
* *Anvers Wines at Lot 11, Main Road,
  McLaren Vale.*
* *Galah at Ashton Hills.*
* *Geoff Hardy Wines at Pertaringa Wines,
  Cnr Hunt & Rifle Range Rds, McLaren Vale.*
* *Petaluma at Bridgewater Mill,
  Mt Barker Rd, Bridgewater.*

The Region 🌿

CLIMATE

Altitude is the key to the climate; Mount Lofty and the Piccadilly Valley are a bare 25 minutes' drive from the centre of Adelaide, but the contrast in climate throughout much of summer has to be experienced to be believed. The veritable maze of valleys and sub-valleys means there is much meso-climatic variation, making generalisations hazardous. However, most of the Adelaide Hills has an unequivocally cool climate; it is not until one reaches the northern extremity of the region, and the west-facing slopes, that one moves out of a climate suited principally to early-ripening varieties such as Chardonnay, Pinot Noir and Sauvignon Blanc, and into terrain which satisfactorily ripens Cabernet Sauvignon and Shiraz.

SOIL & TOPOGRAPHY

The Adelaide Hills have predominantly grey, grey-brown or brown loamy sands and clay loams; there are also patches of much sandier and more weakly structured soils of lesser quality. Fertility varies, tending to be higher in the southern and central areas.

PRINCIPAL GRAPE VARIETIES

Overall, 55 per cent white, 45 per cent red. In descending order:

CHARDONNAY

PINOT NOIR

SAUVIGNON BLANC

SHIRAZ

MERLOT

SEMILLON

RIESLING

VIOGNIER.

[ABOVE & RIGHT] NEPENTHE VINEYARDS, ADELAIDE HILLS.

🌿 WHITE WINE STYLES

Chardonnay. Complex but elegant wines are par for the course; the variety flourishes and the resulting wines are invariably full of character, responding in marked fashion to the winemaking philosophies and practices of the numerous distinguished producers in the region. The natural levels of acidity are good, allowing makers to use malolactic fermentation to increase complexity without making the wines soft and flabby, nor threatening their longevity.

Sauvignon Blanc. As vineyard plantings have begun to mature, and as experience in making the variety has increased, so has the quality and consistency of the Hills' Sauvignon Blanc soared to the point where it is one of Australia's best, with great intensity and length.

Sparkling. Substantial quantities of the Pinot Noir and Chardonnay grown in the Adelaide Hills are used in the making of sparkling wines, with Petaluma's Croser commonly accepted as being one of Australia's finest. The style is extremely refined, the flavour long and lingering.

🌿 RED WINE STYLES

Pinot Noir, after a slow and at times uncertain start, is now asserting itself in the fashion that the climate has long suggested it should. The arrival of new Burgundian clones should ensure continued impetus and interest. Indeed, there is no doubt that the Adelaide Hills is and will remain South Australia's leading producer of Pinot Noir.

Cabernet Sauvignon and Merlot. Although not widely grown in this region, several producers have managed to make outstanding wines from Cabernet Sauvignon and Merlot, none more so than Henschke at Lenswood. There is an increasing number of quality offerings as experience (and vine age) grows.

Shiraz. The rapid acceptance of cool-climate Shiraz, and the judicious use of a little Viognier, has seen an acceleration in plantings across all parts of the Adelaide Hills. Intensely aromatic and spicy wines are the result.

Wineries of the Adelaide Hills

Anvers Wines Est. 1998

Lot 11, Main Rd, McLaren Vale 5171
www.anvers.com.au

[icon] (at McLaren Vale); exports to US

Myriam and Wayne Keoghan established Anvers Wines near Kangarilla in the Adelaide Hills with the emphasis on quality rather than quantity. The first Cabernet Sauvignon was made in 1998, and volume has increased markedly since then. The quality of the wines is exemplary, no doubt underwriting the increase in production and expansion of markets both across Australia and in most major export markets other than the UK.

Signature wine: Adelaide Hills Semillon Sauvignon Blanc

Ashton Hills Est. 1982

Tregarthen Rd, Ashton 5137
(08) 8390 1243

[icon] exports to UK, US

Stephen George wears three winemaker hats: one for Ashton Hills, drawing upon a 3.5 ha estate vineyard high in the Adelaide Hills; one for nearby Galah Wines; and one for Wendouree in the Clare Valley. It would be hard to imagine three wineries producing more diverse styles, with the elegance and finesse of Ashton Hills at one end of the spectrum, the awesome power of Wendouree at the other. The Ashton Hills Riesling, Chardonnay and Pinot Noir have moved into the highest echelon.

Signature wine: Pinot Noir

Barratt Est. 1993

Uley Vineyard, Cornish Rd,
Summertown 5141
info@barrattwines.com.au

[icon] exports to UK

Lindsay and Carolyn Barratt own two vineyards at Summertown: the Uley Vineyard and the Bonython Vineyard. They have 8.4 ha of vines, adding Sauvignon Blanc and Merlot to the Chardonnay and Pinot Noir from 2002. Part of the production from the vineyards is sold to other makers, with Jeffrey Grosset the maker of the superbly flavoured and balanced Chardonnay and Reserve Pinot Noir. Since 2003 Barratt has established a winery facility at the Adelaide Hills Business and Tourism Centre at Lobethal.

Signature wine: Reserve Pinot Noir

Chain of Ponds Est. 1993

Adelaide Rd, Gumeracha 5233
www.chainofponds.com.au

[icon] [icon] exports to UK, US

Chain of Ponds is the largest grower in the Adelaide Hills, with 100 ha of vines at Gumeracha and 120 ha at Kersbrook, producing 1000 tonnes of grapes a year. Former Southcorp senior winemaker Neville Falkenberg has the pick of the crop to make a large range of wines, which have had deserved show success, the bulk of the grapes being sold to other makers. The Vineyard Balcony Restaurant is open for lunch on weekends and public holidays.

Signature wine: Morning Star Chardonnay

Geoff Hardy Wines Est. 1993

c/o Pertaringa Wines
Cnr Hunt and Rifle Range Rds,
McLaren Vale 5171
www.k1.com.au

[icon] (at Pertaringa Wines)

Leading viticulturist and viticultural consultant Geoff Hardy has 20 ha of estate vineyards established in the early 1990s; while the major part of the grape production is sold, some of the best is kept back for a limited range of high-quality Pinot Noir, Chardonnay, Shiraz and Cabernet Sauvignon contract-made by Ben Riggs. This is a parallel operation to Pertaringa in McLaren Vale.

Signature wine: K1 Adelaide Hills Shiraz

Geoff Weaver Est. 1982

2 Gilpin Lane, Mitcham 5062 (postal)
www.geoffweaver.com.au

[icon] exports to UK, US

This is the full-time business of former Hardy Group chief winemaker Geoff Weaver. He has a little over 11 ha of vineyard established between 1982 and 1988; for the time being, at least, the physical winemaking is carried out by him at Shaw & Smith. He produces invariably immaculate Riesling and Sauvignon Blanc, and one of the longest-lived Chardonnays to be found in Australia, which has intense grapefruit and melon flavour. The beauty of the labels ranks supreme with that of Pipers Brook.

Signature wine: Lenswood Chardonnay

Nepenthe Vineyards Est. 1994

Jones Rd, Balhannah 5242
www.nepenthe.com.au

[icon] exports to UK, US

The Tweddell family has established a little over 160 ha of close-planted vineyards at Lenswood since 1994, with an exotic array of varieties reflected in the wines. In late 1996 it obtained the second licence to build a winery in the Adelaide Hills, Petaluma being the only other successful applicant, back in 1978. A large winery has been constructed, with the highly skilled Peter Leske as chief winemaker. Nepenthe goes from strength to strength as the largest estate producer of Adelaide Hills wines, thanks to the high-quality wines and energetic marketing.

Signature wine: Adelaide Hills Chardonnay

Paracombe Wines Est. 1983

Main Rd, Paracombe 5132 (postal)
www.paracombewines.com

[icon] exports to UK, US

The Drogemuller family have established 12 ha of vineyards at Paracombe, reviving a famous name in South Australian wine history, and becoming one of the pioneers in the renaissance of the Adelaide Hills wine region. The wines are ever-stylish and consistent, ranging across Sauvignon Blanc, Riesling, Chardonnay, Shiraz, Reuben (a Bordeaux blend) and even Cabernet Franc.

Signature wine: Adelaide Hills Sauvignon Blanc

Petaluma Est. 1976

Spring Gully Rd, Piccadilly 5151
www.petaluma.com.au

🍷🍴 (both at Bridgewater Mill)
exports to UK, US

The Petaluma empire comprises Knappstein Wines, Mitchelton, Stonier and Smithbrook. In late 2001 the Petaluma group was acquired by New Zealand brewer Lion Nathan, but left Brian Croser in place; in 2005 he moved to a consultancy role. The Clare Valley Riesling is almost monotonously good; the Adelaide Hills Chardonnay is a category leader, Tiers a super-reserve; and the Coonawarra Merlot is another marvellously succulent wine to buy without hesitation.

Signature wine: Tiers Chardonnay

Setanta Wines Est. 1997

RSD 43 Williamstown Rd
Forreston 5233 (postal)
www.setantawines.com.au

📦 exports to UK, US

The Sullivan family (first-generation Australians, but of Irish parentage) chose Setanta, Ireland's most mythological hero, as their brand name, carrying on the allusion with striking and very beautiful labels for their Speckled House Riesling, Emer Chardonnay, Cuchulain Shiraz and Black Sanglain Cabernet Sauvignon. The contract-made wines are uniformly excellent.

Signature wine: Emer Chardonnay

Shaw & Smith Est. 1989

Lot 4, Jones Rd, Balhannah 5242
www.shawandsmith.com

🍷 exports to UK

This is a highly successful partnership between winemaker Martin Shaw and Michael Hill Smith MW, the first Master of Wine not to come from the UK. Shaw & Smith has progressively moved from a contract grape-grown base to estate production with the development of a 40 ha vineyard at Balhannah in the Adelaide Hills, followed by the erection prior to the 2000 vintage of a state-of-the-art, beautifully designed and executed winery, ending the long period of tenancy at Petaluma. Each one of the wines is immaculately crafted, with ultimate attention to detail.

Signature wine: Sauvignon Blanc

TK Wines Est. 1991

c/o Kilikanoon Wines
Penna Lane, Penwortham 5453
www.tkwines.com.au

📦 exports to UK, US

Yet another name change for the wine business of Tim and Annie Knappstein, although on this occasion doing no more than reflecting the difficulty of using the Lenswood Vineyards name, thanks to the Geographic Indication legislation. The label will be used for all of the wines, regardless of whether they come entirely from the Lenswood Vineyard, and hence Lenswood GI. The wines are made by Tim Knappstein, his near-obsessive attention to detail paying handsome dividends with the wines' consistent quality.

*Signature wine: The Palatine
(Cabernet dominant blend)*

[OPPOSITE MIDDLE] Geoff Weaver. [opposite right] Peter Leske. [this page left] Michael Hill Smith and Martin Shaw. [above] Speckled House Riesling, Setanta Wines.

Mount Lofty Ranges Zone
Clare Valley ❦

More than any other district, the Clare Valley throws into question the accuracy of the heat summation index as a measure of climate, although it still remains the best shorthand method we have. The HDD summation is 1770, the same as that of Rutherglen and in excess of the 1710 for Nuriootpa. The style of the wines is inconsistent with a climate seemingly so warm; the continental climate and cold nights in the growing season provide the answer. Over 60 per cent of the annual rainfall is between May and September. The growing season rainfall, of a mere 200 millimetres, makes irrigation highly desirable, although the absence of groundwater makes this difficult to supply in many parts of the Clare Valley, and the vines have traditionally been grown using dryland farming techniques. The low humidity means fungal diseases are seldom a threat, but water stress late in the growing season may lead to partial or total defoliation of the vines, and occasional ripening problems with Riesling.

Clare was founded by an extraordinary Englishman, John Horrocks, when he established Hope Farm in 1840 and planted the first vines. Minerals provided the first surge in population shortly thereafter: copper was discovered at Burra in 1845 and at Wallaroo and Moonta between 1859 and 1861. When the first flush of minerals was depleted, a wheat boom started, creating great wealth in a short time. High-quality slate was then discovered at Mintaro, and in 1885 the Broken Hill Proprietary Company Limited was formed to mine silver at Broken Hill. Clare was the town through which much of the trade and the food (and the people) generated by these developments passed: it became known as 'The Hub of the North'.

Vineyards (and wineries) grew steadily. Sevenhill planted its first vines in 1852, those of Spring Vale (later to become Quelltaler) in 1853. By 1890 there were 100 hectares of vineyards, but expansion (at a rate reminiscent of the late 1960s in the Hunter Valley) lifted hectareage by almost 500 per cent in the next seven years. By 1897 there were 580 hectares under vine, and in 1903 the Stanley Wine Company produced 450 000 litres of wine (mostly exported to London), the same quantity as Penfolds. The twentieth century slowed the rate of growth, and a number of the nineteenth-century wineries disappeared. The Stanley Wine Company and Quelltaler dominated production, but Sevenhill and Wendouree both continued to make and market wines to a small but appreciative market.

The 1980s saw significant corporate investments and ownership changes. Hardys now owns Stanley Leasingham, Beringer Blass owns Quelltaler Estate (now known as Annie's Lane) and both Beringer Blass and Penfolds have established major vineyards on the Polish Hill River side of the valley. But the atmosphere has not changed, and the Clare Valley vignerons remain one of the most dedicated and harmonious of groups. One of many achievements has been the annual wine and food weekend held in May, at which the public is given the rare opportunity of tasting the weeks-old wines from the current vintage (on the Saturday) and touring the wineries on the Sunday (when each winery teams up with a prominent local or Adelaide restaurant to provide a matched glass of wine and small plate of food).

But whenever you visit the Clare Valley, you will be assured of an especially warm welcome and be seduced by its gentle beauty. The feeling stems in part from its abundant stone buildings (banks, halls, houses, wineries, farmhouses and sheds); in part from its convoluted geography, ever promising a little creek or a spring, though not always providing it; in part from the interplay between eucalypts and vines; in part from its people; and in part from its surrounding districts, notably Mintaro (with such wonderful places as The Magpie and Stump Hotel and Martindale Hall) and Burra (the old copper mining town with its unique terraces of miners' cottages, now converted to bed-and-breakfast accommodation). The late Mick Knappstein summed it up beautifully when he said, 'There are only two kinds of people: those who were born in Clare, and those who wish they were born in Clare'. He, of course, was in the former category; I am in the latter.

[OPPOSITE & BELOW] CLARE VALLEY.

THE COVER DRIVE

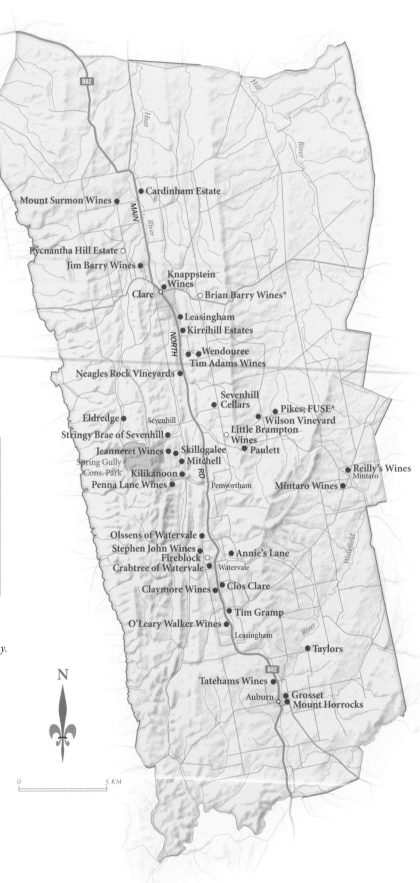

CLARE VALLEY

Latitude **33˚50'S**

Altitude **400–500 m**

Heat degree days **1770**

Growing season rainfall **200 mm**

Mean January temp. **21.9˚C**

Harvest **Early March to late April**

Chief viticultural hazards **Frost; drought**

Cellar Doors
* Brian Barry Wines at 10–12 Union St, Stepney.
* FUSE has no cellar door tastings.

Adelaide ●

Mount Surmon Wines ●
Cardinham Estate ●
Rycnantha Hill Estate ○
Jim Barry Wines ●
Knappstein Wines ●
Clare ○
Brian Barry Wines* ○
Leasingham ●
Kirrihill Estates ●
Wendouree ●
Tim Adams Wines ●
Neagles Rock Vineyards ●
Sevenhill Cellars ○
Pikes; FUSE* ●
Eldredge ●
Sevenhill
Wilson Vineyard ●
Little Brampton Wines ○
Stringy Brae of Sevenhill ●
Jeanneret Wines ●
Paulett ●
Spring Gully Cons. Park
Skillogalee ●
Mitchell ●
Kilikanoon ●
Reilly's Wines ●
Mintaro
Penna Lane Wines ●
Penwortham
Mintaro Wines ●
Olssens of Watervale ●
Stephen John Wines ●
Annie's Lane ●
Fireblock ○
Crabtree of Watervale ●
Watervale
Claymore Wines ●
Clos Clare ●
Tim Gramp ●
O'Leary Walker Wines ●
Leasingham
Taylors ●
Tatehams Wines ●
Auburn ○
Grosset ●
Mount Horrocks

N

0   5 KM

The Region

CLIMATE

The paradoxical nature of the Clare Valley's climate has already been canvassed. Both Brian Croser and John Gladstones separately suggest the official figure of 1770 HDD is due to an inappropriately sited weather station, and that the true figure is close to 1600.

SOIL & TOPOGRAPHY

With the exception of the open expanses of the Polish Hill River to the west, and Auburn to the south, the region is broken into a series of sub-valleys running in every direction, with numerous creeks or creek beds. The higher altitude or west-facing slopes often produce the best vineyard sites in a very beautiful region. The soils vary, but are by and large excellent, red to brown-grey in colour, and with a significant limestone content, particularly in the more southerly subregions.

PRINCIPAL GRAPE VARIETIES

Overall, 65 per cent red, 35 per cent white.
In descending order:

SHIRAZ

CABERNET SAUVIGNON

RIESLING

CHARDONNAY

MERLOT

SEMILLON

MALBEC

GRENACHE

SAUVIGNON BLANC.

[OPPOSITE] THE COVER DRIVE CABERNET SAUVIGNON, JIM BARRY WINES. [ABOVE] CLARE VALLEY. [RIGHT] KILIKANOON, CLARE VALLEY.

WHITE WINE STYLES

Riesling typically starts life in a fairly austere mode, with faint aromas of passionfruit, a touch of lime, and a steely strength. Almost immediately a telltale touch of lightly browned toast starts to emerge, and as the wine ages and becomes more complex, the intensity of that toasty character grows. These are long-lived wines: only in the weakest years will they not benefit from five years in bottle, many of the better wines improving for up to 20 years, a future underwritten by the universal use of screw-cap closures. Much of Australia's finest Riesling is grown in the Clare Valley.

Semillon made from the 55-year-old plantings of Semillon at Annie's Lane (formerly Quelltaler Estate), originally sourced from the Hunter Valley, is high quality, rich and long lived. Other producers add their weight with more opulently oaked styles.

Chardonnay is an unqualified and almost consistent failure.

RED WINE STYLES

Shiraz. Believed by many to be equal to or better than Cabernet Sauvignon, and over the years the two have frequently been blended, sometimes with the addition of a little Malbec. The Shiraz is deep in colour and flavour, rounder and softer than the Cabernet Sauvignon, but with similar strength and depth.

Cabernet Sauvignon is the other great red wine of the region. Here the character and the style are less homogenous, in part reflecting the philosophy of the winemaker and in part the imperatives of the vineyard terroir. The wines are seldom less than full bodied, at times as strikingly dense, rich and concentrated as any wine to be found in Australia. A regional specialty is the Cabernet Malbec blend.

Wineries of the Clare Valley

Annie's Lane Est. 1851

Quelltaler Rd, Watervale 5452
www.annieslane.com.au

🍷 exports to UK, US

The Clare Valley portfolio of Beringer Blass – formerly made at the historic Quelltaler winery – is sold under the Annie's Lane label, the name coming from Annie Weyman, a turn-of-the-century local identity. Since 1996, a series of outstanding Rieslings, Semillons, Shirazs and Grenache Mourvèdres have appeared under the Annie's Lane label. The two Copper Trail wines (Riesling and Shiraz) are in effect Reserve wines, made in small quantities.

Signature wine: Copper Trail Shiraz

Grosset Est. 1981

King St, Auburn 5451
www.grosset.com.au

🍷 exports to UK, US

The quietly spoken, seemingly ascetic, Jeffrey Grosset crafts the wines with the utmost care from grapes grown to the most exacting standards; all need a certain amount of time in bottle to achieve their ultimate potential, not the least the Rieslings (one from Polish Hill, one from Watervale) and Gaia (Bordeaux blend), among Australia's best examples of their kind. At a Riesling Summit held in Hamburg in 1998, Grosset was voted Riesling Winemaker of the Year. He is also an articulate advocate of the use of screw-caps on all wines, red and white, and rather unexpectedly, drives a gold M3 BMW.

Signature wine: Polish Hill Riesling

Jim Barry Wines Est. 1959

Craig's Hill Rd, Clare 5453
jbwines@jimbarry.com

🍷 exports to UK, US

The large Barry family, with the late patriarch Jim, winemaker son Mark and wine marketer extraordinaire Peter, has 247 ha of priceless old-vine vineyards in the Upper Clare district. Riesling and Shiraz across a number of price points offer great value, the Shiraz being typically concentrated and full flavoured, the Rieslings coming (in whole or part) from the famed Florita Vineyard, purchased for a song from Lindemans' fire-sale a decade ago.

Signature wine: The Armagh (Shiraz)

Kilikanoon Est. 1997

Penna Lane, Penwortham 5453
www.kilikanoon.com.au

🍷 🍴 exports to UK, US

Kevin Mitchell has 20 ha of estate vineyards at Leasingham and Penwortham, giving rise to consistently outstanding, trophy-winning Riesling, Shiraz and Cabernet Sauvignon. All wines are built to last, the red wines with maximum possible fruit, and appropriate levels of oak and tannins. The success of the Clare Valley wines has allowed Mitchell to spread his vinous wings with reds from the Barossa Valley and McLaren Vale.

Signature wine: Oracle Shiraz

Knappstein Wines Est. 1976

2 Pioneer Ave, Clare 5453
www.knappsteinwines.com.au

🍷 exports to UK

Very much part of the Petaluma empire, with winemaker-manager Paul Smith having taken over from Andrew Hardy, who has returned to Petaluma headquarters. The 90 ha of mature estate vineyards in prime locations supply grapes both for the Knappstein brand and for wider Petaluma use. Riesling and Shiraz are the cornerstones, Enterprise the reserve soubriquet, but Knappstein does better than most with its top-end cabernets.

Signature wine: Single Vineyard Cabernet Sauvignon

Leasingham Est. 1893

7 Dominic St, Clare 5453
www.leasingham-wines.com.au

🍷 exports to UK, US

Successive corporate ownerships and various peregrinations in labelling and branding have not resulted in any permanent loss of identity or quality. With a core of high-quality, aged vineyards to draw on, Leasingham has flourished under Hardys' direction. The stentorian red wines (Shiraz and Cabernet Sauvignon) take no prisoners, compacting densely rich fruit and layer upon layer of oak into every long-lived bottle; the Bin 7 Riesling often excels.

Signature wine: Classic Clare Shiraz

Mount Horrocks Est. 1982

The Old Railway Station, Curling St Auburn 5451
www.mounthorrocks.com

🍷 exports to UK, US

Owned by ultra-feisty winemaker Stephanie Tool (Jeffrey Grosset's partner in life), Mount Horrocks has well and truly established its own identity. Positive marketing and, equally importantly, wine quality, has resulted in both show success and critical acclaim. Riesling, Semillon, Shiraz and Cabernet Merlot are all first-class wines.

Signature wine: Clare Valley Cabernet Merlot

O'Leary Walker Wines Est. 2001

Main Rd, Leasingham 5452
www.olearywalkerwines.com

🍷 exports to UK, US

Large company, veteran winemakers David O'Leary and Nick Walker took the plunge, leaving employment security for the uncertain waters of small winery production of super-premium wines. With vineyard resources in the Clare Valley and Adelaide Hills, they have succeeded admirably, producing elegant but intensely varietal wines which fully reflect their differing terroirs.

Signature wine: Watervale Riesling

Pikes Est. 1984

Polish Hill River Rd, Sevenhill 5453
www.pikeswines.com.au

🍷 exports to UK, US

Owned by the Pike brothers, one of whom (Andrew) was for many years the senior viticulturist with Southcorp, the other (Neil) a former winemaker at Mitchell. Pikes now has its own winery, with Neil Pike presiding. Generously constructed and flavoured wines are the order of the day, the now mature vineyards providing Riesling, Chardonnay, Shiraz, Merlot and Cabernet Sauvignon of high quality. Success has led to the establishment of a related brand, Pike and Joyce, using estate-grown Adelaide Hills grapes vinified at Pikes.

Signature wine: The Merle Reserve Riesling

Sevenhill Cellars Est. 1851

College Rd, Sevenhill 5453
www.sevenhillcellars.com.au

🍷 exports to UK

One of the historical treasures of Australia; the oft-photographed stone wine cellars are the oldest in the Clare Valley, and winemaking is still carried out under the direction of the Jesuit Manresa Society, and the semi-retired, infinitely charming Brother John May. Quality is very good, especially the Riesling and the powerful Shiraz, but all the wines reflect the estate-grown grapes from old vines.
Signature wine: St Ignatius (Bordeaux blend)

Stringy Brae of Sevenhill
Est. 1991

Sawmill Rd, Sevenhill, 5453
www.stringybrae.com.au

🍷 exports to UK

Donald and Sally Willson began the planting of their 10 ha vineyard in 1991, having purchased the property eight years earlier. In 2004 daughter Hannah Rantanen took over day-to-day management from Donald, but skilled contract-making of the Riesling and Cabernet Merlot by O'Leary Walker continues to pay big dividends.
Signature wine: Clare Valley Riesling

Taylors Est. 1969

Taylors Rd, Auburn 5451
www.taylorswines.com.au

🍷 exports to UK, US

The family-founded and -owned Taylors continues to flourish and expand, with yet further extensions to its vineyards, now totalling over 500 ha, by far the largest holding in the Clare Valley. There have also been substantial changes on the winemaking front, both of the winemaking team and in

terms of the wine style and quality, particularly through the outstanding St Andrews range. That said, the standard varietal range (led by Riesling and Shiraz) offers outstanding value for money, as does the recently introduced multi-regional Jaraman range.
Signature wine: St Andrews Cabernet Sauvignon

Wendouree Est. 1895

Wendouree Rd, Clare 5453
(08) 8842 2896

🍷

The iron fist in a velvet glove best describes these extraordinary wines. They are fashioned with passion and yet precision from the very old vineyard with its unique terroir by owners Tony and Lita Brady (with Stephen George as executive winemaker), who rightly see themselves as custodians of a priceless treasure. The 110-year-old stone winery is virtually unchanged from the day it was built; this is in every sense a treasure beyond price. It is almost impossible to choose between the Shiraz, Shiraz Malbec, Shiraz Mataro, Cabernet Malbec and Cabernet Sauvignon; all need an absolute minimum of 20 years' bottle age.
Signature wine: Cabernet Malbec

Wilson Vineyard Est. 1974

Polish Hill River, Sevenhill via Clare 5453
www.wilsonvineyard.com.au

🍷 exports to US

Dr John Wilson was a tireless ambassador for the Clare Valley and for wine (and its beneficial effect on health) in general. His wines were made using techniques and philosophies garnered early in his wine career and can occasionally be idiosyncratic (particularly the Zinfandel), but in recent years the mainstream varietals have been most impressive as a seamless handover to son Daniel Wilson has taken place.
Signature wine: DJW Riesling

MOUNT LOFTY RANGES ZONE
Adelaide Plains 🌿

The Adelaide Plains run due north of the city of Adelaide, north-west of the Adelaide Hills and west of the Barossa Valley. The region is a significant producer of low-cost grapes, which come from high-yielding vineyards with a low incidence of disease. The laser-flat topography is another factor assisting in the economics of grape production, facilitating broad-acre planting and a high degree of mechanisation.

Primo Estate, under the direction of winemaker (and owner) Joe Grilli, encapsulates the reasons why Australia has been so successful in attracting worldwide markets for its wines. On the one hand there is the abundant sunshine and warmth, factors which guarantee ripe, lush grapes. Indeed, in the case of the Adelaide Plains, there is theoretically too much sun and too much warmth for high-quality grapegrowing.

It is here that the other hand comes into play: the skill and innovative brilliance of Joe Grilli. It is not just that he was dux of his year when he graduated with a viticulture degree from Roseworthy, nor that he was head-hunted to join Australia's Flying Winemakers in Italy. It is rather that he has been able to transcend the limitations of the vineyard environment, making crisp, Sauvignon Blanc-like Colombard, suave Shiraz, complex Joseph Cabernet Merlot (using the 'Moda Amarone' borrowed from Italy) and Botrytis Riesling, all wines of quality, and all of startlingly different styles. It is the sort of ingenuity, of daring, which lies outside the imagination of the Old World winemakers and which stands Australia in such good stead.

There is another solution to the limitations of the climate which so many Australian wineries employ. That is simply to look to other regions for grapes (as does Joe Grilli), and to transport those grapes to their wineries for processing. This may seem blindingly obvious to Australians, but it is a solution (and freedom) that is denied to any European winemaker seeking to make wine within the official framework of the Appellation Laws, and thereby have access to the subsidies offered within the European Union. Freedom, it seems, always has a price, but in this instance Australians would say it is well worth it.

In a final twist of the knife, the three most recent arrivals on the local winemaking scene (all, like Joe Grilli, with Italian parentage) have elected to run with single-region, estate-grown grapes, to further expand the quality horizons of the region.

ADELAIDE PLAINS

Latitude **34°41'S**

Altitude **20 m**

Heat degree days **2081**

Growing season rainfall **130 mm**

Mean January temp. **23°C**

Harvest **Mid February to early March**

Chief viticultural hazard **Nil**

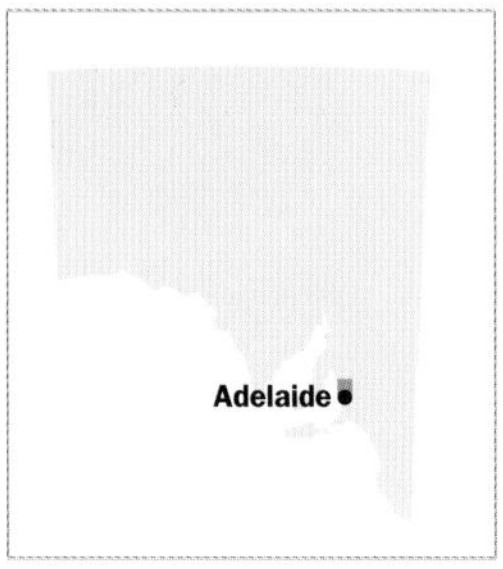

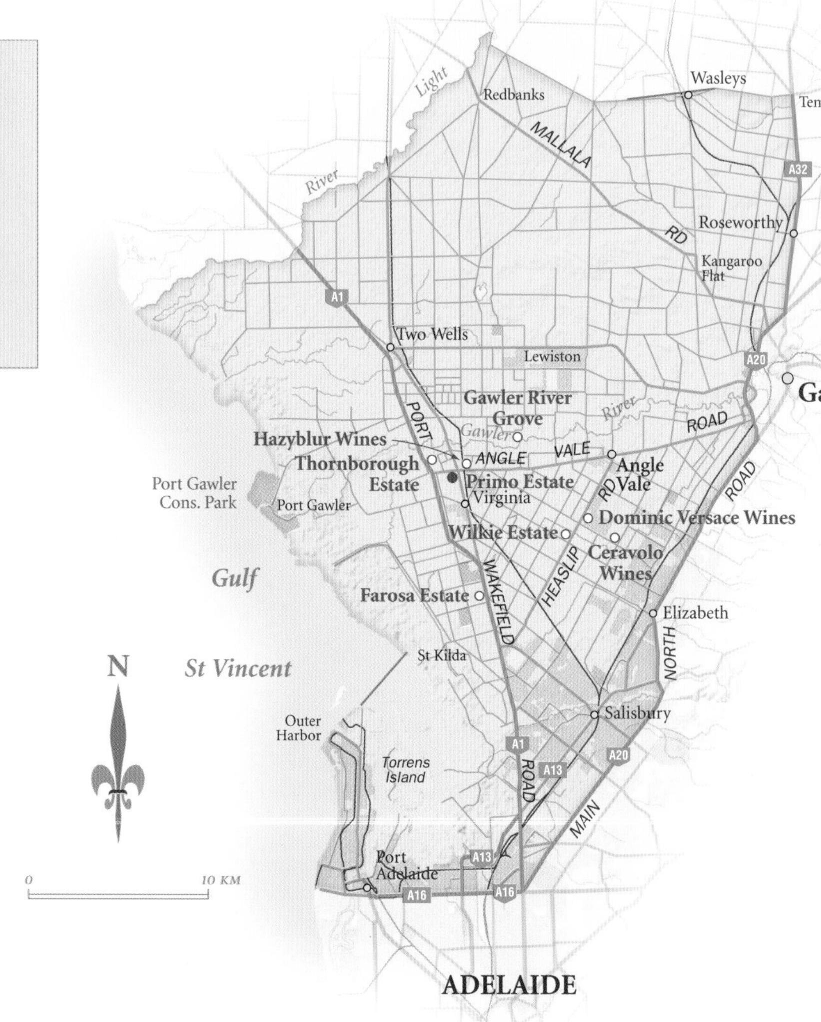

The Region

CLIMATE

Given the proximity of the Adelaide Plains to Adelaide and the Southern Ocean, and the absence of any mountain range between the Plains and the ocean, the hot to very hot climate comes as a surprise. It is warmer than the Hunter Valley, and not far behind the Riverland region of South Australia. Indeed, its rainfall during the growing season, of only 130 mm, is the same as the Swan Valley, making the region totally dependent on irrigation.

SOIL & TOPOGRAPHY

There are two soil types. First, the ubiquitous red-brown loamy sands found through so much of south-eastern Australia, with alkaline subsoils and free limestone at deeper levels. These are excellent viticultural soils which readily support the typically high yields of the region. Then there are also smaller patches of heavier loam and cracking clay soils which are strikingly different in structure, but once again tend to be alkaline rather than acidic, and once again promote vigorous vine growth.

PRINCIPAL GRAPE VARIETIES

Overall, 25 per cent white, 75 per cent red. In descending order:

SHIRAZ

CABERNET SAUVIGNON

GRENACHE

CHARDONNAY

MERLOT.

Wineries of the Adelaide Plains

Ceravolo Wines Est. 1995

Suite 16, Tranmere Village, 172 Glynburn Rd, Tranmere 5073 (postal)
www.ceravolo.com.au

 exports to UK

Parents Joe and Heather Ceravolo, and dental son Dr Joe Ceravolo, have moved from grapegrowing into grapegrowing and winemaking (via contract) with considerable success. Both mainstream varietals and the new arrivals of Sangiovese and Petit Verdot, estate-grown with controlled yields, have produced wines with real character. Conspicuous success with Shiraz at the London International Wine Challenge led both to exports and the registration of the Adelaide Plains region under the GI legislation.

Signature wine: Sangiovese

 WHITE WINE STYLES

Chardonnay. Most of the 1200 or so tonnes of Chardonnay grown here each year disappears into the anonymity of casks or lower-priced bottles, which in all probability will show South East Australia as the area of origin, and in fact be multi-regional blends. In this respect the Adelaide Plains' wine is no different from that produced throughout much of the Riverland, and is none the worse for that.

Colombard. It is true the variety is particularly well suited to hot climates, thanks to its ability to retain relatively high levels of natural acidity, and is much prized as a blend component for this very reason in the casks and generic white wines to which it is usually directed. But it can produce a wine which looks disconcertingly like Sauvignon Blanc, so fresh and bracing is it (particularly if, as the law allows, 15 per cent is in fact cool-grown Sauvignon Blanc).

 RED WINE STYLES

Shiraz can produce wines of remarkable quality, showing a totally unexpected touch of spice and fine-grained tannins. Winemaking skills no doubt play a part, but it demonstrates what can be achieved with grapes grown on mature vines and with controlled yields.

Cabernet Sauvignon. Primo Estate's Cabernet Merlot, made using a modified Amarone method and incorporating some Coonawarra material, stands supreme.

Sangiovese. With so much Italian influence in the wineries, it is not surprising that Sangiovese is making an appearance, although statistically the area under vine is as yet insignificant. More can be expected in the future.

Diloreto Wines Est. 2001

45 Wilpena Terrace, Kilkenny 5009 (postal)
diloreto@chariot.net.au

The Diloreto family has been growing grapes since the 1960s; second-generation Tony and wife Gabriell (the latter with winemaking experience in Germany) undertook short winemaking courses, and proceeded to make small quantities of Shiraz that won trophies in the Australian Amateur Wine Show, leading to the decision to come out and make small quantities for professional sale.

Signature wine: Shiraz

Dominic Versace Wines Est. 2000

Lot 258, Heaslip Rd, MacDonald Park 5121
www.versacewines.com.au

At first simply called Versace Wines, 'Dominic' has since been added, and it's not hard to guess why. In fact, Dominic Versace and brother-in-law Armando Verdiglione have a long association with wine in both Italy and (since 1980) Australia. In that year Dominic Versace planted 4.5 ha of Shiraz, Grenache and Sangiovese (one of the earliest such plantings in Australia), selling grapes to Primo Estate until 1999. The pair now vinify the near-organically grown grapes from the Versace vineyard, deliberately using a basket press and minimum technology.

Signature wine: Limited Release Shiraz

Primo Estate Est. 1979

Old Port Wakefield Rd, Virginia 5120
www.primoestate.com.au

 exports to UK, US

Roseworthy dux Joe Grilli has risen way above the constraints of the hot Adelaide Plains to produce an innovative and always excellent range of wines. However, the core lies with the zingy, fresh Colombard, trendy and stylish 'il briccone' Shiraz Sangiovese, the velvet-smooth Adelaide Shiraz and the distinguished, complex Joseph Moda Cabernet Merlot. Then there is the biennial release of the Joseph Sparkling Red, which sells out immediately, and Australia's best olive oil.

Signature wine: Joseph Moda Cabernet Merlot

Fleurieu Zone 🌿

Given its numerous population of five regions, the climatic homogeneity of the Fleurieu Zone is in stark contrast to most others in the state; only the Limestone Coast comes close, but not as close. The reason is the profound sea influence, which provides 24-hour, 365-days-a-year air conditioning.

Lake Alexandrina is a very large volume of water, with an important impact on Langhorne Creek, but – of course – pales into insignificance compared to the Southern Ocean. Nonetheless, few Australian wine lovers or critics living outside South Australia realise just how cool the climate of Langhorne Creek is, although they very likely know it can ripen generous yields of grapes, a rare double.

The partial exception to this is McLaren Vale, or at least the parts of it closest to Adelaide and furthest from the coast, where the sea influence diminishes to a degree. A second point of difference is that McLaren Vale has severe water restrictions, including a moratorium on the building of further dams for the collection of surface water (and there is no additional suitable underground water, thanks to salinity).

Thus the style of McLaren Vale wines, notably its reds, but also its whites, has always been full-bodied, or at least towards the end of that spectrum. Rhône Valley red varietals, notable Grenache and Shiraz but also Mourvèdre, flourish here, achieving maximum flavour at high alcohol levels (14% to 16.5% by volume, with an optimum average of 14.5% by volume). Cabernet Sauvignon is also an important variety.

Each of the four remaining regions produces medium-bodied red wines, and light to medium-bodied whites. Grenache and Mourvèdre are sparingly grown; rather, it is Shiraz and the Bordeaux varieties, both white (Semillon and Sauvignon Blanc) and red (Cabernet Sauvignon, Merlot and Malbec). As ever, Chardonnay is a common denominator across all the regions.

Another common denominator is the soft, beguiling fruit character of the red wines in particular. This was recognised by Wolf Blass in the early 1970s, and became the cornerstone of his red wine style: soft, fruity and gently mouthfilling right from the time the wines were bottled and sold.

[OPPOSITE] McLaren Vale.

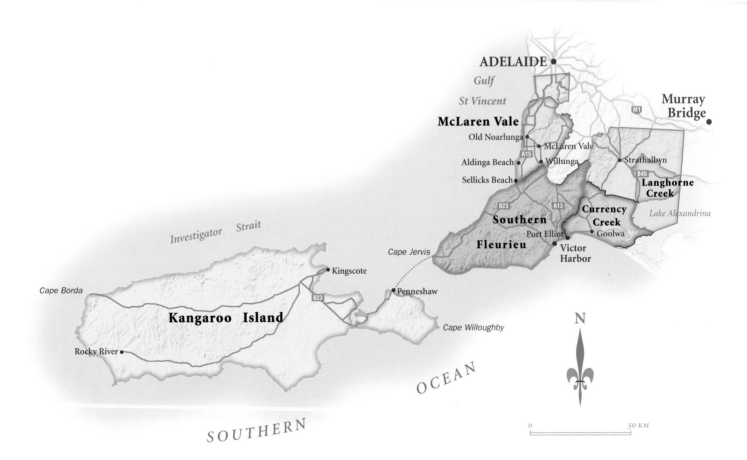

Fleurieu Zone
McLaren Vale ❧

Unlike the Silesian background of the Barossa and Clare Valleys, the development of the Southern Vales – from Reynella to McLaren Vale to Langhorne Creek – was almost exclusively due to the efforts of Englishmen. More precisely, to the efforts of three men: John Reynell, Thomas Hardy and Dr A. C. Kelly, with a lesser contribution from George Manning at Hope Farm and Frank Potts at Langhorne Creek.

Despite the early start – John Reynell laid the foundations for Château Reynella in 1838 – viticulture initially played second fiddle to wheat, which enjoyed a brief boom during the 1850s and 1860s. As in the Clare Valley, the soil's fertility was soon exhausted; the wheat fields disappeared as quickly as they had arrived.

In large part due to the success of Thomas Hardy, who acquired Tintara from Dr A. C. Kelly in 1876, the pace of viticultural development steadily picked up through the 1880s and 1890s. In 1903 over three million litres of wine (almost entirely red table and fortified) was made by the 19 wineries in the district. Thomas Hardy was the largest, followed (in order) by Reynella, Horndale, Vale Royal, Tatachilla, The Wattles, Kay Brothers Amery, Clarendon Vineyard, Pirramimma, Wirra Wirra, Mount Hurtle, Potts Bleasdale, Hope Vineyard, Mrs Douglas, Ryecroft, Katunga, Formby and E. Potts.

The prosperity was in large part founded on the English trade, with the staple export dark-coloured, high-alcohol, tannic dry red wine of legendary medicinal value. This trade continued (with a brief hiatus between 1940 and 1945) until well into the 1950s, largely through the agency of the Emu Wine Company, which was ultimately acquired by Thomas Hardy from its English owners.

McLaren Vale shared in the prosperity of the 1960s and 1970s, and quickly became the spiritual home of the small winery in Australia, then (but no more) boasting more small wineries than any other region by the early 1970s. The one threat was urban sprawl, which progressively swallowed the large vineyards that once existed between Reynella and Adelaide, and reduced those around Reynella to token levels.

Hopefully, there will be no more major inroads. Because Adelaide's population base is small, it exerts less pressure on McLaren Vale than, for example, Melbourne does on the Yarra Valley, and winemaking plays a much greater role in the economy and hence the political consciousness of South Australia than it does elsewhere.

On the other hand, the opportunities for expansion are extremely limited; not so much by urban pressure as by a severe shortage of water for irrigation. The underground watertable is severely depleted, and additional surface catchment has been prohibited since the mid 1990s while an extensive water resource study is carried out. The long-term solution would seem to be with diverting and piping part of the Murray River flow, but the cost of such a scheme makes it an improbable dream.

Notwithstanding these limitations, the region is experiencing prosperity reminiscent of its golden days at the end of the nineteenth century. Its traditional staples of Grenache and Shiraz (and also Mourvèdre) have come thundering back into vogue (supported, of course, by Cabernet Sauvignon) at the same time as it has forged a reputation for its Chardonnay, Sauvignon Blanc and Semillon. Only Riesling seems impervious to the charms of McLaren Vale, obdurately producing a rather heavy, oily wine.

McLaren Vale is not much over 35 kilometres south of Adelaide, and – once clear of the city traffic – the drive is a pleasant one. The scenery is varied, the ocean never far away. Winery restaurants exist in profusion, offering excellent food at yesterday's prices. (Adelaide residents refuse point-blank to pay more than a pittance for their restaurant meals.) While most visitors come in summer, those who are clever go in winter, the vineyards shimmering with yellow soursobs between the rows, tasting rooms uncrowded, and hearty food to go with hearty red wine in abundance.

[OPPOSITE & BELOW] McLaren Vale.

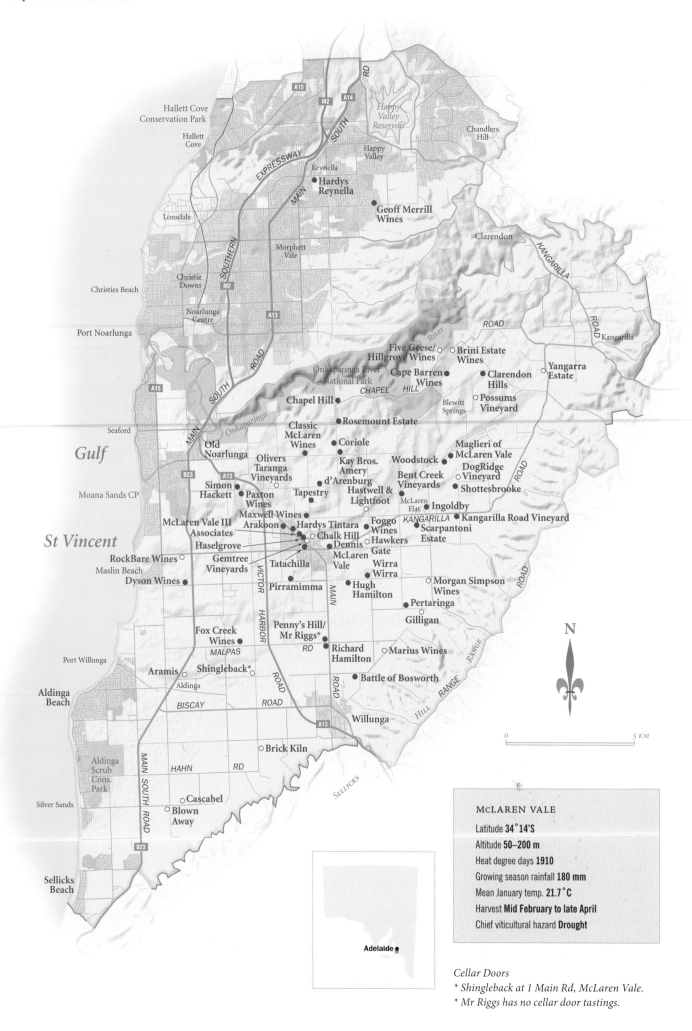

Hallett Cove
Conservation Park

Hallett
Cove

Happy
Valley
Reservoir

Chandlers
Hill

Reynella

**Hardys
Reynella**

**Geoff Merrill
Wines**

Lonsdale

Clarendon

Morphett
Vale

Christie
Downs

Christies Beach

Noarlunga
Centre

Port Noarlunga

River

Five Geese/
Hillgrove Wines

**Brini Estate
Wines**

Kangarilla

*Onkaparinga River
National Park*

**Cape Barren
Wines**

**Clarendon
Hills**

*Yangarra
Estate*

CHAPEL HILL

Blewitt
Springs

**Possums
Vineyard**

Chapel Hill

Seaford

Onkaparinga

Rosemount Estate

Gulf

**Classic
McLaren
Wines**

Coriole

**Maglieri of
McLaren Vale**

**Old
Noarlunga**

Woodstock

**Olivers
Taranga
Vineyards**

**Kay Bros.
Amery**

**DogRidge
Vineyard**

**Bent Creek
Vineyards**

Shottesbrooke

**Simon
Hackett**

d'Arenburg

Moana Sands CP

**Paxton
Wines**

Tapestry

**Hastwell &
Lightfoot**

*McLaren
Flat*

Ingoldby

Maxwell Wines

**McLaren Vale III
Associates**

Arakoon

Hardys Tintara

**Foggo
Wines**

KANGARILLA

Kangarilla Road Vineyard

St Vincent

Haselgrove

Chalk Hill

Dennis

**Hawkers
Gate**

**Scarpantoni
Estate**

RockBare Wines

**Gemtree
Vineyards**

**McLaren
Vale**

**Wirra
Wirra**

Maslin Beach

Tatachilla

**Morgan Simpson
Wines**

Dyson Wines

Pirramimma

**Hugh
Hamilton**

Pertaringa

**Penny's Hill/
Mr Riggs***

Gilligan

**Fox Creek
Wines**

MALPAS

RD

**Richard
Hamilton**

Marius Wines

Port Willunga

Aramis

Shingleback*

Battle of Bosworth

Aldinga

**Aldinga
Beach**

BISCAY

ROAD

Willunga

Brick Kiln

HAHN   *RD*

Aldinga
Scrub
Cons.
Park

Silver Sands

Cascabel

**Blown
Away**

Sellicks
Beach

N

0   5 KM

MCLAREN VALE

Latitude **34°14'S**

Altitude **50–200 m**

Heat degree days **1910**

Growing season rainfall **180 mm**

Mean January temp. **21.7°C**

Harvest **Mid February to late April**

Chief viticultural hazard **Drought**

Adelaide

Cellar Doors

* Shingleback at 1 Main Rd, McLaren Vale.

* Mr Riggs has no cellar door tastings.

The Region

CLIMATE

There is substantial meso-climatic variation throughout McLaren Vale, due to varying exposure to the cooling influence of the nearby ocean (or conversely, to protection from it). There are also significant changes in altitude as the region merges with the Adelaide Hills. Summer rainfall is low, and irrigation is considered essential for young vines. Site selection, and site/variety marriage, are all-important.

SOIL & TOPOGRAPHY

There is a wide variety of soil types, even though red-brown loamy sands dominate. The structurally similar grey-brown loamy sand with yellow clay subsoils interspersed with limey deposits, and a slightly more sandy version of the same, are common. This tendency to a more sandy character reaches a peak around the Blewitt Springs region. Finally, there are patches of black or red friable loams of the Coonawarra terra rossa.

PRINCIPAL GRAPE VARIETIES

Overall, 80 per cent red, 20 per cent white.
In descending order:

Shiraz

Cabernet Sauvignon

Chardonnay

Grenache

Merlot

Semillon

Sauvignon Blanc

Riesling

Pinot Noir

Cabernet Franc

Chenin Blanc

Petit Verdot.

[above] Grenache end post, Hardys Reynella, McLaren Vale. [right] Foggo Wines, McLaren Vale.

 ## WHITE WINE STYLES

Chardonnay has established a stranglehold on white grape plantings in the region since its introduction a little over 25 years ago. The style varies according to site, maker input and vintage conditions, ranging from elegant, citrus-tinged wines through to richer, fleshier, peachy/buttery versions.

Sauvignon Blanc. Arguably, the cooler sites in McLaren Vale are among Australia's better areas for Sauvignon Blanc; while vintage variation does play a role, in most years the wines have good varietal character without becoming coarse or heavy. Semillon is often incorporated as a blend component to good effect.

RED WINE STYLES

Shiraz was the backbone of the industry for much of the twentieth century. It produces a densely coloured, richly flavoured wine with a velvety texture. This is not the region for the peppery/spicy type of Shiraz, but the style of Australian wine which, in bygone years, was always labelled Burgundy. The regional signatures are a frequent dash of dark, bitter chocolate (non-controversial) and levels of alcohol which frequently reach or exceed 15% by volume (decidedly more controversial). The fact is that some high-alcohol wines show 'dead fruit' character, making them less attractive, while others suffer not at all.

Cabernet Sauvignon is full-bodied and rich, often with a touch of dark chocolate intermixed with blackcurrant, but normally avoids overripe, jammy characteristics. The tannins are plentiful but soft, and the wines have the structure for long ageing when made in cooler vintages.

Grenache enjoyed a spirited renaissance in the latter part of the 1990s, continuing into the new millennium; the older plantings produce incredibly richly flavoured wines, high in alcohol and with an almost juicy sweetness. From the sandy hillsides around Blewitt Springs more spicy, lively wines can be made. All are of excellent quality.

Other varieties. Viognier, Sangiovese, Petit Verdot and Tempranillo are statistically unimportant as yet, but all show considerable promise.

Wineries of McLaren Vale

Brini Estate Wines Est. 2000
RSD 600 Blewitt Springs Rd,
McLaren Vale 5171 (postal)
briniwines@bigpond.com

The Brini family has been growing grapes in the Blewitt Springs area of McLaren Vale since 1953. In 2000 brothers John and Marcello Brini established Brini Estate Wines to vinify a portion of the grape production that up to that time was exclusively sold to companies such as Penfolds, Rosemount Estate and d'Arenberg. The flagship Sebastian Shiraz is produced from dry-grown vines planted in 1947, the Shiraz Grenache from dry-grown vines planted in 1964. Skilled contract winemaking by Brian Light, coupled with impeccable fruit sources, has resulted in a new star in the McLaren Vale firmament.
Signature wine: Sebastian Shiraz

Clarendon Hills Est. 1989
Brookmans Rd, Blewitt Springs 5171
clarendonhills@bigpond.com

exports to UK

Age and experience, it would seem, have mellowed owner/winemaker Roman Bratasiuk – and the style of his wines; the formerly stratospheric prices have also somewhat diminished. Once formidable and often rustic, they are now far more sculpted and smooth, at times bordering on downright elegant. Clarendon Hills has no vineyards of its own, but has sought out special parcels of old-vine vineyards to make its exclusively red wines, focussing on Shiraz, Grenache and Cabernet Sauvignon.
Signature wine: Hickinbotham Vineyard Shiraz

Coriole Est. 1967
Chaffeys Rd, McLaren Vale 5171
www.coriole.com

exports to UK, US

Justifiably best known for its Shiraz, which – both in the rare Lloyd Reserve and standard forms – is extremely impressive. Coriole has spread its wings in recent years, being one of the first wineries to catch on to the Italian fashion with its Sangiovese, but its white varietal wines (Semillon, Semillon Sauvignon Blanc and Chenin Blanc) lose nothing by comparison. It is also a producer of high-quality olive oil distributed commercially throughout Australia.
Signature wine: Lloyd Reserve Shiraz

d'Arenberg Est. 1912
Osborn Rd, McLaren Vale 5171
www.darenberg.com.au

exports to UK, US

Originally a conservative, traditional business (albeit successful), d'Arenberg adopted a much higher profile in the second half of the 1990s, with a cascade of volubly worded labels and the opening of a spectacularly situated and high-quality restaurant, d'Arry's Verandah. Happily, wine quality has more than kept pace with the label changes, covering an ever-increasing range of mainstream and more exotic varieties. Energetic marketing by perpetual motion Chester Osborn (also chief winemaker and son of industry legend d'Arry Osborn) has built worldwide exports and domestic sales alike.
Signature wine: The Dead Arm Shiraz

Foggo Wines Est. 1999
Lot 21, Foggos Rd, McLaren Vale 5171
www.foggowines.com.au

exports to US

Herb and Sandie Van De Wiel have been grapegrowers in McLaren Vale for 16 years, and in 1999 they were able to purchase the former Curtis winery, which, after refurbishment, gave them the opportunity to establish Foggo Wines. They have three vineyards, the oldest (on Foggo Road) is 9 ha of Shiraz dating back to 1915; their 80-year-old Grenache, 45-year-old Cinsaut and 20-year-old Chardonnay and Sauvignon Blanc come from the other vineyards, totalling 25 ha in all. With help from winemaker son Ben, they have a range of Shiraz, Grenache, Grenache Shiraz Cinsaut and Cabernet Sauvignon equal to the best.
Signature wine: Hubertus Reserve Shiraz

Gemtree Vineyards Est. 1992
PO Box 164, McLaren Vale 5171
www.gemtreevineyards.com.au

exports to UK, US

The Buttery family, headed by Paul and Jill and with the involvement of Melissa as viticulturist for Gemtree Vineyards, has been actively involved as grapegrowers in McLaren Vale since 1980, when it purchased its first vineyard. Today the family owns a little over 130 ha of vines, and produces Chardonnay, Shiraz, Tempranillo and a Cabernet blend. Only the best grapes are kept for the lush, supple red wines, the lion's share of the production sold to other makers.
Signature wine: Paragon Shiraz

Geoff Merrill Wines Est. 1980
291 Pimpala Rd, Woodcroft 5162
www.geoffmerrillwines.com

exports to UK, US

If Geoff Merrill ever loses his impish sense of humour or his zest for life, high and not-so-high, we shall all be the poorer. He has lifted the profile of his wines on the domestic market; in 1998 the product range was rearranged into three tiers: premium (in fact simply varietal); reserve, the latter being the older (and best) wines, reflecting the desire for elegance and subtlety of this otherwise exuberant winemaker; and at the top, Henley Shiraz. Constant overseas travel, particularly to the UK, has built a substantial export base.
Signature wine: Henley Shiraz

Hardys Reynella/Tintara
Est. 1853/1876
Reynell Rd, Reynella 5161
www.hardys.com.au

exports to UK, US

Rather like the little old lady who swallowed a fly, the old, established firm of Thomas Hardy merged with Berri Renmano in 1992, going from strength to strength thereafter until it, in turn, was swallowed by the giant US Constellation Group, to form the largest wine group in the world. The wide range of product, from fighting varietal to ultra-premium, (so far at least) remains unaffected. Hardys has a dedicated and highly talented winemaking team which often seems to be one step ahead of the field.

Signature wine: Eileen Hardy Chardonnay/Eileen Hardy Shiraz

Mitolo Wines Est. 1999

34 Barossa Valley Way, Tanunda 5352 (postal)
www.mitolowines.com.au

 exports to UK, US

Frank Mitolo began making wine in 1995 as a hobby, and soon progressed to undertaking formal studies in winemaking. His interest grew year by year, but it was not until 2000 that he took a hugely successful plunge into the commercial end of the business, retaining Ben Glaetzer to make the wines for him. Since that time, a remarkably good series of wines have been released, focussing on old-vine Shiraz from Barossa Valley and McLaren Vale vineyards.

Signature wine: G.A.M. McLaren Vale Shiraz

Mr Riggs Wine Company
Est. 2001

PO Box 584, McLaren Vale 5171
www.pennyshill.com.au

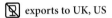 exports to US

After 20 years as winemaker at Wirra Wirra (and elsewhere) lanky and personable Ben Riggs decided to establish his own business. His major activity is as a consultant winemaker here and overseas, sourcing grapes for and making commercial batches of wine, adopting a 'grape to plate' approach. He also makes stylish wine for the Mr Riggs label, initially from old vines in McLaren Vale, and in due course from his own recently planted vineyard with 6.5 ha of Shiraz, Viognier and Petit Verdot.

Signature wine: Shiraz

Pirramimma Est. 1892

Johnston Rd, McLaren Vale 5171
www.pirramimma.com.au

exports to UK

A long-established, conservative, family-owned company with outstanding vineyard resources. After a quiet period, it has turned those resources to full effect, with a series of intense, old-vine varietals including Shiraz, Grenache, Cabernet Sauvignon and Petit Verdot. Upgraded packaging and a much-lifted approach to marketing has given the still modestly priced wines the attention they deserve.

Signature wine: Reserve Petit Verdot

Rosemount Estate Est. 1888

Chaffeys Rd, McLaren Vale 5171
www.rosemountestate.com.au

exports to UK, US

The specialist red-wine arm of Rosemount Estate, responsible for its prestigious Balmoral Syrah, Show Reserve Shiraz and GSM (Grenache Shiraz Mourvèdre), as well as most of the other McLaren Vale-based Rosemount brands. These wines come in large measure from 325 ha of estate plantings, and are consistently the best in the entire Rosemount portfolio. There is nothing to suggest much will change in the wake of the acquisition of Southcorp (and hence Rosemount) by Fosters Wine Estates, unless it be the sale of Rosemount as a whole.

Signature wine: Balmoral Syrah

Tatachilla Est. 1901

151 Main Rd, McLaren Vale 5171
www.tatachillawinery.com.au

exports to UK, US

Between 1901 and 1995 the chequered history of Tatachilla could have given rise to a long-running television soap series. Even since then, it has passed through three ownerships, now being part of the Lion Nathan Group. For all that, it produces a range of red and white varietal wines from McLaren Vale and the Adelaide Hills which represent excellent value. Chardonnay, Shiraz, Merlot and Cabernet Sauvignon are its strengths.

Signature wine: Foundation Shiraz

Wirra Wirra Est. 1969

McMurtie Rd, McLaren Vale 5171
www.wirrawirra.com

exports to UK, US

Founded by the late, much-loved, highly eccentric Greg Trott. Long-respected for the consistency of its white wines, Wirra Wirra has now established an equally formidable reputation for its reds. Right across the board, the wines are of exemplary character, quality and style, The Angelus Cabernet Sauvignon and RSW Shiraz battling with each other for supremacy.

Signature wine: RSW Shiraz

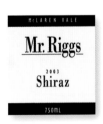

N

Bletchley

Belvidere

WELLINGTON

ROAD

LANGHORNE

Ben Potts Wines

Bremerton Wines ● *RD*
Cleggett Wines;
Angas Plains Estate;
Raydon Estate;
Oddfellows Wines

CREEK

Langhorne
Creek

Zonte's
Footstep

Bleasdale Vineyards

Angas
Vineyards

WELLINGTON   *ROAD*

Lake Breeze Wines

MILANG

Angas

Step Road
Winery

Bremer

LAKE

Temple
Bruer

Brothers in Arms

River

PLAINS

Marandoo
Estate

Dog Lake

ROAD

BALLANDOWN   *ROAD*

Casa
Freschi

River

TOLDEROL   *ROAD*

Tolderol Game Res.

ROAD

ROAD

LAKE

LAKE   ALEXANDRINA

Milang

0   5 *KM*

B45

B45

LANGHORNE CREEK

Latitude **35˚15'S**

Altitude **30 m**

Heat degree days **1520**

Growing season rainfall **140 mm**

Mean January temp. **19.9˚C**

Harvest **Late February to late April**

Chief viticultural hazard **Nil**

Adelaide ●

FLEURIEU ZONE
Langhorne Creek ❦

Alfred Langhorne left Sydney in 1841 with a mob of cattle and drove them all the way to the flood plain of the Bremer River. He crossed the river, and decided far was far enough, squatting on the fertile ground and giving his name to Langhorne's Crossing. When a bridge was built it was likewise named after him, and the region became known as Langhorne's Creek.

Frank Potts had arrived in South Australia even earlier (in 1836), and when the government subdivided the area in 1850, he acquired 130 hectares, reputedly attracted by the fertile soils and vast red gums. Ten years later he planted a little over 12 hectares of Shiraz and Verdelho on either side of the Bremer River, constructing a unique weir and channel system by which he was able to divert the river during winter, flood irrigating (to a depth of several feet) the vineyard and providing the subsoil with sufficient moisture to last through the entire growing season.

Five generations later the Potts family still presides over Bleasdale, but Langhorne Creek is a different place these days. The enduring link with the past is the Stonyfell Vineyard, established in 1890 by Arthur Formby, but which soon passed into the ownership of Ronald Martin of Stonyfell, and hence into that of Saltram. The individually numbered and strikingly labelled bottles of Stonyfell Metala Cabernet Shiraz remain one of the most immediately recognisable of all Australian wine labels.

Another label, less enduring, was that of Lindemans Oeillade Shiraz Bin 426, introduced in the 1960s. Another name for Cinsaut in Australia, the Oeillade Shiraz was significant as a forerunner for the arrival en masse (initially as grape purchasers) of major South Australian wine companies. Wolf Blass discovered the merits of Langhorne Creek early in the piece; not only did it play a major role in the building of his large personal empire, but also gave rise to his famous observation that only a fool would bother investing in Coonawarra – an area which, in his view, could not produce decent wine.

Emphatic though the endorsement by Wolf Blass may have been, an even more significant one was made by Orlando Wyndham, which in the mid 1990s invested $15 million in a purpose-designed state-of-the-art vineyard planted specifically to meet the needs of its world brand, Jacob's Creek. Using GPS and laser-guided planting machinery, vineyards of 300 to 500 hectares were planted in a single season, ultimately lifting the planted area from 1650 hectares to over 4400 hectares. Today Langhorne Creek is one of the most intensively planted regions in Australia, the vineyards a precise pattern of oblong mosaics making a vivid picture from the air.

While the major wineries and highly efficient broad-acre farming of vines remain the driving force of Langhorne Creek, the quality of the wines coming from its rapidly increasing number of resident wineries leaves no doubt this region is well capable of producing premium-quality wines.

BREMERTON WINES, LANGHORNE CREEK.

The Region 🍇

CLIMATE

The growing season climate is predominantly shaped by the on-shore southerly winds blowing in from the Southern Ocean and across Lake Alexandrina. While intermittently broken by periods of hot weather associated with northerly winds emanating from Central Australia, the prevailing southerlies normally reduce diurnal temperature fluctuations; they also decrease sunshine hours and overall summer temperatures, while increasing the relative humidity. The winter–spring rainfall pattern persists, however, and irrigation is universally practised, these days utilising conventional drip irrigation.

SOIL & TOPOGRAPHY

The flat river delta landscape is ideally suited for large-scale, relatively low-cost vineyard developments, all with a high degree of mechanisation. These are predominantly deep alluvial sandy loams varying from red-brown to dark grey, with patches of black, self-mulching clays. All promote vine vigour and generous canopies and cropping levels.

PRINCIPAL GRAPE VARIETIES

The split is 85 per cent red and 15 per cent white. In descending order:

CABERNET SAUVIGNON

SHIRAZ

CHARDONNAY

MERLOT

RIESLING

GRENACHE

VERDELHO.

The lion's share is Cabernet Sauvignon and Shiraz; Petit Verdot and Sangiovese are waiting in the wings.

[ABOVE] BEN POTTS WINES, LANGHORNE CREEK.
[RIGHT] LUCY WILLSON & REBECCA WILLSON, BREMERTON WINES, LANGHORNE CREEK.

 WHITE WINE STYLES

Verdelho, although produced in relatively small quantities, is a regional specialty, originally as a fortified wine in the style of Madeira, but now handled as a soft, early-maturing table wine.

 RED WINE STYLES

Cabernet Sauvignon and Blends. Cabernet Sauvignon is of equal importance in its own right with Shiraz, but is often blended with smaller amounts of Merlot, Malbec and Petit Verdot, which increases the overall volume. The wines have a soft generosity of red and black fruits, the tannins never hard or harsh. The plush fruit allows plenty of new oak to be absorbed without dominating the wine, all adding up to a style which is attractive from the word go.

Shiraz and Blends. After lagging behind Cabernet Sauvignon, Shiraz is now on equal terms in plantings, the two dominating the landscape. The best wines retain regional softness, but have great depth of flavour, ranging through blackberry, prune, liquorice, bitter chocolate, sometimes detouring into a red fruit/raspberry spectrum. Shiraz Cabernet and Shiraz Malbec blends also work well.

Wineries of Langhorne Creek

Ben Potts Wines Est. 2002
Step Rd, Langhorne Creek 5255 (postal)
www.benpottswines.com.au

Ben Potts is the sixth generation to be involved in grapegrowing and winemaking in Langhorne Creek, the first being Frank Potts, founder of Bleasdale Vineyards. Ben completed an oenology degree at Charles Sturt University, and (aged 25) ventured into winemaking on a commercial scale in 2002. Fiddle's Block Shiraz is named after great-grandfather Fiddle; Lenny's Block Cabernet Malbec after grandfather Len; and Bill's Block Malbec after father Bill.
Signature wine: Lenny's Block Cabernet Malbec

Bleasdale Vineyards Est. 1850
Wellington Rd, Langhorne Creek 5255
www.bleasdale.com.au
exports to UK, US

For many decades the only functioning winery in Langhorne Creek, and one of the most historic wineries in Australia (established by Frank Potts in 1850, and still in family ownership). Frank Potts' ingenious scheme of diverting water from the Bremer River was a forerunner of the harnessing of the Murray River by the Chaffey brothers 40 years later. The wines offer excellent value for money, all showing that particular softness which is the hallmark of the Langhorne Creek region, but moving with the times with super-cuvees such as Frank Potts.
Signature wine: Frank Potts (Bordeaux blend)

Bremerton Wines Est. 1988
Strathalbyn Rd, Langhorne Creek 5255
www.bremerton.com.au
exports to UK, US

Several generations of the Willson family have seen a relatively small grapegrowing business flourish, plantings doubling to over 100 ha (predominantly Cabernet Sauvignon, Shiraz and Merlot), and second-generation sisters Rebecca and Lucy taking conduct of the business in 2004. High-quality wines are being supported by revamped labels and packaging.
Signature wine: Old Adam Shiraz

Brothers in Arms Est. 1998
PO Box 840, Langhorne Creek 5255
www.brothersinarms.com.au
exports to UK, US

Five generations of the Adams family have been growing grapes at Langhorne Creek since 1891, when the first vines at the famed Metala vineyards were planted. Tom and Guy Adams have both improved the viticulture and expanded the plantings to the present 40 ha of Shiraz and Cabernet Sauvignon. It was not until 1998 that they took the next step, deciding to hold back a small proportion of the production for vinification under the Brothers in Arms brand, with David Freschi as contract winemaker.
Signature wine: Shiraz

Casa Freschi Est. 1998
30 Jackson Ave, Strathalbyn 5255
www.casafreschi.com.au
exports to US

David Freschi graduated with a degree in oenology from Roseworthy in 1991, and spent most of the decade working overseas in California, Italy and New Zealand. In 1998 he and his wife decided to trade in the corporate wine world for a small family-owned winemaking business, with a core of 2.5 ha of vines established by Freschi's parents in 1972. An additional 2 ha of Nebbiolo has been planted adjacent to the original vineyard.
Signature wine: Profondo
(Cabernet Shiraz Malbec)

Lake Breeze Wines Est. 1987
Step Rd, Langhorne Creek 5255
www.lakebreeze.com.au
exports to UK, US

The Folletts have been farmers at Langhorne Creek since 1880, grapegrowers since the 1930s. Since 1987 a small proportion of their grapes has been made into wine, and a cellar-door sales facility was opened in early 1991. The quality of the releases made by Greg Follett (Chardonnay, Shiraz, Grenache, Cabernet Sauvignon) has been exemplary.
Signature wine: Bernoota (Cabernet Shiraz)

Oddfellows Wines Est. 1997
PO Box 88, Langhorne Creek 5255
wine@oddfellowswines.com.au
exports to US

An export-oriented business (to China, Singapore, US, Canada and Belgium), buying its grapes from a range of Langhorne Creek grapegrowers. Two wines only are made, Shiraz and Shiraz Cabernet, by Lake Breeze winemaker Greg Follett, and the quality is unimpeachable. Exports are supplemented by direct sales in Australia.
Signature wine: Shiraz Cabernet

Temple Bruer Est. 1980
Milang Rd, Strathalbyn 5255
www.templebruer.com.au
exports to US

Always known for its eclectic range of wines, Temple Bruer (which also carries on a substantial business as a vine propagation nursery) has seen a sharp but consistent lift in wine quality. Clean, modern, redesigned labels add to the appeal of a stimulatingly different range of red wines. Part of the production from the 24 ha of estate vineyards is sold to others, the remainder being made under the Temple Bruer label. The vineyard is now certified organic, and Temple Bruer has become one of the major players in the organic movement.
Signature wine: Reserve Organically Grown Cabernet Petit Verdot

Zonte's Footstep Est. 1997
PO Box 53, Langhorne Creek 5255
www.zontesfootstep.com.au
exports to UK

The 215 ha vineyard of Zonte's Footstep was created when a group of old schoolmates banded together to purchase the land and established the vineyard under the direction of viticulturist Geoff Hardy and long-term vigneron John Pargeter. Obviously enough, a large percentage of the grapes are sold to others, a small part skilfully made by Ben Riggs. The wine quality is as good as the prices are modest, the snappy marketing masterminded by Zar Brooks.
Signature wine: Cabernet Malbec

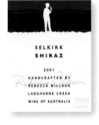

FLEURIEU ZONE
Currency Creek

The region was first explored by Captain Charles Sturt, who travelled down the Murray River in 1829–30, and whose last campsite was near the present town of Goolwa, which was the first (or last, depending which way you were travelling) port on the Murray River. In 1837 Hindmarsh Island and the town of Currency Creek were officially named, and an elaborate town plan for Currency Creek was laid out in 1840.

Agriculture, river transport and recreation developed over the next 50 years, but it was not until 1969 that the first vines were planted, by Wally and Rosemary Tonkin: one acre each of Riesling, Grenache, Shiraz and Cabernet Sauvignon. Despite local cynicism, the vines flourished and the first vintage followed in 1972, for what was then called Santa Rosa Winery (now Currency Creek Estate). In that same year the first vines (2.6 hectares) were planted at what is now Middleton Winery, and were likewise successful.

The region's very low growing-season rainfall means that irrigation is essential; fortunately, abundant high-quality water is available, with no restrictions on its use.

Hindmarsh Island, the subject of a celebrated and long-running battle over Aboriginal 'secret women's business' and the government's desire to build a bridge linking the island to the mainland, is part of the region, and home to one of its best wineries, Angus Wines.

Currency Creek's proximity (on the west) to Victor Harbor, Adelaide's favourite seaside holiday resort, must ultimately be an asset and help to sustain more small wineries, but for the time being the region has a surprisingly low profile.

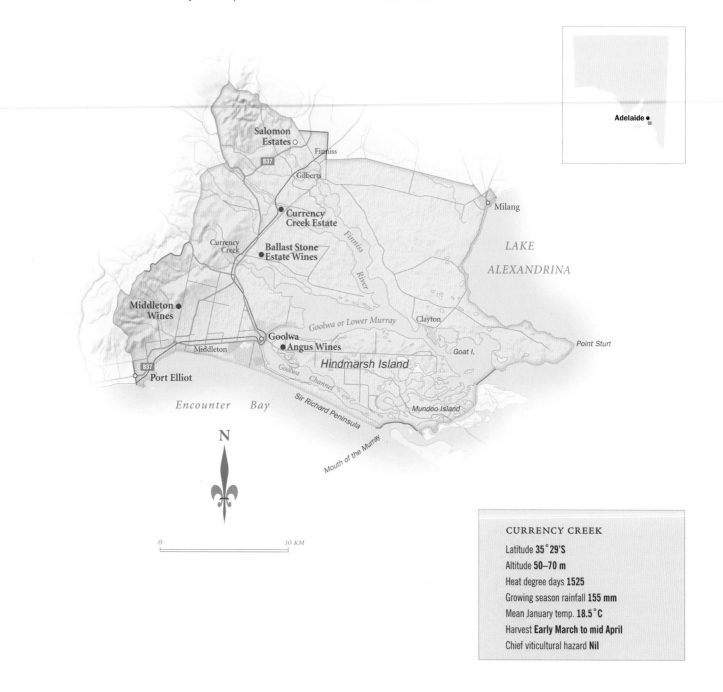

CURRENCY CREEK

Latitude **35°29'S**

Altitude **50–70 m**

Heat degree days **1525**

Growing season rainfall **155 mm**

Mean January temp. **18.5°C**

Harvest **Early March to mid April**

Chief viticultural hazard **Nil**

The Region

CLIMATE

The climate of Currency Creek is slightly warmer than that of Langhorne Creek and Coonawarra, on a par with that of Margaret River and California's Carneros. In common with those regions, it is strongly maritime (due to Lake Alexandrina and the Southern Ocean), avoiding extremes of cold or heat.

SOIL & TOPOGRAPHY

Dominant rolling sandy slopes (which allow easy infiltration of water) overlaying friable cracking clays, easily accessed by the vines' roots. The other suitable soils are loams with red alkaline clayey subsoils.

PRINCIPAL GRAPE VARIETIES

Overall, 85 per cent red, 15 per cent white. In descending order:

CABERNET SAUVIGNON

SHIRAZ

MERLOT

SAUVIGNON BLANC

CHARDONNAY

SEMILLON.

WHITE WINE STYLES

Sauvignon Blanc is the dominant white variety, sometimes assisted by a little Semillon. The varietal definition is better than that of McLaren Vale, the wines having greater delicacy and freshness.

Semillon has a freshness, intensity and delicacy reminiscent of the Hunter Valley at its best.

RED WINE STYLES

Shiraz has fragrance and lifted aromatics, the palate with elegance and finesse, utterly unlike near-neighbour McLaren Vale. The wines are medium-bodied, low in tannin and extract, with Rhône Valley-like spicy fruit and a silky texture.

Cabernet Sauvignon is ideally suited to the temperate, mild climate of the region, producing complete and rounded wines with clear varietal definition. As the ripening curve increases, the flavours move from coffee to blackberry to blackcurrant/cassis at optimum ripeness. The style has more similarity to that of Coonawarra than either Langhorne Creek or McLaren Vale.

Merlot, while not widely planted so far, performs very well, with good perfume and varietal character, providing a synergistic blend with Cabernet Sauvignon. It would also seem to offer potential as a varietal wine in its own right.

Wineries of Currency Creek

Angus Wines Est. 1995

Captain Sturt Rd, Hindmarsh Island 5214
www.anguswines.com.au

🍷 exports to UK

Susan and Alistair Angus were the pioneer viticulturists on Hindmarsh Island, now connected to the mainland by a once highly controversial bridge opposed by the local indigenous population. They have established 4.5 ha of Shiraz and 1.5 ha of Semillon, the wine being contract-made for them by Mike Farmilo at The Fleurieu Winery in McLaren Vale. Part is bottled under the Angus Wines label, a larger amount being sold in bulk to other wineries. Every aspect of packaging and marketing the wine has a sophisticated touch, with quality to match.

Signature wine: Sturt Ridge Semillon

Ballast Stone Estate Wines

Est. 2001
Myrtle Grove Rd, Currency Creek 5214
www.ballaststone.com.au

🍷 exports to UK

The Shaw family had been grapegrowers in McLaren Vale for 25 years before deciding to establish a large vineyard in Currency Creek in 1994. Two hundred and fifty ha have been planted, mainly Cabernet Sauvignon and Shiraz, with much smaller quantities of eight other trendy varieties. A large on-site winery has been built, but only a small part of the production is being sold under the Ballast Stone Estate label, albeit covering eight mainstream varieties.

Signature wine: Shiraz

Currency Creek Estate

Est. 1969
Winery Rd, Currency Creek 5214
www.currencycreekwines.com.au

🍷 🍴 exports to US

By far the oldest winery in the region, travelling under various names (Santa Rosa and Tonkins) but always having its wine made off-site under contract. Now part of the Ballast Stone Estate group, where the typically elegant wines are made, under a new, trendy series of brand names.

Signature wine: The Creek Station Semillon Sauvignon Blanc

Salomon Estates

Est. 1997
PO Box 621, McLaren Vale 5171
sallyp@senet.com.au

🚫

Bert Salomon is an Austrian winemaker who became acquainted with Australia as the first importer of Australian wines (Penfolds) into Austria, and was so taken by Adelaide that he moved his family there for the first few months each year, setting in place an Australian red winemaking venture. He is now a full-time travelling winemaker, running the family winery in the northern hemisphere vintage, and overseeing the making of the excellent Salomon Estates wines at Boar's Rock in the first half of the year.

Signature wine: Finniss River Cabernet Merlot

NEAR CURRENCY CREEK ESTATE.

FLEURIEU ZONE
Kangaroo Island ❧

The synergy between wine and tourism is well known, but Kangaroo Island has the potential to develop it to an unprecedented degree. This third-largest island off the coast of Australia (nine times larger than Singapore Island, 60 times larger than Hong Kong Island) offers an extraordinary range of attractions for the tourist, the best known being its native flora and fauna, unpolluted beaches and coastal scenery. It is also rapidly gaining a reputation for high-quality food products (witness Kangaroo Island chicken, Ligurian bee honey, and of course all manner of seafood), with vineyards now making their contribution.

While the native habitat has been in existence for untold centuries, early attempts to settle on the island proved more difficult than might be imagined today. Likewise sporadic moves to establish vines in the early 1900s (by the Potts family of Bleasdale), then in 1951, next in 1955, and in the 1970s, all came to nothing. It was not until 1985 that Michael and Rosi Florance succeeded in establishing 1 hectare of Cabernet Sauvignon, Merlot and Cabernet Franc vines, although birds proved a major problem, delaying the first vintage until 1990.

In conjunction with the Florances, Caj Amadio (of Chain of Ponds in the Adelaide Hills) established Kangaroo Island Trading Co., which buys grapes from a number of growers and sells the wine under the Kangaroo Island Vines brand name.

The highest profile development on the island is that of French Flying Winemaker Jacques Lurton, who has a 300 hectare property so far planted with 11 hectares of Sangiovese, Cabernet Franc, Malbec, Shiraz, Grenache, Semillon and Viognier. The Islander Estate, as it is known, is the most important single wine venture on Kangaroo Island, with its own on-site winery and a 100 per cent estate-based focus.

The island's slopes are gentle, with the north and north-east facing sites being preferred for viticulture. Obviously, there is no frost risk in the coastal areas that benefit from the maritime influence. A measure of protection from the prevailing south-easterly winds is the major consideration in site selection.

This is an unspoilt and largely undiscovered treasure island for tourists. Daily light plane access (a 25-minute flight from Adelaide airport) and increased sea crossings (for motor vehicles) will result in greater visitation, but hopefully not degrade the island's freshness and beauty.

[ABOVE] THE ISLANDER ESTATE VINEYARDS, KANGAROO ISLAND. [OPPOSITE] JACQUES LURTON, THE ISLANDER ESTATE VINEYARD, KANGAROO ISLAND.

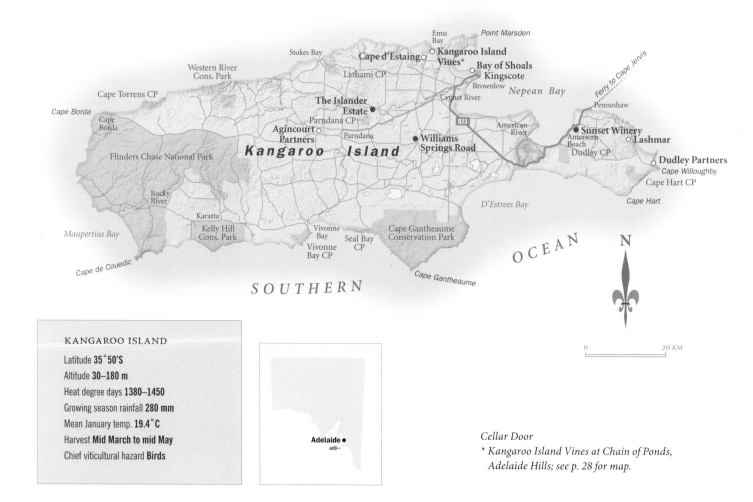

KANGAROO ISLAND

Latitude **35°50'S**

Altitude **30–180 m**

Heat degree days **1380–1450**

Growing season rainfall **280 mm**

Mean January temp. **19.4°C**

Harvest **Mid March to mid May**

Chief viticultural hazard **Birds**

Cellar Door
* Kangaroo Island Vines at Chain of Ponds, Adelaide Hills; see p. 28 for map.

The Region

CLIMATE

Self-evidently, the climate is wholly maritime-influenced, with the prevailing winds during the growing season (and in particular December to March) coming directly from the Southern Ocean. The average summer temperature is 25°C, significantly cooler than that of Adelaide, while the winter temperatures are several degrees warmer. The low growing season rainfall makes irrigation desirable, but the quite high relative humidity of 74 per cent renders the vineyards moderately susceptible to the mildews and to botrytis. Overall, the climate is temperate and devoid of extremes, with a particularly even accumulation of heat.

SOIL & TOPOGRAPHY

The soils are chiefly weakly structured, shallow red-brown sands overlying limestone in some sites, and have limited water-holding capacity, which emphasises the need for irrigation. Generally speaking, the soils are similar to those of Padthaway, and can sustain good yields if adequate water is applied.

PRINCIPAL GRAPE VARIETIES

Overall, 80 per cent red, 20 per cent white. In descending order:

SHIRAZ

CABERNET SAUVIGNON

CHARDONNAY

MERLOT

SANGIOVESE

CABERNET FRANC

RIESLING

SEMILLON.

WHITE WINE STYLES

Chardonnay is light to medium-bodied, usually either unoaked or made with modest amounts of oak.

Semillon can make wine of considerable complexity.

Riesling performs better here than in McLaren Vale, but is nonetheless a soft, early maturing style.

RED WINE STYLES

Cabernet Sauvignon Merlot provides the longest established style, consistently showing fragrant aromas, and elegant spicy/cedary overtones to red berry fruit, sometimes with touches of leaf and mint.

Sangiovese is the principal choice of Jacques Lurton, blended with Cabernet Franc for The Islander – spicy, savoury and elegant.

Shiraz makes surprisingly rich, ripe wines, with ample blackberry fruit in warmer vintages.

Wineries of Kangaroo Island

Bay of Shoals Est. 1994

19 Flinders Ave, Kingscote,
Kangaroo Island 5223 (postal)
veronica@kin.on.net

John Willoughby's vineyard overlooks the Bay of Shoals, which is the northern boundary of Kingscote, Kangaroo Island's main town. Planting of the vineyard began in 1994, and has now reached 10 ha of Riesling, Chardonnay, Sauvignon Blanc, Cabernet Sauvignon and Shiraz. In addition 460 olive trees have been planted to produce table olives. The wines are contract-made by Bethany Wines in the Barossa Valley.

Signature wine: Cabernet Sauvignon

Cape d'Estaing Est. 1994

PO Box 214, Kingscote, Kangaroo Island 5223
www.capedestaingwines.com
 exports to US

Partners Graham and Jude Allison, Alan and Ann Byers, Marg and Wayne Conaghty and Robin and Heather Moody have established 9 ha of Cabernet Sauvignon and Shiraz near Wisanger. Robin Moody was a long-serving senior employee of Southcorp, with a broad knowledge of all aspects of grapegrowing and winemaking; it's he who joins with contract winemaker Mark Farmilo each year. There is limited retail distribution in Adelaide; the wines are also available by mail order.

Signature wine: Shiraz

Kangaroo Island Vines Est. 1990

c/o 413 Payneham Rd, Felixstow 5070
(08) 8365 3411

(at Chain of Ponds, Adelaide Hills)

Kangaroo Island is the venture of Caj and Genny Amadio, with the wines being sold through the Chain of Ponds cellar door. The Amadios were the first to commercially sell Kangaroo Island wines and have been the focal point of the development of vineyards on the island, producing the wines not only from their own tiny planting of 450 vines on quarter of an acre (0.1 ha), but buying Shiraz, Merlot and Cabernet Sauvignon from other vignerons on the island.

Signature wine: Florance Cabernet Merlot

The Islander Estate Vineyards

Est. 2000
Jumbuck–Bark Hut Rd, Parndana 5220
www.islanderestatevineyards.com.au

The island showpiece, founded by one of the most famous Flying Winemakers in the world, Bordeaux-born, -trained and part-time resident Jacques Lurton, who has established 10 ha of close-planted vineyard and an on-site winery. The principal varieties are Sangiovese and Cabernet Franc; then lesser amounts of Semillon, Viognier, Grenache, Malbec and Merlot. The wines are made and bottled on-site, in true estate style. The ultimate flagship wine will be an esoteric blend of Sangiovese, Cabernet Franc and Malbec. Production of this wine will be limited to 2000 cases, with another 2000 cases of Bark Hut Road.

Signature wine: Bark Hut Road
(Cabernet Shiraz Viognier)

FLEURIEU ZONE
Southern Fleurieu ❧

As with Kangaroo Island, the vineyards and wineries are but one of numerous tourist attractions. The undulating slopes and gentle hills pose no limitations to viticulture, simply enhancing the beauty of the vineyards and the diversity of the scenery. This is quite distinct from any other part of the zone, and the quality of the wines made to date will almost certainly lead to further plantings and developments.

Settlement began in the middle of the nineteenth century, and rapidly diversified with flour mills for locally grown wheat, a brewery and extensive grazing. Viticulture began with the arrival of Buxton Laurie (the ancestor of a distinguished wine family in the regions around Adelaide) in the 1860s. By 1876 his Southcote Vineyards near Port Elliot covered 180 hectares, but were destroyed by massive bushfires in the 1890s. Other vineyards in the region escaped, although by the turn of the century activity had ceased, only reactivated after a gap of nearly 90 years.

The eminent viticultural climate researcher, Dr John Gladstones, has written in *Viticulture and Environment*, 'At least in climatic terms, the lower Fleurieu Peninsula has arguably the best conditions in all of mainland South Australia for table wine production.'

That said, the best wines to date are the fragrant, elegant Chardonnays, Sauvignon Blancs and Semillon Sauvignon Blancs. The red wines share the same elegance, but – particularly in cooler vintages – can struggle with mid-palate vinosity and fruit sweetness. Merlot and Shiraz seem most likely to adapt as the vines mature.

> ### SOUTHERN FLEURIEU
>
> Latitude **34°44'S**
> Altitude **250 m**
> Heat degree days **1628**
> Growing season rainfall **121 mm**
> Mean January temp. **19.6°C**
> Harvest **Mid February to April**
> Chief viticultural hazard **Mildew**

Adelaide •

Cellar Doors
* Minko Wines at 13 High St, Willunga.
* Parri Estate at Ingoldby Rd,
  McLaren Vale; see p. 44 for map.

The Region

CLIMATE

The climate is Mediterranean, very strongly maritime influenced by the expanses of water which surround the Peninsula, and in particular its southern end. Thus temperatures are 1–2°C cooler in summer than McLaren Vale, with an average summer maximum of only 25°C. The Mediterranean pattern means the rainfall is winter dominant and the minimal growing-season rainfall makes irrigation essential. Spring frosts are simply not an issue, and the prevailing southerly winds seldom blow with sufficient force to inhibit growth. Overall, the climate is cooler than one envisages and reflects itself in the wine styles.

SOIL & TOPOGRAPHY

There are two soil types in the vineyard areas: first, a friable sandy to more clayey loam over a limestone subsoil; and, second, a buckshot gravel again over limestone. Both are suited to viticulture, and support moderately vigorous vine growth.

PRINCIPAL GRAPE VARIETIES

Overall, 75 per cent red, 25 per cent white. In descending order:

SHIRAZ

CABERNET SAUVIGNON

SEMILLON

CHARDONNAY

MERLOT

SAUVIGNON BLANC.

Wineries of Southern Fleurieu

Minko Wines Est. 1997

13 High Street, Willunga 5172

minkowines@bigpond.com

Mike Boerema, Inger Kellett, and children Nick and Margo (the winery name uses letters from each of the family names) established their vineyard on the slopes of Mt Compass at an altitude of 300 m. Minko practises sustainable eco-agriculture, and is a member of the Compass Creek Care group; the Nangkita and Tookayerta Creeks flow through the property, providing wetlands and associated native vegetation.

Signature wine: Mount Compass Merlot Rosé

WHITE WINE STYLES

Chardonnay produces light- to medium-bodied wines, with elegance the keynote, citrus and apple flavours dominant.

Sauvignon Blanc and Semillon are either made as single varietal or as a blend; these varieties do well, producing wines with elegance, finesse and length.

RED WINE STYLES

Cabernet Sauvignon in the warmer years produces a wine with a most attractive mix of gently herbaceous/tobacco characters plus sweeter red and blackberry flavours; the tannins are fine and supple, and the wine is of medium body. In the cooler vintages, herbaceous characters are more evident, though not unpleasantly so.

Shiraz has classic temperate climate characters, fine and medium-bodied, with blackberry, spice, and savoury flavours supported by fine tannins.

Merlot. If there is to be significant expansion of plantings in the region, Merlot should be one of the front runners. Not only is it in demand overall, but it appears particularly well suited to the climate (and soil) of the Peninsula, producing wine of bell-clear varietal character. The flavours run through a spectrum of leaf, mint and red berry, the bouquet appropriately fragrant.

Mt Billy Est. 2000

18 Victoria St, Victor Harbor 5211 (postal)

www.mtbillywines.com.au

🗷 exports to UK, US

John Edwards and wife Pauline bought a 3.75 ha property on the hills behind Victor Harbor in 1983, and the sheep and goats ultimately gave way to plantings of 1.2 ha each of Chardonnay and Pinot Meunier. The intention was to sell the grapes, but low yields persuaded Edwards that making and selling a bottle-fermented sparkling wine was the way to go. Additionally, in 1999 one tonne each of Grenache and Shiraz were purchased in the Barossa Valley, and David Powell of Torbreck agreed to make the wine. Mt Billy was born. A Riesling, and the estate-based sparkling wine, complete the portfolio.

Signature wine: Antiquity Shiraz

Parri Estate Est. 1998

Sneyd Rd, Mount Jagged 5210

www.parriestate.com.au

🖵 (at Ingoldby Rd, McLaren Vale)

exports to UK

Alice, Peter and John Phillips have established a substantial business with a clear marketing plan, and an obvious commitment to quality. Thirty-three ha of Chardonnay, Viognier, Sauvignon Blanc, Semillon, Pinot Noir, Cabernet Sauvignon and Shiraz have been planted using modern trellis and irrigation systems. The protected valley in which the vines are planted has a creek which flows throughout the year, and which has been rejuvenated by the planting of 3000 trees. The white wines are particularly impressive.

Signature wine: Viognier Chardonnay

Whale Coast Wines Est. 1994

65 Ocean St, Victor Harbor 5211

www.whalecoastwines.com.au

🗷 exports to UK

This is the venture of obstetrician David Batt, partner Chris and their five children; no longer a hobby, one of the daughters is completing oenology studies at Adelaide University. Since purchasing the 64 ha farm in 1994, 25 ha of vineyard has been planted to Shiraz, Cabernet Sauvignon, Riesling, Sauvignon Blanc, Viognier, Tempranillo, Merlot and Petit Verdot. Most of the grapes have been sold to Cascabel, where Duncan Fergusson and Susanna Fernandez also make limited quantities of The Crows Nest Shiraz, Kondole Cabernet and Balaena Cabernet Shiraz for Whale Coast Wines.

Signature wine: The Crows Nest Shiraz

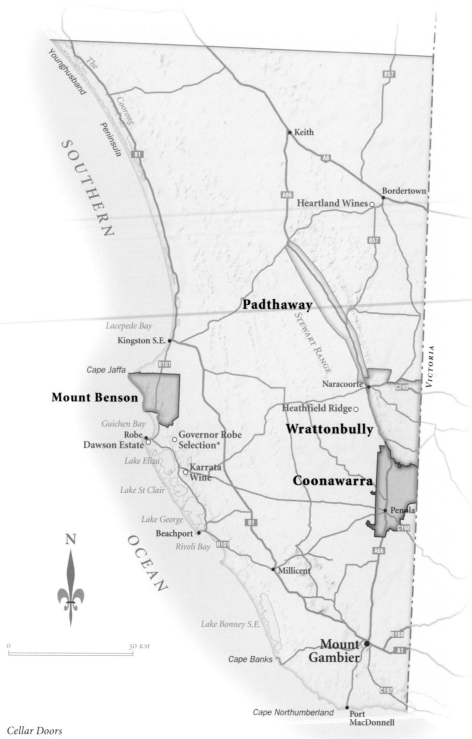

Younghusband

The

Coorong

Peninsula

B1

SOUTHERN

Keith

A8

A66

Bordertown

Heartland Wines

B57

B57

Padthaway

STEWART RANGE

VICTORIA

Lacepede Bay

Kingston S.E.

Cape Jaffa

B101

Naracoorte

C240

Mount Benson

Heathfield Ridge

Guichen Bay

Robe

Governor Robe

Selection*

Wrattonbully

Dawson Estate

Lake Eliza

Karrata

Wine

Coonawarra

Lake St Clair

Penola

Lake George

C198

N

B1

Beachport

OCEAN

Rivoli Bay

B101

A66

Millicent

Lake Bonney S.E.

B160

0   50 KM

Mount

Gambier

A1

Cape Banks

C192

Cape Northumberland   Port

MacDonnell

Cellar Doors

* Frog Island at Ralph Fowler Wines,
  Mount Benson; see p. 70 for map.

* Governor Robe Selection at Attic House, Robe.

Limestone Coast Zone 🌿

The Limestone Coast may have four regions, one (Coonawarra) being of national and international fame, but there is still a long way to go before the legal boundary mapping of these is completed. Coonawarra took years of litigation and tens of millions of dollars in legal fees, Wrattonbully was a smaller imitation, but still costly and time consuming.

There are three further parts of the zone which seem more likely than not to seek recognition as regions some time in the future:

Robe, adjacent to Mount Benson; Bordertown, as its name implies on the Victorian border; and Mount Gambier.

Bordertown, well to the north, has the warmest climate and has several large vineyards, one owned by Southcorp. Mount Gambier, the most southerly and by far the coolest, has the greatest potential in the zone for Pinot Noir table wine, as well as for Sauvignon Blanc and sparkling. Robe is very similar to Mount Benson, both in terms of climate and soil.

Whatever be the outcome, the Limestone Coast will remain the second-largest grower of grapes in South Australia (second only to the Lower Murray in terms of tonnage) and by far the most important in terms of the value of its production.

LINDEMANS, ROBE, LIMESTONE COAST.

Wineries of the Limestone Coast Zone

Frog Island Est. 2003
PO Box 423, Kingston SE 5275
www.frogisland.com.au
🍷 (at Ralph Fowler Wines, Mount Benson);
exports to UK

Sarah Squire (née Fowler) has decided to do her own thing, with full support from father Ralph. The quixotic name is taken from a small locality inland from the seaside town of Robe, and the wines are deliberately made in a fresh, fruit-forward style. They include Chardonnay, Shiraz, Cabernet Merlot and Sparkling Red.
Signature wine: Cabernet Merlot

Governor Robe Selection
Est. 1998
Waterhouse Range Vineyards,
Lot 11, Old Naracoorte Rd, Robe 5276
www.waterhouserange.com.au
🍷 (at Attic House, Robe)

Brothers Bill and Mick Quinlan-Watson, supported by a group of investors, began the development of Waterhouse Range Vineyards Pty Ltd in 1995, progressively planting 60 ha. The majority of the grapes are sold, with a lesser amount retained and contract-made at Cape Jaffa winery. The unusual name comes from the third Governor of South Australia, Frederick Holt Robe, who in 1845 selected the site for a port and personally put in the first survey peg at Robe.
Signature wine: Shiraz

Heartland Wines Est. 2001
Level 1, 205 Greenhill Rd, Eastwood 5063
www.heartlandwines.com.au
🚫 exports to UK

This is a joint venture between four industry veterans: winemakers Ben Glaetzer and Scott Collett, viticulturist Geoff Hardy and wine industry management specialist Grant Tilbrook. It draws upon grapes grown in the Limestone Coast, Barossa Valley and McLaren Vale, predominantly from vineyards owned by the partners. Its sights are firmly set on exports of Semillon, Chardonnay, Viognier, Rose, Shiraz, Sangiovese, Cabernet Merlot and Cabernet Sauvignon. Red wine quality is admirable, the venture very successful.
Signature wine: Limestone Coast Shiraz

Heathfield Ridge Wines
Est. 1997
PO Box 94, Kensington Park 5068
www.heathfieldridgewines.com.au
🚫

Having leased the former Heathfield Ridge winery to Orlando Wyndham, the Tidswell family has retained the two large vineyards, totalling 114 ha, the lion's share planted to Shiraz and Cabernet Sauvignon, with smaller plantings of Merlot, Chardonnay and Sauvignon Blanc. Part of the production is vinified under the Heathfield Ridge label by the Irvine Consultancy group, the remainder sold to Russet Ridge.
Signature wine: Caves Road Shiraz

Karatta Wine Est. 1994
43/22 Liberman Close, Adelaide 5000 (postal)
www.robewineregion.com.au
🚫

This is the former Anthony Dale vineyard, planted to 12 ha of Shiraz, Cabernet Sauvignon, Pinot Noir, Malbec, and more recently Sauvignon Blanc and Chardonnay. It is owned by Karatta Wine Company in association with the Tenison Vineyard. The wines are sold through regional outlets, and by mail order, but with further developments planned.
Signature wine: Lake Butler Reserve Tenison Vineyard Shiraz

LIMESTONE COAST ZONE
Coonawarra ❧

Coonawarra's pre-eminent position as Australia's greatest Cabernet Sauvignon wine region today stands in stark contrast to Bill Redman's famous dictum: 'From 1890 to 1945 you can write failure across the face of Coonawarra.' For much of that time most of the wine was distilled into brandy, while in the 1930s the South Australian government implemented a mini Vine Pull Scheme, offering all ex-servicemen in the area a bounty of four pounds and ten pence an acre (0.4 hectare) for removing their vines and converting the land to dairying.

Indeed, there is every reason to argue that '1951' should be substituted for '1945', for at that time what is now Wynns Coonawarra Estate was nearly sold to the Department of Lands and Forests. Had that occurred, the only working winery would have been the then tiny Rouge Homme of the Redman family. It was in 1951 that David Wynn made his fateful decision to buy the now famous stone winery and cellars which had been built with such hope and enterprise by John Riddoch exactly 60 years earlier. Until this time the only table wine made in Coonawarra was Redman's Shiraz, which had been sold in bulk to Woodley Wines since 1920. Woodley bottled some of the wine, and sold the rest in bulk to other South Australian wineries. From 1952 Redman started selling to those companies direct, while continuing to supply Woodley

with its requirements for bottling (and which gave rise to the famous Treasure Chest series).

Thomas Hardy, Reynella, Leo Buring and Yalumba were among the first purchasers of Redman's wine; in 1953 Ronald Haselgrove of Mildara joined the queue, and – unable to buy as much as he needed – commissioned Bill Redman to find a suitable block and develop a vineyard. This was done in 1955, and Penfolds followed suit in 1957. The quest for land was on in earnest, and has still not run its course.

More than that, the unrelenting pressure caused problems which Ronald Haselgrove did not foresee when in 1955 he observed that 'within 15 years every major wine company will be clamouring for Coonawarra vineyard land'. A battle-royal erupted when application was made to register Coonawarra as a Geographic Indication, over, in particular, how and where the boundaries should be drawn. At the core of the dispute was the famous terra rossa, or red soils, on which all of the early vineyards were planted.

Even at that point, however, there were problems, because fingers of black soil ran into vineyard blocks which, by their very nature, had straight-line boundaries. There were also significant patches of terra rossa some distance away from the historical centre, known as the Hundred of Comaum. Seven years of hugely expensive litigation ultimately led to the borders being drawn on a far wider and more

expansive scale than any proposal by the most liberal of the original litigants. The eastern border of the Coonawarra GI, indeed, is the border between Victoria and South Australia, the western an even longer straight line which pays no respect to soils, except for a little appendix reaching out to encompass a patch of terra rossa just to the south of the town of Coonawarra. It is nothing if not ironic that the cigar shape of Padthaway would also be that of Coonawarra if terra rossa (and not lawyers) were to have determined the boundaries.

Another problem confronted Coonawarra: its coupling of isolation and ultra-compact size. As the early winewriter Dr Sam Benwell wrote, 'It lies between Melbourne and Adelaide, but is never quite on the way between the two cities, no matter which way one goes.' It is completely flat, and is bitterly cold in winter, wet in spring and chancy in autumn. Tourist infrastructure was slow to develop: for long Wynns Coonawarra Estate was the only winery with aesthetic appeal, and Chardonnay Lodge the only modern hotel accommodation.

Things are now very different: the town of Penola has realised its old homes have great historical value. New wineries have been built with excellent tasting facilities and, in a number of instances, with restaurants open each day for lunch, competing with the ever-growing Chardonnay Lodge and its own excellent restaurant.

[OPPOSITE & BELOW] COONAWARRA.

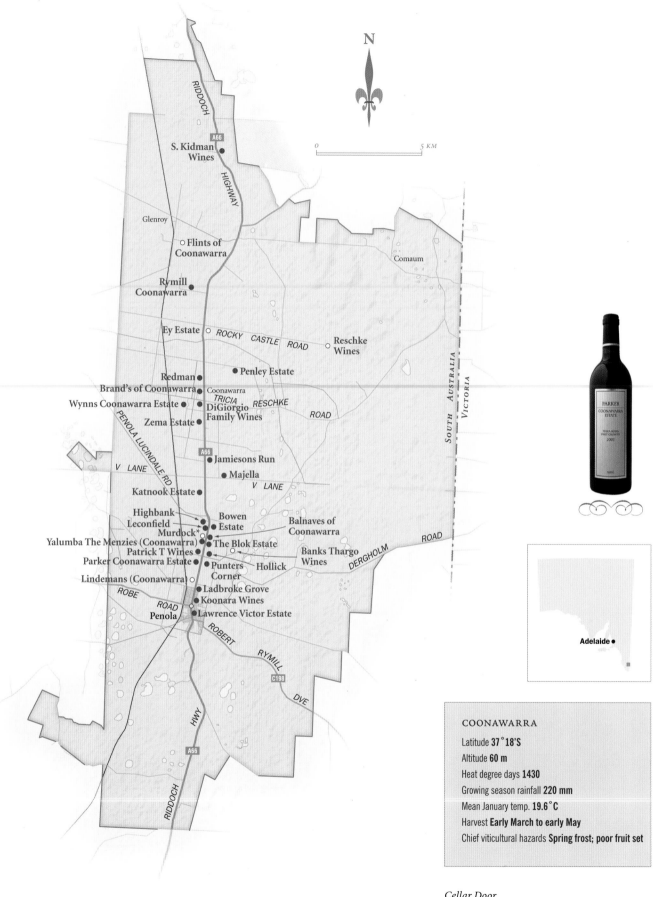

N

0   5 KM

S. Kidman
Wines

Glenroy

Flints of
Coonawarra

Comaum

Rymill
Coonawarra

Ey Estate   ROCKY CASTLE ROAD   Reschke
Wines

Redman   Penley Estate

Brand's of Coonawarra   Coonawarra

Wynns Coonawarra Estate   TRICIA   RESCHKE

DiGiorgio   ROAD

Zema Estate   Family Wines

Jamiesons Run

Majella

V LANE   V LANE

Katnook Estate

Highbank   Bowen

Leconfield   Estate

Murdock*   Balnaves of
Coonawarra

Yalumba The Menzies (Coonawarra)   The Blok Estate

Patrick T Wines   Banks Thargo
Wines

Parker Coonawarra Estate   Hollick   DERGHOLM   ROAD

Punters
Corner

Lindemans (Coonawarra)

ROBE   Ladbroke Grove

ROAD   Koonara Wines

Penola   Lawrence Victor Estate

ROBERT

RYMILL

C198

DVE

RIDDOCH

HWY

A66

Adelaide ●

COONAWARRA

Latitude **37˚18'S**

Altitude **60 m**

Heat degree days **1430**

Growing season rainfall **220 mm**

Mean January temp. **19.6˚C**

Harvest **Early March to early May**

Chief viticultural hazards **Spring frost; poor fruit set**

Cellar Door
* Murdock at Lightpass Rd, Tanunda;
   see pp. 16–17 for map.

The Region

CLIMATE

Coonawarra, with a heat degree summation of 1430, was the first cool-climate viticultural region to gain national prominence. Due to the limited maritime influence, the winters are cold, wet and windy, and throughout much of the growing season the night-time temperatures are likewise low. In almost all vintages Coonawarra receives intermittent bursts of very hot weather in February–March; the other climatic problems in a basically favourable climate are wind and rain during flowering.

SOIL & TOPOGRAPHY

Coonawarra boasts the most celebrated vineyard soil in Australia, commonly known as terra rossa, a distinctive, albeit thin, band of at times vivid red soil 10–50 cm deep overlying a bed of soft limestone. The colour comes from iron impurities in the limestone which have oxidised and become red-brown. The soil is extremely friable and well drained; the adjoining soils to the west and east are far less suited to viticulture.

PRINCIPAL GRAPE VARIETIES

Overall, 90 per cent red, 10 per cent white.
In descending order:

CABERNET SAUVIGNON

SHIRAZ

MERLOT

CHARDONNAY

RIESLING

PINOT NOIR

SAUVIGNON BLANC

CABERNET FRANC.

WHITE WINE STYLES

Riesling. While overshadowed by the reputation of the red wines, its fragrant, flowery and appealingly fruity style (so different from that of the Clare Valley) is slowly but surely gaining the recognition it deserves.

Chardonnay is still the bridesmaid in Coonawarra, with much of the tonnage being directed to sparkling wine, but nonetheless capable of producing table wine of considerable quality. Some heavy-handed oak treatment in earlier years tended to hide the Chardonnay light under a bushel, but it is now being given the opportunity to emerge.

RED WINE STYLES

Cabernet Sauvignon. Whatever yardstick one adopts, Coonawarra produces most of Australia's great Cabernet Sauvignon. These wines cover a broad spectrum of individual fruit flavours, ranging from blackcurrant to plum to red cherry to prunes, always with elegance. Notwithstanding the impact of oak tannins, the wines are seldom astringent or tannic, and indeed Coonawarra winemakers invest much effort in extracting every last grain of available tannin.

Shiraz was, to all intents and purposes, the only wine grape grown in Coonawarra between 1900 and 1950; there were a few vines of Cabernet Sauvignon and a little Grenache. The grape that in effect created Coonawarra's reputation seemed to be taking a slow ride to obscurity in the face of the success of Cabernet Sauvignon until Wynns Coonawarra Estate turned the tide. Notwithstanding the Shiraz boom elsewhere in Australia, in Coonawarra there is still three times as much Cabernet Sauvignon as there is Shiraz. The style is medium bodied and notably elegant, and some of the greatest Coonawarra reds are blends of Shiraz and Cabernet Sauvignon.

Merlot is a fairly recent arrival in Coonawarra, but an important one, with plantings 40 per cent of those of Shiraz. It is used both to make elegant varietal wines, and as a blend component in various configurations with the other two principal red varieties.

[ABOVE] COONAWARRA TERRA ROSSA RED SOIL OVER LIMESTONE. [RIGHT] COONAWARRA.

Wineries of Coonawarra

Balnaves of Coonawarra

Est. 1975
Main Rd, Coonawarra 5263
www.balnaves.com.au
⚲ exports to UK, US

This is one of Coonawarra's foremost producers, founded on viticulturist-owner Doug Balnaves' 52 ha of high-quality estate vineyards. The pick of the crop is made in the winery – built in 1996 – by the immensely talented Pete Bissell. The wines (ranging through Chardonnay to Shiraz, Cabernet Merlot blends and Cabernet Sauvignon) are invariably excellent, often outstanding.

Signature wine: The Tally Reserve
Cabernet Sauvignon

Brand's of Coonawarra

Est. 1966
Riddoch Hwy, Coonawarra 5263
www.mcwilliams.com.au
⚲ exports to UK, US

Part of a very substantial investment in Coonawarra by McWilliam's, which first acquired a 50 per cent interest from the founding Bill Brand family then moved to 100 per cent, and followed this with the purchase of 100 ha of additional vineyard land. Significantly increased production of the smooth wines for which Brand's is known has followed. The standard varietal releases (Riesling, Chardonnay, Shiraz, Merlot, Cabernet Sauvignon) offer excellent value. A priceless block of 115-year-old Shiraz provides Stentiford's Reserve Shiraz, on a par with the Patron's Reserve.

Signature wine: Patron's Reserve
(Bordeaux blend)

Jamiesons Run Est. 1955

Penola–Naracoorte Rd, Coonawarra 5263
www.jamiesonsrun.com.au
⚲ exports to UK, US

The vineyard (and winery) was once the prized possession of a stand-alone Mildara, which spawned a child called Jamiesons Run to fill the need for a cost-effective second label. Now the name Mildara is very nearly part of ancient wine history, and the child has usurped the parent. A five-tiered range of wines, headed by Rothwell Cabernet Sauvignon; then a single annual Winemakers Reserve; next three single vineyard wines, followed by Red Terra Reserve; then the varietal core range of four reds and a Chardonnay. In late 2005 Fosters Wine Estates announced it would sell the winery while retaining the brand.

Signature wine: Winemakers Reserve Dry Red

Katnook Estate Est. 1979

Riddoch Hwy, Coonawarra 5263
www.katnookestate.com.au
⚲ exports to UK, US

Freixinet, the Spanish cava maker, quietly acquired 60 per cent of Katnook some years ago, underpinning its position as one of the largest contract grapegrowers and suppliers in Coonawarra. The historic stone woolshed in which the second vintage in Coonawarra (1896) was made and which has served Katnook since 1980 has been restored, leading to the subsequent release of flagships Odyssey Cabernet Sauvignon and Prodigy Shiraz. Then follow the Katnook varietals (including Riesling, Sauvignon Blanc and Chardonnay), with the Riddoch label, the third and lowest level, offering good value.

Signature wine: Prodigy Shiraz

Ladbroke Grove Est. 1982

Riddoch Hwy, Coonawarra 5263
www.ladbrokegrove.com.au
⚲

Since its acquisition by John Cox and Marie Valenzuela, this relatively long-established producer has gone from strength to strength, with a variety of owned and leased vineyards producing (via contract winemaking) Shiraz, Shiraz Viognier and Cabernet Sauvignon at the top of a tree which also includes Chardonnay and Riesling.

Signature wine: Killian Vineyard
Cabernet Sauvignon

Leconfield Est. 1974

Riddoch Hwy, Coonawarra 5263
www.leconfieldwines.com
⚲ exports to UK, US

Sydney Hamilton was 76 years old when he purchased the land to found Leconfield in 1974, proceeding to make a series of seminal Cabernet Sauvignons between 1977 and 1981 (the back label famously disclosing the grapes had been picked by experienced women) before reluctantly selling the property to nephew Richard Hamilton when aged 84. These days, with former Lindemans winemaker Paul Gordon in charge, Old Vines Riesling, Cabernet Sauvignon, Merlot and Chardonnay are all excellent.

Signature wine: Cabernet Sauvignon

Lindemans (Coonawarra)

Est. 1908
Riddoch Hwy, Coonawarra 5263
www.lindemans.com.au
⚲ exports to UK, US

The establishment date harks back to the first vintage made by strict legend Bill Redman; Lindemans acquired the Redman Rouge Homme brand, winery and vineyards in 1965. The vineyards are of ever-increasing significance because of the move towards regional identity in the all-important export markets, which has led to the emergence of a new range of regional/varietal labels.

Signature wine: Limestone Ridge
(Shiraz Cabernet)

Majella Est. 1969

Lynn Rd, Coonawarra 5263
www.majellawines.com.au

exports to UK, US

With 61 ha of mature Shiraz and Cabernet Sauvignon (and a little Riesling and Merlot) Majella is one of the foremost high-quality grape suppliers in the district. 'Prof' Brian Lynn has slowly eased into winemaking with the on-site winery under control of winemaker Bruce Gregory, and demand always exceeds supply. The Shirazs and Cabernets are invariably among the best the region produces.

Signature wine: The Malleea Shiraz Cabernet

Murdock Est. 1998

Riddoch Hwy, Coonawarra 5263
www.murdockwines.com

(at Murdock, Barossa Valley);
exports to US

The Murdock family has established 10.4 ha of Cabernet Sauvignon, 2 ha of Shiraz, 1 ha of Merlot, and 0.5 ha each of Chardonnay and Riesling, and produces small quantities of an outstanding Cabernet Sauvignon, contract-made by Pete Bissell at Balnaves. Former senior Southcorp viticulturist David Murdock has overall responsibility for the brand and its marketing. A second vineyard has been added in the Barossa Valley, with 5.8 ha of Shiraz and 2.1 ha each of Semillon and Cabernet Sauvignon. The labels, incidentally, are ultra-minimalist; no flood of propaganda here.

Signature wine: Cabernet Sauvignon

Parker Coonawarra Estate

Est. 1985

Riddoch Hwy, Coonawarra 5263
www.parkercoonawarraestate.com.au

exports to UK, US

Acquired by the Rathbone family (of Yering Station fame) in 2004, Parker Estate has always taken the high ground, rigidly focussing on quality rather than quantity. Lavish fruit is supported by lavish oak, with stunning results in the better vintages for the three wines, Terra Rossa Merlot, Terra Rossa Cabernet Sauvignon and Terra Rossa First Growth Cabernet Sauvignon. There is every reason to suppose the focus on quality will continue.

Signature wine: Terra Rossa First Growth Cabernet Sauvignon

Penley Estate Est. 1988

McLeans Rd, Coonawarra 5263
www.penley.com.au

exports to UK, US

Owner-winemaker Kym Tolley describes himself as a fifth-generation winemaker, the family tree involving both the Penfolds and the Tolleys. He worked 17 years in the industry before establishing Penley Estate (with 91 ha of estate plantings) and has made every post a winner since, producing a succession of rich, complex, full-bodied red wines and stylish Chardonnays. The red wine range also extends to lower-priced blends of Coonawarra and other South Australian-sourced grapes.

Signature wine: Reserve Cabernet Sauvignon

Punters Corner Est. 1988

Cnr Riddoch Hwy and Racecourse Rd, Coonawarra 5263
www.punterscorner.com.au

exports to UK, US

The quaintly named Punters Corner started life in 1975 as James Haselgrove, but in 1992 was acquired by a group of investors who quite evidently had few delusions about the uncertainties of viticulture and winemaking, even in a district as distinguished as Coonawarra. The arrival of Pete Bissell as contract winemaker (at Balnaves) paid immediate (and continuing) dividends. Sophisticated packaging and label design add to the appeal of the wines.

Signature wine: Spartacus Reserve Shiraz

Wynns Coonawarra Estate

Est. 1891

Memorial Drive, Coonawarra 5263
www.wynns.com.au

exports to UK, US

The large-scale production has in no way prevented Wynns from producing excellent wines covering the full price spectrum from the bargain-basement Riesling, Chardonnay and Shiraz through to the deluxe John Riddoch Cabernet Sauvignon and Michael Shiraz. Even with steady price increases, Wynns offers extraordinary value for money. Good though that may be, there is even greater promise for the future: the vineyards are being rejuvenated by new trellising or replanting, and a regime directed to quality rather than quantity has been introduced.

Signature wine: John Riddoch Cabernet Sauvignon

Zema Estate Est. 1982

Riddoch Hwy, Coonawarra 5263
www.zema.com.au

exports to UK

Zema is one of the last outposts of hand-pruning in Coonawarra, the various members of the Zema family (headed by patriarch Demetrio Zema) tending a 60 ha vineyard progressively planted since 1982, principally to Shiraz and Cabernet Sauvignon, in the heart of Coonawarra's terra rossa soil. Winemaking practices are straightforward; if ever there was an example of great wines being made in the vineyard, this is it.

Signature wine: Family Selection Shiraz

Limestone Coast Zone
Padthaway ❧

If Coonawarra is not quite on the way to anywhere, Padthaway is on the way to nowhere. If you can pass through Coonawarra without noticing very much, you can pass through Padthaway without noticing anything at all. Its birth was both recent and humble, and initially the major wine companies (which have a near monopoly on its plantings) entirely misread its potential. Yet 40 years after the first vines were planted there, and notwithstanding the degree of trial and error, it is an unambiguously important producer of premium-quality wines.

The region's potential was pinpointed by a Seppelt committee appointed in the early 1960s to select suitable vineyard sites for large-scale planting of early-ripening grape varieties. The requirements were ready availability of land (at a modest price), a cool climate and plentiful water for irrigation. The committee's research turned up a 1944 CSIRO (Commonwealth Scientific and Industrial Research Organisation) report which had focused on a 3200 hectare strip of country north of Naracoorte – about 300 kilometres south-east of Adelaide, near the South Australia–Victoria border – and which concluded: 'The soil type is variable in depth and there are usually some stony portions on each of the small patches in which it occurs. It is a terra rossa soil … the deeper sites of the terra rossa soils should make first-class garden soils.'

Only then did the Seppelt viticulturists visit the region, and duly identified a strip running for 16 kilometres along the Naracoorte to Padthaway road, and which fell within the narrow 550 mm rainfall zone – but with unlimited underground water. One of the nearby principal farming and grazing properties was Keppoch Park, and Seppelt gave the name Keppoch to the region, a choice initially adopted by Thomas Hardy when it purchased its first land in 1968. Lindemans arrived the same year, but selected land further north, at Padthaway, and used that name. Wynns, the other big company landholder, has never made a regional wine (all of its production is blended, some into sparkling wine) so did not enter the tug-of-war over the name.

After a decade or more of confusion, all agreed on Padthaway, which went some way to giving the region a sense of identity. However, it was not until 1998 that any of the major players installed more than field crushing stations. In that year Stonehaven, an $18 million, 10 000-tonne winery on land south of the Padthaway township, was built by Hardys.

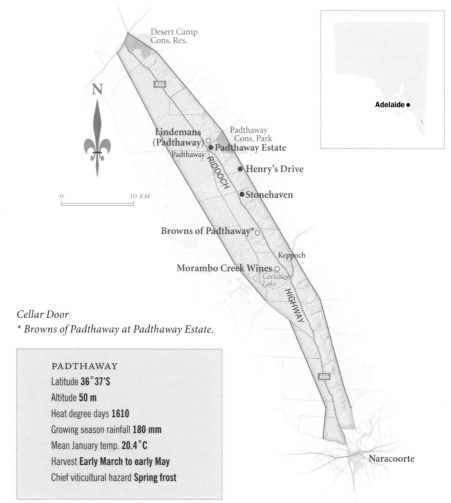

Cellar Door
* Browns of Padthaway at Padthaway Estate.

PADTHAWAY
Latitude **36°37'S**
Altitude **50 m**
Heat degree days **1610**
Growing season rainfall **180 mm**
Mean January temp. **20.4°C**
Harvest **Early March to early May**
Chief viticultural hazard **Spring frost**

To add historical insult to injury, Seppelt initially decided to concentrate on red wines (relying on Drumborg in far south-west Victoria to produce the white wines), while Lindemans envisaged the region as a producer of medium-quality white and red wine to go into its lower- to mid-priced bottle range (casks were then but a bright idea for the future, with numerous technical problems unsolved).

Padthaway falls within a buffer zone between Victoria and South Australia which imposes strict controls on water usage. No further irrigation rights are being granted, and this has restricted (and will in the future restrict) the spread of viticulture. The first major independent grower (the Brown family) supplies Orlando, which acquired 165 hectares of land and established a vineyard of its own in the latter part of the 1980s. Local farmers and graziers, the Longbottom and Bryson families, followed suit in the mid 1990s, both with large vineyards, selling most of the grapes, but having part contract-made for their respective brands, Henry's Drive and Morambro Creek. The only other acquisitions (in 1989) have been by Andrew Garrett Wines (now part of Beringer Blass) and by Angove's.

To this day the one great drawcard is Padthaway Estate, a magnificent two-storey Victorian homestead now offering luxurious Relais et Châteaux-type accommodation to a handful of lucky guests. Padthaway Estate has also established its own sparkling and table wine winery on the property, in a superb stone shearing shed.

What is more, it has only been since the mid 1990s that Padthaway has been given a chance to show what it can really do. Prior to that, flood irrigation (leading, incidentally, to ever-increasing levels of salinity), minimal pruning, and management practices solely designed to maximise yield per hectare were the rule rather than the exception, and still continue to be practised in some lesser vineyard blocks.

The move to give greater regional identity to the wines of the large wine companies, the establishment of Stonehaven, and the emergence of part-grower, part-winemaker businesses, have all acted synergistically to put more focus and expenditure on producing quality rather than quantity.

[OPPOSITE] DESTEMMING THE FRUIT.

The Region

CLIMATE

As one would expect, given its proximity to Coonawarra, and given the absence of any significant mountains, the climate of Padthaway is similar to that of Coonawarra, but warmer. It was no doubt the climatic statistics which led to its founders realising it would ultimately succeed better as a red wine area. Irrigation is essential, water availability being a strictly limiting factor in an area of otherwise vast potential, with spring frosts a major threat.

SOIL & TOPOGRAPHY

The landscape avoids the dead-flat monotony of Coonawarra, but the slopes are gentle. The principal 'garden soil' identified by the CSIRO in 1944 is in fact the same soil which dominates the Barossa Valley, Clare Valley, Watervale and McLaren Vale: red-brown loamy sand soils. There are also patches of surface soil identical to the bright red soil of Coonawarra.

PRINCIPAL GRAPE VARIETIES

Overall, 60 per cent red, 40 per cent white. In descending order:

SHIRAZ

CHARDONNAY

CABERNET SAUVIGNON

RIESLING

MERLOT

PINOT NOIR

SEMILLON

GEWÜRZTRAMINER

SAUVIGNON BLANC

MALBEC

VERDELHO.

[RIGHT & OPPOSITE] PADTHAWAY.

WHITE WINE STYLES

Chardonnay is clearly the most successful of all of the white table wines of this region. There is a particular character to the fruit flavour which is evident in the majority of the vintages, and which (without the intervention of oak) is strongly reminiscent of grapefruit, although the flavours also extend to more conventional melon, fig and white peach.

Riesling is, once again, frequently used as a workhorse, albeit to good effect with major brands. Intermittent releases of high-quality botrytised Rieslings are among the best of this style to be found in Australia, and are indeed of international standard, with intense lime, apricot and cumquat aromas and flavours.

RED WINE STYLES

Cabernet Sauvignon is made either as a single varietal, or blended with Merlot; the wine is typically of medium body, fragrant and with cool (rather than warm) climate characters to the fore. The tannins are fine and soft, and the wine does not need (nor is it usually given) significant oak influence.

Shiraz is, like Cabernet, frequently blended with wines from other South Australian regions, but as from time to time appears either as a single-region varietal, or as a significant component. Yield has to be controlled if Shiraz is to give of its best in the region, and the reality has been that much of the production is of above optimum yields and hence directed to lower-priced products. Orlando's Lawson Vineyard Shiraz is a wine of the highest quality.

Wineries of Padthaway

Browns of Padthaway Est. 1993

Keith Rd, Padthaway 5271

www.browns-of-padthaway.com

 (at Padthaway Estate)

The Brown family has for many years been the largest independent grapegrower in Padthaway, a district in which most of the vineyards were established and owned by Wynns, Seppelt, Lindemans and Hardys respectively. After a slow start, the winery has produced some excellent wines since 1998, and production has increased accordingly. While Riesling, Sauvignon Blanc, Chardonnay and Verdelho are included in the range, Shiraz and Cabernet Sauvignon are the focus.

Signature wine: Ernest Family Reserve Shiraz

Henry's Drive Est. 1998

PMB 182, Naracoorte 5271

www.henrysdrive.com

exports to UK, US

Brian and Kay Longbottom, owners of Henry's Drive, are part of a family which has been farming in Padthaway since the 1940s, a diverse operation from sheep and cattle to growing crops and onions. In 1992 a decision was made to further diversify and plant a few vines. Now with almost 300 ha, the vineyard consists mainly of Shiraz and Cabernet Sauvignon and other varieties such as Chardonnay, Merlot, Verdelho and Sauvignon Blanc. The lion's share of the grapes is sold elsewhere, with limited amounts being made under various labels from Shiraz and Cabernet Sauvignon.

Signature wine: Parsons Flat Padthaway Shiraz Cabernet

Morambro Creek Wines

Est. 1994

Riddoch Hwy, Padthaway 5271 (postal)

mcwine@rbm.com.au

The Bryson family has been involved in agriculture for more than a century, moving to Padthaway in 1955 as farmers and graziers. In the early 1990s it began the establishment of 125 ha of vines, planted principally to Chardonnay, Shiraz and Cabernet Sauvignon, but with further plantings planned. Most of the grapes are sold; the three wines made (Chardonnay, Shiraz and Cabernet Sauvignon) have had consistent wine show success.

Signature wine: Shiraz

Padthaway Estate Est. 1980

Riddoch Hwy, Padthaway 5271

www.padthawayestate.com

For many years, until the opening of Stonehaven, this was the only functioning winery in Padthaway, set amid superb grounds in a large and gracious old stone wool shed. The homestead is in the Relais et Châteaux mould, offering luxurious accommodation and fine food. Initially sparkling wine (a nice Pinot Chardonnay) was the only product, the range since being extended with Chardonnay, Merlot and Cabernet Sauvignon table wines.

Signature wine: Eliza Pinot Chardonnay

Stonehaven Est. 1998

Riddoch Hwy, Padthaway 5271

www.stonehavenvineyards.com.au

exports to UK, US

It is, to say the least, strange that it should have taken 30 years for a substantial winery to be built at Padthaway; in the interim, either open-air 'crush pads' on concrete slabs were used for first-stage processing. However, when Hardys took the decision it was no half-measure: $18 million was invested in what was then the largest greenfields winery built in Australia for more than 20 years. The mainstream varietals come at several price levels; more often than not, the quality of the wine far exceeds its price.

Signature wine: Limited Vineyard Release Chardonnay

LIMESTONE COAST ZONE
Mount Benson 🌿

The plantings here at Mount Benson and at nearby Robe are among the most recent in Australia, and there was no history of viticulture prior to 1989. But the potential is exciting, notwithstanding the lack of prior experience and some teething problems with frost (chiefly in Mount Benson) and wind.

So far, at least, access to the vast underground watertable of the south-east has not been restricted, nor is salinity yet a problem. One day the situation may change; if it does, the viticultural wheel may turn full circle, and we shall see dryland, unirrigated vineyards in production again.

But that day is a long way off. In the meantime the relatively sparse landscape, formerly home to sheep but little else, will continue to blossom with the spread of verdant vineyards among the bleached, brown summer grasses. Only the charming seaside town of Robe,

20 kilometres to the south of Mount Benson, with its fleet of crayfishing boats, provides much for the tourist. But it alone is sufficient reason to make the hour's drive across from Coonawarra and see the region first-hand.

The first vines were planted in 1989 by Peter and Leah Wehl, gradually extending to 24 hectares of Shiraz, Cabernet Sauvignon and (eventually) a little Merlot and Sauvignon Blanc. Derek Hooper of Cape Jaffa followed next, in 1993.

The famous Rhône Valley firm of M. Chapoutier & Co placed its imprimatur on the region in 1998, when it headed a joint venture to establish a 38 hectare biodynamic vineyard planted to Shiraz (almost half the total), Cabernet Sauvignon, Marsanne, Viognier and Sauvignon Blanc. While Chapoutier has since shown signs of second thoughts (seeking to sell the vineyard before withdrawing it

from the market) the Belgian-based firm of G. & C. Kreglinger – with significant family connections to several highly-ranked Pomerol, Bordeaux producers – has shown no hesitation. Kreglinger's Norfolk Rise has a 160 hectare vineyard and a 2000 tonne winery. This is the most important local venture by far, and will do much to determine just how successful the region will be in the long term.

MOUNT BENSON

Latitude **31°09'S**

Altitude **50–150 m**

Heat degree days **1226**

Growing season rainfall **217 mm**

Mean January temp. **22.7°C**

Harvest **Late March to late April**

Chief viticultural hazards **Spring frost; poor fruit set**

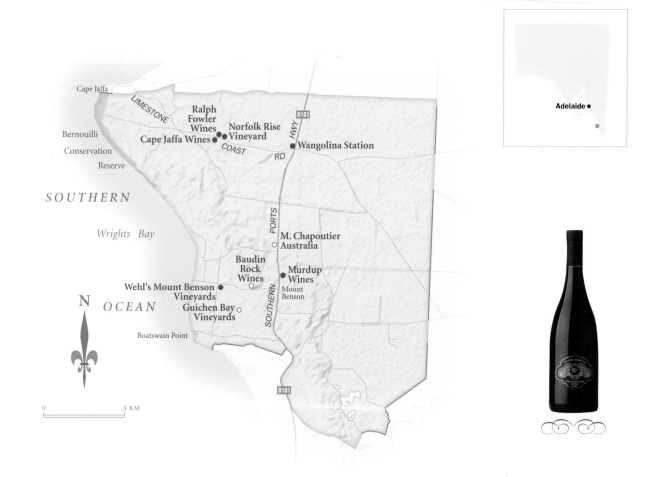

The Region

CLIMATE

The climate is unequivocally cool, strongly maritime-influenced by the nearby ocean on one side and (at Robe) the lakes on the other. The winters are cold and wet, the growing season is long, cool and dry. The winds are predominantly from the south, south-east and south-west, and are particularly strong during the spring and early summer. Overall, summer temperatures are 3°C lower than Coonawarra; budburst, though, occurs two weeks earlier yet harvest is at much the same time.

SOIL & TOPOGRAPHY

The principal soil type is generally described as terra rossa, a red-brown soil that varies from sandy to loamy and which is typically associated with limestone. The limestone may outcrop or occur 10–50 centimetres below the surface. The terrain on which the vineyards have been planted is gently undulating, the surrounding natural bushland scrubby, and giving little clue of the potential of the area from a viticultural viewpoint.

PRINCIPAL GRAPE VARIETIES

Overall, 75 per cent red, 25 per cent white. In descending order:

SHIRAZ

CHARDONNAY

MERLOT

SAUVIGNON BLANC

PINOT NOIR

SEMILLON.

Wineries of Mount Benson

Cape Jaffa Wines Est. 1993

Limestone Coast Rd, Cape Jaffa 5276
www.capejaffawines.com.au

exports to UK

Cape Jaffa Wines was the first Mount Benson winery to be established, owned jointly by the Hooper and Fowler families. The split-level winery was built with local paddock rock, designed with future expansion in mind. Most of the wines come from the 25 ha of estate plantings, which feature the four major Bordeaux red varieties, as well as Shiraz, Chardonnay, Sauvignon Blanc and Semillon.

Signature wine: Sauvignon Blanc

 WHITE WINE STYLES

Chardonnay leads the white grape plantings by a considerable distance. The wines are slightly finer and more elegant than those of either Padthaway or Coonawarra, but with excellent intensity and length.

Sauvignon Blanc produces crisp, grassy, herbaceous wines, very different from those of Padthaway (which are far richer, reflecting the distinctly warmer climate there), but do have attractive touches of gooseberry and passionfruit.

 RED WINE STYLES

Shiraz. The status of Shiraz in the region was given a major boost by the Chapoutier investment and the subsequent success of Norfolk Rise. The wine quality and style is exciting, with cherry, black pepper and spice flavours in a medium-bodied frame lending itself to the use of French oak.

Cabernet Sauvignon and Merlot avoid any suggestion of outright herbaceousness, but are more Bordeaux-like than those of Coonawarra. Natural tannin levels are now good, and the overall extract and weight more than satisfactory.

Norfolk Rise Vineyard

Est. 2000

Limestone Coast Rd, Mount Benson 5265
www.norfolkrise.com.au

exports to UK

The largest and most important development in the Mount Benson region, ultimately owned by a privately held Belgian company, G. & C. Kreglinger, established in 1797. Kreglinger Australia was established in 1893 as an agribusiness export company specialising in sheep skins. In early 2002 it acquired Pipers Brook Vineyard in Tasmania, and will maintain the separate brands of each venture. Norfolk Rise has 160 ha of Riesling, Sauvignon Blanc, Pinot Gris, Shiraz, Merlot and Cabernet Sauvignon, supported by a state-of-the-art 2000 tonne winery built into the side of a gentle slope, to minimise its impact on the landscape.

Signature wine: Shiraz

Ralph Fowler Wines Est. 1999

Limestone Coast Rd, Mount Benson 5275
www.ralphfowlerwines.com.au

exports to UK

Established by the Fowler family, headed by well-known winemaker Ralph Fowler, with wife Deborah and children Sarah and James all involved in the 40 ha vineyard property at Mount Benson. Ralph Fowler began his 30-year winemaking career at Tyrrell's, and ultimately the Hamilton/Leconfield group, before moving to Mount Benson to make fine Sauvignon Blanc, Viognier, Shiraz and Cabernet Sauvignon. In 2005 he handed the reins to Sarah, and moved to Château Tanunda in the Barossa Valley.

Signature wine: Shiraz Viognier

Wehl's Mt Benson Vineyards

Est. 1989

Wrights Bay Rd, Mount Benson 5275
wehls.mountbenson@bigpond.com

Peter and Leah Wehl were the first to plant vines in the Mount Benson area, beginning the establishment of their 24 ha vineyard, two-thirds Shiraz and one-third Cabernet Sauvignon, in 1989. Their grapes were primarily sold to the Beringer Blass-owned Cellarmaster operation to make the multi-gold medal winning Black Wattle Cabernet Sauvignon. While primarily grapegrowers, they have moved into winemaking via contract makers, and plan to increase the range of wines available by grafting 1 ha of Merlot and 1.5 ha of Sauvignon Blanc on to the existing plantings.

Signature wine: Shiraz

[LEFT] GEESE, RALPH FOWLER WINES.

LIMESTONE COAST ZONE
Wrattonbully 🌿

This is another important region to emerge with a separate identity in the wake of the Geographical Indications process. Only Pemberton (in Western Australia) has generated as much debate over its correct name. The commonsense solution would have been to name the region Koppamurra, making special arrangements to accommodate the particular position and needs of Koppamurra Wines. (It not only made wines from estate-grown grapes, but also from grapes grown outside the putative Koppamurra region. This would have led to insuperable problems under the Geographic Indications legislation,

restricting Koppamurra Wines to sole use of grapes grown within the region.) Just when it seemed that commonsense would prevail, negotiations collapsed, a situation which displeased many inside and outside the region. However, the die has been cast, and with the registration process finalised, the name is Wrattonbully. The ultimate irony is that the Koppamurra Vineyard has been purchased by a distinguished consortium headed by Brian Croser and renamed Tapanappa.

After a slow start (the Koppamurra Vineyard was established in 1973) the pace of development accelerated dramatically

during the 1990s. There are over ten major vineyard developments and 2000 hectares of vineyards have been established. As in the case of Padthaway, much of the production is used by major wine companies (notably Hardys, Beringer Blass and Yalumba) in blended wines, but Yalumba's Smith and Hooper range is regionally identified.

In 1998 a large contract crush and winery was constructed. Its primary purpose was to service the needs of the major grape (and bulk wine) buyers from the region. In 2001 the winery was leased to Orlando Wyndham and is now called Russet Ridge.

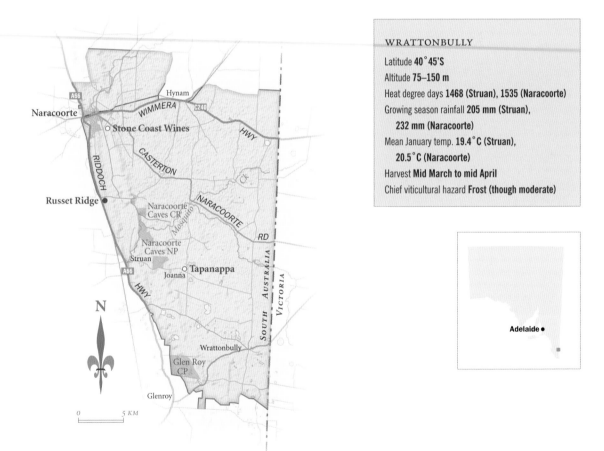

WRATTONBULLY

Latitude **40°45'S**

Altitude **75–150 m**

Heat degree days **1468 (Struan), 1535 (Naracoorte)**

Growing season rainfall **205 mm (Struan),**
232 mm (Naracoorte)

Mean January temp. **19.4°C (Struan),**
20.5°C (Naracoorte)

Harvest **Mid March to mid April**

Chief viticultural hazard **Frost (though moderate)**

The Region

CLIMATE

The climate is poised between that of Coonawarra and Padthaway, warmer than the former and cooler than the latter, although there is surprising variation across the region. Relative humidity and rainfall (and hence the risk of disease) are slightly lower than the other two regions, and the risk of frost is significantly less. Irrigation is essential, but there is sufficient underground water of appropriate quality (salinity is not a problem) to irrigate 10 000 hectares of vines in the region if no other irrigated agriculture is carried on.

SOIL & TOPOGRAPHY

The Naracoorte Ranges are the last in a series extending from the coast, and has permitted the establishment of vineyards at an elevation of 75–100 metres above sea level on gently undulating slopes. The vineyards are almost exclusively planted on the so-called terra rossa soils made famous in Coonawarra, deriving from the ancient coastal dunes and seabed formations which give the Limestone Coast its name. Technically known as non-cracking, subplastic clays, they are very friable and free draining.

PRINCIPAL GRAPE VARIETIES

In descending order:

CABERNET SAUVIGNON

SHIRAZ

MERLOT

CHARDONNAY.

🌿 WHITE WINE STYLES

Chardonnay barely makes a blip on the radar screen, a rarity in Australia, and not likely to change in the early years of the new millennium.

🌿 RED WINE STYLES

Cabernet Sauvignon. Both the large and small players alike have put their money where their mouths are by planting this variety to the seeming exclusion of all others. Quite evidently, it ripens easily even when crop levels are generous, producing a pleasantly soft, red-berry fruited wine with moderate tannin levels.

Shiraz provides much the same play as Cabernet Sauvignon; the flavour register is of course different, but the mouthfeel, weight and texture is similar. Wines such as these are valuable blending tools, filling in gaps and smoothing out the rough edges in other wines from other varieties and/or regions.

Merlot is the one wine of the region to have consistently asserted individual character and quality; here the flavours are in a positively varietal leafy/cedary/cigar box spectrum.

Wineries of Wrattonbully

Russet Ridge Est. 2000
**Cnr Caves Rd and Riddoch Hwy,
Naracoorte 5271**
russetridge@orlando-wyndham.com
🍷 **exports to UK**

This is the former Heathfield Ridge winery, built in 1998 as a contract crush and winemaking facility for multiple clients, but leased by Orlando Wyndham in 2000. It is the only winery in the large Wrattonbully region, and also receives Orlando's Coonawarra and Padthaway grapes, and other Limestone Coast fruit. Ironically, Russet Ridge is a Coonawarra brand.
*Signature wine: Coonawarra
Cabernet Shiraz Merlot*

Stone Coast Est. 1997
18 North Terrace, Adelaide 5000 (postal)
www.stonecoastwines.com

The names of the two wines produced, The Struggle Shiraz and The Commitment Cabernet Sauvignon, hint at the problems encountered with the development of the 33 ha of Cabernet Sauvignon and 11 ha of Shiraz which constitute the vineyard. It is situated on a terra rossa ridge top, but had unusually thick limestone slabs running through it, which had caused others to bypass the property. A 95 tonne bulldozer was hired to deep rip the limestone, but was unequal to the task, and ultimately explosives had to be used to create sufficient inroads to allow planting. Fifteen per cent of the production from the vineyard is used to have the wines contract-made.
*Signature wine: The Commitment
Cabernet Sauvignon*

Tapanappa Est. 2003
PO Box 174, Crafers 5152
bcroser@adelaide.on.net
exports to UK

Arguably the most interesting of all new ventures to be announced in Australia over the past few years. Its partners are Brian Croser of Petaluma, Jean-Michel Cazes of Château Lynch-Bages in Pauillac, and Société Jacques Bollinger, the parent company of Champagne Bollinger. The core of the business is the Koppamurra vineyard, acquired from Koppamurra Wines prior to the 2003 vintage; the 2003 vintage of Cabernet Sauvignon Shiraz and Merlot was released under the Tapanappa brand in late 2005. In the meantime, the vineyard has been entirely reworked on to vertical spur positioning, and given that it was planted in 1973 (one of the two original vineyards in the Koppamurra area), will undoubtedly produce fruit of great quality.
Signature wine: Cabernet Shiraz Merlot

Lower Murray Zone
Riverland ❧

When Californian George Chaffey fell foul of political duplicity in Victoria in 1887, the South Australian government quickly stepped in to capitalise on the expertise he and his brother William had developed in pioneering irrigation in California. With unconditional government support the Chaffeys selected Renmark, on the west bank of the Murray, as the site for the commencement of irrigation in South Australia. With formidable energy, the brothers had quickly laid out the site of the town, with the wide streets and parklands which remain a feature to this day.

It was not long, however, before the Chaffeys were back in Victoria, developing Mildura for a by then chastened Victorian government. In 1893 the Renmark Irrigation Trust took over responsibility for the area, and for maintaining the irrigation channels, which had already started to fall into disrepair. The Trust has since been responsible both for the town of Renmark and for 4800 hectares of orchards and vineyards in the district; it is in turn effectively run by local landholders.

The Riverland has long been recognised as the 'engine-room' that has driven the Australian wine industry. The region produces over 55 per cent of all of South Australia's grapes, and that translates to almost 25 per cent of Australia's grape production. Until recently, the area has been mostly known for the quantity of wine it produces, but this has now changed, with the focus switching to the quality of its wines.

Increased quality is being achieved by better viticultural practices (trellising and canopy management), better water usage (less total water, improved monitoring of soil moisture and the gradual replacement of flood or overhead irrigation with drip irrigation), and improved grape varieties and clones.

The process of change is set to continue well into the current century. Many of the Riverland's white and red varieties are in fact a mix of inferior wine grape varieties or the so-called multi-purpose grapes which can be used for wines, for drying into sultanas and raisins, or as table grapes. Slowly but surely these will be replaced by the better-quality wine grapes, in particular by Chardonnay and Shiraz.

[OPPOSITE] HARVESTING BY HAND.
[BELOW] BANROCK STATION, RIVERLAND.

The Region ✿

CLIMATE

The climate is hot, with high evaporation rates and low rainfall, making irrigation essential; it is also continental, resulting in long sunny days and noticeably cooler nights. Modern viticultural and winemaking techniques mean this climate can be seen as one of the region's strengths. Long sunshine hours ensure fruit ripeness, while a strongly winter dominant rainfall results in low disease incidence and allows the viticulturists the choice of how much moisture the vine receives during the growing season.

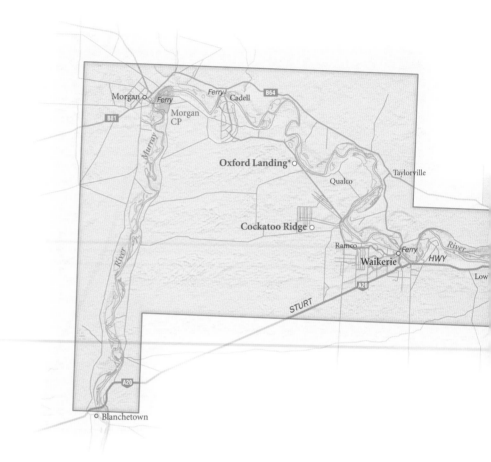

SOIL & TOPOGRAPHY

The soils are red-brown sandy loams often overlying a limestone substrate. Fertility rates are moderate. As with the entire Murray Darling basin, salinity is an increasingly important issue and will affect all aspects of land use in future generations.

PRINCIPAL GRAPE VARIETIES

The overall mix is 60 per cent red and 40 per cent white. In descending order:

CABERNET SAUVIGNON

CHARDONNAY

MUSCAT GORDO BLANCO

GRENACHE

MERLOT

COLOMBARD

PETIT VERDOT.

[ABOVE] BANROCK STATION, RIVERLAND.
[RIGHT] OXFORD LANDING, RIVERLAND.

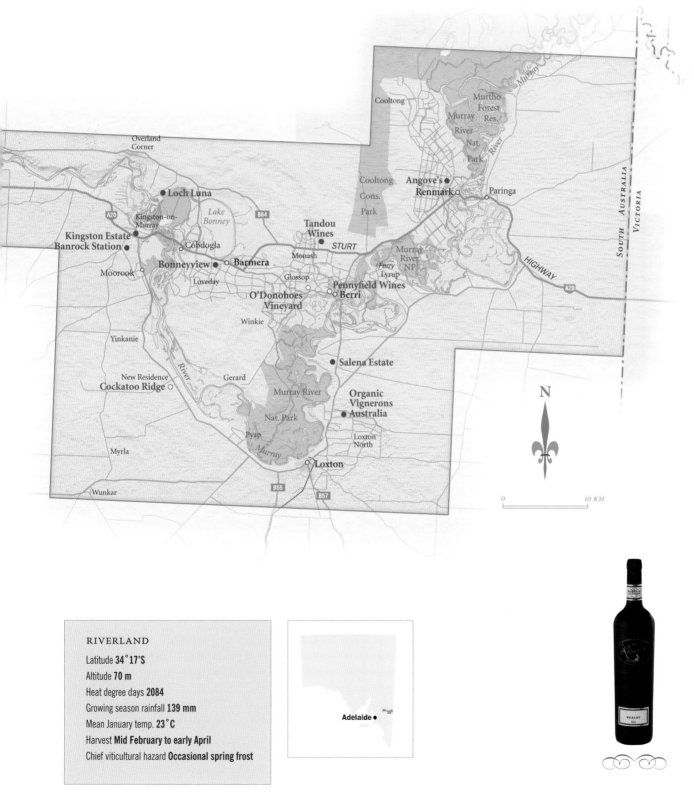

RIVERLAND

Latitude **34°17'S**

Altitude **70 m**

Heat degree days **2084**

Growing season rainfall **139 mm**

Mean January temp. **23°C**

Harvest **Mid February to early April**

Chief viticultural hazard **Occasional spring frost**

Cellar Door
* Oxford Landing at Yalumba, Eden Valley; see p. 23 for map.

WHITE WINE STYLES

Chardonnay, as ever, proves itself to be incredibly flexible. Cropped heavily here, and fermented in vast stainless steel fermenters with or without the use of oak chips, it produces a perfectly pleasant but unremarkable wine, which sells at an attractive price.

Other White Varietals. Varieties such as Colombard, Chenin Blanc and Verdelho are increasingly being used to lift the quality of white wines in the region.

RED WINE STYLES

Shiraz. If limiting the yield is important in maximising the potential of Chardonnay, it is quite critical with Shiraz. Of course, all things are relative: a low crop in the Murray is still substantial, and the best wines are soft and round, recommended to be consumed while young.

Cabernet Sauvignon plantings in excess of 3400 hectares are not going to disappear overnight, nor even decline appreciably in the years ahead. But it is likely the high-water mark has been reached, however important 'fighting varietal' Cabernet Sauvignon may be in some markets.

Mourvèdre and Grenache. While there are many young vineyards in the Riverland, there are also significant areas with vines over 80 years old. Many of these consist of Grenache and Mourvèdre which were until recently seen as workhorse varieties for use in cask reds and fortifieds. Fruit from these old vines, often in combination with Shiraz, is now being used to produce medium-bodied spicy red wines which exemplify the sunny, fruit-driven Australian style.

Petit Verdot here, as elsewhere in similar Australian regions, is on the march, producing wine of deep colour and abundant flavour – notwithstanding high yields.

[ABOVE] BANROCK STATION, RIVERLAND.
[BELOW] OXFORD LANDING, RIVERLAND.
[OPPOSITE LEFT] JOHN AND VICTORIA ANGOVE.
[OPPOSITE RIGHT] WETLANDS, BANROCK STATION.

Wineries of Riverland

Angove's Est. 1886

Bookmark Ave, Renmark 5341

www.angoves.com.au

exports to UK, US

The 510 ha Angove's vineyard at Renmark exemplifies the economies of scale achievable in the Riverland without compromising potential quality. Very good technology provides wines which are never poor and which can sometimes exceed their theoretical station in life; the white varietals are best. Angove's expansion into Padthaway has resulted in estate-grown premium wines at the top of the range, but don't challenge the core wines when it comes to value for money.

Signature wine: Long Row Sauvignon Blanc

Banrock Station Est. 1994

Holmes Rd, off Sturt Hwy,
Kingston-on-Murray 5331

www.banrockstation.com

exports to UK, US

A $1 million visitors centre at Banrock Station was opened in 1999. Owned by Hardys, the Banrock Station property covers over 1700 ha, with 240 ha of vineyard, the remainder being a major wildlife and wetland preservation area. The full range of varietal wines have consistently offered excellent value for money in the sub-$10 price bracket, The Reserve varietals (incluidng Durif) breaking the $10 barrier with authenticity.

Signature wine: The Reserve Merlot

Kingston Estate Est. 1979

Sturt Hwy, Kingston-on-Murray 5331

www.kingstonestatewines.com

exports to UK

Kingston Estate, under the direction of Bill Moularadellis, still has its production roots in the Riverland region, but has also set up long-term purchase contracts with growers in the Clare Valley, the Adelaide Hills, Coonawarra, Langhorne Creek and Mount Benson. It has spread its net to take in a wide range of varietals, mainstream and exotic, under a number of different brands at various price points. Since 2002, a consistent over-achiever.

Signature wine: Echelon Shiraz

Organic Vignerons Australia

Est. 2002

Section 395, Derrick Rd, Loxton North 5333

www.ova.com.au

Organic Vignerons Australia is a very interesting winemaking business. It consists of the owners of five certified organic South Australian properties: Claire and Kevin Hansen at Padthaway, Bruce and Sue Armstrong at Waikerie, Brett and Melissa Munchenberg here at Loxton, Terry Markou at Adelaide Plains and David and Barbara Bruer at Langhorne Creek. The wines are made by David Bruer at Temple Bruer, which is itself a certified organic producer.

Signature wine: Shiraz Cabernet Sauvignon

Oxford Landing Est. 1958

Qualco 5322

www.yalumba.com

(at Yalumba, Eden Valley);

exports to UK, US

A large and highly successful vineyard and brand owned by Yalumba: 260 ha of vineyard produce a core range of Sauvignon Blanc, Chardonnay, Shiraz, Merlot and Cabernet Sauvignon, which ably contest the fierce fighting varietal battleground. It has many points in common with Angove's and Hardys' Banrock Station.

Signature wine: Cabernet Sauvignon

FAR NORTH ZONE
Southern Flinders Ranges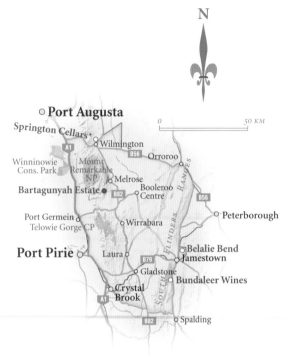

The Southern Flinders Ranges is at the southern extremity of the Far North Zone, and its only region – the latter not a situation likely to change in the foreseeable future. The well-known Goyder's Line, drawn by surveyor George Goyder in the nineteenth century, runs east–west through the region, marking the northernmost limits of feasible agriculture. The Spencer Gulf marks the western edge of the region, which is sandwiched between the Peninsulas Zone to the west, and the Mount Lofty Ranges Zone to the south-east.

The beauty of the region is well known to campers and tourists, the Mount Remarkable National Park one of its jewels. In geological terms, it has two parts, the ridgeline of the Flinders Ranges separating the Wild Dog Creek land system to the east from the coastal Baroota land system to the west. The soils of the former range from deep red loams to shallower stony loams on the slopes; those of the latter are deep sandy loams.

Most of the vineyards have been established on the slopes of the Flinders Ranges at a height of 350–550 metres; both the altitude and sea breezes from the Gulf temper the otherwise hot climate. The limitation on viticulture is the low annual rainfall of between 450 and 650 millimetres, making irrigation nigh-on essential during the establishment phase of the vineyards.

While most of the mainstream varieties are planted, the focus is on Shiraz, Merlot and Cabernet Sauvignon. The major part of the grape production is sold to Barossa Valley makers, a minor part vinified for the handful of wineries in the region.

Wineries of Southern Flinders Ranges

Bartagunyah Estate Est. 2000
7 Survey Rd, Melrose 5483
www.smartaqua.com.au/bartagunyah

Rob and Christine Smart have established 3 ha of Shiraz, 2 ha of Cabernet Sauvignon and 1 ha of Viognier on a property adjoining the southern ridge of the beautiful and rugged Mount Remarkable. It is hidden away in a valley in the hills about 5 km south of Melrose along the historic Survey Road. It is a hop, step and jump into the Flinders Ranges, and the Smarts offer four-wheel drive tours and mountain bike tours to take in both the scenery and the abundant wildlife.

Signature wine: Shiraz

Belalie Bend Est. 2001
PO Box 288, Jamestown 5491
www.belaliebend.com.au

In 2001 farmers Guy and Emma Bowley decided to diversify by planting 1 ha each of Shiraz, Cabernet and Riesling, followed by 1.5 ha each of Mourvèdre and Shiraz the following year. The vineyard is situated beneath Mount Remarkable at an elevation of over 400 m, and there is provision for farm/vineyard stay for self-contained motor homes.

Signature wine: Connection Clare Valley Shiraz Cabernet

Bundaleer Wines Est. 1998
41 King St, Brighton 5048 (postal)
www.bundaleerwines.com.au

Bundaleer is a joint venture between third-generation farmer Des Meaney and manufacturing industry executive Graham Spurling (whose family originally came from the Southern Flinders). Planting of the 8 ha vineyard began in 1998, the first vintage coming in 2001. It is situated in a region known as the Bundaleer Gardens, on the edge of the Bundaleer Forest, 200 km north of Adelaide, at an altitude of 500 m. The wines are made under the care of industry veteran Angela Meaney at Paulett Winery in the Clare Valley.

Signature wine: Shiraz

Springton Cellars Est. 1991
14 Miller St, Springton 5235
www.agale.com.au/winery.htm
(at Springton Cellars, Springton)

Dr Allen E. Gale, together with Chris Thomas, has established 1 ha of vines at Wilmington in the Southern Flinders Ranges, a very promising area which will shortly be officially recognised as a region under the legislation. The Cabernet Sauvignon and Shiraz are made off-site by Chris Thomas, and are chiefly sold from the cellar door, together with hotels and restaurants throughout the mid and far north.

Signature wine: Old Gunyah Road Shiraz

Cellar Door
* Springton Cellars at 14 Miller St, Springton, Eden Valley; see p. 23 for map.

Southern Eyre Peninsula 🌿

The Southern Eyre Peninsula – and the Yorke Peninsula on the eastern side of the Spencer Gulf – is still at an embryonic state viticulturally, although the two wineries on the Eyre Peninsula are over 20 years old. It seems remoteness, rather than lack of appropriate conditions for grapegrowing, has held back the rate of development.

The strong maritime influence of the Spencer Gulf, combined with patches of terra rossa over limestone soils similar to Coonawarra, make the area particularly suited to full-bodied red wine production from Shiraz, Merlot and Cabernet Sauvignon, while Riesling and Chardonnay have also performed quite well.

Viticulture on the Yorke Peninsula has been slower to develop, although the climate and terra rossa sandy loams on its south-eastern quadrant seem equally suited to quality grapegrowing.

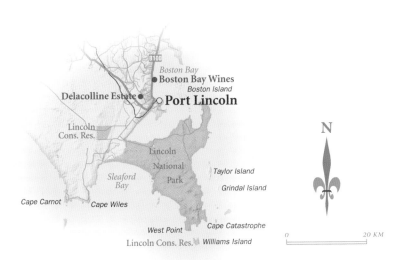

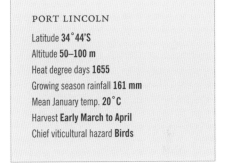

PORT LINCOLN

Latitude **34°44'S**

Altitude **50–100 m**

Heat degree days **1655**

Growing season rainfall **161 mm**

Mean January temp. **20°C**

Harvest **Early March to April**

Chief viticultural hazard **Birds**

Wineries of Southern Eyre Peninsula

Boston Bay Wines Est. 1984
Lincoln Hwy, Port Lincoln 5606
www.bostonbaywines.com.au

A strongly tourist-oriented operation which has extended the viticultural map in South Australia. It is situated at the same latitude as Adelaide, overlooking the Spencer Gulf at the southern tip of the Eyre Peninsula. Say proprietors Graham and Mary Ford, 'It is the only vineyard in the world to offer frequent sightings of whales at play in the waters at its foot.' The wines are professionally contract-made by O'Leary Walker from the 7 ha estate plantings of Riesling, Chardonnay, Shiraz, Merlot and Cabernet Sauvignon, but are seldom seen outside the region.

Signature wine: Riesling

Delacolline Estate Est. 1984
Whillas Rd, Port Lincoln 5606
(08) 8682 5277

Joins Boston Bay as the second Port Lincoln producer; the white wines are made under contract in the Clare Valley. The 3 ha vineyard, planted to Riesling, Sauvignon Blanc and Cabernet Sauvignon and run under the direction of Tony Bassett, reflects the cool maritime influence, with ocean currents that sweep up from the Antarctic. Like Boston Bay, its wines seldom travel outside the region.

Signature wine: Sauvignon Blanc

SHIRAZ GRAPES.

Victoria

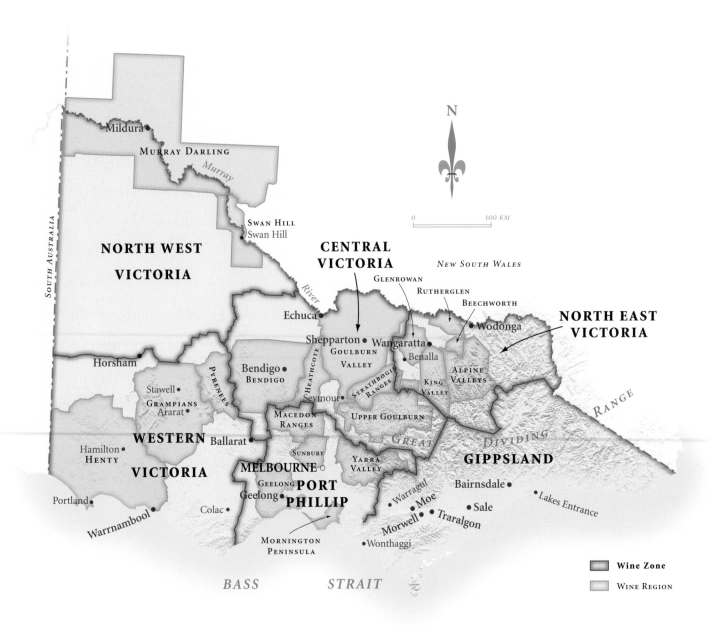

N

0   100 KM

MILDURA •

MURRAY DARLING

Murray

SWAN HILL
Swan Hill

NORTH WEST

VICTORIA

CENTRAL
VICTORIA

NEW SOUTH WALES

GLENROWAN

RUTHERGLEN

BEECHWORTH

NORTH EAST
VICTORIA

River

Echuca •

Wodonga •

SOUTH AUSTRALIA

Horsham •

Shepparton •   Wangaratta •
GOULBURN   • Benalla
VALLEY

Stawell •

PYRENEES

Bendigo •
BENDIGO

HEATHCOTE

Seymour •

STRATHBOGIE
RANGES

KING
VALLEY

ALPINE
VALLEYS

GRAMPIANS
Ararat •

MACEDON
RANGES

UPPER GOULBURN

RANGE

WESTERN

Ballarat •

GREAT

DIVIDING

GIPPSLAND

Hamilton •
HENTY

VICTORIA

SUNBURY

MELBOURNE ○

Yarra
Valley

Bairnsdale •

Portland •

Colac •

Geelong
Geelong •

PORT
PHILLIP

Warragul •
Morwell • Moe •
Traralgon •

Sale •

Lakes Entrance •

Warrnambool •

MORNINGTON
PENINSULA

• Wonthaggi

BASS   STRAIT

■ Wine Zone

▢ Wine Region

Introduction ❧

The viticultural map of Victoria is more densely populated than that of any other state: it has more regions and it has more wineries than South Australia, its western neighbour, and – in production terms – its big brother. Moreover, the percentage of its total surface area covered by wine regions is far greater than that of any other state. Small wonder that Hubert de Castella called his 1886 book about the wines of Victoria *John Bull's Vineyard*. He was convinced all the wine needs of England could be supplied by Victoria.

To a far greater degree than in any other part of Australia, wine and gold formed a potent blend here throughout the second half of the nineteenth century. The Victorian goldfields are now largely a memory – however glorious in places such as Ballarat – but wine has prospered to the present, notwithstanding the impact of phylloxera which arrived in Geelong in 1875 or 1876, and worked its destructive path north to Rutherglen by the end of that century.

Other than Tasmania, Victoria is the smallest state in the Commonwealth, yet it has the greatest diversity of regional and site climates, from the very cool Macedon Ranges to the very warm regions stretching along the Murray River, from the north-east to the north-west of the state.

As with all the other states, however, there are anomalies of various kinds. Gippsland is a zone – and a very large one at that – without regions, notwithstanding that climate and commonsense would suggest at least three regions. The problem is it simply doesn't grow enough grapes for regions to be registered.

At the other end of the spectrum, some significant small wineries within the Port Phillip, Central Victoria, Western Victoria and North East Victoria Zones find themselves outside the regions falling with those zones. These wineries are covered in the zonal introductions.

Finally, for the sake of convenience and logic, I cover the North West Victoria Zone and its two regions, Murray Darling and Swan Hill, in this section of the book, rather than in the Big Rivers Zone of New South Wales. Both of these regions fall partly in Victoria and partly in New South Wales, but most, if not all, of the wineries are in Victoria.

[PREVIOUS] YARRA VALLEY, VICTORIA.
[OPPOSITE] SCOTCHMANS HILL, GEELONG.
[RIGHT] COLDSTREAM HILLS, YARRA VALLEY.

Port Phillip Zone

I have long described the regions of the Port Phillip Zone as the dress circle of Melbourne, around which they are more or less equally distributed. They share a fundamentally similar climate: cool Mediterranean, meaning the rainfall is winter–spring dominant, and without the extremes of day–night, and winter–summer, temperatures. These extremes are to be found in continental (or inland) climates.

They can all be reached by car from Melbourne's CBD within an hour plus (Mornington Peninsula) or less (Sunbury, Macedon Ranges). With the qualified exception of parts of Sunbury and Geelong, they offer spectacular scenery, while the Mornington Peninsula (especially) and Yarra Valley cater for every wish of the day tourist.

However close and compact the regions may be, there are some parts of the zone not included in those regions, leaving wineries metaphorically marooned in some surprising locations although deserving a place in this *Atlas*.

[RIGHT & OPPOSITE] COLDSTREAM HILLS, YARRA VALLEY.

Wineries of the Port Phillip Zone

Brunswick Hill Wines Est. 1999

34 Breeze St, Brunswick 3056
patkins@alphalink.com.au

Peter Atkins owns Brunswick Hill Wines, which is claimed to be Melbourne's only urban winery, situated in the heart of Brunswick, 15 minutes from the CBD. Studley Park Vineyard is even closer to the city centre, but its wines are made at Granite Hills. A member of the Eltham and District Winemakers Guild, Atkins moved to commercial winemaking after ten years as an amateur. Brunswick Hill Wines takes grapes from a number of Victorian regions, ranging from cool to warm. 1999 was the first fully-fledged commercial vintage, and a number of vintages are available by mail order and the cellar door on Saturdays.
Signature wine: Yarra Valley Chardonnay

Cannibal Creek Vineyard

Est. 1997
260 Tynong North Rd, Tynong North 3813
www.cannibalcreek.com.au

 exports to UK

The Hardiker family moved to Tynong North in 1988 to graze beef cattle, but aware of the viticultural potential of the sandy clay loam and bleached subsurface soils weathered from the granite foothills of Tynong North. Planting of the 5 ha vineyard ultimately began in 1997, using organically based cultivation methods, and by 1999 it was already producing grapes. The decision was taken to (very successfully) make their own wine, with Patrick Hardiker in charge, and a heritage-style shed built from locally milled timber has been converted into a winery and small cellar-door facility.
Signature wine: Chardonnay

Jinks Creek Winery Est. 1981

Tonimbuk Rd, Tonimbuk 3815
www.jinkscreekwinery.com.au

 exports to US

Situated between Gembrook and Bunyip, bordering the evocatively named Bunyip State Park. While owner-winemaker (and wine consultant to others) Andrew Clarke did not build a winery until 1992, planting of the 3.6 ha vineyard started back in 1981, and all of the Gippsland wines are estate-grown. The intake is supplemented by purchases of (separately labelled) Heathcote Shiraz and Yarra Valley Shiraz; all three Shirazs speak strongly of their very different terroirs.
Signature wine: Longford Gippsland Shiraz

Limbic Est. 1997

295 Morrison Rd, Pakenham Upper 3810
limbic@cyberspace.net.au

Jennifer and Michael Pullar have established a vineyard on the hills between Yarra Valley and Gippsland, overlooking the Mornington Peninsula and Western Port. They have planted a total of 6.2 ha of Pinot Noir, Chardonnay and Sauvignon Blanc, increasingly utilising organic and thereafter biodynamic practices. The first five years of grape production was sold, with trial vintages under the Limbic label commencing in 2001, followed by the first commercial releases in 2003. A winery and cellar door have been constructed, and the 2005 vintage was made on-site, which will see production increase from 600 to 1200 cases. 'Limbic' is the word for a network of neural pathways in the brain that links smell, taste and emotion.
Signature wine: Sauvignon Blanc

Studley Park Vineyard Est. 1994

5 Garden Terrace, Kew 3101 (postal)
www.studleypark.com

Geoff Pryor's Studley Park Vineyard is one of Melbourne's best-kept secrets. It is situated on a bend of the Yarra River barely 4 km from the Melbourne CBD on a half-hectare block originally planted to vines, but for a century used for market gardening until replanted with Cabernet Sauvignon. Immediately across the river, and looking directly towards the CBD, is the epicentre of Melbourne's light industrial development, while on the northern and eastern boundaries are suburban residential blocks. Sales take place directly over the internet.
Signature wine: Cabernet Sauvignon

Woongarra Estate Est. 1992

95 Hayseys Rd, Narre Warren East 3804
www.woongarrawinery.com.au

Dr Bruce Jones, and wife Mary, purchased their 16 ha property many years ago. In 1992 the Joneses planted 1 ha of Sauvignon Blanc, a small patch of Shiraz and a few rows of Semillon. Total plantings now comprise 3.2 ha of Pinot Noir, 1.4 ha of Sauvignon Blanc and a splash of the other two varieties. The spectacular success has come with the Three Wise Men Pinot Noir, jointly owned by Woongarra and Passing Clouds, and which is available from Woongarra direct.
Signature wine: Three Wise Men Pinot Noir

Port Phillip Zone
Yarra Valley ❧

As I have acknowledged elsewhere, I am hopelessly biased when it comes to the Yarra Valley, for it is where I live, where I work – making wine and writing about it – and it is where I hope I will die when my time comes. It is a place of extreme beauty, of constantly changing light, of colour and of mood. It offers landscapes on an heroic scale with the same profligacy as it offers intimate vistas. Once you have seen it, you cannot help but love it.

Yet my love affair started before I set foot in it, when I tasted the first vintages of Seville Estate, Yeringberg and Mount Mary, followed soon thereafter by Yarra Yering. In the second half of the 1970s these wines opened up a new horizon; the Pinot Noirs, a new world.

Within a year I had traversed its length, and although I did not know it then, my fate was sealed, my life was to change direction from that of a senior partner in a major law firm specialising in corporate law to that of full-time wine writer and winemaker without (as I am fond of saying) visible means of support.

The antecedents of the Yarra Valley were (and are) impeccable, with a proud and rich history of grapegrowing and winemaking stretching back to the first settlers (in 1838) and reaching the height of fame in 1881. Its renaissance burst like a spring flower between 1968 and 1971, inexplicably all but stopped throughout the rest of the 1970s and flourished in an extraordinary fashion in the 1980s and, even more, in the 1990s through to 2005.

Until the 1990s the Yarra Valley was the exclusive preserve of the small winery, most of them producing wines in the super-premium category. De Bortoli Wines of Griffith was the first large, commercial company to invest, acquiring (and renaming) Millers Chateau Yarrinya in 1987. Then in the 1990s, and in quick succession, Mildara Blass acquired Yarra Ridge (and later St Huberts via its Rothbury Estate takeover); Hardys acquired the large Hoddles Creek Vineyards and then Yarra Burn; McWilliam's purchased Lilydale Vineyards; and Southcorp (now part of Fosters Wine Estates) followed up its acquisition of Fernhill Vineyards by taking over Coldstream Hills (which I had founded) in 1996.

There was also a rash of large-scale invest-ment in new wineries initiated by Moët et Chandon with Domaine Chandon in the late 1980s, followed by the Cowan family in Eyton-on-Yarra (since acquired by the Konecsny family and renamed Rochford), the Rathbone family with Yering Station, and (in 1997) the Zitzlaff family with Oakridge Estate, since acquired by Evans & Tate.

Back in the 1980s Dr Tony Jordan of Domaine Chandon wrote a paper suggesting that by 2010 the Yarra Valley could have 5000 hectares of vineyards and 100 wineries producing three million cases of wine a year. At the time, it seemed a fanciful dream; however, with the national and international acceptance of the Yarra Valley as one of Australia's foremost fine-wine regions, it has become a realistic target. By 2005 the number of wineries was over a hundred, the grape harvest sufficient to make 1,400,000 cases.

[OPPOSITE] Domaine Chandon, Yarra Valley. [BELOW] Amphitheatre Vineyard, Coldstream Hills, Yarra Valley. [OVERLEAF] Kangaroos, Coldstream Hills, Yarra Valley.

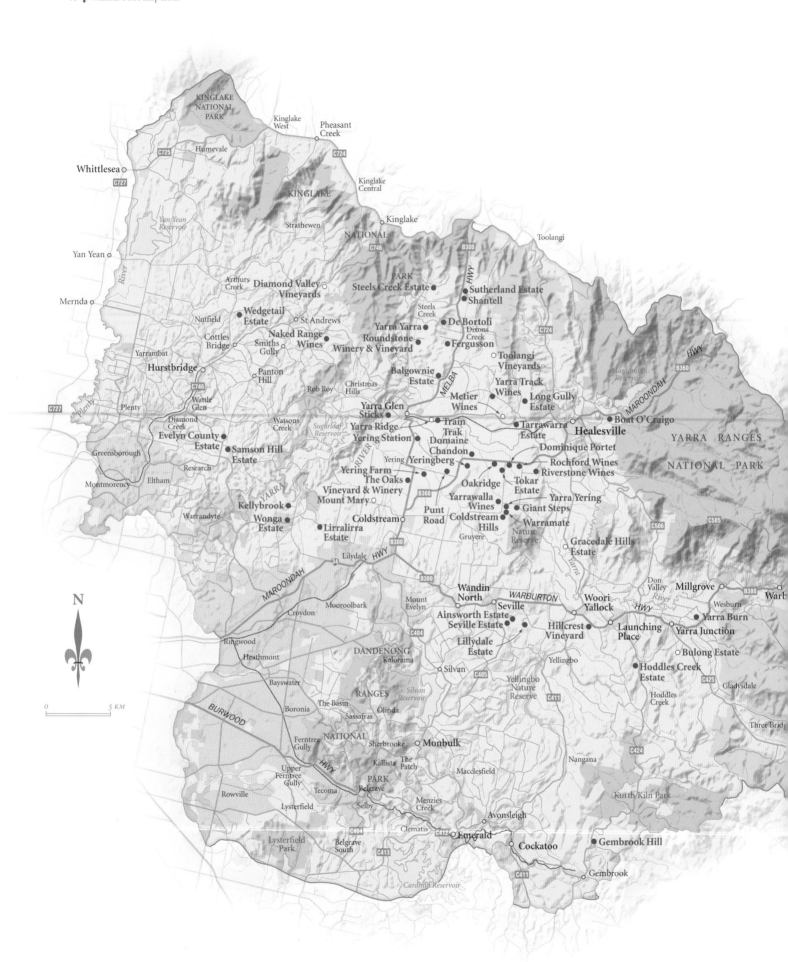

KINGLAKE
NATIONAL
PARK

Kinglake
West

Pheasant
Creek

C725

Humevale

C724

Whittlesea

C727

KINGLAKE

Kinglake
Central

Yan Yean
Reservoir

Strathewen

Kinglake

NATIONAL

Toolangi

C746

B300

Yan Yean

Mernda

Arthurs
Creek

Diamond Valley
Vineyards

Steels Creek Estate

PARK

Sutherland Estate
Shantell

Steels
Creek

Nutfield

Wedgetail
Estate

St Andrews

Yarra Yarra

De Bortoli

Dixons
Creek

C724

Cottles
Bridge

Naked Range
Wines

Smiths
Gully

Roundstone
Winery & Vineyard

Fergusson

Toolangi
Vineyards

MELBA

Yarrambat

Hurstbridge

C746

Panton
Hill

Balgownie
Estate

Yarra Track
Wines

Long Gully
Estate

Plenty

C727

Wattle
Glen

Rob Roy

Christmas
Hills

Yarra Glen
Sticks

Metier
Wines

Plenty

Diamond
Creek

Watsons
Creek

Sugarloaf
Reservoir

Yarra Ridge
Yering Station

Train
Trak

Tarrawarra
Estate

Boat O'Craigo

Healesville

Maroondah
Reservoir

MAROONDAH

B360

Greensborough

Evelyn County
Estate

Samson Hill
Estate

Research

Domaine
Chandon

Dominique Portet

YARRA RANGES

Eltham

Yering

Yeringberg

Rochford Wines

NATIONAL PARK

Montmorency

Yering Farm
The Oaks

Oakridge

Riverstone Wines

Vineyard & Winery
Mount Mary

B360

Yarrawalla
Wines

Tokar
Estate

Yarra Yering

C506

C505

Kellybrook

Warrandyte

Coldstream

Punt
Road

Coldstream
Hills

Giant Steps

Warramate

Wonga
Estate

Lirralirra
Estate

Gruyere

Nature
Reserve

Gracedale Hills
Estate

Lilydale

B300

Don
Valley

Millgrove

B380

Warb

Mooroolbark

MAROONDAH

Croydon

Mount
Evelyn

Wandin
North

WARBURTON

Woori
Yallock

Wesburn

Yarra Burn

Ringwood

Heathmont

C404

Ainsworth Estate
Seville Estate

Seville

Hillcrest
Vineyard

Launching
Place

Yarra Junction

Lilydale
Estate

Bayswater

DANDENONG

Kalorama

Silvan

C405

Yellingbo

Bulong Estate

BURWOOD

Boronia

RANGES

The Basin

Silvan
Reservoir

Yellingbo
Nature
Reserve

C411

Hoddles Creek
Estate

Gladysdale

Sassafras

Olinda

Hoddles
Creek

C425

Three Bridg

Ferntree
Gully

NATIONAL

Sherbrooke

Kallista

Monbulk

Macclesfield

Nangana

C424

Upper
Ferntree
Gully

PARK

The
Patch

Tecoma

Belgrave

Menzies
Creek

Kurth Kiln Park

Rowville

Lysterfield

Selby

Avonsleigh

Clematis

C404

C412

Emerald

Cockatoo

Gembrook Hill

Lysterfield
Park

Belgrave
South

C413

C411

Gembrook

Cardinia Reservoir

N

0   5 KM

YARRA RANGES

NATIONAL

PARK

Upper Yarra
Reservoir

YARRA   RANGES

NATIONAL   PARK

McMahons
Creek

C511

rton

Pats
ek

vn

Melbourne ●

YARRA VALLEY

Latitude **37˚49'S**

Altitude **50–400 m**

Heat degree days **1250–1352**

Growing season rainfall **400 mm**

Mean January temp. **17.9–19.4˚C**

Harvest **Early March to early May**

Chief viticultural hazards **Birds; mildew**

The Region

CLIMATE

Given the considerable variation in altitude throughout the Yarra Valley, and the significance of aspect (i.e. north or south) on the many hillside vineyards, it is not surprising that there is substantial variation in meso-climate. However, even the warmest sites are, comparatively speaking, cool; the Mean January Temperature (MJT) at Healesville is 19.4°C, which is lower than at Bordeaux or Burgundy.

SOIL & TOPOGRAPHY

There are two radically different soil types: grey-brown sandy clay loam with a mixed rock and clay subsoil, deriving from ancient sandstone of the Great Dividing Range. The other is a much younger, vivid red soil of volcanic origin, very deep and well drained. The grey soils are on the Maroondah and Melba highways (i.e. northern) sides of the Valley, the red soils on the Warburton (southern) Highway.

PRINCIPAL GRAPE VARIETIES

Overall, two-thirds red, one-third white.
In descending order:

PINOT NOIR AND CHARDONNAY (ALMOST EQUAL)

CABERNET SAUVIGNON

SHIRAZ

MERLOT

SAUVIGNON BLANC.

[OPPOSITE] TARRAWARRA ESTATE, YARRA VALLEY.
[ABOVE, TOP] PINOT GRIS, YARRA VALLEY.
[ABOVE] YERING STATION, YARRA VALLEY.
[RIGHT] COLDSTREAM HILLS, YARRA VALLEY.

WHITE WINE STYLES

Chardonnay. Curious though it may seem, the quality of Yarra Valley Chardonnay took longer to assert itself than that of its Pinot Noir. However, since the 1990s both the quality and range of style has increased dramatically; while there is a distinctive regional melon/fig/white peach flavour substrate to all Yarra Valley Chardonnays, there is tremendous diversity in weight, texture and richness, partly reflecting vintage variation and partly the different winemaking philosophies and techniques. What is undoubted is the capacity of the Yarra Valley to produce long-lived Chardonnay of the highest quality.

Sauvignon Blanc is sparingly grown, with demand substantially in excess of valley-grown supply. The wines show a range of herb, gooseberry and tropical flavours. Even smaller quantities of Semillon are grown, and – where available – it is usually blended with Sauvignon Blanc to good effect.

RED WINE STYLES

Pinot Noir takes pride of place simply because the Yarra Valley has achieved more with this difficult variety than any other mainland Australian wine region. Slowly, too, the essential nature of Pinot Noir is becoming better understood; while some wine drinkers dismiss it because it is so different from that of Cabernet Sauvignon or Shiraz, others appreciate its haunting delicacy and surprising length of flavour. For those who understand true Burgundy the sappy/strawberry/plum spectrum of fruit flavours to be found in the Yarra is exciting.

Shiraz. Appropriate site selection is essential, with warm, north-facing slopes highly desirable, and in that circumstance the region is capable of producing intensely coloured and flavoured wines, redolent of black cherry, spice and pepper, but with those fine, silky Yarra Valley tannins. Since the late 1990s, Viognier has made its appearance as a minor blend component with Shiraz to produce wines of startling aroma and flavour, akin to the best of Côte Rotie.

Cabernet Sauvignon is often blended with 15 per cent (sometimes more) of Cabernet Franc and Merlot. The wines are invariably elegant, but can vary from light-bodied through to full-bodied. The common feature is the softness of the tannins – they are almost silky. This can trap the unwary into assuming the wines will not cellar well, but they do, as anyone who has tasted a 100-year-old Yeringberg will attest.

Wineries of the Yarra Valley

Coldstream Hills Est. 1985
31 Maddens Lane, Coldstream 3770
www.coldstreamhills.com.au

⬚ exports to UK

Co-founded by the author, who lives on the property and continues to be involved as a consultant notwithstanding the acquisition of Coldstream Hills by Southcorp in 1996. It has in excess of 100 ha of owned or managed estate vineyards as the base, situated in both the Lower and Upper Yarra areas. Pinot Noir and Chardonnay continue to be the prime focus, with support from Sauvignon Blanc, Merlot, Cabernet Sauvignon and Shiraz. All except the Sauvignon Blanc and Shiraz are offered both in varietal and Reserve versions, if the vintage justifies a Reserve release, and all are closed with screw-caps.
Signature wine: Reserve Pinot Noir

De Bortoli Est. 1987
Pinnacle Lane, Dixons Creek 3775
www.debortoli.com.au

⬚ ⫙ exports to UK, US

The highly successful quality arm of the bustling De Bortoli group, run by Leanne De Bortoli and husband Stephen Webber, ex-Lindemans winemaker. Originally called Château Yarrinya, the first vines were planted in 1971 by then owners Graeme and Denise Miller, who caused a sensation by winning the Jimmy Watson Trophy in 1978 with their 1977 Cabernet Sauvignon. The top label (De Bortoli), the second (Gulf Station) and the third label (Windy Peak) offer wines of consistently good quality and excellent value – the complex Chardonnay is of outstanding quality, the Pinot Noir hot on its heels. The value for money at each price point is all the more remarkable given that this is by a long distance the largest producer in the Yarra Valley.
Signature wine: Yarra Valley Chardonnay

Domaine Chandon Est. 1986
Green Point, Maroondah Hwy,
Coldstream 3770
www.yarra-valley.net.au/domaine_chandon/

⬚ exports to UK

Wholly owned by Moët et Chandon, and one of the three most important wine facilities in the Yarra Valley, the Green Point tasting room has a national and international reputation and has won a number of major tourism awards in recent years. Not only has the sparkling wine product range evolved, but there has been increasing emphasis placed on the table wines. The return of Dr Tony Jordan, the first CEO of Domaine Chandon, has further strengthened both the focus and quality of the brand. The ZD Blanc de Blanc was the first quality sparkling wine to be released with a stainless steel crown seal.
Signature wine: ZD Blanc de Blanc

Gembrook Hill Est. 1983
Launching Place Rd, Gembrook 3783
www.gembrookhill.com.au

⬚

The 6 ha Gembrook Hill vineyard is owned by Melbourne dentist Ian Marks and family. It is situated on rich, red volcanic soils 2 km north of Gembrook in the coolest part of the Yarra Valley. The vines are not irrigated, with consequent natural vigour control, and naturally low yields. Harvest usually spans mid April, three weeks later than the traditional northern parts of the valley, and the style is consistently elegant. The recent completion of an on-site winery marks the success of the brand.
Signature wine: Sauvignon Blanc

Metier Wines Est. 1995
Tarraford Vineyard, 440 Healesville Rd,
Yarra Glen 3775 (postal)
www.metierwines.com.au

⬚ exports to UK, US

'Metier' is the French word for craft, trade or profession; the business is that of Yarra Valley-based winemaker Martin Williams, MW, who has notched up an array of degrees and winemaking stints in France, California and Australia which are, not to put too fine a word on it, extraordinary. The focus of Metier is to produce individual vineyard wines, initially based on grapes from the Tarraford and Schoolhouse Vineyards, both in the Yarra Valley. The wines are made in limited quantities; Williams' main occupation is with MasterWineMakers, the major contract winemaking business in the Yarra Valley.
Signature wine: Tarraford Vineyard Chardonnay

Mount Mary Est. 1971
Coldstream West Rd, Lilydale 3140
(03) 9739 1761

⬚

Owner-winemaker and former doctor Dr John Middleton has become a legend in his own lifetime, both for the quality of his wines and the scathing prose in his annual newsletter directed at the many wine-related evils in the world. Superbly refined, elegant and intense Cabernets and usually outstanding and long-lived Pinot Noirs fully justify Mount Mary's exalted reputation; the only problem is securing access to the wines, for total production is a mere 3000 cases. The Triolet (white Bordeaux) blend is very good, more recent vintages of Chardonnay even better. It is regarded by many as the best producer in the Valley.
Signature wine: Cabernets

Seville Estate Est. 1970
65 Linwood Rd, Seville 3139
www.sevilleestate.com.au

⬚ exports to UK

The changes have come thick and fast for this long-established Yarra Valley producer founded by former medical practitioner Peter McMahon. In 1997 it was jointly acquired by Brokenwood (based in the Hunter Valley) and associated shareholders. Late in 2002 it was decided to move the business to Beechworth, but retain the brand, selling the winery and vineyard in the Yarra Valley to a shareholding group (closely associated with Brokenwood, but no longer including Brokenwood itself), but with a grape supply agreement from the estate back to the vendors.
Signature wine: Old Vine Reserve Shiraz

TarraWarra Estate Est. 1983
Healesville Rd, Yarra Glen 3775
www.tarrawarra.com.au

⬚ ⫙ exports to UK, US

Established by clothing magnate Marc Besen and wife Eva (of Sussan fame), from the word go every aspect of the business has been undertaken without regard to the cost. Slowly developing Chardonnay of great structure and complexity is the winery specialty; its Pinot Noir also needs time and evolves impressively if given it. The opening of the large on-site art gallery (and its attendant cafe/restaurant) in early 2004 adds another dimension to the tourism tapestry of the Yarra Valley. For the time being, the gallery is only open from Wednesday to Sunday, but as the *Michelin Guide* would have it, is definitely worth a detour. Tin Cows is a second label.
Signature wine: Chardonnay

Toolangi Vineyards Est. 1995

PO Box 5046, Glenferrie South 3122 (postal)
www.toolangi.com

🗷 exports to UK

Garry and Julie Hounsell acquired their property in the Dixons Creek subregion of the Yarra Valley, adjoining the bottom edge of the Toolangi State Forest, in 1995. Plantings have taken place progressively since that year, with 13 ha now in the ground. The primary accent is on Pinot Noir, Chardonnay and Cabernet, accounting for all but 1 ha, which is predominantly Shiraz, and a few rows of Merlot. Winemaking is split between Tom Carson of Yering Station, Rick Kinzbrunner of Giaconda and Trevor Mast of Mount Langi Ghiran, as impressive a trio of contract winemakers as one could wish for, the wines of outstanding quality.

Signature wine: Estate Chardonnay

Yarra Burn Est. 1975

Settlement Rd, Yarra Junction 3797
www.hardywines.com.au/brands/yarra.html

🗓 🍴 exports to UK, US

Yarra Burn was established by David and Christine Fyffe, pioneers of the very cool southern side of the Yarra Valley. It was acquired by Hardys in 1995 and is the headquarters of Hardys' very substantial Yarra Valley operations, the latter centring on the large production from its Hoddles Creek vineyards. The new brand direction has largely taken shape, but care needs to be taken in reading the back labels of Yarra Burn wines other than the Bastard Hill duo of Chardonnay and Pinot Noir, for the majority are regional blends, albeit with a substantial Yarra Valley component.

Signature wine: Bastard Hill Chardonnay

Yarra Yarra Est. 1979

239 Hunts Lane, Steels Creek 3775
wine@yarrayarravineyard.com.au

🗓 exports to UK

Despite its small production, the wines of Yarra Yarra have found their way on to a veritable who's who listing of Melbourne's best restaurants, encouraging Ian Maclean to increase the estate plantings from 2 ha to over 7 ha in 1996 and 1997. The demand for the beautifully crafted wines continued to exceed supply, so the Macleans have planted yet more vines and increased winery capacity. With the exception of a hatful of Syrah, this is a Bordeaux-inclined winery, with a Semillon Sauvignon Blanc blend and the flagship red a blend of Cabernet Sauvignon and the other Bordeaux varieties.

Signature wine: The Yarra Yarra

Yarra Yering Est. 1969

Briarty Rd, Coldstream 3770 (postal)
yy@hotkey.net.au

🗓 (first Saturday in May); exports to UK, US

Dr Bailey Carrodus has a Ph.D. in plant physiology, and had a long career at the CSIRO, but when he established Yarra Yering he turned back the clock to his post-Second World War degree in oenology from Roseworthy, and brief tenure there as a lecturer. He makes extremely powerful, complex, occasionally idiosyncratic, long-lived wines from his 35-year-old, low-yielding, unirrigated vineyards. The labelling is likewise idiosyncratic, Dry White No. 1 being a Sauvignon Blanc Semillon blend, Dry Red No. 1 a Bordeaux blend, Dry Red No. 2 a Rhône blend. More conventional is Chardonnay, Underhill Shiraz, Merlot and Sangiovese, before the idiosyncrasies pick up again with Portsorts, a vintage port style made from the correct varieties.

Signature wine: Dry Red No. 1

Yering Station Est. 1988

38 Melba Hwy, Yarra Glen 3775
www.yering.com

🗓 🍴 exports to UK, US

This part of the historic Chateau Yering property was purchased by the Rathbone family in January 1996 and is now the site of a joint venture with the French Champagne house Devaux. A spectacular and large winery has been erected, which handles the Yarrabank sparkling wines and the Yering Station and Yarra Edge table wines. It has immediately become one of the focal points of the Yarra Valley, with Chateau Yering next door offering luxury accommodation. Yering Station's own restaurant is open every day for lunch, providing the best cuisine in the Valley. Winemaker Tom Carson has produced an endless stream of trophy-winning wines of exceptional quality, winning the accolade of International Winemaker of the Year from England's International Wine and Spirit Competition in 2005.

Signature wine: Reserve Shiraz Viognier

Yeringberg Est. 1863

Maroondah Hwy, Coldstream 3770
(03) 9739 1453

🗓 exports to UK, US

Yeringberg has been owned by the Swiss-descended de Pury family since 1863, Baron Guillame de Pury (universally known simply as Guill) being the third generation, with children ready to take on the mantle. It makes wines for the new millennium from low-yielding vines re-established in the heart of what was one of the most famous vineyards of the nineteenth century. In the riper years, the red wines have a velvety generosity of flavour yet never lose varietal character, while the Yeringberg Marsanne Roussanne takes students of history back to Yeringberg's fame in the nineteenth century. The original three-storey wooden winery, erected in the 1880s, is still in great condition, the outstanding wine landmark in the Valley.

Signature wine: Yeringberg (Cabernet blend)

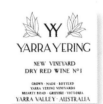

Port Phillip Zone
Mornington Peninsula 🌿

Contrary to most accounts, vineyards did exist on the Mornington Peninsula (chiefly in the Hastings area) in the nineteenth century, albeit on a small scale. They disappeared without trace, and the next attempt to establish a vineyard was in 1948, when a member of the Seppelt family planted Riesling on a 68 ha property on Harrison's Road, Dromana. Two years later the property was sold to the Broadhurst family, close relatives of a Melbourne retailer and wine judge, Doug Seabrook, who maintained the vineyard (and made the wine) until the vines were killed by a bushfire in 1967.

A chance lunchtime conversation between David Wynn and Baillieu Myer at Elgee Park in 1971 ignited the flame once more, this time to burn brightly. Wynn told Myer of the Seabrook experiment, and expressed regret that it had lapsed. Baillieu Myer resolved to establish a vineyard, which he did the following year.

The subsequent rapid and continuing growth in the number of wineries and vineyards is a reflection of the many advantages the Peninsula has. Moreover, as the link between tourism and wine continues to strengthen, so does the underlying business base of the region. While the Mornington Peninsula winemakers may not welcome the idea, there are parallels to be drawn with the Hunter Valley and its symbiotic relationship with Sydney. For the Peninsula is Melbourne's foremost holiday playground, its foremost weekend retreat. This is both bane and blessing: on the one hand it provides a populous and active local clientele; on the other hand it places inexorable pressure on land use and hence land prices.

The net result is a patchwork quilt of small wineries and even smaller vineyards, and the absence of larger wine producers. In some regions this can result in winemaking practices (and wines) which might charitably be described as rustic, less charitably as downright unpleasant. No such problem exists in the Mornington Peninsula: the affluence of the majority (though by no means all) of the vignerons means they have not hesitated to spend the money necessary to acquire the human and material resources to maximise wine quality and guarantee consistency.

It has also resulted in the establishment of numerous attractive cellar-door facilities and many winery restaurants and cafés. The sheer beauty of the softly rolling hillsides, the green grass of much of the year, the white-railed horse studs, the groves of native and imported trees, and the sweeping sea vistas are a perfect backdrop for visitor or resident alike. Fortuitously, too, concentrated urban development is largely restricted to the seaside suburbs and towns, leaving large tracts of the centre of the Peninsula unscarred.

A quick glance at the map will tell you how important the sea is in shaping the overall climate, even in the centre of the Peninsula. What it does not so clearly show is the diversity of site or subregional climate in what is a deceptively large region. As the vineyards have started to mature, and experience has been gained over many vintages, the differences between the Red Hill area at the coolest end of the spectrum and Moorooduc at the warmer end are increasingly evident in the wine styles.

That said, only the Bellarine Peninsula and Langhorne Creek can lay claim in Australia to such a profoundly maritime-influenced climate. The wind is either blowing from the north and west across Port Phillip, or from the south and east across Bass Strait – and usually, in this part of the world, it is blowing from somewhere. That the climate is cool is not in dispute; exactly how cool is strongly dependent on site and aspect, for weather stations provide heat summations ranging from about 1080 near Main Ridge to 1240 at Dromana, higher again at Merricks South. Certain it is that whatever heat is measured will have been evenly accumulated, for frosts are as rare as hot, dry winds. Relative humidity is high, stress is low, sunshine hours are abundant, and rainfall plentiful during winter and spring. In the outcome, there is no argument: the drier, warmer vintages are the best.

[OPPOSITE] Paringa Estate, Mornington Peninsula. [BELOW] Moorooduc Estate, Mornington Peninsula.

The Region

CLIMATE

The strongly maritime, cool yet site-specific climate has been discussed on page 97.

SOIL & TOPOGRAPHY

Yellowish brown and brown soils over a friable, well-drained clay are the first of the principal soil types; around Red Hill and Main Ridge red soils of volcanic origin predominate, deep and fertile; much sandier soils are in evidence at Moorooduc.

PRINCIPAL GRAPE VARIETIES

Overall, slightly more red grapes are crushed than white, thanks solely to Pinot Noir.
In descending order:

PINOT NOIR (85 PER CENT OF THE RED CRUSH)

CHARDONNAY

SHIRAZ

PINOT GRIS.

TEN MINUTES BY TRACTOR WINE CO., MORNINGTON PENINSULA.

 WHITE WINE STYLES

Chardonnay is the Mornington Peninsula's most distinctive wine, which – if made in the style favoured by most producers – is distinctively different from any other Chardonnay produced in Australia. The background fruit flavour is quite delicate, with flavours in the melon/citrus/fig spectrum, and is sensitive to the influence of winemaking technique, and in particular to the effect of malolactic fermentation – it overlays a strong nutty/cashew character.

Pinot Gris and Viognier. Viognier has been in the district for decades, Pinot Gris for a lesser time. The contrast between the performance of the two underlines how cool the climate is: too cool to bring out the best in Viognier, but ideally suited – so it would seem – to Pinot Gris.

Sauvignon Blanc is light, bright, crisp and fresh, usually stainless steel fermented and early bottled, with relatively few Sauvignon Blanc Semillon blends.

 RED WINE STYLES

Pinot Noir. There is enormous range in depth and style of the region's Pinot Noirs, ranging from hauntingly delicate to intense and lingering. The constant factor is the bell-clear varietal character; as many are at the lighter end of the spectrum, that varietal clarity is all the more pronounced.

Shiraz. Ultra-classic, cool-climate Shiraz (picked as late as June) is stacked with spice, black pepper and liquorice, and is the only Mornington Peninsula red variety other than Pinot Noir to convince, but is only made in small quantities.

Queenscliff

The Rip

Point Nepean

Portsea

Mornington

MORNINGTON PENINSULA

Latitude **38°20'S**

Altitude **25–250 m**

Heat degree days **1080–1570**

Growing season rainfall **320–386 mm**

Mean January temp. **18.8–20°C**

Harvest **End March to early June**

Chief viticultural hazards **Autumn rain; birds**

N

0   5 KM

Cellar Door
* Kooyong at Port Phillip Estate.

Wineries of the Mornington Peninsula

Dromana Estate Est. 1982

Cnr Harrison's Rd & Bittern–Dromana Rd, Dromana 3936

www.dromanaestate.com.au

⌾ ⍩ exports to UK

Founder Garry Crittenden (with a successful career in wholesale plant nurseries) played a role far larger than simply establishing Dromana Estate, developing cool-climate viticulture techniques at a time when there was little practical understanding of the requirements and alternatives. Dromana Estate is now owned by a group of investors, and Garry Crittenden has moved on to re-establish a much smaller operation, but son Rollo remains in charge of winemaking, continuing the elegant style for which Dromana Estate became well known.
Signature wine: Reserve Chardonnay

Eldridge Estate Est. 1985

120 Arthurs Seat Rd, Red Hill 3937

www.eldridge-estate.com.au

⌾

Since acquiring the Eldridge Estate vineyard in 1995, the energetic, indeed dynamic, duo of Wendy and David Lloyd has transformed both viticulture and winemaking, lifting the quality of the wines to new heights, including one of Australia's best two Gamays. The focus is primarily on Pinot Noir, with French clone selections playing a prominent role.
Signature wine: Pinot Noir

Kooyong Est. 1996

PO Box 153, Red Hill South 3937

www.kooyong.com

⌾ (at Port Phillip Estate); exports to UK, US

Kooyong, owned by Giorgio and Dianne Gjergja, is one of the larger new entrants on the Mornington Peninsula scene, releasing its first wines in June 2001. Thirty-four ha of vines are in bearing, two-thirds Pinot Noir and one-third Chardonnay. Winemaker Sandro Mosele, a graduate of Charles Sturt University, having previously gained a science degree, has worked at Rochford and learnt from Sergio Carlei, of the Green Vineyards, and makes the classy wines at an on-site winery which also provides contract-making services for others.
Signature wine: Chardonnay

Main Ridge Estate Est. 1975

80 William Rd, Red Hill 3937

www.mre.com.au

⌾ exports to UK

The second-oldest winery on the Peninsula, fully deserving its iconic status. Nat White gives meticulous attention to every aspect of his viticulture, doing annual battle with one of the coolest and highest sites on the Peninsula and welcoming the prospects of global warming. The same attention to detail extends to the winery and the winemaking. The flavour of the 1000 case enterprise is encapsulated in the names of the two wines: Chardonnay and Half Acre Pinot Noir. Unsurprisingly, the wines are seldom seen on retailers' shelves, cellar door and mail order, restaurants and exports being the principal sales channels.
Signature wine: Chardonnay

Montalto Vineyards Est. 1998

33 Shoreham Rd, Red Hill South 3937

www.montalto.com.au

⌾ ⍩

John Mitchell and family established Montalto Vineyards in 1998, although the core of the vineyard goes back to 1986. There are 3 ha of Chardonnay and 5.6 ha of Pinot Noir, with 0.5 ha each of Semillon, Riesling and Pinot Meunier. Intensive vineyard work opens up the canopy, with low yields, and the majority of the fruit is hand-harvested. Wines are released under two labels, the flagship Montalto and Pennon, the latter lower-priced; the Chardonnay is quite superb. All of the wines are contract-made by Robin Brockett at Scotchmans Hill in Geelong. The high-quality restaurant features guest chefs and cooking classes.
Signature wine: Montalto Chardonnay

Moorooduc Estate Est. 1983

501 Derril Rd, Moorooduc 3936

www.moorooduc-estate.com.au

⌾ ⍩

Dr Richard McIntyre regularly produces one of the richest and most complex Chardonnays in the region, with melon/fig/peach fruit set against sumptuous spicy oak, and that hallmark soft nutty/creamy/regional texture. Wild yeast fermentation and abstention from filtration add to the market persona (and quality) of

the Chardonnays, which now come in three tiers: at the bottom, Devil Bend, then simply Chardonnay, and at the top, The Moorooduc Chardonnay. His skills have led to increasing demand for his contract winemaking services.
Signature wine: The Moorooduc Chardonnay

Paringa Estate Est. 1985

44 Paringa Rd, Red Hill South 3937

www.paringaestate.com.au

⌾ ⍩

Schoolteacher turned winemaker Lindsay McCall has shown an absolutely exceptional gift for winemaking across a range of styles, but with immensely complex Pinot Noir and Shiraz leading the way, Chardonnay in close attendance. The wines have an unmatched level of success in the wine shows and competitions Paringa Estate is able to enter, the limitation being the relatively small size of the production. His skills are no less evident in contract winemaking for others. One of the best, if not the best, wineries on the Peninsula.
Signature wine: Estate Pinot Noir

Port Phillip Estate Est. 1987

261 Red Hill Rd, Red Hill 3937

www.portphillip.net

⌾ exports to UK, US

Situated as it is in the same area as Paringa Estate, it is not surprising that Lindsay McCall should have played a leading role in originally establishing the reputation of the winery as contract winemaker for then owner Melbourne QC Jeffrey Sher. The property is now owned by Giorgio and Dianne Gjergja, the main signs of change being enhanced cellar door facilities, redesigned labels, and the introduction of Sandro Mosele as winemaker (at Kooyong, also owned by the Gjergjas).
Signature wine: Pinot Noir

Red Hill Estate Est. 1989

53 Redhill–Shoreham Rd,
Red Hill South 3937
www.redhillestate.com.au

☐ ☐ exports to UK, US

Red Hill has three vineyard sites: Range Road of 31 ha, Red Hill Estate (the home vineyard) of 10 ha, and The Briars of 2 ha. Together, the vineyards make Red Hill Estate one of the largest producers of Mornington Peninsula wines, the wines made on-site by Michael Kyberd. The business was established by Sir Peter Derham and family, but majority ownership now rests with a group of investors headed by Tony Palazzo, who has had a lifelong involvement in all aspects of the industry. The tasting room and ever-busy restaurant have a superb view across the vineyard to Western Port and Phillip Island.

Signature wine: Classic Release Chardonnay

Stonier Wines Est. 1978

362 Frankston–Flinders Rd, Merricks 3916
www.stoniers.com.au

☐ exports to UK, US

One of the most senior wineries on the Mornington Peninsula, now part of the Petaluma group, which is in turn owned by Lion Nathan of New Zealand. Founder Brian Stonier is still involved in a godfather role, and wine quality is assured, as is the elegant, restrained style of the majority of the wines. Core varietals Chardonnay and Pinot Noir are released at three quality levels: a simple varietal designation, then Reserve, and at the top, KBS Vineyard.

Signature wine: KBS Vineyard Pinot Noir

Ten Minutes by Tractor Wine Co. Est. 1999

111 Roberts Rd, Main Ridge 3928
www.tenminutesbytractor.com.au

☐ ☐

Ten Minutes by Tractor was sold to Martin Spedding in early 2004, but the same three families (Judd, McCutcheon and Wallis), with their vineyards ten minutes by tractor distant from each other, continue to supply the fruit, and the contract winemaking continues. There are now three wine ranges: Individual Vineyard at the top; Reserve in the middle; and 10 x Tractor, with its striking label graphics, the base range. There are strong elements of the Da Vinci code in the new labels for the Reserve and Individual Vineyard, but I suppose a $60 bottle of Pinot is not an impulse buy.

Signature wine: Wallis Vineyard Pinot Noir

Tuck's Ridge Est. 1988

37 Shoreham Rd, Red Hill South 3937
www.tucksridge.com.au

☐ exports to US

Tuck's Ridge has gone through a series of roles since it was founded, at one time being one of the largest vineyard holders on the Peninsula, before selling its largest Red Hill vineyard for several million dollars in 2002. Production continues to be substantial (around 14,000 cases), the second label Callanans Road providing good value for money. The top-end varietals of Pinot Noir and Pinot Gris are impressive.

Signature wine: Buckle Vineyard Pinot Noir

Willow Creek Est. 1989

166 Balnarring Rd, Merricks North 3926
www.willow-creek.com.au

☐ ☐ exports to US

Has an outstanding winery and restaurant site, with panoramic views and quality food seven days a week. The wines are released under two labels: Tulum at the top, Willow Creek the second, with bigger volume. The warmer site is one of the better places for Cabernet Sauvignon on the Peninsula, but Willow Creek also produces high-quality Pinot Noir and (unusually for the region) Unwooded Chardonnay.

Signature wine: Tulum Cabernet Sauvignon

Yabby Lake Est. 1998

112 Tuerong Rd, Tuerong 3933
www.yabbylake.com

☒

This high-profile winery is owned by Robert and Mem Kirby (of Village Roadshow fame) who have been involved as landowners in the Mornington Peninsula for decades. It was not until 1998 that they established Yabby Lake Vineyard under the direction of founding vineyard manager Keith Harris; it is favourably positioned on a north-facing slope capturing maximum sunshine while also receiving sea breezes. Thirty-six ha of Pinot Noir, Chardonnay and Pinot Gris are the main focus, with 2 ha each of Shiraz and Merlot taking a back seat. Tod Dexter (the long-term winemaker at Stonier) and Larry McKenna (ex-Martinborough Vineyards and now the Escarpment in New Zealand) are the skilled winemaking team.

Signature wine: Chardonnay

PORT PHILLIP ZONE
Geelong

It may come as a major surprise to find that 140 years ago Geelong was the most important winemaking district in Victoria, if not Australia. In 1861 there were 225 hectares under vine, and by the end of that decade 400 hectares. It also shares with the Yarra Valley the unusual distinction of being primarily established by Swiss vignerons, drawn to Australia by the Swiss-born wife of the first governor of Victoria.

By 1875 the vineyards extended along each side of the valleys formed by the Moorabool, Leigh and Barwon rivers; on the slopes and plains around Ceres and Waurn Ponds, and on to German Town (or Marshall, as it is called today). Either in that year, or a little later, phylloxera was discovered at Fyansford, and neither for the first nor the last time, the politicians became involved and demonstrated that – whatever their understanding of the political process – they knew nothing whatsoever about the wine industry. In a knee-jerk reaction to public pressure (some say fuelled by a jealous Rutherglen industry, then vying for pre-eminence with Geelong) the government ordered the wholesale eradication of the Geelong vineyards.

It has been generally accepted that this spelt the end of local viticulture until Daryl and Nini Sefton planted Idyll Vineyard (since sold) in 1966, but Francois de Castella, speaking in 1942, said Pilloud and Deppler – descendants of some of the original Swiss vignerons – still owned vineyards planted subsequent to the government-ordered eradication. There is, however, no record of winemaking or surviving vines from the interregnum, so for the time being the honour for the revival of the district must go to the Seftons, followed almost immediately by Tom Maltby at Mount Anakie.

While outstanding wines have been made in Geelong since its rebirth, and while land values – relatively speaking – remain modest, and broad-hectare viticulture likewise remains free from urban or alternative land use pressure, the rate of growth was much slower than that of the Yarra Valley or the Mornington Peninsula up to the mid 1990s. Quite why this should be so is not easy to say. A facile explanation is that the district had only one market-oriented operator prior to the arrival of Scotchmans Hill. A slightly more convincing thesis is that the nineteenth century was far more accommodating financially to modest yields in good seasons and to derisory yields in poor ones. For Geelong today is not an easy place to grow grapes. Spring frosts, wind during flowering and fruit set, the mysterious abortion of varieties such as Sauvignon Blanc after fruit set, generally hard soils and a miserable rainfall (making irrigation all but a necessity) have an impact in one year or another somewhere in the district.

Nonetheless, the tide has turned. An ever-increasing number of small wineries is producing wines of the highest quality, and on the other side three substantial (million dollar plus) wineries have been built in the new century: Pettavel, Shadowfax, and most recently, Austin's Barrabool. For good measure, the Littore Group established its Jindalee headquarters at the former Idyll Winery in 1977, even though its 500 000 case production comes almost exclusively from the Murray Darling.

SCOTCHMANS HILL, GEELONG.

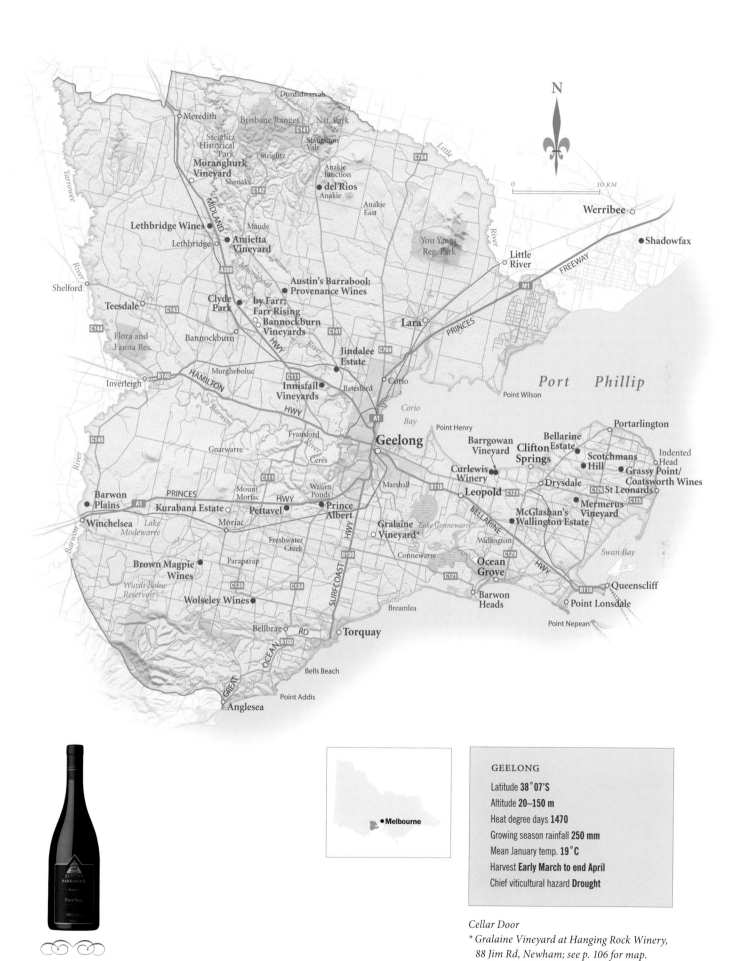

N

0 ────── 10 KM

Durdidwarrah

Meredith

Brisbane Ranges   Nat. Park

C141

Steiglitz
Historical
Park   Steiglitz   Staughton
Vale
**Moranghurk
Vineyard**   Sheoaks
C142
Anakie
Junction
● **del Rios**
Anakie

Anakie
East

C704

You Yangs
Reg. Park   Little
River

Werribee ○

Lethbridge Wines ●   Maude   Little
River   **Shadowfax** ●
Lethbridge ○   ● **Amietta
Vineyard**   FREEWAY

A300   Moorabool   M1

Shelford ○

**Clyde   ● by Farr;
Park** ○   **Farr Rising**
**Bannockburn
Vineyards**   **Austin's Barrabool;
Provenance Wines** ●

Teesdale ○   **Lara** ●
C143   HWY   C141

C144   Bannockburn ○   C704   PRINCES

Flora and
Fauna Res.   Murgheboluc   **Jindalee
Estate** ●   **Port   Phillip**

HAMILTON   C111   Corio ○   Point Wilson

B140   **Innisfail
Vineyards** ●   Batesford
Inverleigh ○   HWY   **Geelong**   Corio
Bay   Point Henry   **Portarlington** ○

C145   Fyansford   **Barrgowan
Vineyard**   **Bellarine
Estate**
River   Gnarwarre   Ceres   **Clifton
Springs**   **Scotchmans   Indented
Head**
**Curlewis
Winery**   **Hill** ●
**Barwon
Plains** ●   PRINCES   Mount   Waurn
Moriac   Ponds   Marshall   B110   **Drysdale** ●   **Grassy Point/
Coatsworth Wines**
Kurabana Estate ●   HWY   **Leopold**   ● St Leonards
A1   **Prince   B110   C123   C126
Winchelsea ○   Lake   **Pettavel** ●   **Albert**   **Mermerus
Vineyard**
Modewarre   Moriac ○   **Gralaine   Lake Gonnewarre   **McGlashan's   C125
Vineyard*   **Wallington Estate**
Freshwater   Wallington   C129
Creek   **Ocean   Swan Bay
Brown Magpie   Paraparap   Conewarre   Grove
Wines** ●
C135   C134   **Barwon   Point Lonsdale** ○
Wurdi Boluc   **Wolseley Wines** ●   Heads**   **Queenscliff** ○
Reservoir
Breamlea   B110

Bellbrae   **Torquay** ●   Point Nepean
B100

Bells Beach
GREAT
Point Addis

Anglesea ●

GEELONG

Latitude **38˚07'S**

Altitude **20–150 m**

Heat degree days **1470**

Growing season rainfall **250 mm**

Mean January temp. **19˚C**

Harvest **Early March to end April**

Chief viticultural hazard **Drought**

● **Melbourne**

Cellar Door
** Gralaine Vineyard at Hanging Rock Winery,
88 Jim Rd, Newham; see p. 106 for map.*

The Region

CLIMATE

This open, and strongly maritime-influenced region, has a climate roughly halfway between that of Bordeaux and Burgundy in terms of ripening temperatures and sunshine hours. The long, cool and usually dry autumn means that Chardonnay and Pinot Noir achieve optimum ripeness almost every year, but the later-ripening Cabernet Sauvignon can struggle in cooler, wetter vintages. Yields are low to moderate, with both wind and lack of rainfall inhibiting vigour, particularly on the more exposed slopes and hardened soils.

SOIL & TOPOGRAPHY

The principal soil type is one of the commonest to be found in viticultural regions in Australia: red-brown clay loam over a hard clay base, ranging from mildly acidic to mildly alkaline. There are also patches of a not dissimilar-looking group of dark black cracking clays. Almost all the vineyards are established on gentle to moderate slopes.

PRINCIPAL GRAPE VARIETIES

Overall, 65 per cent red, 35 per cent white.
In descending order:

PINOT NOIR

SHIRAZ

CHARDONNAY

CABERNET SAUVIGNON

RIESLING

SAUVIGNON BLANC.

WHITE WINE STYLES

Chardonnay has shown it can produce a wine of exceptional strength and complexity, developing pronounced Burgundian overtones with age, but can also be made in a more simple and easily accessible form on the Bellarine Peninsula.

Sauvignon Blanc is fine, crisp and tangy, showing clear varietal character.

RED WINE STYLES

Pinot Noir has established itself as the leading grape variety in the region simply because of the symbiosis between the vine, the soil and the climate. Naturally low yields and a high degree of sophistication in the winemaking produces Pinot Noirs of ultimate complexity: one does not need flights of fancy to find plums, tobacco, violets, strawberries and truffles appearing in the wines.

Shiraz. If there is a unifying feature in all of the Geelong wines it is their strength and depth of colour, bouquet and flavour. Almost all the wineries produce striking Shiraz which sometimes shows pepper/spice overtones, but more often than not relies on potent dark cherry fruit with persistent but balanced tannins providing structure and longevity.

Cabernet Sauvignon. The area is capable of producing concentrated, powerful and long-lived Cabernets, with intense blackcurrant/cassis characters at their best. The winemakers have split down the middle in deciding whether to leave it as a single varietal wine, blend it with Shiraz or blend it with Merlot, most opting for a blend of some description.

Wineries of Geelong

Austin's Barrabool Est.1982

870 Steiglitz Rd, Sutherlands Creek 3331
www.abwines.com.au

Owned by Richard and Pamela Austin, this typifies the recent expansion in Geelong, moving from the original Waurn Ponds vineyard and winery established in 1982 to the much larger, 60 ha Sutherland Creek vineyard in the Moorabool Valley. The overall property is 565 ha in size, and it is here that the new and much larger winery and cellar door have been opened. Winemaker Scott Ireland makes Riesling, Chardonnay, Pinot Noir, Merlot and Cabernet Sauvignon, all with great style. He doubles up as contract winemaker for others, as well as for his own excellent Provenance Wines.
Signature wine: Reserve Pinot Noir

Bannockburn Vineyards

Est.1974
Midland Hwy, Bannockburn 3331
www.bannockburnvineyards.com

☒ exports to UK, US

The grand old man of Geelong, with low-yielding, 30-year-old vines producing wines of exceptional concentration, power and complexity courtesy of former winemaker Gary Farr. It is often difficult to separate the sublime quality of the Shiraz, Pinot Noir and Chardonnay, the Sauvignon Blanc and Cabernet Merlot a pace or so back. The ultra-close-planted Serre Pinot Noir competes vigorously for top honours in Australia's Pinot Noir stakes.
Signature wine: Serre Pinot Noir

by Farr and Farr Rising

Est.1999
PO Box 72, Bannockburn 3331
kalvos@datafast.net.au,
nickfarr01@hotmail.com

☒ exports to UK, US (by Farr)

The father and son brands of Gary and Nicholas (Nick) Farr respectively. The by Farr wines come from 11 ha of densely planted, clonally selected Viognier, Chardonnay, Pinot Noir and Shiraz, on a vineyard block adjacent to Bannockburn; Farr Rising casts its net wider to take in both Geelong and Mornington grape sources. All of the wines are of very high quality and considerable complexity.
Signature wines: Shiraz by Farr and Farr Rising Geelong Chardonnay

Curlewis Winery Est.1998

55 Navarre Rd, Curlewis 3222
www.curlewiswinery.com.au

Rainer Breit and partner Wendy Oliver purchased their property at Curlewis in 1996 with 1.6 ha of what were then 11-year-old Pinot Noir vines; previously, and until 1998, the grapes had been sold to Scotchmans Hill. They established an on-site winery, with Rainer Breit as a self-taught winemaker, but the full bag of Pinot Noir winemaking tricks is used: cold-soaking, hot-fermentation, post-ferment maceration, part inoculated and partly wild yeast use, prolonged lees contact, and bottling the wine neither fined nor filtered.
Signature wine: Reserve Pinot Noir

del Rios Est.1996

2320 Ballan Rd, Anakie 3221
www.delrios.com.au

German del Rio came from northern Spain, where his family owned vineyards. After three generations in Australia, his family established 15 ha of vines on their 104 ha property on the slopes of Mount Anakie, the principal focus being Chardonnay, Pinot Noir and Cabernet Sauvignon (4 ha each), then Marsanne, Sauvignon Blanc, Merlot and Shiraz (1 ha each). Vintage 2000 was the first commercial release; winemaking moved on-site in 2004.
Signature wine: Reserve Pinot Noir

Pettavel Est.2000

65 Pettavel Rd, Waurn Ponds 3216
www.pettavel.com

☒ ⑪ exports to UK, US

This is a major landmark in the Geelong region. Mike and wife Sandi Fitzpatrick (and children) sold their large Murray Darling winery and vineyards, and moved to Geelong where, in 1990, they began developing vineyards at Sutherlands Creek (65 ha) and Waurn Ponds (12 ha). A striking and substantial winery was opened in time for the 2002 vintage, prior to which time the wines were contract made at Mount Langi Ghiran. The development also includes a modern tasting area adjacent to a large (140 seats) restaurant which is open seven days a week for lunch.
Signature wine: Platina Merlot Petit Verdot

Scotchmans Hill Est.1982

190 Scotchmans Rd, Drysdale 3222
www.scotchmanshill.com.au

☒ exports to UK

Owned and founded by the fiercely competitive Vivienne and David Browne, Scotchmans Hill is situated on the Bellarine Peninsula, south-east of Geelong. With a well-equipped winery and first-class vineyards, it has a strong following for its astutely priced, well-made wines, with Robin Brockett long-term winemaker. A doubling in production (it is by far the largest Geelong producer) has led to exports to the UK and elsewhere. The second label is Swan Bay (from cool-climate Victorian regions), and, at the top, individual vineyard wines. All levels focus on Sauvignon Blanc, Chardonnay, Pinot Noir and (more recently) Shiraz.
Signature wine: Chardonnay

Shadowfax Vineyard and Winery Est.2000

K Rd, Werribee 3030
www.shadowfax.com.au

☒ ⑪ exports to UK

Shadowfax is part of an awesome development at Werribee Park, a mere 20 minutes from Melbourne towards Geelong. The truly striking winery, designed by Wood Marsh architects, was erected in time for the 2000 vintage crush, adjacent to the extraordinary 60-room private home built in the 1880s by the Chirnside family and known as The Mansion, then the centrepiece of a 40 000 ha pastoral empire. The impressive packaging and the quality of the wines both underline the serious nature of this quite amazing venture. Estate production is supplemented by Heathcote Shiraz and Adelaide Hills Pinot Gris and Sauvignon Blanc, all the wines being made on-site by Matt Harrop.
Signature wine: Chardonnay

[OPPOSITE] SCOTCHMANS HILL, GEELONG.
[ABOVE] MATT HARROP.

N

0   10 KM

Melbourne

MACEDON RANGES

Latitude **37°25'S**

Altitude **300–700 m**

Heat degree days **970–1050**

Growing season rainfall **290–370 mm**

Mean January temp. **17.2–18.5°C**

Harvest **Mid March to early June**

Chief viticultural hazards **Cool season; frost**

Port Phillip Zone
Macedon Ranges

Even in the new millennium, there is an improbably wild and untamed feeling about this region – improbable given its proximity to the immediate north of Melbourne. The winds blow hard for much of the year, more often cold than hot, even in summer. Much is hard, sheep-grazing country, with granitic outcrops common, remnants of ancient volcanic activity. On the other hand, Daylesford and Hepburn Springs have regained their nineteenth- and early twentieth-century reputations as weekend and holiday resorts, a reminder of the diversity of scenery within the region.

Burke and Wills passed through in 1860 on their ill-fated journey north, a legacy being the Burke and Wills Track road-name used to this day. Small vineyards and wineries sprang up from 1860 onwards, mainly at the southern end of the region around Riddells Creek, but all had disappeared by 1916.

The renaissance began when celebrated Melbourne restaurateur Tom Lazar began to plant Virgin Hills vineyard in 1968, soon followed by Gordon Knight at Granite Hills in 1970. Two more different personalities cannot be imagined, the mercurial Lazar being worthy of a biography in his own right. Gordon Cope-Williams came next in 1977, then John Ellis at Hanging Rock in 1982. Many others have followed since, but none have found viticultural life particularly easy, the scale of most very small.

Site selection (altitude, protection from wind and spring frosts, and maximum sun interception from north- and north-east-facing slopes), the careful matching of site and grape variety, razor-sharp canopy management, and relatively low yields are all prerequisites for success. Even then success will not come every year; there have to be those extra few degrees of heat, those extra hours of sunshine in the warmer Melbourne summers to get the best results. This is the coolest wine region on the Australian mainland.

That said, there are some producers who create top-class wines of one kind or another in virtually every vintage: Bindi with Pinot Noir and Chardonnay, more recently, Curly Flat likewise; Granite Hills Riesling and Shiraz; Hanging Rock Sauvignon Blanc and Sparkling; Portree Chardonnay; and Virgin Hills Cabernet Shiraz Merlot blend.

Finally, virtually every producer to make a sparkling wine succeeds, led by Cope-Williams and Hanging Rock (which also provide contract winemaking facilities for sparkling wines and, in the case of Hanging Rock, table wines too).

Little more than 45 minutes' drive north of Melbourne Airport, the region is often overlooked by wine tourists, who miss the small, historic towns and sweeping vistas. For those who do go, there are none of the cellar-door crowds, nor traffic, of the better-known regions of the Port Phillip Zone.

Curly Flat, Macedon Ranges.

The Region

CLIMATE

Altitude is a factor in determining just how cool a given site is, and this varies significantly in the Macedon Ranges (Mount Macedon is a fraction over 1000 metres high). However, wind is another key force in determining just how well vines grow, and is an unseen factor in statistics – vines suffer wind chill every bit as keenly as do humans.

SOIL & TOPOGRAPHY

The majority of the soils are relatively skeletal mountain soils, most typically granitic sandy loams which further restrict yields. However, there are patches of deep loams in valleys and on the lower slopes and occasional plains.

PRINCIPAL GRAPE VARIETIES

Sixty-five per cent red, 35 per cent white.
In descending order:

CHARDONNAY, PINOT NOIR (MORE OR LESS EQUAL)

SHIRAZ

CABERNET SAUVIGNON

MERLOT

RIESLING

CABERNET FRANC

GEWÜRZTRAMINER

PINOT GRIS.

WHITE WINE STYLES

Sparkling. The preponderance of Chardonnay and Pinot Noir in the vineyards confirms what the climatic statistics suggest: this is an extremely good region for the production of sparkling wine, with a number of high-profile boutique brands within its borders. The intense flavours and high natural acidity of the base wines encourages the use of avant-garde winemaking processes, and the winemakers have been quick to respond.

Chardonnay. Fine, elegant, lightly structured and potentially long-lived wines are the order of the day from plantings on and around Mount Macedon. The warmer years give fuller-flavoured styles, as do the warmer sites in the lower altitude and more northerly parts of the region.

Riesling has long been transformed to another art form by Granite Hills, ageing superbly around a diamond-like core of fine, lemony/minerally acidity.

Other White Varieties. Despite their disparate nature, Gewürztraminer, Sauvignon Blanc and Pinot Gris are all defined by the very cool climate, with ultra-delicate aromas and flavours, which nonetheless show varietal character.

RED WINE STYLES

Pinot Noir is used both to produce sparkling and table wines, arguably with equal success. Here the logic of the match of climate and wine style is immediately obvious, with both old and new arrivals producing wines of unimpeachable varietal character, fine and tending to lighter-bodied in style in the cooler vintages.

Shiraz. Virgin Hills, Granite Hills and Craiglee (the latter in Sunbury) were the first three Australian wineries to introduce consumers to the striking pepper, liquorice and black cherry aromas and flavours of genuinely cool-climate Shiraz.

[TOP] HANGING ROCK WINERY, MACEDON RANGES. [LEFT] PICKING FRUIT, CURLY FLAT, MACEDON RANGES. [ABOVE] HANGING ROCK WINERY, MACEDON RANGES.

Wineries of the Macedon Ranges

Bindi Wine Growers Est. 1988

343 Melton Rd, Gisborne 3437 (postal)
(03) 5428 2564

 exports to UK, US

Few winemakers are more committed to making the best possible wines than Michael Dhillon (and eminence gris Stuart Anderson in the background). The Chardonnay is top-shelf, the Pinot Noir as remarkable (albeit in a very different idiom) as Bass Phillip, Bannockburn or any of the other tiny-production, icon wines. The Heathcote-sourced Shiraz under the Bundaleer label simply confirms Bindi as one of the greatest small producers in Australia.

Signature wine: Original Vineyard Pinot Noir

Candlebark Hill Est. 1987

Fordes Lane, Kyneton 3444
www.candlebarkhill.com.au

Candlebark Hill was established by David Forster on the northern end of the Macedon Ranges, enjoying magnificent views over the central Victorian countryside north of the Great Dividing Range. The 3.5 ha vineyard is planted to Pinot Noir (1.5 ha) together with 1 ha each of Chardonnay and the three main Bordeaux varieties, completed with 0.5 ha of Shiraz and Malbec. Wine quality is excellent, the warmer-than-most site (in Macedon Ranges terms) giving the wines lush, ripe fruit flavours.

Signature wine: Reserve Pinot Noir

Cobaw Ridge Est. 1985

31 Perc Boyer's Lane,
East Pastoria via Kyneton 3444
www.cobawridge.com.au

exports to UK

Nelly and Alan Cooper established Cobaw Ridge's 6 ha vineyard at an altitude of 610 m in the hills above Kyneton complete with self-constructed pole-framed mudbrick house and winery. The plantings of Cabernet Sauvignon have been removed and partially replaced by Lagrein, a north-east Italian variety typically used to make delicate Rosé, but at Cobaw Ridge it is made into an impressive full-bodied dry red. The aromatic and spicy Shiraz Viognier and Chardonnay are also of high quality.

Signature wine: Lagrein

Curly Flat Est. 1991

Collivers Rd, Lancefield 3435
www.curlyflat.com

exports to UK

Former banker Phillip and Jeni Moraghan at Curly Flat have drawn in part upon the inspiration Phillip experienced when working in Switzerland in the late 1980s. With ceaseless guidance from the late Laurie Williams (who died unexpectedly in 2001) the Moraghans have painstakingly established 14 ha of vineyard, principally Pinot Noir with lesser amounts of Chardonnay and Pinot Gris. A multi-level, gravity-flow winery was commissioned for the 2002 vintage. Ranks next to Bindi Wine Growers for its Chardonnay and Pinot Noir.

Signature wine: Pinot Noir

Domaine Epis Est. 1990

812 Black Forest Drive, Woodend 3442
domaineepis@primus.com.au

Three legends are involved in the Epis wines. They are long-term Essendon guru and former player, Alec Epis; Stuart Anderson, who guides the winemaking at the on-site winery, with Alec Epis doing all the hard work; and the late Laurie Williams, the father of viticulture in the Macedon region, who established the Flynn and Williams vineyard in 1976. Alec Epis purchased that vineyard from Laurie Williams in 1999; the Cabernet Sauvignon comes from it, the Chardonnay and Pinot Noir from the vineyard at Woodend.

Signature wine: Macedon Ranges Pinot Noir

Granite Hills Est. 1970

1481 Burke and Wills Track, Baynton,
Kyneton 3444
www.granitehills.com.au

exports to UK, US

Garrulous founder Gordon Knight has passed the winemaking baton to quietly spoken, self-effacing son Llew Knight, making Granite Hills one of the enduring classics; it pioneered the successful growing of Riesling and Shiraz in an uncompromisingly cool climate. It is based on 12 ha of Riesling, Chardonnay, Shiraz, Cabernet Sauvignon, Merlot and Pinot Noir (the last mainly used in its sparkling wine). The Rieslings age superbly, and the Shiraz is at the forefront of the cool-climate school in Australia.

Signature wine: Knight Riesling

Hanging Rock Winery

Est. 1982
88 Jim Rd, Newham 3442
www.hangingrock.com.au

exports to UK

The Macedon area has proved very marginal in spots, and the Hanging Rock Jim Jim vineyard, with its lovely vista towards the Rock, is no exception. John Ellis has thus elected to source additional grapes from various parts of Victoria to produce an interesting and diverse style of wines. The Jim Jim trio of Gewürtraminer, Pinot Gris and Sauvignon Blanc are at the delicate end of the extreme, Heathcote Shiraz at the richest end, while the Non Vintage Macedon Cuvee Sparkling Wine is one of the most complex sparkling wines in Australia.

Signature wine: Macedon Cuvee

Portree Est. 1983

72 Powells Track via Mt William Rd,
Lancefield 3455
www.portreevineyard.com.au

exports to UK

Owner-winemaker Ken Murchison selected his 5 ha Macedon vineyard after studying viticulture at Charles Sturt University. The wines show distinct cool-climate characteristics, the Quarry Red (Cabernet Franc) reminiscent of Chinon in the Loire Valley. However, it is with long-lived Chardonnay that Portree has done best and which is its principal wine (in terms of volume).

Signature wine: Chardonnay

Straws Lane Est. 1987

1282 Mt Macedon Rd, Hesket 3442
carowe@strawslane.com.au

The 3 ha Straws Lane vineyard was planted in 1987, but the Straws Lane label is a relatively new arrival on the scene; after a highly successful 1995 vintage, adverse weather in 1996 and 1997 meant that little or no wine was made in those years, but the pace picked up again with subsequent vintages. Stuart Anderson guides the making of the Pinot Noir, Hanging Rock Winery handles the Gewürztraminer and the sparkling wine base. It's good to have co-operative neighbours.

Signature wine: Gewürztraminer

Virgin Hills Est. 1968

Salisbury Rd, Lauriston West
via Kyneton 3444
www.virginhills.com.au

exports to UK, US

Founded by flamboyant Melbourne restaurateur Tom Lazar, who ignored the universal advice that it would be impossible to ripen grapes at this location. Subsequent ownership changes, and a period during which no sulphur dioxide was added to the wine, have somewhat undermined the once 24-carat reputation of Virgin Hills. It produces a single Cabernet Sauvignon Shiraz Merlot blend simply called Virgin Hills; from time to time there has been an occasional limited Reserve release. The varietal composition of the wine varies from year to year in much the same way as Bordeaux.

Signature wine: Virgin Hills

PORT PHILLIP ZONE
Sunbury ❧

While a relatively small region, Sunbury has a marvellously rich history, some of which has been miraculously preserved. In 1858 James Goodall Francis, a former Victorian Premier, planted the first vines at Goona Warra – an Aboriginal name chosen long before Coonawarra was even a twinkle in John Riddoch's eye. He subsequently built a magnificent bluestone winery, and while winemaking ceased there in the early 1900s, the buildings were preserved. In 1982 Goona Warra was purchased by Melbourne lawyer John Barnier and family, and brought back to life with estate vineyards, winery and restaurant.

James S. Johnstone followed quickly in the footsteps of Francis, establishing Craiglee in 1864. A fellow parliamentarian, he also established the *Argus* newspaper, and in 1872 made a Shiraz which I have been lucky enough to taste on several occasions – bottles from a cache long forgotten and unearthed in the 1950s. Still with remarkable life and vinosity, they were a powerful testament to the suitability of the region for the production of elegant but long-lived Shiraz.

The four-storey stone winery remains at Craiglee, but in this instance public health bureaucracy has decreed that Pat Carmody (whose family purchased the property in 1961, forty years after wine production had ceased, and re-established the vineyard in 1976) should have to make the wine in a new building. This,

it must be said, has not prevented him from making the best and most consistent wines from the region, most notably the multi-trophy-winning Craiglee Shiraz.

Where the Macedon Ranges (with which Sunbury was once lumped) are hilly, indeed mountainous, Sunbury is almost, but not quite, flat. Situated 15 minutes past Melbourne Airport, and the closest wine region to the Melbourne CBD, it is not particularly well known. It can be a chilly place, at times downright forbidding, particularly when the wind blows hard from the north, sweeping the plain with frigid air drawn up from the Southern Ocean and circulated over the mountains to the north before rushing back whence it came. But Sunbury's proximity to Melbourne, its historic wineries and the quality of its wines are more than enough to compensate for these shortcomings.

GOONA WARRA VINEYARD, SUNBURY.

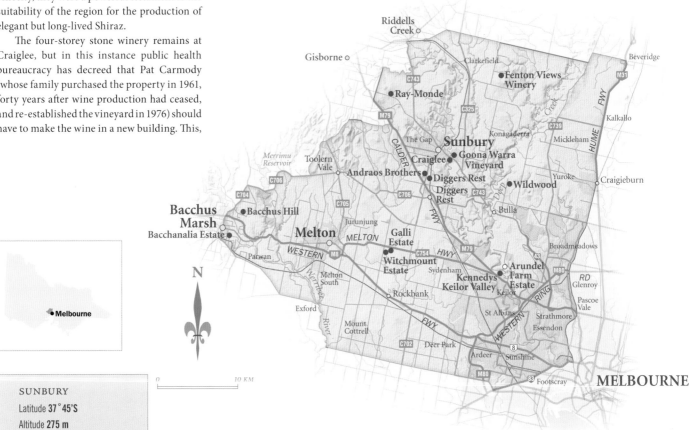

SUNBURY

Latitude **37°45'S**

Altitude **275 m**

Heat degree days **1380**

Growing season rainfall **310 mm**

Mean January temp. **19.2°C**

Harvest **Late March to early May**

Chief viticultural hazard **Birds**

The Region

CLIMATE

The growing season climate, in particular, is much influenced by the wind which sweeps across the plain, further cooling an already cool region. The nearby Macedon Ranges to the north and the sea to the south each also exercise moderating though different influences; this is a cool climate, however measured.

SOIL & TOPOGRAPHY

The soils are typically dark, and – except on old alluvial river terraces with free-draining sandy loams – not particularly fertile. Their depth and structure varies significantly from lower-level plains to hillsides, ranging from alkaline to acidic.

PRINCIPAL GRAPE VARIETIES

Sixty-five per cent red, 35 per cent white. In descending order:

SHIRAZ

CHARDONNAY

PINOT NOIR

CABERNET SAUVIGNON

SAUVIGNON BLANC

SEMILLON.

 WHITE WINE STYLES

Chardonnay. Unlike Macedon, most of the Chardonnay grown in the region is used to make table wine. As one would expect given the cool climate, the style is elegant, with good natural acidity. The resulting wines are not dissimilar to those of Geelong, a region with which Macedon has many things in common, but with a touch of Yarra Valley elegance.

Sauvignon Blanc and Semillon both perform well, either in unison or separately, but are sparingly grown.

RED WINE STYLES

Shiraz is, without question, the most noble grape for the region even though (paradoxically) only Craiglee concentrated on it initially. It produces wines with a splendid array of black pepper, spice and black cherry aromas and flavours; the body can be deceptively light, as it is seldom more than medium bodied; the alcohol level seldom rises much beyond 13% by volume, and the tannins are typically soft and fine. There seems no logical reason why the best vintages should not age as well as the 1872 which, after all, was produced from relatively young vines and was of quite low alcohol.

Pinot Noir is another paradox, for one would have expected more to be grown and made in the region. Nonetheless, since the mid 1990s the number of makers of Pinot Noir has increased significantly, with wines of subtle but intense and long flavour.

Wineries of Sunbury

Craiglee Est. 1864

Sunbury Rd, Sunbury 3429
www.craiglee.com.au
📦 exports to UK, US

Winemaker and owner (with his family) Pat Carmody produces one of the finest cool-climate Shirazs in Australia, redolent of cherry, liquorice and spice in the better (i.e. warmer) vintages, lighter bodied in the cooler ones. Maturing vines and improved viticulture have made the wines more consistent (and even better) since the start of the 1990s. A little Sauvignon Blanc, stylish Chardonnay and Pinot Noir and a hatful of Cabernet Sauvignon complete a distinguished portfolio.
Signature wine: Shiraz

Galli Estate Est. 1997

1507 Melton Hwy, Rockbank 3335
www.galliestate.com.au
📦 🍴

Galli Estate may be a relative newcomer, but it is a substantial one. The Galli family has planted 38 ha of vineyard, the lion's share to Cabernet Sauvignon and Shiraz, but with 1.5–2.5 ha each of Semillon, Sauvignon Blanc, Pinot Grigio, Chardonnay, Sangiovese and Pinot Noir. A 50 m long underground cellar has been constructed, due to be extended in the future. A cellar door sales, bistro and administration centre was completed in 2002, with former Coldstream Hills winemaker Stephen Phillips in charge. The quality is as high as the prices are low.
Signature wine: Rockbank Chardonnay

Goona Warra Vineyard

Est. 1863
Sunbury Rd, Sunbury 3429
www.goonawarra.com.au
📦 🍴 exports to UK

Another part of the great history of Sunbury, which, after a brief interlude under investor ownership, has reverted to the Barnier family. History to one side, it adds another dimension to the wines of the region, its Semillon Sauvignon Blanc and Cabernet Franc included as part of a more conventional portfolio of Chardonnay, Pinot Noir, Shiraz and Cabernet blends. The wines are as elegant and stylish as the climate would suggest. The bluestone winery houses the well-patronised restaurant and reception centre.
Signature wine: Sunbury Shiraz

Wildwood Est. 1983

St John's Lane, Wildwood, Bulla 3428
www.wildwoodvineyards.com.au
📦 🍴

Wildwood is situated just 4 km past Melbourne Airport, at an altitude of 130 m in the Oaklands Valley, which provides unexpected views back to Port Phillip and the Melbourne skyline. Plastic surgeon Wayne Stott has taken what is very much a part-time activity rather more seriously than most by undertaking (and completing) the Wine Science degree at Charles Sturt University. Chardonnay, Pinot Noir, Shiraz and Cabernets are made, all with success when drought does not intervene.
Signature wine: Pinot Noir

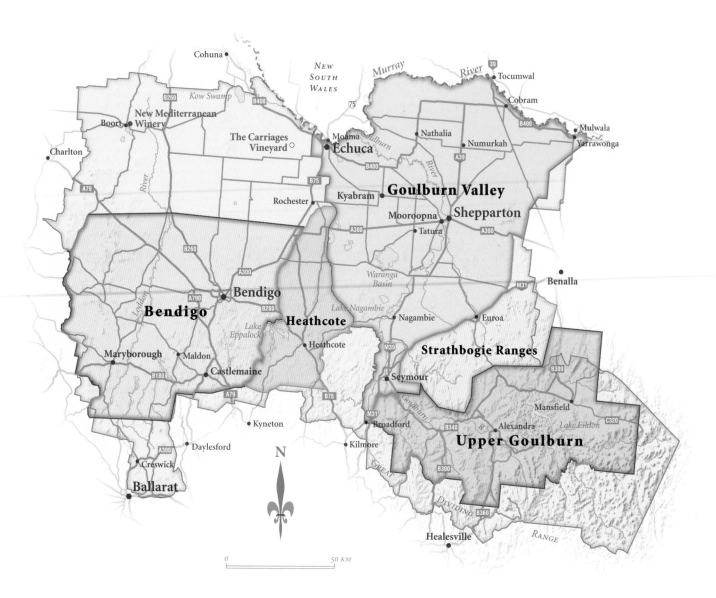

Cohuna

New
South
Wales

Murray   River   Tocumwal
39

Cobram
B400

B260   Kow Swamp   B400   75   Mulwala
Yarrawonga

New Mediterranean
Winery

Boort   Nathalia   Numurkah

Charlton   The Carriages
Vineyard

Moama   Goulburn   A39

Echuca

B400   Goulburn Valley

River   Kyabram   **Goulburn Valley**

B75   Mooroopna   Shepparton

Rochester   Tatura

A300

B260   Waranga
Basin   Benalla

A790   **Bendigo**   M31

Bendigo   Lake Nagambie   Euroa

B280

Heathcote   Nagambie

Lake
Eppalock   **Strathbogie Ranges**

Maryborough   Maldon   Heathcote   B300

Castlemaine   M39

B180   Seymour   Mansfield

A79   B75   C320

Kyneton   Broadford   Alexandra   Lake Eildon

M31   B340

Daylesford   Kilmore   **Upper Goulburn**

A300   B300

Creswick

Ballarat   B360

Healesville   RANGE

N

0   50 KM

Central Victoria Zone 🌿

This is another densely populated zone in terms of regions and of wineries, an important part of the crucible which has seen Victoria spawn more new wineries since 1985 than any other state. Thus it leads the tally count of wineries on a state-by-state basis, returning it to the former glory days of the third quarter of the nineteenth century. It is perhaps no accident that this was the time that gold mining reached a peak of activity: wine and gold are inextricably woven together in Victoria's history, no more so than in the Central Victoria and Victoria zones.

The regions of the Central Victoria Zone are on the inland, or northern, foothills of the Great Dividing Range, which swings west and starts to lose altitude as it nears Melbourne. Warm days are offset by cold nights, although the rainfall (as is the case further south) remains winter–spring dominant, making irrigation economically essential. It is red wine country first and foremost, with Shiraz leading the way.

Winery of the Central Victoria Zone

New Mediterranean Winery
Est. 1997
35 Holloway St, Boort 3537
www.akrasiwine.com.au

🍷

It is a reasonably safe bet that you will not come across Boort by accident. It falls roughly between the Calder and Loddon Highways as they wend their way north towards the Murray River; Kerang, 51 km to the north, is the nearest landmark of any significance. George Tallis commenced home winemaking in the early 1990s, initially simply for his own benefit and that of his immediate family. Success at this level led to relatively small commercial winemaking, strongly influenced by Tallis's Greek ancestry.
Signature wine: Shiraz

[RIGHT] MAYGARS HILL WINERY, STRATHBOGIE RANGES. [BELOW] BLACKJACK VINEYARDS, BENDIGO.

Kurraca
West

Glenalbyn

Kurraca

CALDER

Old
Loddon
Wines

Kamarooka

Fentons
Creek

Glenalbyn
Passing Clouds
Blanche Barkly
Wines

Inglewood

Kingower

Rheola

Bridgewater
on Loddon

A79

Water
Wheel

Pondalowie
Vineyards

Raywood

Campbells
Forest

Summerfield
Greater Bendigo

Neilborough
National

Avonmore
Estate

Karee Estate

Elmore

A300

Burkes Flat

B240

LODDON

VALLEY

Goornong

Mount Moliagul

Moliagul

Arnold

Llanelly

Murphys
Creek

HIGHWAY

Newbridge

Leichardt

Sandhurst Ridge

Marong

Park

Huntly

MIDLAND

Bagshot

Barnadown

Bealiba

Goldsborough

Tarnagulla

B240

Balgownie Estate

Eaglehawk

Epsom

Fosterville

Lockwood

Bendigo

Laanecoorie

Shelbourne

A790

Chateau
Leamon

McIVOR

Axedale

Dunolly

Eddington

Eastville

Big Hill
Vineyard

A300

A79

Strathfieldsaye

Tannery
Lane
Vineyard

Eppalock

B280

Lake
Eppalock

Knowsley

Dunluce

Betley

Bet Bet

Laanecoorie

Ravenswood

Sedgwick

Lake
Eppalock

Rathscat

Havelock

Timor

Nuggety
Vineyard

Ravenswood
South

Pilchers
Bridge

Bowenvale

Baringhup

Cairn Curran
Reservoir

Maldon

Sutton
Grange
Winery

Maryborough

Carisbrook

Paddys
Ranges
SP

Bress

Harcourt

Sutton
Grange

Harcourt Valley
Vineyards

Langanook Wines

Avoca

B180

PYRENEES

Welshmans
Reef

BlackJack
Vineyards

A79

Minto Wines

Bung
Bong

Daisy
Hill

Majorca

Castlemaine

Campbells
Creek

B180

Chewton

Elphinstone

Amherst

Newstead

Yapeen

A300

Talbot

Guildford

Glengower

Campbelltown

Evansford

Clunes

N

0   10 KM

● Melbourne

BENDIGO

Latitude **36°45'S**

Altitude **240–390 m**

Heat degree days **1579**

Growing season rainfall **267 mm**

Mean January temp. **21°C**

Harvest **Mid March to end April**

Chief viticultural hazards **Frost; drought**

CENTRAL VICTORIA ZONE
Bendigo 🌿

Whether vines preceded or followed the discovery of gold at the end of 1851 is not clear, but in 1864 there were more than 40 vineyards in the Bendigo region. By 1880, 216 hectares supported over 100 wineries – a term which one must suppose included a lean-to at the back of a house containing a few wine barrels and a motley assortment of Heath Robinson-inspired pieces of winemaking equipment.

Phylloxera heralded a brutal end to winemaking when it arrived in 1893, but no doubt the bank crash of the same year and the move in popular taste to fortified wines also played their part in the cessation of winemaking in the region.

A gap of over 60 years followed until Bendigo pharmacist Stuart Anderson planted vines at Balgownie in 1969, and within five years had captured the imagination of wine drinkers from Melbourne to Sydney with his startling red wines – wines with a colour, character and strength which were to set the pace for the many who followed in his path.

The eucalypt-forested countryside is undulating, with small, generally dry, creek beds relatively common, but with little significant variation in altitude. Some care is needed in site selection to minimise the risk of spring frost, but the major limitation for viticulture is the absence of readily available water for irrigation.

This is red wine country first, second and last, with red grapes accounting for 93 per cent of the regional crush. In turn, Shiraz provides 65 per cent of the red grape total, with Cabernet Sauvignon at 30 per cent.

There are few other regions in Australia in which there is such a disparity between the white and red crush; equally unusual is the two-to-one dominance of Sauvignon Blanc over Chardonnay. The climate should suit Chardonnay better than Sauvignon Blanc, the latter being pulled by Australia-wide demand for the variety, a phenomenon of the twenty-first century.

There is no reason to suppose this pattern will change in the foreseeable future. The Italian designer varietals are represented by Sangiovese and Nebbiolo, Spain by Tempranillo; the other four varieties are Bordeaux-style blend mates for Cabernet Sauvignon: Cabernet Franc, Malbec, Merlot and Petit Verdot. In absolute tonnage terms these varieties are insignificant compared to Shiraz and Cabernet Sauvignon. Sangiovese may prove the (smallish) dark horse.

OLD OAK BARRELS WEATHER OUTDOORS.

The Region

CLIMATE

The climate is strongly continental, with warm to hot days and cool to cold nights in summer, the diurnal differential diminishing in autumn. It is ideally suited to the making of full-bodied dry reds, the principal limitation being the shortage of water for irrigation. The modest annual rainfall (500 millimetres) falls mainly in winter and spring, and supplementary water (particularly in drought years) is essential if excessive vine stress is to be avoided.

SOIL & TOPOGRAPHY

The majority of the soils are those found in much of south-eastern Australia, with brownish loamy sand over a relatively acidic stony clay base, needing additions of lime and gypsum if reasonable yields are to be obtained. Other than the lower slopes of the Great Dividing Range on which most of the vineyards nestle, the two geographic features are Mount Alexander (744 metres) and Mount Tarrangower.

PRINCIPAL GRAPE VARIETIES

Ninety-three per cent red, seven per cent white. In descending order:

SHIRAZ

CABERNET SAUVIGNON

SAUVIGNON BLANC

MERLOT

CHARDONNAY.

[ABOVE] WATER WHEEL, BENDIGO.
[RIGHT] SANDHURST RIDGE, BENDIGO.

WHITE WINE STYLES

Sauvignon Blanc performs best only in the cooler vintages, but has nonetheless well surpassed Chardonnay.

Chardonnay produces generously flavoured wines in either oaked or unoaked mode. Viognier is sometimes blended with it. Could make a comeback.

RED WINE STYLES

Shiraz. Only in the wettest, coldest vintages does Shiraz (and Cabernet Sauvignon) lose its characteristic richness, and even then not to any great degree. Paradoxically, such years tend to increase the distinctive eucalypt/mint aroma which was first noticed and described 140 years ago as 'a faint aroma of sandalwood'. The wines have excellent texture, with substantial but supple tannins; as elsewhere, Viognier is starting to appear (with success) as a six to seven per cent blend component, adding a lift to the aromatic qualities of the wines.

Cabernet Sauvignon. The style is similar to that of Shiraz, with an abundance of blackcurrant and cassis fruit, but without excessive alcohol or extract. Merlot is used by some as a blend-mate, but Shiraz also works particularly well in tandem with Cabernet Sauvignon.

Wineries of Bendigo

Balgownie Estate Est. 1969

Hermitage Rd, Maiden Gully 3551
www.balgownieestate.com.au
 🍷🍴 exports to UK, US

Founded by then-pharmacist Stuart Anderson, and once again the most respected name in the region, having recovered from the loss of focus and direction in the latter years of Beringer Blass's ownership. Substantial investment in a winery upgrade and vineyard extension by the Forrester family, the new owners, has paid handsome dividends, with powerful, intense Cabernet Sauvignon and Shiraz both outstanding.
Signature wine: Cabernet Sauvignon

BlackJack Vineyards Est. 1987

**Cnr Blackjack Rd & Calder Hwy,
Harcourt 3453**
www.blackjackwines.com.au

Established by the McKenzie and Pollock families on the site of an old apple and pear orchard in the Harcourt Valley, best known for some trophy-winning Shirazs (Cabernet Merlot is the only other wine produced). Ian McKenzie, incidentally, is not to be confused with Ian McKenzie formerly of Seppelt Great Western.
Signature wine: Block 6 Shiraz

Bress Est. 2001

**Mt Alexander Vineyard, 3894 Calder Hwy,
Harcourt 3453**
www.bress.com.au
🍷

Adam Marks won the Ron Potter Scholarship in 1991 to work as assistant winemaker to Rodney Hooper at Charles Sturt University. Since that time he has made wine in all parts of the world, before taking the brave decision (during his honeymoon in 2000) to start his own business. He has selected Margaret River Semillon and Sauvignon Blanc as the best source of white Bordeaux-style wine; Yarra Valley as the best Pinot Noir region; and Shiraz from Heathcote for precisely the same reason. In early 2005 the Marks family acquired the former Mount Alexander Vineyard and cellar door at Harcourt.
Signature wine: Unfiltered Heathcote Shiraz

Chateau Leamon Est. 1973

5528 Calder Hwy, Bendigo 3550
www.chateauleamon.com.au
🍷 exports to UK

Owned by Alma Leamon and winemaker son Ian, this is one of the longest-established wineries in the region, with fully mature estate plantings complemented by contract-grown grapes, some from cool sites on the Strathbogie Ranges. Ian Leamon shows a nice touch with all of the wines, the Shiraz with liquorice, spice, anise, blackberry and black cherry, the Cabernet Sauvignon and Cabernet blends with a little more mint and leaf.
Signature wine: Reserve Shiraz

Passing Clouds Est. 1974

RMB 440 Kurting Rd, Kingower 3517
www.passingclouds.com.au
🍷 exports to US

Graeme Leith is one of the great personalities of the industry, with a superb sense of humour, and he makes lovely regional wines with cassis, berry and mint fruit. The winery places the accent on medium-bodied, fruit-driven wines, oak playing a pure support role. He also shares with the author a lifelong love of fly fishing for trout, and has recently showed his versatility with Three Wise Men Pinot Noir, grown at Woongarra Estate.
Signature wine: Angel Blend (Cabernet Sauvignon dominant)

Pondalowie Vineyards

Est. 1997
6 Main St, Bridgewater-on-Loddon 3516
www.pondalowie.com.au
🍷 exports to UK

Flying Winemakers Dominic and Krystina Morris collectively worked many vintages in Portugal, France and various parts of Australia while establishing Pondalowie. Their eclectic vineyard plantings of 5.5 ha of Shiraz, 2 ha each of Tempranillo and Cabernet Sauvignon, and a little Viognier, Malbec and Touriga, reflect their international background. The wines are excellent, and will only get better as the vineyard ages.
Signature wine: Shiraz Viognier

Sandhurst Ridge Est. 1990

156 Forest Drive, Marong 3515
www.sandhurstridge.com.au
🍷 exports to US

Brothers Paul and George Greblo, with experience in business, agriculture, science and construction, have constructed a purpose-built, 400-barrique winery alongside the 6 ha of estate plantings, predominantly given over to Shiraz and Cabernet Sauvignon, but with small amounts of Sauvignon Blanc, Merlot and Nebbiolo. The quality of the full-bodied, full-blooded red wines is most impressive; the white wine has some distance to go.
Signature wine: Reserve Shiraz

Water Wheel Est. 1972

Bridgewater-on-Loddon 3516
www.waterwheelwine.com
🍷 exports to UK, US

A stalwart of the region, with winemaker/owner Peter Cumming producing significant quantities of Sauvignon Blanc, Chardonnay, Shiraz and Cabernet Sauvignon, ever-reliable and competitively priced. There is nothing showy or flashy about the wines, in keeping with Peter Cumming's personality.
Signature wine: Bendigo Shiraz

New South Wales

MURRAY

Barmah
State
Park

Picola
North

VALLEY

Strathmerton

Koonoomoo

Bearii

Tocumwal

Barooga

Cobram

Picola

B400

Katunga

Mulwala

Barwo

Monichino
Wines

RIVER

HIGHWAY

B400

Cape Horn
Vineyard

Nathalia

Waaia

A39

Numurkah

Yarrawonga

Moama

Kanyapella

C361

Katamatite

Echuca

Yambuna

Katunga

Telford

B400

Kotupna

Wunghnu

Wyuna

Goulburn

Invergordon

Youanmite

MURRAY

Undera
North

Marungi

Tungamah

Strathallan

Tongala

C351

C355

C358

Tallygaroopna

C363

C371

Undera

Goulburn
Valley
Estate

Katandra

Rochester

Nanneella

Kyabram

Lancaster

Congupna

Timmering

C362

Dookie

Girgarre

Merrigum

Mooroopna

Shepparton

C364

Tallis Wine

Byrneside

HWY

MIDLAND

Gentle Annie

Corop

MIDLAND

Tatura

A300

HWY

Nalinga

Stanhope

A300

Kialla

C356

Toolamba

Caniambo

Koonda

Colbinabbin

C348

Waranga
Basin

C357

Tamleugh
North

C365

Rushworth

Arcadia

Miepoll

Tamleugh

C345

Whroo

Murchison

Murchison East

C366

Murchison

GOULBURN

Earlston

C345

Violet Town

Twelve Acres

Goulburn
Weir

M39

Kirwan's Bridge Wines

Bailieston

Nagambie

Goulburn Terrace

Euroa

David Traeger

Burramurra

Graytown

McPherson Wines

Tahbilk

Dalfarras*

Longwood

M31

Mitchelton

Tabilk

Locksley

Avenel Park

Avenel

HUME

Hankin
Estate

M39

Mangalore

Seymour

B340

Tallarook

M31

Sugarloaf Creek
Vineyard

Broadford

0   20 KM

N

Melbourne

GOULBURN VALLEY

Latitude **36°42'S**

Altitude **130–350 m**

Heat degree days **1694**

Growing season rainfall **250 mm**

Mean January temp. **21.2°C**

Harvest **Early March to early May**

Chief viticultural hazard **Spring frost**

Cellar Door
* Dalfarras at Tahbilk.

CENTRAL VICTORIA ZONE
Goulburn Valley & Nagambie Lakes 🌿

The story of the establishment of viticulture in the Goulburn Valley has all the ingredients for a television epic: high-stakes gambling, initial failure, glory and premature death quickly followed by overnight success. The success was that of a syndicate headed by R. H. Horne and John Pinney Bear, which in 1860 raised 25 000 pounds sterling ($50 000) for the purpose of forming the company to be entitled 'The Tahbilk Vineyard Proprietary'.

Within two years 80 hectares had been planted with 700 000 vines, and by the end of the decade 90 metre-long 'old' cellars had been constructed, followed by the 'new' cellars in 1875. By this time Tahbilk was producing the equivalent of 70 000 cases of wine a year, and even though production declined somewhat in the ensuing years to around 35 000 cases, a thriving trade with England was quickly established.

Phylloxera spelt the end for the other smaller vineyards and wineries in the district, and when the Purbrick family purchased Chateau Tahbilk in 1925, it was the only operating winery. Indeed, the only other significant winery (in commercial terms) to be established in the Goulburn Valley has been Mitchelton (in 1969), and even it had a prolonged struggle before becoming successful.

These two wineries more than compensate for the lack of numbers: the National Trust-classified Tahbilk retains more of its nineteenth-century atmosphere than any other winery in Australia. New buildings have been added with the utmost care and sensitivity, and are barely noticed.

Tahbilk is surrounded by the billabongs and backwaters of the Goulburn River (and by the river itself on one side), a setting it shares with Mitchelton. The special qualities of this part of the Goulburn Valley have resulted in the creation of the Nagambie Lakes subregion. It is within this slightly cooler area that most of the best-performed wineries in the greater Goulburn Valley region are to be found.

The essentially flat countryside is never boring: white-trunked eucalypts (frequently massive), a profusion of bird life and the wandering watercourses create a unique atmosphere. In the height of summer, when the temperatures soar and the canopy of the vines starts to wilt under the heat, a cool and shady spot is never far away.

The country around Tahbilk and Mitchelton is nearly perfect for viticulture, allowing generous yields while still retaining plenty of flavour and extract. Moreover, the patches of sandy soil have held phylloxera at bay in some places – most notably the vineyard at Tahbilk on which the gnarled and twisted old vines planted in 1860 continue to provide a precious quantity of grapes made into a special wine by Tahbilk. This is history encapsulated in a bottle.

TALLIS WINES, GOULBURN VALLEY.

The Region

CLIMATE

As befits its status as primarily a producer of full-bodied red wines, this is a relatively warm region if judged by its centre, around the towns of Seymour and Nagambie. Nor is the rainfall especially generous: at 560 millimetres, irrigation, or vine access to the underground watertable (as in the case of Tahbilk), is essential.

SOIL & TOPOGRAPHY

There are three principal soil types: red and brown sandy clay loams; similar hard duplex soils, but yellow-brown in colour; and gritty/gravelly quartzose sands laid down by the prehistoric wanderings of the Goulburn River. The sandy soils held phylloxera at bay, and it is for this reason that Tahbilk has Shiraz vines in production which date back to 1860.

PRINCIPAL GRAPE VARIETIES

Fifty-six per cent red, 44 per cent white. In descending order:

SHIRAZ

CHARDONNAY

CABERNET SAUVIGNON

SAUVIGNON BLANC

MARSANNE

MERLOT.

 WHITE WINE STYLES

Chardonnay has forged to the lead in white grape plantings, for it is capable of producing good yields at high sugar levels, and a peachy/buttery richness attesting to the climate.

Sauvignon Blanc has swept to second place behind Chardonnay; its primary use is as a blend component in multi-regional, lower-priced varietal Chardonnays.

Marsanne. At one point of time Tahbilk had the largest single planting of Marsanne in the world, and this is still the only region (or, technically, subregion) in Australia in which Marsanne has an important place in the scheme of things. Delicate and honeysuckle-accented when young, it can flower majestically with ten or more years in bottle.

Riesling. Victoria is not a noted producer of Riesling, but the continental climate of the Nagambie Lakes subregion produces some consistently good wines, with Mitchelton to the fore.

RED WINE STYLES

Shiraz. This is full-bodied red wine country, producing long-lived, strongly structured wines. The 145-year-old vines of Tahbilk take Shiraz into another dimension, but all the producers in the region make wines with abundant flavour and character.

Cabernet Sauvignon follows much in the footsteps of Shiraz, making solidly framed wines with plenty of dark fruit flavours supported by ripe tannins.

DAYBREAK AT SUGARLOAF CREEK VINEYARD, GOULBURN VALLEY.

Wineries of the Goulburn Valley & Nagambie Lakes

Dalfarras Est. 1991

PO Box 123, Nagambie 3608
(Nagambie Lakes)
ajp@tahbilk.com.au
🍷 (at Tahbilk); exports to UK

The family project of Alister Purbrick and artist-wife Rosa (nee) Dalfarra, whose paintings adorn the labels of the wines. Alister, of course, is best known as winemaker at Tahbilk, the family winery and home, but this range of wines is intended to (in Alister's words) 'allow me to expand my winemaking horizons and mould wines in styles different to Tahbilk'. It now draws upon 23 ha of its own plantings in the Goulburn Valley, but the wines are made at Tahbilk.
Signature wine: Shiraz

David Traeger Est. 1986

139 High St, Nagambie 3608
(Nagambie Lakes)
dtw1@bigpond.com
🍷 exports to UK

David Traeger learned much during his years as assistant winemaker at Mitchelton, and knows Central Victoria well. The red wines are solidly crafted, the Verdelho interesting and surprisingly long-lived. In late 2002 the business was acquired by the Dromana Estate group, but David Traeger has stayed on as winemaker.
Signature wine: Verdelho

Gentle Annie Est. 1997

455 Nalinga Rd, Dookie 3646
(Goulburn Valley)
www.gentle-annie.com
🍷

Gentle Annie (named after an early settler renowned for her beauty and gentle temperament) was established by Melbourne businessman Tony Cotter, together with wife Anne and five daughters assisting with sales and marketing. The vineyard is a substantial one, with 4 ha of Verdelho, 41 ha of Shiraz and 23 ha of Cabernet Sauvignon planted on old volcanic ferrosol soils, similar to the red Cambrian loam at Heathcote. The winemaking team is headed by David Hodgson, who also heads up the Oenology faculty at Dookie College.
Signature wine: Shiraz

McPherson Wines Est. 1993

PO Box 529, Artarmon 1570
(Nagambie Lakes)
www.mcphersonwines.com
📵 exports to UK, US

The 300 000-case McPherson Wines is not well known in Australia but is, by any standards, a substantial business. Its wines are mainly directed at the export market, with sales in Australia through the Woolworths/Safeway group and First Estate. The wines (in two ranges, Varietal and Reserve) are made at various locations from contract-grown grapes and represent very good value at their low price points. For the record, McPherson Wines is a joint venture between Andrew McPherson and Alister Purbrick of Tahbilk, both with a lifetime of experience in the industry.
Signature wine: Reserve Goulburn Valley Shiraz

Mitchelton Est. 1969

Mitchellstown via Nagambie 3608
(Nagambie Lakes)
www.mitchelton.com.au
 🍴 exports to UK, US

Acquired by Petaluma in 1994, having already put the runs on the board in no uncertain fashion (200 000 cases annually) with the gifted winemaker Don Lewis, who retired in 2004. Boasts an impressive array of wines across a broad spectrum of style and price, but each carefully aimed at a market niche. It has built on its legacy of Marsanne by taking the oak out of play on the one hand, but introducing wines such as The Airstrip Marsanne Roussanne Viognier on the other.
Signature wine: Print Shiraz

Monichino Wines Est. 1962

1820 Berrys Rd, Katunga 3640
(Goulburn Valley)
www.monichino.com.au
🍷

Carlo Monichino (since joined by son Terry) was an early pacemaker for the region, making clean, fresh wines in which the fruit character was (and is) carefully preserved; Monichino also showed a deft touch with its Botrytis Semillon. It has moved with the times, introducing an interesting range of varietal wines while preserving its traditional base.
Signature wine: Sangiovese

Murchison Est. 1975

105 Old Weir Rd, Murchison 3610
(Goulburn Valley)
www.murchisonwines.com.au
🍷

Sandra and Guido Vazzoler acquired the long-established 8 ha Longleat Estate vineyard in 2003. The wines are estate-grown, and the red wine style has softened – and improved – under the direction of Guido Vazzoler. Its Semillon, Riesling, Shiraz and Cabernet Sauvignon are all eminently reliable wines.
Signature wine: Longleat Estate Cabernet Sauvignon

Sugarloaf Creek Vineyard

Est. 1998
20 Zwars Rd, Broadford 3658
(Goulburn Valley)
www.sugarloafcreek.com
🍷

The 2 ha vineyard, planted exclusively to Shiraz, was established by the Blyth and Hunter families in the 1990s, the first vintage following in 2001. While situated in the Goulburn Valley, it is in fact near the boundaries of the Upper Goulburn and Macedon Ranges regions, and the climate is significantly cooler than that of the major part of the Goulburn Valley. Matched with skilled winemaking by Adrian Munari, it became immediately apparent that this is a distinguished site, the first two vintages having notable wine show success.
Signature wine: Central Victoria Shiraz

Tahbilk Est. 1860

Goulburn Valley Hwy, Tabilk 3608
(Nagambie Lakes)
www.tahbilk.com.au
 🍴 exports to UK, US

The quietly spoken, highly intelligent Alister Purbrick runs a winery steeped in tradition (with high National Trust classification), which should be visited at least once by every wine-conscious Australian, and which makes wines – particularly red wines – utterly in keeping with that tradition. The essence of that heritage comes in the form of the tiny quantities (plus or minus 200 cases) of Shiraz made entirely from vines planted in 1860. The Wetlands nature reserve opened in 2005, and should not be missed.
Signature wine: 1860 Vines Shiraz

Tallis Wine Est. 2000

PO Box 10, Dookie 3646
(Goulburn Valley)
www.talliswine.com.au
📵

Richard, Mark and Alice Tallis have a substantial vineyard with 16 ha of Shiraz, 5 ha of Cabernet Sauvignon, 2 ha of Viognier and 1 ha of Merlot. While most of the grapes are sold, they have embarked on winemaking with the aid of Gary Baldwin of the consultancy Wine Net group, and done so with considerable success. The philosophy of their viticulture and winemaking is to adopt a low-input and sustainable system; all environmentally harmful sprays are eliminated. The relatively warm climate produces rich red wines, and is particularly suited to Shiraz.
Signature wine: Dookie Hills Shiraz

N

Rochester o

Lake Cooper
Estate

Corop

*Green
Lake*

MIDLAND   HWY

A300

Elmore o

*Lake
Cooper*

Mount
Burrumboot
Estate

NORTHERN

Colbinabbin
West

Colbinabbin o

MOUNT   CAMEL   RANGE

Myola

Campaspe

Barnadown

Muskerry
East

Dead Horse Hill ●

Barnadown
Run

Toolleen

● St Michael's Vineyard

HWY

○ Domaines Tatiarra

0   10 KM

B75

Redcastle

Heathcote
Estate

● Munari Wines

Lake
Eppalock

Jasper Hill Vineyard;
Occam's Razor

Graytown

McIVOR

B280

Sanguine
Estate

Knots Wines
Mount Ida
Vineyard

● Paul Osicka Wines

*Lake
Eppalock*

Costerfield

Baptista*

Milvine Estate Vineyard
Heathcote Winery

○ Heathcote

Eppalock
Ridge

Red Edge

HWY

Argyle

Wild Duck
Creek Estate

River

Redesdale
Estate

NORTHERN

Mia Mia

Grace
Devlin
Wines

Redesdale

B75

Coliban

Burke & Wills
Winery

HWY

Coliban Valley
Vineyards

Barfold

Tooborac

Shelmerdine
Vineyards

● Barfold Estate

McIvor Estate ●

● Melbourne

HEATHCOTE

Latitude **36°54'S**

Altitude **160–320 m**

Heat degree days **1490**

Growing season rainfall **279 mm**

Mean January temp. **21°C**

Harvest **Mid March to early May**

Chief viticultural hazards **Drought; frost**

Cellar Door
*Baptista at David Traeger, Nagambie;
see p. 118 for map.*

CENTRAL VICTORIA ZONE
Heathcote ❧

As elsewhere in Central Victoria, at Heathcote wine followed gold in the 1860s. The vineyards were not as numerous as might have been expected, and, with one remarkable exception, were wiped out by phylloxera prior to the end of the nineteenth century. The one vineyard to survive was planted in the eye of the phylloxera storm in 1891, at Majors Creek near Graytown by Baptista Governa, and is now owned by district veteran winemaker David Traeger.

The last-minute excision of Heathcote from the proposed Bendigo region provoked more angst and argument from the potential winegrowers of Heathcote than it did from Bendigo, which lost one of the most exciting new areas in the whole of Australia. The argument from within Heathcote was a familiar one: where should the boundaries be drawn?

The western side was effectively the eastern boundary of Bendigo, the Siamese-twin join now to be sundered. The question was how far north, south and east should Heathcote's boundaries extend. In a minor way, it was a mirror image of the Coonawarra boundary dispute between those who had been there longest and adventitious newcomers, in turn focussed on the dark red Cambrian soil which so distinguishes this outstanding region. Unlike Coonawarra, the dispute did not get locked in lengthy and expensive court battles, and the extended boundaries were adopted.

The Cambrian red soil deposits start 20 kilometres south-east of the town of Heathcote, continuing south of the town before immediately turning north and running along the Mount Ida Range and thereafter Mount Camel Range for a distance of over 60 kilometres, passing Colbinabbin.

Viewed from the air, the red soil country is a spectacular scene: square or oblong patterns of vivid red alternating with verdant green rows of vines as the planting of new vineyards continues. On the ground, the slopes of the Mount Camel Range are equally impressive, and it is easy to see why land values have soared.

As ever, water availability is an issue, and has slowed plantings in those parts which do not have access to the Waranga Western Channel irrigation scheme. Some of the early arrivals, such as Jasper Hill, Red Edge and Mount Ida, were content to persevere with the lengthy establishment phase and have dry-grown vines with sufficiently deep root systems to withstand drought, wine quality repaying their commitment.

Substantial vineyards have been developed here by wineries as far afield as Hanging Rock and Tyrrell's; the largest (175 hectares) is that of Brown Brothers, with a diverse range of varieties. Most of these are in the northern end of the region, around Colbinabbin, where the warmer climate and greater water availability make economic sense.

REDESDALE ESTATE, HEATHCOTE.

The Region

CLIMATE

Site variations due to altitude and aspect to one side, the climate is similar to that of Bendigo, but a fraction cooler in terms of total growing season warmth in the south around Heathcote, and warmer in the northern end past Colbinabbin. Warm to hot summer days and cool to cold nights are ideal for full-bodied red wines, but with the scope for varieties as diverse as Viognier, Sangiovese, et cetera.

SOIL & TOPOGRAPHY

The prized soil is decomposed Cambrian era igneous intrusion rock known as greenstone, created 500 million years ago and forming the then higher spine of the Mount Camel range. Progressive weathering caused it to move down the side of the range covering sedimentary layers which now form the subsoil. It has the all-important combination of being well drained while keeping good moisture retention capacity.

PRINCIPAL GRAPE VARIETIES

Ninety per cent red, 10 per cent white.
In descending order:

SHIRAZ (ABSOLUTELY DOMINANT)

CABERNET SAUVIGNON

MERLOT

CABERNET FRANC

SANGIOVESE

CHARDONNAY

VIOGNIER

RIESLING

MARSANNE.

There are many more varieties in experimental lots.

 WHITE WINE STYLES

Chardonnay is typically rich, but not overblown, and with the structure for medium-term cellaring.

Viognier is used both as a component with Shiraz, and as a varietal wine in its own right.

RED WINE STYLES

Shiraz. The mature, dry-grown vines of Jasper Hill and Red Edge show just how compelling Shiraz is from this region. It is mouthfilling and mouth-coating, densely coloured and richly flavoured, its texture akin to a great tapestry, helping to highlight its multi-faceted taste. The fruit flavours may range over blackberry, black and red cherry, plum, liquorice, leather and spice, the tannins supple and ripe.

Cabernet Sauvignon is arguably more suited to the warmer, northern end of the region, where full ripeness and luscious blackcurrant/cassis flavours are par for the course. At the southern end, notes of mint and spice are more evident in more elegant, medium-bodied wines.

Merlot is a logical choice for the region, either as a blend-mate for Cabernet Sauvignon, or as a straight varietal. More is in the pipeline.

Sangiovese and Nebbiolo. Impressive results have already been achieved with these varieties. Once again, production is likely to increase, albeit still insignificantly compared to Shiraz.

[RIGHT] MUNARI WINES, HEATHCOTE.

Wineries of Heathcote

Domaines Tatiarra Est. 1991
2/102 Barkers Rd, Hawthorn 3124 (postal)
www.cambrianshiraz.com

 exports to UK

An investor-owned business with a single purpose (to make the best) from a single variety (Shiraz). Its 60 ha vineyard on vivid red Cambrian soil takes its name from an Aboriginal word meaning beautiful country. The wine is made by consultant Ben Riggs in leased winery space, his long-term McLaren Vale connections providing the 50 per cent McLaren Vale component of Trademark Shiraz. The wines are of outstanding richness and character.
Signature wine: Caravan of Dreams
Shiraz Pressings

Heathcote Estate Est. 1999
206 Bourke St, Melbourne 3000 (postal)
www.heathcoteestate.com

An investor-owned

Heathcote Estate is a partnership between Louis Bialkower, founder of Yarra Ridge, and businessman Robert G. Kirby, also owner of Yabby Lake Vineyard. They purchased a prime property on Drummonds Lane in 1999 with an experienced and skilled winemaking team in the form of Tod Dexter (ex Stonier) and Larry McKenna (of New Zealand) as consultant (who are also responsible for the Yabby Lake wines). Forty ha of vines have been planted, 85 per cent Shiraz and 15 per cent Grenache, the latter an interesting variant on Viognier. A single wine is to be produced, and one suspects that the percentage of Grenache will vary from year to year: it was eight per cent in 2002. The wines are matured exclusively in French oak, 50 per cent new and 50 per cent old.
Signature wine: Shiraz

Heathcote Winery Est. 1978
183–185 High St, Heathcote 3523
winemaker@heathcotewinery.com.au

exports to UK

One of the first movers in the Heathcote region, but initially choosing to head in the wrong direction by planting only white varieties. Emerged under new ownership with an impressive portfolio, turning the estate plantings of Viognier to excellent use, both as a single variety and as a blend component with Shiraz. The wines offer good value across all price points, never lacking for generosity of flavour.
Signature wine: Curagee Shiraz

Jasper Hill Est. 1975
Drummonds Lane, Heathcote 3523
(03) 5433 2528

One of the top producers of Shiraz in Australia. Ron and Alva Laughton named their wines after their children and (appropriately enough) there is little to choose between Georgia's Paddock Shiraz and Emily's Paddock Shiraz Cabernet Franc. A little Riesling and Semillon has always been made, now joined by a small amount of Georgia's Paddock Nebbiolo. Ron Laughton insists he is not seeking high alcohol wines, but does acknowledge alcohol levels have risen (to 15 per cent by volume or more) in his quest for ever-greater complexity, richness and ripeness.
Signature wine: Georgia's Paddock Shiraz

McIvor Estate Est. 1997
80 Tooborac–Baynton Rd, Tooborac 3522
www.mcivorestate.com.au

Not to be confused with the longer-established McIvor Creek. A newcomer, with 5.5 ha of Marsanne, Roussanne, Shiraz, Cabernet Sauvignon, Merlot, Nebbiolo and Sangiovese (plus 7 ha of various types of olive trees). The Marsanne (incorporating a dash of Roussanne) and Sangiovese add a dimension to the more typical reds from the Heathcote region, Adrian Munari's skills as the contract winemaker no doubt helping.
Signature wine: Reserve Heathcote Sangiovese

Munari Wines Est. 1993
1129 Northern Hwy, Heathcote 3523
www.munariwines.com

Adrian and Deborah Munari have quickly established an excellent reputation for the predominantly red wines (Shiraz to the fore) coming from their 8 ha estate. Chardonnay and interesting Viognier (released both as a wine and used in the Schoolhouse Red) add a nice touch of variation.
Signature wine: Lady's Pass Shiraz

Paul Osicka Est. 1955
Majors Creek Vineyard at Graytown, 3608
osvin@mcmedia.com.au

exports to UK

The Osicka vineyard was the first new venture in central and southern Victoria for over half a century following the family's arrival from Czechoslovakia in the early 1950s. They planted 15 ha of principally Shiraz and Cabernet Sauvignon, moving with the times in the 1970s to plant Riesling and Chardonnay. The style is elegant and unforced, perhaps appropriate for a winery which prefers to keep an ultra-low profile.
Signature wine: Shiraz

Red Edge Est. 1971
Golden Gully Rd, Heathcote 3523
(03) 9337 5695

exports to UK, US

Peter and Judy Dredge took over a once illustrious but sadly neglected vineyard prior to the 1997 vintage, renaming it and commencing the process of rehabilitation. Additional plantings have taken the area under vine to 15 ha, with only two varieties: Shiraz and Cabernet Sauvignon. The old vine component (from 1971) produces wines of extraordinary depth of flavour and, at times, monumental extract.
Signature wine: Shiraz

Redesdale Estate Wines
Est. 1982
North Redesdale Rd, Redesdale 3444
www.redesdale.com

Shares many things in common with Red Edge, notably the acquisition of an old, run-down vineyard which required (and received) rehabilitation, and the focus on only two wines: Shiraz and Cabernets. The wines are made under contract at Balgownie, the Shiraz with intense red and black cherry and berry, the Cabernets with luscious cassis/blackcurrant fruit and a supple texture.
Signature wine: Shiraz

Wild Duck Creek Estate
Est. 1980
Spring Flat Rd, Heathcote 3523
(03) 5433 3133

exports to UK, US

The first release of Wild Duck Creek Estate from the 1991 vintage marked the end of 12 years of effort by David and Diana Anderson, who commenced the planting of their 4.5 ha vineyard in 1980, making their first tiny quantities in wine in 1986, moving to commercial production in 1991, followed by winery and cellar door facility in 1993. A quiet enough existence until their wines were discovered by Robert Parker and praised to the skies, since when the 'sold out' sign has been a permanent feature.
Signature wine: Duck Muck

CENTRAL VICTORIA ZONE
Strathbogie Ranges 🌿

The Strathbogie Ranges remains a sparsely populated region, without a single town of any significance other, perhaps, than that of Strathbogie itself. It is an open, windswept place, the original forest felled during the nineteenth century for large-scale grazing and thereafter to provide sleepers for the Melbourne to Sydney railway line.

There is scant record of any early viticulture, the only exception being a vineyard established near Longwood in 1900 by the Tubbs family, which made table and fortified wine, later to disappear without a trace.

The modern era began tentatively in 1968 when a local grazing family, the Plunketts, planted an experimental vineyard of a little over a hectare with no less than 25 varieties. The first commercial venture was that of Dr Peter Tisdall who, after extensive climatic

research, in 1975 purchased the property which became Mount Helen. He planted 13 hectares of Chardonnay, eight hectares each of Pinot Noir and Cabernet Sauvignon, six hectares of Riesling, five hectares of Sauvignon Blanc and four hectares of Traminer.

Given that the vineyard has had a chequered history in the late 1990s, and the Mount Helen brand has long disappeared, its early success is quite remarkable. The 1979 Mount Helen Cabernet Sauvignon won the coveted Stodart Trophy for Best One Year Old Red at the Royal Brisbane Show, and three other capital city gold medals. The 1980 Cabernet Merlot topped its class at the 1981 Royal Canberra National Wine Show, which Chairman of Judges Len Evans described as 'one of the strongest classes of young red wines we have seen for 20 years'.

The Plunkett family, no doubt heartened by this success, began planting a commercial vineyard in 1980, which has since grown to 120 hectares in three locations. As well as the resident winegrowers who followed in the 1980s, Domaine Chandon began the development of a 40 hectare vineyard near Strathbogie in 1987, planting Chardonnay and Pinot Noir for use both in its sparkling wines, and (increasingly) in its table wines.

Overall, the region is different in structure to most others in central and southern Victoria, with a relatively small number of wineries and vineyards of relatively large size. Why? Possibly because it is not a region to attract tourists, however grand the scale of the countryside may be.

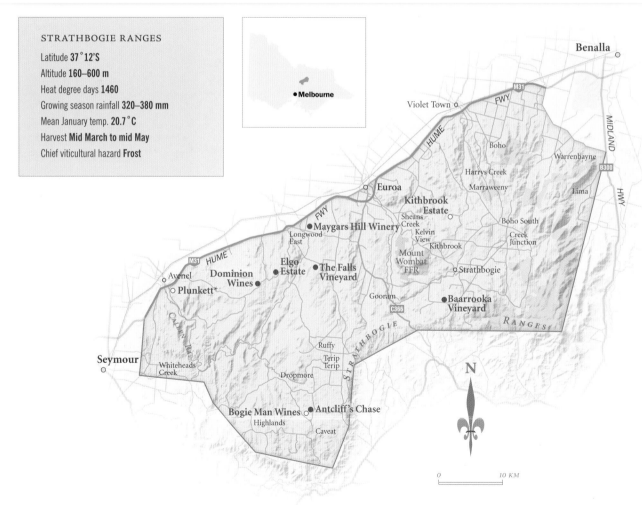

STRATHBOGIE RANGES

Latitude **37°12'S**

Altitude **160–600 m**

Heat degree days **1460**

Growing season rainfall **320–380 mm**

Mean January temp. **20.7°C**

Harvest **Mid March to mid May**

Chief viticultural hazard **Frost**

Cellar Door
* Plunkett at cnr Hume Hwy & Lambing Gully Rd,
  Avenel.

The Region

CLIMATE

Given that vineyards are planted at altitudes between 160 metres and 600 metres, it is not surprising that there is substantial site variation. The region is at its warmest on its north-western boundary with the Goulburn Valley, becoming progressively cooler as the elevation increases with the move east. In the lee of Mount Broughton and Mount Concord in the south, near the quaintly named town of Caveat, Antcliff's Chase is at an elevation of 600 metres, and the Mount Helen vineyard is located between the 420 and 480 metre contour lines.

SOIL & TOPOGRAPHY

Elevation again plays a role, but most of the soils are derived from the granitic base rock of the surrounding mountains, mixed with sand, sandy loams, ironstone gravel and quartz, with a clay subsoil. All of these soils are moderately acidic and devigorating.

PRINCIPAL GRAPE VARIETIES

Sixty-six per cent red, 34 per cent white. In descending order:

CHARDONNAY

CABERNET SAUVIGNON

SHIRAZ

MERLOT

PINOT NOIR

RIESLING

SAUVIGNON BLANC.

Numerous other varieties are grown in smaller quantities.

Wineries of the Strathbogie Ranges

Dominion Wines Est. 1999

Upton Rd, Strathbogie Ranges
via Avenel 3664
www.dominionwines.com

A substantial operation, with 91 ha of vines planted at its Alexander Park vineyard, the predominant varieties being Sauvignon Blanc, Chardonnay, Pinot Noir, Shiraz and Cabernet Sauvignon. Prior to the 2000 vintage a large architect-designed winery was erected with a capacity of 7500 tonnes; it acts as winemaker for the three tiers of Dominion wine brands, and as a contract winemaking service for other growers and wine companies.
Signature wine: Vinus Chardonnay

[RIGHT] CAMERON ATKINS.

 WHITE WINE STYLES

Chardonnay is somewhat variable, but at best with bright grapefruit and nectarine flavours backed by crisp acidity.

Riesling is flavourful, with tropical fruit overtones offset by good acidity; medium-term cellaring.

Sauvignon Blanc is bright and fresh, particularly in cooler vintages.

 RED WINE STYLES

Cabernet Sauvignon is, at its best, very expressive, with attractive cassis and blackcurrant fruit; does best on the north-western perimeter around Longwood in the cooler vintages, and at higher elevations in warmer years.

Shiraz continues its long march in this region as it does elsewhere, offering powerful blackberry, liquorice and spice allied with plenty of extract and tannins.

Pinot Noir is extremely vintage dependent, sometimes lacking varietal character, but coming up with wines of considerable merit and style every now and then. Much is used in sparkling wine.

Elgo Estate Est. 1999

Upton Rd, Upton Hill via Longwood 3665
www.elgoestate.com.au

The Taresch family planted their vineyard at an altitude of 500 m in the Upton area, adjacent to Mount Helen and Plunkett's Blackwood Ridge vineyards. Grant Taresch manages the vineyard, while Cameron Atkins, who oversaw the vintages made up to 2003 at other venues, runs the 800 tonne winery erected for the 2004 vintage. Striking packaging is a feature, wine quality (at three price levels) very good.
Signature wine: Strathbogie Ranges Chardonnay

Maygars Hill Winery Est. 1997

53 Longwood–Mansfield Rd, Longwood 3665
www.strathbogieboutiquewines.com

The 8 ha property known as Maygars Hill was purchased by Jenny Houghton in 1994. She has established on-site bed and breakfast accommodation, and planted 1.6 ha of Shiraz and 0.8 ha of Cabernet Sauvignon; the wines are contract-made at Plunkett. The name comes from Lieutenant Colonel Maygar, who fought with outstanding bravery in the Boer War in South Africa in 1901, where he won the Victoria Cross.
Signature wine: Reserve Cabernet Sauvignon

Plunkett Est. 1980

Cnr Hume Hwy & Lambing Gully Rd,
Avenel 3664
www.plunkett.com.au

🍷 🍴 exports to UK, US

The Plunkett family hides its light under a bushel with its 1980 establishment date. In fact the family planted a little over a hectare of 25 experimental varieties way back in 1968; the move to commercial planting followed in 1980, a vigneron's licence in 1985, and then (finally) winemaking and marketing in 1992. The estate-grown wines are released at various price levels, the cheaper Blackwood Ridge range often representing very good value for money. Winemaker Sam Plunkett also acts as contract maker for Maygars Hill.
Signature wine: Strathbogie Ranges Reserve Shiraz

The Falls Vineyard Est. 1969

RMB 2750 Longwood–Gobur Rd,
Longwood East 3665
www.cameronsbythefalls.com.au

The Falls Vineyard was planted by Andrew and Elly Cameron way back in 1969, as a minor diversification for their pastoral company. Two ha of Shiraz provides both the Longwood Shiraz and the Longwood Reserve Shiraz. With fewer than 1000 cases each year, the intensely flavoured wines are sold by word of mouth, and the cellar door is open only by appointment or if you take advantage of the on-site B&B accommodation.
Signature wine: Longwood Reserve Shiraz

CENTRAL VICTORIA ZONE
Upper Goulburn ❧

Originally a Central Victorian High Country region was proposed, encompassing both the Upper Goulburn and Strathbogie Ranges, but the decision to split the two regions was clearly correct. This is a seriously cool area, with mountains up to 1800 metres, and vineyards planted as high as 800 metres (and as low as 250 metres). It is one of the few Victorian regions without a history of nineteenth-century viticulture: it may well have seemed to be too cold.

The scenery is always beautiful and varied, with alternating areas of dense forest, grazing pasture, and – increasingly – vineyards. Delatite offers spectacular views towards the Australian Alps, snow-clad in winter and (sometimes) well into spring. Mount Buller, one of Victoria's foremost skiing destinations, is accessed through Mansfield.

Lake Eildon, one of Victoria's most important water sources, is in the eastern half of the region, and the Goulburn River runs east to west through its centre. The continuing links with its past are grazing (sheep, dairy cattle and beef cattle), timber logging, and (on a small scale) gold mining.

While the winter–spring rainfall (and snow) is substantial, most vineyards use drip irrigation in summer. This is in turn mainly supplied by surface dams which fill readily; water is not the limiting force here that it is in other parts of Central Victoria.

Wine has added to the tourism attractions of the region: boating on Lake Eildon, trout fishing in the Lake and the numerous streams in its borders, while Delatite is on the road to Mount Buller's ski slopes.

TALLAROOK, UPPER GOULBURN.

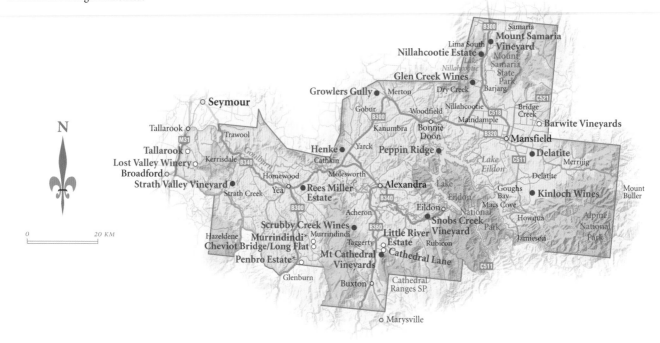

UPPER GOULBURN

Latitude **37°3'S**

Altitude **250–800 m**

Heat degree days **1407**

Growing season rainfall **370 mm**

Mean January temp. **19.9°C**

Harvest **Late March to late May**

Chief viticultural hazard **Spring frost**

Cellar Doors
* Murrindindi at Marmalades Cafe, Yea.
* Penbro Estate at Glenburn Hotel, Glenburn.

The Region

CLIMATE

Both rainfall and growing season temperatures are strongly influenced by altitude. Likewise, north-facing slopes receive more effective heat and light than do south- or south-west-facing slopes.

SOIL & TOPOGRAPHY

Both are varied, with valleys and slopes running in many different directions. The region as a whole is geologically described as the physiographic region of the East Victorian Uplands, with volcanic origins. The soils are most commonly clay and loam, but with sandstone, siltstone, granite, shale, limestone and dolomite all represented.

PRINCIPAL GRAPE VARIETIES

Fifty-five per cent red, 45 per cent white.
In descending order:

CHARDONNAY

SHIRAZ

PINOT NOIR

CABERNET SAUVIGNON

SAUVIGNON BLANC

MERLOT

GEWÜRZTRAMINER

OTHERS, INCLUDING CORTESE, MARSANNE, PINOT GRIS, ROUSSANNE AND VIOGNIER.

Wineries of Upper Goulburn

Cheviot Bridge/Long Flat

Est. 1998
10/499 St Kilda Rd, Melbourne 3004 (postal)
www.cheviotbridge.com.au
 exports to UK, US

Some of the most experienced executives in the wine business formed Cheviot Bridge with the specific intention of building exports to the US. In its own right it has wines at two levels: the Yea Valley varietal range at the top, and the CB range sourced from south-eastern Australia. Subsequently it purchased the Long Flat brand from Tyrrell's for over $10 million, then entering the lists of the Australian Stock Exchange. The extent of future wine releases from the Upper Goulburn region remains to be seen.
Signature wine: Yea Valley Cabernet Merlot

Delatite Est. 1982

Stoneys Rd, Mansfield 3722
www.delatitewinery.com.au

The Ritchie family carried on grazing when it planted the first vines in the region, selling the crop to Brown Brothers. The establishment of the Delatite brand came later; it remains the leading winery in terms of local production. Elegant, delicate Gewürztraminer, Sauvignon Blanc, Pinot Gris and Riesling remain its forte, the red wines struggling in cooler vintages, but doing well in warmer years. Courageously, David Ritchie (with support from winemaker Rosalind Ritchie) has embarked on a program to take the vineyard to biodynamic status.
Signature wine: Limited Edition Riesling

Lost Valley Winery Est. 1995

Strath Creek 3658 (postal)
www.lostvalleywinery.com
 exports to UK

Dr Robert Ippaso planted the vineyard at 450 m on the slopes of Mt Tallarook, with 1.5 ha each of Shiraz, Merlot and the rare Italian grape Cortese. The only such planting in Australia, it pays homage to Dr Ippaso's birthplace: Savoie, in the Franco–Italian Alps. The wines are contract-made off-site by Alex White.
Signature wine: Cortese

Murrindindi Est. 1979

Cummins Lane, Murrindindi 3717
www.murrindindivineyards.com.au
(at Marmalades Cafe, Yea)
The Cuthbertson family, headed by Alan Cuthbertson – son Hugh Cuthbertson having transferred his activities to Cheviot Bridge – has long produced stylish and elegant wines, all

showing a capacity to age well. Over the years, the Chardonnay has been the most consistent, but when conditions are favourable, Cabernet Sauvignon, Merlot and Shiraz are all commendable.
Signature wine: Chardonnay

Rees Miller Estate Est. 1996

5355 Goulburn Hwy, Yea 3717
www.reesmiller.com

When partners Sylke Rees and David Miller purchased the 64 ha property in 1998, it was already planted with 1 ha of Pinot Noir. Since then they have extended the Pinot Noir, and planted 5 ha of Cabernet Sauvignon, Merlot and Shiraz, and a little Cabernet Franc. They use integrated pest management (no insecticides) and irrigate sparingly, the upshot being very low yields of 2.5 tonnes per hectare. All of the wines are expressive and generously flavoured; they are made on-site, part of the grape production being sold.
Signature wine: Wilhemina Pinot Noir

Tallarook Est. 1987

2 Delaney's Rd, Warranwood 3134
www.tallarook.com
exports to UK

Louis Reibl, Tallarook's owner, established 14 ha of vines at an elevation of 200–300 m, the three principal varieties being Chardonnay, Shiraz and Pinot Noir. The wines are made under contract by MasterWineMakers and all show sophistication.
Signature wine: Chardonnay

North East Victoria Zone

Nowhere is it more apparent that the boundaries of zones are purely arbitrary: the legislation makes it clear that a zone is an area of land without any qualifying attributes. Thus it is that two regions, rich in history, famous for their unique fortified wines born of their hot summer climate, are grouped with three much newer, much cooler, mountain regions within the same zone.

Rutherglen and Glenrowan were at the height of their power at the very end of the nineteenth century. The United Kingdom was greatly enamoured of the massively strong wines they produced: there was in fact great argument in the UK as to whether the red table wines were fortified or not. If they were fortified (which the local vignerons hotly denied) a higher rate of duty would have applied. Of course, neither then nor now was there any suggestion the Muscats, Tokays and Ports (vintage or tawny) were not fortified.

But these regions in the zone were brought to their knees as the new century arrived: phylloxera had relentlessly, if arbitrarily, moved north from Geelong, devastating some regions, sparing others. It took courage for the vignerons to replant their vineyards, but this they did.

The three newer regions – Beechworth, King Valley and Alpine Valleys – with overall much cooler climates, have introduced an entirely new suite of aromatic, light to medium-bodied white and red table wines. It is altitude, rather than distance, which leads to such dramatic shifts in climate. The result is that wine tourists can move from hot to cool climates in an hour's drive.

[OPPOSITE & ABOVE] CHRISMONT WINES, KING VALLEY.

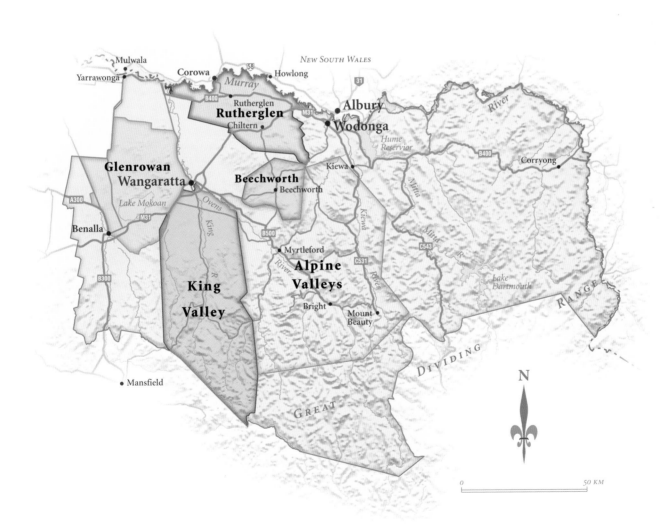

North East Victoria Zone
Rutherglen ❦

This is a part of Australia steeped in history, with character and personality second to none. One of the first vignerons in the north-east was Lindsay Brown, who took up the Gooramadda run in 1839. Gold came later, but Brown was convinced there was greater (and surer) wealth in viticulture. Victoria's great wine historian and chronicler Hubert de Castella records that Brown 'was in the habit of settling miners' discussions as to the depth to which sinking of shafts should be carried. "To get gold", he would say, "you need sink only about 18 inches and plant vines".'

As in so much of Victoria, gold and vines remained intertwined during the extraordinary boom days of 1860 to 1893 – with Ned Kelly and the Murray River providing local colour – each in a different way facilitating the flow of wealth. The bank crash of 1893 and the onset of phylloxera then struck hard at what had become Victoria's most important wine-producing region, but it had the resilience to survive.

Right from the outset it was obvious the shimmering heat of the summer days, not to mention the acid-retention counterbalance of the cold nights, were ideally suited to the production of full-bodied red wines and even more to fortified wines. For reasons which are lost in the mists of time the emphasis fell on Muscat and Tokay, but the significance of the heavy red table wine market that the region developed in the United Kingdom cannot be overemphasised.

It was this market which led to the establishment of the three great vineyards and wineries of the region: Mount Ophir (280 hectares), Fairfield (250 hectares) and Graham's (also 250 hectares). These produced massive quantities of both heavy table and fortified wine, most of which was exported in barrel to the United Kingdom. They survived the Second World War, sustained by the local market, and re-established their export franchise at its conclusion, but the shift away from fortified wine (and heavy table wine) led to their demise in the second half of the 1950s.

Almost all of the smaller wineries and vineyards that were replanted after the onslaught of phylloxera survived, even if some changed names and/or owners. Largely for this reason the north-east is richly endowed with wineries and buildings which are as full of character (and history) as the people who inhabit them. Mercifully, the twentieth century did little to destroy the inheritance of the nineteenth century, and the north-east stands proud among Australia's most interesting wine regions.

The character of the wineries comes in part from the richness of the architecture, whether it be the main street of Rutherglen or the magnificence of the Victorian mansions of Fairfield and Mount Ophir, the humble galvanised iron of the working areas of wineries such as Chambers Rosewood and Morris, or the striking (and bizarre) castellated red brick walls of the pseudo-Scottish castle of All Saints Estate.

The annual Winery Walkabout, held on the Queen's Birthday long weekend in June, is as much an institution as the Barossa Vintage Festival, and is as popular as ever.

[OPPOSITE] PADDOCKS NEXT TO VINEYARD, NORTH EAST VICTORIA.
[BELOW] STANTON & KILLEEN, RUTHERGLEN.

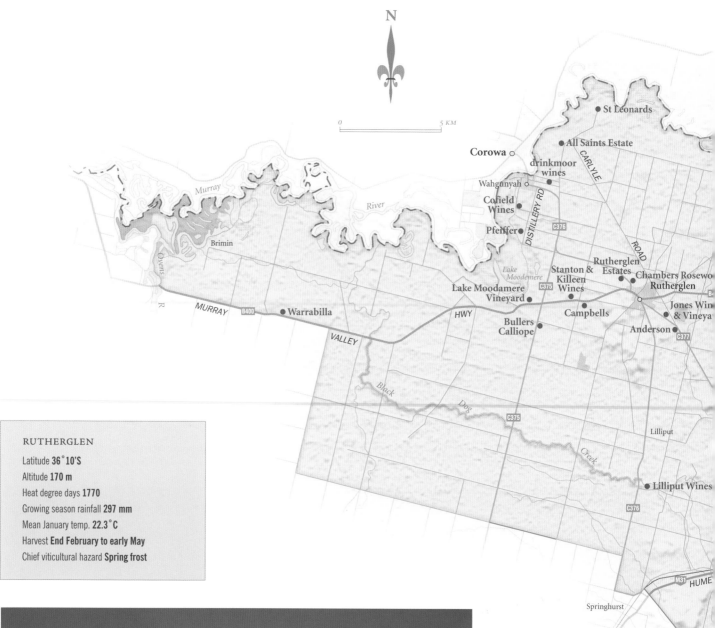

N

0   5 KM

St Leonards

Corowa ○

All Saints Estate

drinkmoor
wines

CARLYLE

Wahgunyah ○

Cofield
Wines

DISTILLERY RD

C376

Pfeiffer

ROAD

Murray

River

Brimin

Lake
Moodemere

Rutherglen
Estates

Stanton &
Killeen
Wines

Chambers Rosewo
Rutherglen

Ovens R.

Lake Moodamere
Vineyard

C375

B-

Jones Win
& Vineya

MURRAY

B400

Warrabilla

HWY

Campbells

Anderson

C377

VALLEY

Bullers
Calliope

Black

Dog

C375

Lilliput

Creek

Lilliput Wines

C376

M31 HUME

Springhurst

RUTHERGLEN

Latitude **36˚10'S**

Altitude **170 m**

Heat degree days **1770**

Growing season rainfall **297 mm**

Mean January temp. **22.3˚C**

Harvest **End February to early May**

Chief viticultural hazard **Spring frost**

1893

THE WORLD'S RICHEST WINE

RUTHERGLEN WINE EXPERIENCE ·

AITKEN & FULLERTON

RIVERINA

HIGHWAY

58 Howlong

Murray

Mount Prior
Vineyard ● ROAD

Gooramadda

C381

WEBBS RD

MIA MIA RD

FALKNERS LA

ADDA

● Morris

MURRAY

Sutherland
Smith Wines

Browns
Plains VALLEY

Gehrig
Estate

Indigo

River

HWY

Barnawartha
North

B400

HUME M31 FWY

Indigo

Barnawartha ○

Chiltern
Mount Pilot
National Park

C377 C381

Chiltern

Creek

Chiltern
Mount Pilot
National
Park

Middle Indigo

FWY

C377

Watchbox ●
Wines

Chiltern
Mount Pilot
National Park

Indigo
Upper

C315

The Region 🍀

CLIMATE

The climate is strongly continental, with very hot summer days and cold nights. The growing season can be threatened at one end by spring frosts (exacerbated by cold air draining down from the mountains to the south) and at the other end by the abrupt arrival of autumn rain. But when conditions are favourable, the exceptionally high sugar levels needed for the fortified wines (and which power the full-bodied red table wines) are attained.

SOIL & TOPOGRAPHY

The great fortified wines for which the region is famous are grown on a band of loam on the lower slopes of the gentle local hills, a band which snakes its way around Rutherglen and extends 2.3 kilometres to the east and 5 kilometres south of the town. It is shared by Morris, Chambers, Campbells and Stanton & Killeen, the leading producers of those wines. The other, entirely different, soil type is sandy flats around All Saints, Cofield, Pfeiffer and St Leonards – with the exception of All Saints, better known for their table wines.

PRINCIPAL GRAPE VARIETIES

Eighty-five per cent red, 15 per cent white. In descending order:

SHIRAZ (50 PER CENT OF ALL PLANTINGS)

CABERNET SAUVIGNON

DURIF

BROWN MUSCAT A PETITS GRAINS

MUSCADELLE

CHARDONNAY

MARSANNE.

🍀 RED WINE STYLES

Shiraz was the traditional red grape of Rutherglen even before it became fashionable. Provided crop levels are restricted, the wine achieves exceptional colour density, weight and overall richness on a scale all of its own.

Durif seems intent on saying to Shiraz, anything you can do, I can do better. On any view of the matter, it is a contest between Australia's super-heavyweights. Despite this, both Shiraz and Durif manage to achieve balance, and avoid (obvious) over-extraction.

Cabernet Sauvignon, like Shiraz, is often sought by companies from other regions (notably the large companies) as a blend component, adding muscle and weight where needed.

Muscat is wrought from the brown clone (or type) of Muscat a Petits Grains, commonly known as Brown Muscat. It is Rutherglen's most famous fortified wine and conventionally regarded as its greatest. Virtually unique in the world, this distilled essence of liquid raisins can achieve undreamt of layers of complexity as it ages (and gently oxidises) in cask. Explosively rich and sweet though the Muscats are, the finish is cleansing and brisk; if not dry in the technical sense, the finish does not cloy nor seem as sweet as the plum pudding flavours of the mid-palate suggest it will be.

Tokay is unique; nowhere else in the world is an aged, fortified wine produced as this is from the Muscadelle grape. Here it has an intense varietal aroma and flavour akin to a mixture of cold tea and fish oil (the latter in the nicest possible sense). Toffee and butterscotch are also commonly used descriptors for a wine which has more feline grace than the all-powerful Muscat, and is preferred by some winemakers and wine judges simply because it has that grace.

Classification Scheme. The winemakers of Rutherglen have agreed on four quality levels for Muscat and Tokay, starting with Rutherglen, then Classic, next Grand and, finally, Rare. It is a self-monitored scheme with regular benchmark tastings, and, while no minimum ages are specified for each level, there is in fact an ascending range of age and complexity.

[OPPOSITE] ANDREW & DAMIEN COFIELD.

Wineries of Rutherglen

All Saints Estate Est. 1864

All Saints Rd, Wahgunyah 3687
www.allsaintswine.com.au

📷 🍴 exports to US

Prior to its acquisition by the late Peter Brown (of the Brown Brothers family), All Saints was forced to sell large quantities of its Muscats and Tokays. At the time, it seemed that the heart of the winery had been ripped out, but it has proved not to be the case. Its range of Classic, Grand and Rare Muscats and Tokays is second to none, the Museum versions quite extraordinary. Nor should the table wines be ignored, especially the Shiraz.

Signature wine: Rare Rutherglen Muscat Museum Release

Anderson Est. 1992

Lot 12 Chiltern Rd, Rutherglen 3685
www.andersonwinery.com.au

📷

Having notched up a winemaking career spanning over 30 years, including a stint at Seppelt Great Western, Howard Anderson and family started their own winery, initially with a particular focus on sparkling wine but now extending across all table wine styles. There are 4 ha of estate Shiraz, and 1 ha each of Durif and Petit Verdot, with yields controlled at a very low 2.5 tonnes per hectare (or, in the old money, 1 ton per acre).

Signature wine: Cellar Block Petit Verdot

Bullers Calliope Est. 1921

Three Chain Rd, Rutherglen 3685
www.buller.com.au

📷 exports to UK, US

Successive generations of the Buller family have kept stewardship over the business, which effectively has three parts: the separately located Bullers Beverford in Swan Hill, making budget-priced fighting varietal wines; small amounts of Calliope Shiraz and Shiraz Mondeuse from old estate plantings; and, most notably, its releases of Muscat and Tokay, the Rare versions having elicited 100-point ratings from Robert Parker, and which are, indeed, immensely complex.

Signature wine: Rare Rutherglen Liqueur Tokay

Campbells Est. 1870
Murray Valley Hwy, Rutherglen 3685
www.campbellswines.com.au
 exports to UK, US

Without undue fuss, Colin Campbell presides over the second-largest producer in Rutherglen. Campbells has a wide range of table and fortified wines of ascending quality and price, which are always honest. As so often happens in this part of the world, the fortified wines are the best, with the extremely elegant Isabella Rare Tokay and Merchant Prince Rare Muscat at the top of the tree.
Signature wine: Merchant Prince Rare Muscat

Chambers Rosewood Est. 1858
Barkly St, Rutherglen 3685
wchambers@netc.net.au
exports to UK, US

Bill Chambers (now joined by son Stephen on the winemaking team) is one of the great characters of the north-east. Bluff-faced, and with startling light blue eyes, he was for many years chairman of the Royal Melbourne Wine Show, but it is his Muscats and Tokays (rather than the table wines) which send the pulse racing. Aficionados say it is not a question of quality, but of style, in determining which of the ancient wines of Chambers or Morris are the greatest. For the author, it is Chambers.
Signature wine: Rare Rutherglen Muscat

Cofield Wines Est. 1990
Distillery Rd, Wahgunyah 3687
scott@cofieldwines.com
exports to US

District veteran Max Cofield, together with wife Karen and sons Damien (in the winery), Ben (in the vineyard) and Andrew, has established a business quite different to most of those in Rutherglen. While making fortified wines, the primary focus is a broad range of both white and red table wines. An off-shoot is the drinkmoor wines business (with its own separate cellar door) run by Damien, its non-vintage range of wines deliberately aimed at taking the fear factor out of play.
Signature wine: Quartz Vein Vineyard Durif

Jones Winery & Vineyard
Est. 1864
Jones Rd, Rutherglen 3685
www.joneswinery.com

Late in 1998 the ultra-historic winery was purchased from Les Jones by Leanne Schoen and Mandy and Arthur Jones (nieces and nephew of Les). The cellar-door sales area is situated in a building from the 1860s, still with the original bark ceiling and walls with handmade bricks fired on-site; it was completely renovated in 2002–03. Wine quality, too, has surged, although the quantity of wine made is very small.
Signature wine: LJ Shiraz

Morris Est. 1859
Mia Mia Rd, Rutherglen 3685
www.morriswines.com
exports to UK

Ownership by Orlando Wyndham has in no way threatened the quality or style of the Morris wines. Most of the table wines released under the Morris label are made elsewhere by Orlando Wyndham, and are not of any significance. The splendidly rich Morris Rutherglen Durif is by a long way the best of the table wines, but it is the Old Premium Rare and Cellar Reserve Grand Muscats and Tokays which are utterly majestic in their quality and style.
Signature wine: Old Premium Rare Rutherglen Muscat

Pfeiffer Est. 1984
167 Distillery Rd, Wahgunyah 3687
www.pfeifferwines.com.au
exports to UK

Ex-Lindemans fortified winemaker Chris Pfeiffer (together with wife Robyn) occupies one of the historic wineries (built 1880) which abound in north-east Victoria and which is worth a visit on this score alone. Drawing upon 32 ha of estate plantings, the range of wines on offer is greater than any other Rutherglen producers, including exotic offerings such as Auslese Tokay, Marsanne, Gamay and (more conventional) Pale Dry Flor Fino.
Signature wine: Christopher's Vintage Port

St Leonards Est. 1860
St Leonards Rd, Wahgunyah 3687
www.stleonardswine.com.au

Owned by the Peter Brown family, and effectively run as a twin business with that of All Saints, although the cellar door (and bistro) is in an entirely separate historic winery on the banks of the Murray River. The accent is firmly on table wines, but with a wide range of white, red, sparkling and fortified wines available, almost all sold through the cellar door and mailing list. Quirky label designs are very much a product of the twenty-first, rather than nineteenth, century.
Signature wine: Wahgunyah Shiraz

Stanton & Killeen Wines
Est. 1875
Jacks Rd, Murray Valley Hwy, Rutherglen 3685
www.stantonandkilleenwines.com.au
exports to UK, US

Another winery which makes a great contribution to the historical fabric of Rutherglen. Three generations of various members of the Stanton and Killeen families have been actively involved in the business over the past 70 years, but it is now the relatively young (by the standards of the longevity of his predecessors) Chris Killeen, making one of Australia's best Vintage Ports, and an outstanding range of other table and fortified wines, including (of course) Tokay and Muscat. He has an excellent palate, and a considerable knowledge of European wines (naturally including Port).
Signature wine: Vintage Port

Warrabilla Est. 1990
Murray Valley Hwy, Rutherglen 3685
www.warrabillawines.com.au

Andrew Sutherland Smith and wife Carol have built a formidable reputation for their wines, headed by the reserve trio of Durif, Cabernet Sauvignon and Shiraz, quintessential examples of Rutherglen red wine at its best. Their 18.5 ha vineyard in the Rutherglen region has been extended with the planting of some Riesling and Zinfandel. Andrew Sutherland Smith spent 15 years with All Saints, McWilliam's, Yellowglen, Fairfield and Chambers before setting up Warrabilla, and his accumulated experience shines through in the wines.
Signature wine: Parola's Limited Release Durif

North East Victoria Zone
King Valley 🌿

The King Valley began life as a tobacco-growing region, the rich soils and hard work of the predominantly Italian farmers ensuring a highly profitable business. But times change, and as the tobacco leaf market dwindled away, other crops had to be found. Graziers, too, were looking to diversify, and with crucial encouragement from Brown Brothers in the early 1970s, viticulture was the route chosen by most.

Encompassing the watershed of the King River, this is an important grapegrowing region, albeit one of considerable physical diversity. The King River joins the Ovens River at Wangaratta, and the King Valley region runs south through the Oxley Plains for 25 kilometres to Moyhu before entering a number of narrow valleys in the foothills of the Alps, with steep, well-timbered hillsides. At its northern end is the long-established location of Milawa which is at the lowest point of 155 metres, at the southern end is the Whitlands plateau, at 800 metres one of the highest viticultural areas in Australia. The Whitlands plateau is, indeed, seeking to separate itself from the King Valley proper by individual regional registration, but as at mid 2005 there was a stand-off between the interested parties.

The King Valley is fertile country capable of producing high yields of good-quality grapes across the full spectrum from Chardonnay to Cabernet Sauvignon, and it supplies grapes to a considerable number of Australia's leading wineries across South Australia, Victoria and New South Wales. An increasing number of producers now make (or have made) part of their grapes into wine, taking up the excess in times of oversupply.

Today it is a thriving region, the Italian heritage coming into its own in the last decade of the twentieth century as interest in lesser-known Italian (plus Russian and Spanish) grape varieties has blossomed, and the wineries have given the King Valley a clearer and more substantial image. In turn, the imaginative use of these so-called 'alternative' varieties in both blends and single varietal offerings has built on that image.

The country ranges from basically flat in the north, to mountainous in the extreme south. However, owing to the abundance of suitable land, most of the vineyards have been established on relatively gentle slopes, typically north- and north-east-facing.

[OPPOSITE] CHRISMONT WINES, KING VALLEY.

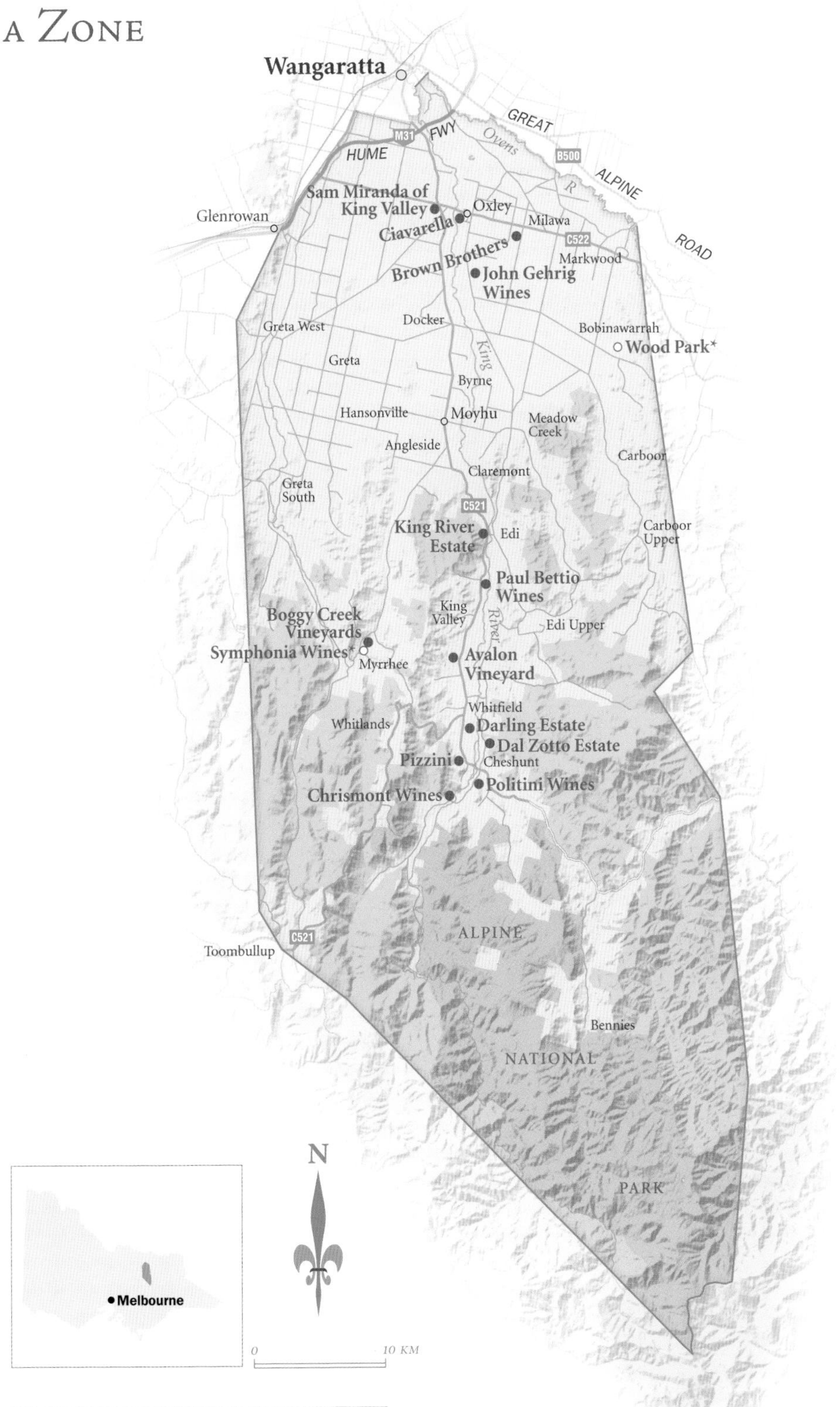

KING VALLEY

Latitude **36°20'S**

Altitude **155–860 m**

Heat degree days **1350–1580**

Growing season rainfall **640–1410 mm**

Mean January temp. **20.8–22°C**

Harvest **Early March to late April**

Chief viticultural hazard **Mildew**

Cellar Doors
* Symphonia Wines at Sam Miranda
of King Valley.
* Wood Park at Milawa Cheese Factory,
Factory Rd, Milawa.

The Region

CLIMATE

The climate changes progressively (and significantly) from north to south, from lower northern elevations to higher southern elevations, with an increase in rainfall and decrease in heat summations. Ripening is progressively delayed, the style of wine changes, and at the highest altitude only the earlier-ripening white varieties are suited to table wines. However, the climate here is ideal for the production of fine sparkling wine base.

SOIL & TOPOGRAPHY

Unsurprisingly, the soil types vary significantly throughout the valley, changing with altitude, slope and site characteristics. However, deep red clay loams abound, at times veering more to grey or brown in colour, but having the same structure. Drainage is good, fertility high, and vigorous growth is encountered in virtually all sites.

PRINCIPAL GRAPE VARIETIES

Seventy-two per cent red, 28 per cent white.
In descending order:

CABERNET SAUVIGNON AND MERLOT (EQUAL)

CHARDONNAY

PINOT NOIR

SHIRAZ

SAUVIGNON BLANC

RIESLING.

[BELOW] SUNRISE AT CHRISMONT WINES, KING VALLEY. [RIGHT] ZACH & JACK AT THE DAM, CHRISMONT WINES, KING VALLEY. [OPPOSITE] THE PIZZINI FAMILY.

WHITE WINE STYLES

Sparkling. Chardonnay and Pinot Noir (principally) are utilised by many of Australia's leading sparkling winemakers as blend components; Brown Brothers' vintage and non-vintage sparkling wines are entirely drawn from King Valley fruit.

Chardonnay is soft and rich, with yellow peach, fig and tropical fruit flavours, and tends to be relatively quick developing; as ever, there are exceptions to prove the rule.

Riesling is principally made as a dry style, but with some late-harvest wines produced. Brown Brothers and De Bortoli (via Windy Peak) are both significant purchasers.

Sauvignon Blanc is rapidly increasing in importance, making a wine with ripe tropical gooseberry flavours.

RED WINE STYLES

Cabernet Sauvignon has its strongest foothold in the low to intermediate elevations. It ripens readily, producing the typically large yields of the region. The resultant wines are soft but flavoursome, making excellent blend components for commercial Cabernet Sauvignon designed for early consumption. The flavours are in the sweet berry spectrum, with just a hint of mintiness and more herbaceous notes. The substantial quantities of Merlot fulfill a similar role; by the nature of the variety, it is, if anything, even softer than the Cabernet Sauvignon.

Other Red Wines. In recent years there has been the experimental development of a wide range of varieties including the Italian grapes Barbera, Dolcetto, Nebbiolo and Sangiovese, and other rarities such as Marzemino, Tannat, Saperavi and Tempranillo. The results have been encouraging.

Wineries of the King Valley

Brown Brothers Est. 1885

Snow Rd, Milawa 3678
www.brownbrothers.com.au
 exports to UK, US

Brown Brothers draws upon a considerable number of vineyards spread throughout a range of site climates, ranging from very warm to very cool, with the climate varying according to altitude. It is also known for the diversity and number of varieties with which it works, and the wines represent good value for money. Deservedly one of the most successful family wineries in Australia, production is in the vicinity of 800 000 cases annually. The wines are exported to over 27 countries throughout Europe and Asia, as well as the UK and (after a long, self-imposed absence) US. Its cellar door is the most sophisticated in Australia, generating very large sales.

Signature wine: Patricia Noble Riesling

Dal Zotto Estate Est. 1987

1944 Edi Rd, Cheshunt 3678
www.dalzottoestatewines.com.au
 exports to UK

Dal Zotto Estate remains primarily a contract grapegrower, with 48 ha of vineyards (predominantly Chardonnay, Cabernet Sauvignon and Merlot, with smaller plantings of Riesling, Pinot Gris, Shiraz, Sangiovese, Barbera and Marzemino). Increasing amounts are made under the Dal Zotto label by Otto Dal Zotto and Michael Dal Zotto.

Signature wine: Family Reserve Shiraz

John Gehrig Wines Est. 1976

Oxley–Milawa Rd, Oxley 3678
www.johngehrigwines.com.au

Honest, well-priced wines are the norm, but with occasional offerings such as the gold medal 2004 Riesling (a cool vintage) of thoroughly impressive quality, all the more given that it comes from the vineyard adjacent to the winery, rather than high in the King Valley. Production is around 5500 cases and the cellar door trade is important – open every day from 9 a.m. to 5 p.m., often manned by the lanky, quietly spoken John Gehrig.

Signature wine: Riesling

King River Estate Est. 1996

3556 Wangaratta–Whitfield Rd, Wangaratta 3678
www.kingriverestate.com.au

Trevor Knaggs, with the assistance of his father Collin, began the establishment of King River Estate in 1990, making the first wines in 1996. The initial plantings were Chardonnay and Cabernet Sauvignon, followed by Merlot and Shiraz. More recent plantings have extended the varietal range with Verdelho, Viognier, Barbera and Sangiovese, lifting the total plantings to a substantial 24 ha. Home-stay accommodation is available in the farm-style guest house. Wine quality across the wide varietal range continues to improve, the Reserve wines deserving the name.

Signature wine: King Valley Reserve Merlot

Pizzini Est. 1980

King Valley Rd, Wangaratta 3768
www.pizzini.com.au

Fred and Katrina Pizzini have been grapegrowers in the King Valley for over 20 years, with 66 ha of mainstream French varietals augmented by Arneis, Nebbiolo, Sangiovese and Verduzzo, all Italian. Grapegrowing (rather than winemaking) still continues to be the major focus of activity, but their move into winemaking has been particularly successful, and the author can personally vouch for their Italian cooking skills. The wines, made by Joel Pizzini, assisted by Alfred Pizzini and with consultancy advice from Mark Walpole, are of reliably good quality.

Signature wine: Sangiovese

Politini Wines Est. 1989

65 Upper King River Rd, Cheshunt 3678
www.politiniwines.com.au

The Politini family has been grapegrowers in the King Valley supplying major local wineries since 1989, selling to Brown Brothers, Miranda and the Victorian Alps Winery. In 2000 the family decided to withhold some Sauvignon Blanc, Chardonnay, Shiraz, Merlot and Cabernet Sauvignon for the purposes of the Politini Wines label, and has established sales outlets at a number of high-class Melbourne restaurants and clubs. The wines are also available through mail order and the cellar door on long weekends and public holidays.

Signature wine: Merlot

Sam Miranda of King Valley

Est. 2004

Cnr Snow & Whitfield Rds, Oxley 3678
sam.miranda@ozemail.com.au

Sam Miranda, grandson of Francesco Miranda, joined the family business in 1991, striking out on his own in 2004 after Miranda Wines was purchased by McGuigan Simeon. The High Plains Vineyard is located in the Myrrhee district of the Upper King Valley at an altitude of 450 m. Thirteen ha of vines are supplemented by some purchased grapes. Wine quality is impressively stylish.

Signature wine: High Plains
King Valley Chardonnay

Symphonia Wines Est. 1998

1699 Boggy Creek Rd, Myrrhee 3732
readsymphonia@bigpond.com
(at Sam Miranda of King Valley)

Peter Read and his family commenced the development of the vineyard in 1981 to supply Brown Brothers. As a result of study tours to both Western and Eastern Europe, Peter Read embarked on an ambitious project to trial a series of grape varieties little known in this country. The process of evaluation and experimentation continues, but Symphonia released the first small quantities of wines in mid 1998 and it has built on that start. A number of the wines have great interest and no less merit, typified by Quintus, a blend of Merlot, Cabernet Sauvignon, Saperavi, Tannat and Tempranillo. In 2005 Sam Miranda acquired Symphonia Wines on a going concern basis.

Signature wine: Quintus

NORTH EAST VICTORIA ZONE
Alpine Valleys

If the name of the region is not sufficiently evocative, then Mount Beauty (snow-clad in winter) and Bright should tell you how spectacularly beautiful the region is, nestled in the northern foothills of the Victorian Alps.

It consists of four river basins or valleys, created by the Ovens, Buffalo, Buckland and Kiewa rivers, which may see the creation of subregions in due course, but it is the altitude which is the prime influence in shaping climate. Thus any subregion would not necessarily represent the boundaries of a single valley.

As with the King Valley, much of the grape production by individual growers/vignerons is sold to larger companies outside the region. In this context, the Victorian Alps Wine Company, whose own brand is Gapsted, plays a crucial role.

The whole of North East Victoria is a declared phylloxera area, and in the last years of the twentieth century much more stringent controls were placed on the movement of grapes out of phylloxera areas. The upshot was that only wine – neither grapes nor fermenting must – can be transported from the region, creating much demand for the services of the Victorian Alps Wine Company and of Michelini Wines.

ANNAPURNA ESTATE, ALPINE VALLEYS.

MYRTLEFORD.

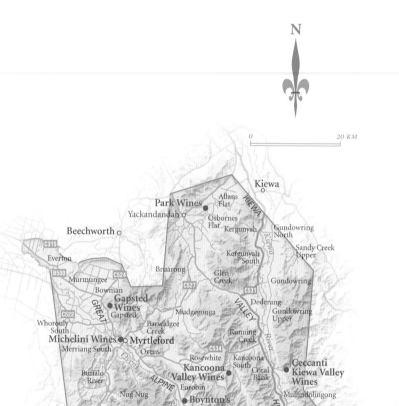

ALPINE VALLEYS

Latitude **36°31'S**

Altitude **150–320 m**

Heat degree days **1482**

Growing season rainfall **425 mm**

Mean January temp. **21.3°C**

Harvest **February to mid April**

Chief viticultural hazard **Spring frost**

The Region

CLIMATE

Altitude rises from 150 metres to over 320 metres, with the highest sites having significantly cooler growing seasons and much higher rainfall. Coupled with the risk of spring frost (and occasional autumn frosts) this makes site selection of prime importance. Harvest begins in mid February for sparkling wine base and continues to the end of April.

SOIL & TOPOGRAPHY

The soils in the four major valleys are all formed on river deposits from similar rocks, mostly granite; all have good structure, ranging from sandy loams to red-brown duplex soils. The common feature is their above-average fertility, which imposes the need for vigour control in most sites.

PRINCIPAL GRAPE VARIETIES

Sixty-five per cent red, 35 per cent white. In descending order:

CHARDONNAY

MERLOT

SHIRAZ

CABERNET SAUVIGNON

SAUVIGNON BLANC.

 WHITE WINE STYLES

Chardonnay is produced for both sparkling and table wine end-use, in part depending on the altitude at which it is grown. Its sparkling use means anonymity, but producers such as Gapsted and Boyntons have consistently produced well-flavoured and structured table wine.

Sauvignon Blanc is of growing importance here as elsewhere, producing a fine flinty/minerally style.

Pinot Gris is following in the footsteps of Sauvignon Blanc, and doing every bit as well.

 RED WINE STYLES

Merlot is a variety which has come from the clouds, and is planted primarily in the higher-elevation vineyards.

Cabernet Sauvignon and Shiraz produce full-bodied red wines at the lower altitudes, wines made famous by the (unhappily now discontinued) Wynns Ovens Valley Burgundy. At times the style can be rustic, but is never short of flavour.

Pinot Noir is used for both sparkling and table wine; at high elevations it is capable of producing table wine of finesse and clear varietal character.

Wineries of the Alpine Valleys

Annapurna Estate Est. 1989

Simmonds Creek Rd, Mt Beauty 3698
www.annapurnawines.com.au

Ezio and Wendy Minutello began the establishment of the 18 ha vineyard at 550 m on Mount Beauty in 1989, planted to Pinot Noir, Chardonnay, Pinot Gris and Merlot. In 1996 Annapurna was named the Victorian Wine Show Vineyard of the Year (assessed purely on viticulture). Appropriately, Annapurna, one of the highest mountains in the Himalayas, is Nepalese for 'goddess of bountiful harvest and fertility'. Frank Minutello makes an amount of high-quality wine each year in a small, on-site winery, but the lion's share of the grapes is sold to other makers.

Signature wine: Pinot Noir

Boynton's Est. 1987

Great Alpine Rd, Porepunkah 3741
boyntons@bright.albury.net.au
 exports to US

The 16 ha vineyard is situated in the Ovens Valley north of the township of Bright, under the lee of Mount Buffalo. Overall, the red wines have always outshone the whites, initially with very strong American oak input, but in more recent years with better fruit/oak balance. Striking, indeed strident, new labelling has led to a minor name change by the dropping of the words 'of Bright', also reflecting the arrival of vine nurseryman Bruce Chalmers as a partner in the business.

Signature wine: Alluvium (Bordeaux blend)

Gapsted Wines Est. 1997

Great Alpine Rd, Gapsted 3737
www.gapstedwines.com.au

Gapsted is the premier brand of the Victorian Alps Wine Co., the latter primarily a contract-crush facility which processes grapes for 48 growers in the King and Alpine Valleys. The estate plantings total 10 ha of Shiraz, Cabernet Sauvignon, Petit Verdot and Merlot, but the Gapsted wines come both from these estate plantings and from a dazzling array of contract-grown varieties, some very obscure. All incorporate the 'Ballerina Canopy' tag, a reference to the open nature of this particular training method which is ideally suited to these regions. The quality of the wines (made by Michael Cope-Williams and Shayne Cunningham) is uniformly high, the best from the region.

Signature wine: Ballerina Canopy Chardonnay

Michelini Wines Est. 1982

Great Alpine Rd, Myrtleford 3737
www.micheliniwines.com.au

The Michelini family is among the best-known grapegrowers in the Buckland Valley. Having migrated from Italy in 1949, the Michelinis originally grew tobacco, diversifying into vineyards in 1982. A little over 42 ha of vineyard have been established on terra rossa soil at an altitude of 300 m, mostly with frontage to the Buckland River. The major part of the production is sold (to Orlando and others), but since 1996 an on-site winery has permitted the Michelinis to process all their grape production. The winery in fact has capacity to handle 1000 tonnes of fruit, thereby eliminating the problem of moving grapes out of a declared phylloxera area; there is no legal barrier to moving wine immediately after fermentation has been completed.

Signature wine: Chardonnay

NORTH EAST VICTORIA ZONE
Beechworth ❦

Beechworth had a dazzling start in the nineteenth century, and there are those who believe its twenty-first century future is every bit as bright; if they are right, it will prove that size does not matter, for the region is a mere pocket handkerchief compared to (say) Geelong. The town of Beechworth was built with gold, discovered in March 1852, the year before the town was proclaimed. Perched precariously on a steep hillside with streets plunging at precipitous, unexpected angles, its stone buildings and array of exotic (European) trees are a sight to behold in autumn.

The first land sales took place in 1855, and a Mr Rochlitz procured 'at very great expense and trouble' 95 vine varieties from Adelaide, which he planted the following year. While a veritable league of nations followed his example, the individual plantings were small, peaking at 70 hectares in 1891. By 1916 only 2 hectares remained, and another 65 years were to pass before a Flying Winemaker called Rick Kinzbrunner – ever a lateral thinker – took the gamble of planting a micro-vineyard of 2.8 hectares of Chardonnay, Pinot Noir and Cabernet Sauvignon. Di and Pete Smith had in fact planted the first vines (in 1978) with the encouragement of Brown Brothers, but were content to sell their grapes to others until 2002.

Stephen and Elizabeth Morris began the planting of their 3 hectare Pennyweight Vineyard in 1982, followed by Barry and Jan Morey in 1984 with the same area for their Sorrenberg Vineyard. So the three winegrowers had less than 10 hectares of vineyards of diverse varieties in an unheralded wine region, yet in the ensuing 15 years it was to become a vinous El Dorado.

Kinzbrunner's Giaconda played the leading role, but Sorrenberg has an intensely loyal following, its wines as conspicuous on leading restaurant wine lists as they are inconspicuous on retail shelves. Castagna has now added its considerable reputation, and half a dozen more labels are coming on to the market, with even more queued up behind.

A significant newcomer has been a syndicate including Brokenwood chief executive Iain Riggs. The group has planted 40 hectares (the largest in the region) with both mainstream and trial varieties over a four-year period from 1999 to 2003. Others are content to simply grow and sell grapes, with demand far exceeding supply. What is also striking is the diversity of varieties, spanning the full range of early- to late-ripening grapes, and the usually concomitant differences in altitude.

BEECHWORTH

Latitude **36°21'S**

Altitude **300–720 m**

Heat degree days **1240–1687**

Growing season rainfall **370–550 mm**

Mean January temp. **19.9–20.4°C**

Harvest **Mid March to end April**

Chief viticultural hazard **Drought**

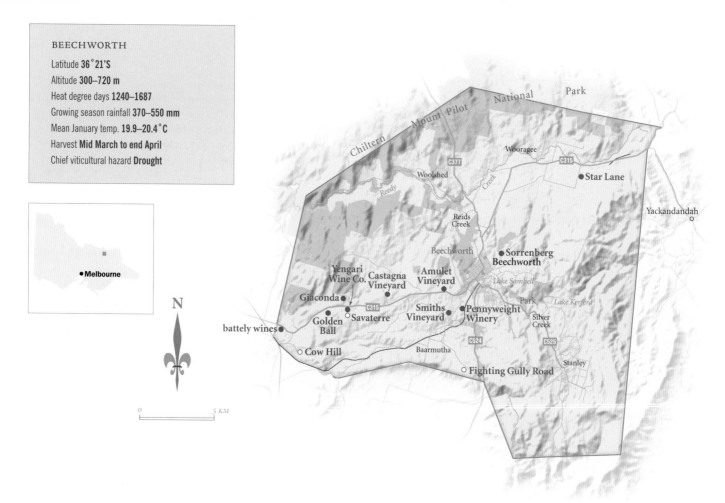

The Region

CLIMATE

The climate is inextricably linked to altitude, with a wide range in all components between the lower and higher parts of the region. Frost risk is site specific; most of the vineyards are planted on slopes with free air drainage taking the frost downhill. The major climatic limitation is restricted water availability, forcing most developments to be dry-grown.

SOIL & TOPOGRAPHY

The precise soil patterns are as complex as the hilly topography, but there are two major soil types: first, very old sandstone gravel and clay derived from marine sediments; second, granitic soil overlying clay derived from volcanic deposits.

PRINCIPAL GRAPE VARIETIES

Sixty per cent red, 40 per cent white.
In descending order:

CHARDONNAY

SHIRAZ

PINOT NOIR

CABERNET SAUVIGNON

MERLOT

SANGIOVESE

SAUVIGNON BLANC

NEBBIOLO.

 WHITE WINE STYLES

Chardonnay. Inevitably, the elegantly complex, long-lived Chardonnays of Giaconda (Sorrenberg sharing some of these qualities) will be seen as defining the style.

Semillon Sauvignon Blanc is usually blended in a fairly tight minerally/gravelly mode.

 RED WINE STYLES

Shiraz is produced by most wineries, but here, too, one maker does better than all others – Castagna, with its Genesis Syrah Viognier, eerily reminiscent of the best of the Côte Rotie in the northern Rhône Valley.

Pinot Noir is strongly influenced by seasonal variation, doing best in the cooler vintages when it retains clear varietal character and good structure.

Gamay. Whether Gamay is a noble variety is a matter of debate, but Sorrenberg clearly does well with it.

Wineries of Beechworth

Castagna Vineyard Est. 1997

Ressom Lane, Beechworth 3747
www.castagna.com.au

Julian Castagna has established 3.3 ha of an eclectic mix of varieties; multi-clonal selections of Shiraz and Viognier make up the bulk of the plantings, the Viognier used both with Shiraz and as a varietal white wine, with a lesser quantity of Sangiovese, and a tiny plot of Nebbiolo. The vineyard is biodynamically run. Notwithstanding his excellent sense of humour, Julian Castagna is as single-minded in his focus on quality as is Rick Kinzbrunner at Giaconda; his very stylish, Rhône-influenced Genesis Syrah is deservedly iconic.

Signature wine: Genesis Syrah

Giaconda Est. 1985

McClay Rd, Beechworth 3747
www.giaconda.com.au

🍷 exports to UK, US

Wines of great quality which have a super-cult status and which, given the tiny production, are extremely difficult to find; they are sold chiefly through restaurants, mail order and (increasingly) the website. All have a cosmopolitan edge befitting owner Rick Kinzbrunner's international winemaking experience. The Chardonnay and Pinot Noir are made in contrasting styles: the Chardonnay tight and reserved, the Pinot Noir more variable, but usually opulent and ripe. Nantua Les Deux, Warner Vineyard Shiraz and Cabernet Sauvignon are also part of the portfolio.

Signature wine: Chardonnay

Golden Ball Est. 1996

1175 Beechworth–Wangaratta Rd, Beechworth 3747
goldenball@iprimus.com.au

The Golden Ball vineyard is established on one of the original land grants in the Beechworth region. The 2.4 ha vineyard was planted by James and Janine McLaurin in 1996, the major parts being Cabernet Sauvignon, Shiraz and Merlot, with lesser plantings of Grenache and Malbec. All of the wines are vinified separately and aged in one-third new French oak, the remainder 2–3 years old.

Signature wine: Gallice Beechworth Cabernet Merlot Malbec

Sorrenberg Est. 1986

Alma Rd, Beechworth 3747
www.sorrenberg.com

Barry and Jan Morey made their first wines in 1989 from the 3 ha vineyard situated on the outskirts of Beechworth. For many years their Gamay was the only serious version of the variety in Australia (one or two others have joined the field since); the stony, minerally Chardonnay, like the Gamay, finds its way on to distinguished restaurant wine lists and the shelves of top end retailers – all in tiny quantities.

Signature wine: Gamay

GIACONDA, BEECHWORTH.

NORTH EAST VICTORIA ZONE
Glenrowan ❧

This is Ned Kelly country, as immersed in history as Rutherglen, but with an added touch of romance from the days of the bushrangers. The feel of the country, too, is subtly different, flanked as it is by the Warby Range on the eastern side and Lake Mokoan on the other (south-western) side

In an oft-repeated story, vines here followed in the footsteps of gold. Richard Bailey and family settled near Glenrowan in the early 1860s, operating the first store in the town to supply the Beechworth and Ovens gold miners. When the gold ran out, they turned to farming on their property Bundarra (Aboriginal for 'meeting of the hills') at the southern foot of the Warby Range.

In 1866 son Varley Bailey planted vines to supplement the grazing activities on the farm, choosing the rich, red granite soil found on part of the property. The first vintage was made in 1870, and demand for the wines – particularly fortified – led to significant expansion of the plantings. By 1892 the wines were sold locally, in Melbourne and exported to England.

Varley Bailey replaced the old slab cellar with concrete cellars which are still in use today. He died in 1931. His son Alan Bailey ran the winery, using the same techniques as his father and grandfather, until 1972 when it was sold to Davis Gelatine (a story in itself); it is now part of Fosters Wine Estates.

Others to establish vineyards included Robert Cox, who established the Herceynia Vineyard; Esca Booth, who in 1904 bought a phylloxera-infested vineyard which he replanted with grafted stock and named Taminick Vineyards, still owned by the Booth family; and in 1987 Michael and Nancy Reid acquired the Herceynia Vineyard which had passed into the ownership of Baileys but was severely run down, rehabilitated it and named it Auldstone Cellars. The new arrivals on the scene are Goorambath and Judds Warby Range Estate.

GLENROWAN

Latitude **36°27'S**

Altitude **190 m**

Heat degree days **1750**

Growing season rainfall **310 mm**

Mean January temp. **22.2°C**

Harvest **End March to end April**

Chief viticultural hazard **Frost**

The Region

CLIMATE

The climate is somewhat warmer than that of Rutherglen, but has less extremes. Thus spring and autumn are warmer (reducing though not eliminating the risk of frost) but the mean January temperature is lower. This is due in part to the moderating influence of Lake Mokoan, which also supplies irrigation water to those vineyards which require it. The rainfall pattern is excellent, and the best soils have good water-holding capacity, so most of the older plantings are in fact not irrigated.

SOIL & TOPOGRAPHY

The soil at the foot of the Warby Ranges is well drained, fertile, deep red clay and loamy clay, derived from granitic material washed down from the Warby Ranges. The soil has good water infiltration and permeability and a high water-holding capacity. The soils around Lake Mokoan are dark clays, loams and silty sands.

PRINCIPAL GRAPE VARIETIES

Ninety-five per cent red, five per cent white. In descending order:

SHIRAZ

CABERNET SAUVIGNON

DURIF

MUSCADELLE

MUSCAT A PETITS GRAINS.

Wineries of Glenrowan

Auldstone Est. 1987

Booths Rd, Taminick via Glenrowan 3675
www.auldstone.com.au

Michael and Nancy Reid have restored a century-old stone winery and have replanted the largely abandoned 26 ha vineyard around it with Riesling, Gewürztraminer, Chardonnay, Shiraz, Merlot and Cabernet Sauvignon. All of the Auldstone varietal and fortified wines have won medals in Australian wine shows at one time or another. Gourmet lunches are available on weekends.

Signature wine: Shiraz

 RED WINE STYLES

Shiraz is without question the leading table wine, in its own idiom as crammed with character as the Muscats and Tokays of the region. Baileys and Taminick Cellars produce monumental Shiraz, the former with a flagship wine from 90-year-old vines. It hardly needs be said these wines have a very long lifespan.

Durif produces wine every bit as, if not more, monumental than Shiraz, opaque in colour and massively mouthfilling, but without hard tannins.

Cabernet Sauvignon is the answer for those who like rich, warm-grown Cabernet styles.

Fortified Wine Styles. The formation of the Winemakers of Rutherglen classification of Muscat and Tokay, and the temporary pause in Baileys' production of the top-of-the-range Winemaker's Selection Muscat and Tokay, saw some of the gloss removed from Glenrowan's fortifieds, but the balance has now been largely rectified; these wines are excellent examples of this unique north-east Victorian style.

Baileys of Glenrowan Est. 1870

Cnr Taminick Gap & Upper Taminick Rds, Glenrowan 3675
www.baileysofglenrowan.com.au

exports to UK

A substantial and hugely historic winery, as noted for its full-blooded, ferruginous red wines as for its Tokays, Muscats and Ports. Since 1998 a major investment program by owner Beringer Blass (now Fosters Wine Estates) has seen the construction of a new winery, planting of additional vineyards (for a total of 143 ha), the preservation of the old winery as a heritage museum, and the reintroduction of top-end Winemaker's Selection Muscat and Tokay.

Signature wine: Winemaker's Selection Old Muscat

Goorambath Est. 1997

103 Hooper Rd, Goorambat 3725
www.goorambath.com.au

Lyn and Geoff Bath have had a long association with the Victorian wine industry. Since 1982 Geoff Bath has been senior lecturer in viticulture with the University of Melbourne at Dookie Campus; they also part-owned a vineyard at Whitlands for 18 years, selling it in 2000 to focus on their small vineyard at Goorambat, hence the clever name. Planting began in 1998 with 1 ha of Shiraz, subsequently joined by 1 ha of Verdelho, 0.5 ha of Orange Muscat and 0.2 ha of Tannat. The ultra-powerful Shiraz is typical of the region at its best.

Signature wine: Shiraz

Judds Warby Range Estate

Est. 1989

Jones Rd, Taminick via Glenrowan 3675
www.warbyrange-estate.com.au

Ralph and Margaret Judd planted their vineyard in 1989 as contract growers for Southcorp. They have 4 ha of Shiraz and 0.5 ha of Durif, plus 100 vines each of Zinfandel, Ruby Cabernet, Cabernet Sauvignon, Petit Verdot, Nebbiolo, Tempranillo and Sangiovese for evaluation. In 1996 the Judds made their first barrel of wine, and have now moved to opening a small cellar door sales facility. The Shiraz and Durif are monumental in flavour and depth, in best Glenrowan tradition, and will richly repay extended cellaring.

Signature wine: Durif

Taminick Cellars Est. 1904

Booth Rd, Taminick 3675
taminick-cellars@iprimus.com.au

Peter Booth continues the family ownership, the winery focussed on Shiraz and Cabernet Sauvignon (its best wines, full of flavour), but flanked by Trebbiano and Chardonnay on the one side, Ports and Muscat on the other. Most of the production is sold to long-term customers and through the cellar door.

Signature wine: Premium Shiraz

Western Victoria Zone ❧

As you move from the Pyrenees Region on the eastern side of the zone, through the Grampians, and finally to Henty, the winery population decreases – dramatically so in the case of Henty. This should not mislead anyone: these are three high-quality regions, with some outstanding wineries and winemakers.

Henty is the odd man out in terms of climate, which is one of the coolest on the Australian mainland. The Pyrenees and the Grampians make full-bodied and medium-bodied red wines respectively, the difference lying purely in style, not quality. Those of the Pyrenees are softer, rounder and more plush; those of the Grampians are finer, more spicy, and more elegant; those of the former can marry well with American oak, those of the latter need French oak.

It is an entirely different ball game in Henty: here Riesling, Sauvignon Blanc, Pinot Gris, Chardonnay and Pinot Noir battle for supremacy, other late-ripening varieties defying the odds and the gods (of weather). Henty ends at the South Australian border; just across that border lies Coonawarra (and Padthaway), which some would argue really belong in Victoria.

There are large vacant expanses in the zone, and it is not surprising some wineries have missed the regional boat.

Wineries of Western Victoria Zone

Empress Vineyard Est. 1998
152 Drapers Rd, Irrewarra 3250
www.empress.com.au

Chief-cum-vigneron Alistair Lindsay has moved his chef's hat to Tasmania, with the intention of also establishing a winery there. It is uncertain whether both vineyard operations will be kept going in tandem; the quality of the wines from the existing Empress Vineyard must tempt Lindsay to maintain the operation, or someone else to buy it.

Signature wine: Chardonnay

Norton Estate Est. 1997
Plush Hannan Rd, Lower Norton 3400
nortonestate@netconnect.com.au

Donald Spence worked for the Victorian Department of Forests for 36 years before retiring. In 1996 he and his family purchased a farm at Lower Norton, and instead of following the regional wool, meat and wheat farming, trusted their instincts in planting Sauvignon Blanc, Shiraz and Cabernet Sauvignon on the lateritic buckshot soil. The vineyard is 6 km north-west of the Grampians GI region, and will have to be content with the Western Victoria Zone until a sufficient number of others follow suit and plant on the thousand or so hectares of suitable soil in the area. The quality of the wines (contract-made by Michael Unwin) is encouragement enough.

Signature wine: Shiraz

Red Rock Winery Est. 1981
Red Rock Reserve Rd, Alvie 3249
www.redrockwinery.com.au

The former Barongvale Estate, which takes its new name from the now dormant Red Rock volcano that created the lakes and craters of the Western Districts when it last erupted, 8000 years ago. The winery has progressively established 10 ha of Sauvignon Blanc, Semillon, Pinot Noir, and Shiraz; a part-time occupation for Rohan Little, with wines sold under both the Red Rock and Otway Vineyards labels. A winery café opened in early 2002.

Signature wine: Semillon Sauvignon Blanc

DALWHINNIE, PYRENEES.

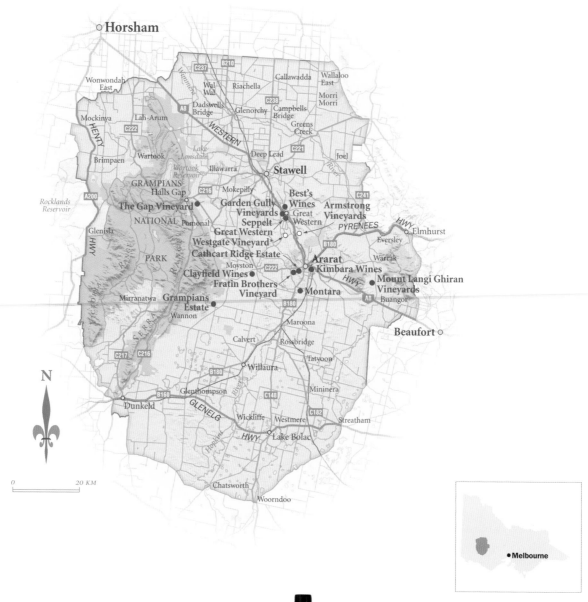

Cellar Door
* *Westgate Vineyard at Garden Gully Vineyard.*

GRAMPIANS

Latitude **37°09'S**

Altitude **240–440 m**

Heat degree days **1460**

Growing season rainfall **240 mm**

Mean January temp. **20.2°C**

Harvest **Mid March to mid May**

Chief viticultural hazards **Spring frost; drought**

Western Victoria Zone

Grampians 🌿

This is quintessential Australian bush country, much of the slopes still covered with stringybark eucalypts, grudgingly yielding up grazing land in the flatter areas. The vineyards of today are widely dispersed, often not visible from the highway. Growth in the number of vineyards has been muted, but the region has a rich history.

Gold fever reached its nineteenth-century peak in central west Victoria: the towns of Ballarat, Beechworth and Bendigo are all testaments to the extraordinary changes it wrought on the fabric, not just of Victoria but of Australian society. But nowhere is its legacy for the wine industry more evident than in the vast underground tunnels (or drives) at what is now Seppelt Great Western.

Grampians (formerly known as Great Western, which may become a subregion) is also unique in that it is the only district in Australia to have directly and significantly benefited from French winemaking experience: Trouette,

Blampied, Pierlot in the nineteenth century, Landragin in the late twentieth century. Pierlot played a key role in establishing the reputation of the district as a sparkling wine producer and (after a 70-year hiatus) Dominique Landragin continued that role for a time during stints both with Seppelt and thereafter Yellowglen.

Simply because Great Western is the best-known sparkling wine brand in Australia, and because of the historic Seppelt winery and cellars, the assumption is that it is indeed still a major producer. The reality is that only a tiny percentage of the grapes used in the Seppelt sparkling wines is grown in the region. As with the Pyrenees, this is a red wine region first and foremost.

For 30 years (1932 to 1963) Great Western was home base for one of Australia's three greatest winemakers of the twentieth century: Colin Preece of Seppelt. (The other two were Maurice O'Shea and Max Schubert.) Preece

had an uncanny ability to blend small parcels of various red varieties from up to three or four vintages to make as little as 500 dozen cases of the wine in question. The vintage ascribed would normally be the youngest component: wine labelling laws were all but non-existent prior to 1963.

His other winemaking practice was to wait until he was satisfied the grapes had achieved the flavour he was looking for, and then to use either water or blocks of ice to pull the alcohol back to between 12.5 per cent and 13 per cent by volume, simultaneously lowering the pH. Many would argue it is a great shame this type of adjustment is now illegal, particularly those who have had the opportunity of recently tasting his superlative red wines from the 1940s and 1950s.

Mount Langi Ghiran Vineyards, Grampians.

The Region

CLIMATE

In part due to its location on the fringes of the Great Dividing Range, which in turn provides altitude, the region has a significantly cooler climate than those areas to its east. The low heat summation is, however, offset by high ratios of growing season sunshine hours, and to a lesser degree by moderate relative humidity. Growing season rainfall is particularly low, and the disappearance of old, low-yielding vineyards throughout the region has been due in large part to lack of available water.

SOIL & TOPOGRAPHY

Grey-brown loamy sands and clay loam surface soils which are quite acid and which need lime adjustment; the subsoils are less permeable than the surface soil, and can lead to drainage problems. Unless the pH is significantly increased by liming both the surface and the subsoil, it will militate against vine vigour and restrict crop levels.

PRINCIPAL GRAPE VARIETIES

Seventy-five per cent red, 25 per cent white.
In descending order:

SHIRAZ

CABERNET SAUVIGNON

CHARDONNAY

SAUVIGNON BLANC

PINOT NOIR

RIESLING

MERLOT.

[ABOVE & RIGHT] GRAMPIANS ESTATE, GRAMPIANS. [OPPOSITE LEFT] SIMON CLAYFIELD. [OPPOSITE RIGHT] MOUNT LANGI GHIRAN VINEYARDS.

 WHITE WINE STYLES

Chardonnay. You barely notice it, yet once again Chardonnay is the leading white variety in terms of plantings, producing wine which is moderately intense, with a mix of citrus, white peach and cashew nut flavours.

Riesling is sparingly grown, but is high-quality wine. The style shows tropical/lime juice aroma and flavour in the warmer years, and reserved, toasty wines in the cooler vintages.

RED WINE STYLES

Shiraz is the district's finest variety, white or red. It makes wines of diverse but great style, ranging from silky smooth, almost understated, red cherry/plum wines of Best's to complex, black cherry, chocolate and spice wines of Seppelt Great Western, then moving up the scale of intensity and finally arriving at superbly concentrated, textured dark fruits and potent pepper/spice of Mount Langi Ghiran.

Sparkling Burgundy is also made from Shiraz (in this region) and in the case of Seppelt Show wines, from the same old vines adjacent to the winery which produce the still table wine. The name Sparkling Burgundy has gone, but not the quality or style of this unique and quite wonderful wine, great at ten years of age, superlative at 20 and beyond praise at 30 to 50 years.

Cabernet Sauvignon has, over the years, been sparingly grown but performs well in adverse conditions and wonderfully when everything goes right. The blackcurrant, blackberry and even raspberry flavours run riot without even threatening that elegant, almost svelte, Grampians style.

Wineries of the Grampians

Best's Wines Est. 1866

111 Bests Rd, Great Western 3377
www.bestswines.com

🍷 exports to UK

This is one of the best-kept secrets of Australia. Indeed the vineyards, with vines dating back to 1867, have secrets which may never be revealed: certain vines planted in the Nursery Block defy identification and are thought to exist nowhere else in the world. The cellars, too, go back to the same era, constructed by butcher-turned-winemaker, Joseph Best, and his family. Since 1920, the Thomson family has owned the property, with father Viv and sons Ben, Bart and Marcus representing the fourth and fifth generations, consistently producing elegant, supple wines, which deserve far greater recognition than they in fact receive.

Signature wine: Thomson Family Shiraz

Clayfield Wines Est. 1997

Wilde Lane, Moyston 3377
www.clayfieldwines.com

🍷 exports to US

Former long-serving Best's winemaker Simon Clayfield and wife Kaye are now doing their own thing. They planted 2 ha of Shiraz between 1997 and 1999; the quantity of rich, juicy blackberry Shiraz has slowly increased year by year. Contract winemaking and consulting keeps the wolf from the door.

Signature wine: Grampians Shiraz

Grampians Estate Est. 1989

Mafeking Rd, Willaura 3379
www.grampiansestate.com.au

🍷

In 1989 local graziers Sarah and Tom Guthrie decided to diversify while continuing to run their fat lamb and wool production. So they planted 3.2 ha of Shiraz and Chardonnay, and opened the Thermopylae Host Farm business. This offers two farm-stay buildings, a five-bedroom shearer's cottage which sleeps 12, and a five-room miner's cottage which sleeps 10. They also secured the services of Simon Clayfield to produce the Grampians Estate wines, which are superb.

Signature wine: Streeton Reserve Shiraz

Mount Langi Ghiran Vineyards Est. 1969

Warrak Rd, Buangor 3375
www.langi.com.au

🍷 exports to UK, US

A maker of outstanding cool-climate peppery Shiraz, crammed with flavour and vinosity, and very good Cabernet Sauvignon. The Shiraz has long pointed the way for cool-climate examples of the variety, for weight, texture and fruit richness all accompany the vibrant pepper-spice aroma and flavour. The business was acquired from founder Trevor Mast by the Rathbone family in 2002, joining Yering Station and Parker Coonawarra Estate in an impressive triumvirate.

Signature wine: Langi Shiraz

Seppelt Great Western

Est. 1865

Moyston Rd, Great Western via Ararat 3377
www.seppelt.com.au

🍷 exports to UK

Should by rights be Victoria's foremost producer of quality table wine, but constant changes in marketing strategy over the past 30 years have not served its image well. A new three-tier structure and cleaner, simpler label designs, with the winemakers' selection of Jaluka Chardonnay and St Peters Great Western Shiraz at the top, may allow it to claim its rightful place.

Signature wine: St Peters Great Western Shiraz

Westgate Vineyard Est. 1997

180 Westgate Rd, Armstrong 3377
www.westgatevineyard.com.au

🍷 (at Garden Gully)

Westgate has been in the Dalkin family ownership since the 1860s, the present owners Bruce and Robyn Dalkin being the sixth-generation owners of the property, which today focuses on grape production, a small winery, accommodation, and wool production. Fourteen ha of vineyards have been progressively established since 1969, including a key holding of 10 ha of Shiraz, the remainder Riesling and Cabernet Sauvignon; most of the grapes are sold to Mount Langi Ghiran and Seppelt Great Western, but a vigneron's licence was obtained in 1999 and a small amount of high-quality wine is made under the Westgate Vineyard label, with richly deserved show success. Both 2002 and 2003 Shiraz were gold medal winners at the Ballarat Wine Show.

Signature wine: Endurance Shiraz Viognier

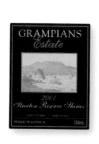

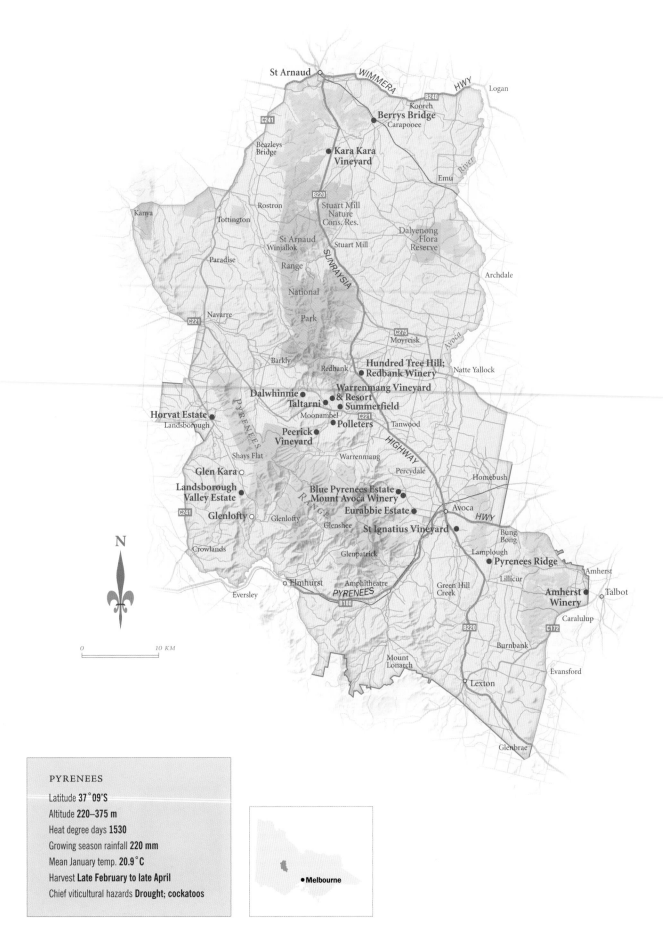

St Arnaud
WIMMERA HWY
Logan
B240
Kooreh
Berrys Bridge
C241
Carapooee
Beazleys
Bridge
Kara Kara Vineyard
Rostron
B220
Emu River
Tottington
Kanya
Stuart Mill
Nature
Cons. Res.
Dalyenong
Flora
Reserve
St Arnaud
Winjallok
Stuart Mill
Paradise
Range
Archdale
SUNRAYSIA
National
C221
Navarre
Park
Barkly
Moyreisk
C275
Avoca
Redbank
**Hundred Tree Hill;
Redbank Winery**
Natte Yallock
Dalwhinnie
**Warrenmang Vineyard
& Resort**
Taltarni
Summerfield
Horvat Estate
Moonambel
C221
Polleters
Landsborough
Tanwood
PYRENEES
**Peerick
Vineyard**
Shays Flat
Warrenmang
HIGHWAY
Glen Kara
Percydale
Homebush
**Landsborough
Valley Estate**
Blue Pyrenees Estate
Mount Avoca Winery
Avoca
HWY
C241
Glenlofty
Glenlofty
RANGE
Eurabbie Estate
Bung
Bong
Crowlands
Glenshee
St Ignatius Vineyard
Lamplough
N
Glenpatrick
Pyrenees Ridge
Lillicur
Amherst
Elmhurst
Amphitheatre
Green Hill
Creek
**Amherst
Winery**
Talbot
Eversley
PYRENEES
B180
Caralulup
Mount
Lonarch
B220
Burnbank
C172
Evansford
Lexton
Glenbrae

0   10 KM

PYRENEES

Latitude **37°09'S**

Altitude **220–375 m**

Heat degree days **1530**

Growing season rainfall **220 mm**

Mean January temp. **20.9°C**

Harvest **Late February to late April**

Chief viticultural hazards **Drought; cockatoos**

● Melbourne

WESTERN VICTORIA ZONE

Pyrenees

The near-schizophrenic wine history of the region might be said to commence with its name: the hills and slopes may well be ideal for viticulture, but the scale of the Pyrenees Ranges is puny compared to the alps on the Franco–Spanish border.

When gold was found in 1853, it didn't inspire the initiation of vineyards as it did in so much of central Victoria. It was not until 1887 that Edwin Horatio Mackereth planted vines. As the size of his family grew, so did that of the vineyard and winery; the enterprise was sufficiently successful for one of his daughters to establish a wine café in High Street, Avoca. The youngest son, Alfred, was able to write in 1962 (at the age of 91) telling how successful the winery had been – particularly with its 'pinneau' – producing both prize-winning red wines and ports.

Alfred's brother Edwin ran the winery, and at the end of the First World War began negotiations to sell the business to Seppelt. It still had 90 000 litres' storage capacity and supported three wine shops in Avoca. At the last moment Seppelt withdrew: Edwin wished to retain some winemaking equipment and

Seppelt suspected he intended to set up in competition. Instead, Seppelt purchased Hans Irvine's Great Western winery. When a Methodist minister bought the Mackereth property in 1929, he promptly smashed all the winemaking equipment and pulled out the vines, a bizarre twist.

The only other winery was established by a Mr Adams near Moonambel; it became known as Kofoed's Mountain Creek. In 1941 Francois de Castella wrote that 'the vineyard still flourishes', but it went out of production in 1945.

There was then a hiatus until 1963 when Remy Martin (of France) formed a joint venture with Melbourne wine merchant Nathan and Wyeth to establish a brandy-making business, named Chateau Remy, planting Trebbiano and Doradillo. When the local brandy market collapsed in the wake of the imposition excise duty, Remy Martin (for various periods the owner of Krug, Charles Heidsieck and Piper Heidsieck) decided to switch to sparkling winemaking, yet another bizarre twist, for if the Pyrenees is suited to anything, it is to the production of full-throated red wines.

Chateau Remy is now Blue Pyrenees, which, having finally rid itself of the Trebbiano and Doradillo, produces pleasant but not remarkable sparkling wine from Chardonnay and Pinot Noir (and table wines). The subsequent growth of vineyards and wineries, Mount Avoca following next in 1970, was leisurely, and it was not until the late 1990s that the large Glenlofty Vineyard of Southcorp (now Fosters Wine Estates) and the even larger adjacent Glen Kara Vineyard (investor funded) brought the Pyrenees up to speed.

It is a quintessential Australian wine region, the vineyards appearing sporadically between the ever-present eucalypts. The wineries cluster in two groups: the larger between the towns of Moonambel and Redbank, the smaller around the rather larger town of Avoca. For tourists, there is one outstanding destination: the Warrenmang Resort, with a top-flight restaurant and much cabin-style accommodation along a hillside overlooking the vineyard.

DALWHINNIE, PYRENEES.

The Region

CLIMATE

The inland location (and to a certain degree the altitude of 220–375 metres) gives rise to low midsummer relative humidity and substantial diurnal temperature ranges in spring and early summer. Late summer daytime temperatures are moderate, lowering the overall heat summation. The major limitation on viticulture is low growing season rainfall, and the absence of underground water. This is true, also, of the new areas on the southern side of the Pyrenees Ranges, which are significantly cooler, but the requirement of water (and danger of spring frosts) is still substantial.

SOIL & TOPOGRAPHY

A mixture of grey-brown sandy and brown loamy sand soils; all have a relatively hard and acidic subsoil, improved by liberal applications of gypsum. Coupled with the climate, they result in moderate rather than vigorous growth.

PRINCIPAL GRAPE VARIETIES

Seventy-five per cent red, 25 per cent white. In descending order:

SHIRAZ

CHARDONNAY

CABERNET SAUVIGNON

MERLOT

PINOT NOIR

SAUVIGNON BLANC

RIESLING.

[ABOVE] KYM LUDVIGSEN, TALTARNI VINEYARDS, PYRENEES. [RIGHT] DALWHINNIE, PYRENEES.

WHITE WINE STYLES

Chardonnay, in typical fashion, responds positively to the differing site climates, relatively full-bodied but not coarse on the southern side of the Ranges, tighter and more citrussy on the northern side.

Sauvignon Blanc has a similar pattern to that of Chardonnay, but performs best in cooler vintages.

Sparkling. Blue Pyrenees and Taltarni are the largest producers, taking a major slice of the Chardonnay and Pinot Noir grown in the region. The Blue Pyrenees wines are full flavoured, but without the finesse of cooler regions; Taltarni adds a Tasmanian component to good effect.

RED WINE STYLES

Shiraz. Whatever other surprises the region may throw up, Shiraz is not one of them. Gloriously sweet and rich fruit flavours easily absorb new oak and are complexed by naturally abundant but ripe tannins. Spice and mint flavours appear in some vintages, but the principal fruit spectrum lies between black cherry and blackberry, with splashes of dark chocolate here and there.

Cabernet Sauvignon produces a wine which is never less than substantial and can be of awesome proportions, on a par with the richest Shiraz. The best wines are both balanced and have good mid-palate fruit (sometimes the Achilles heel of Cabernet) with flavours of blackcurrant, earth and (sometimes) mint.

Merlot has enjoyed the same meteoric rise as in other parts of Australia, and is offered as a straight varietal or blended with Cabernet Sauvignon. Sally's Paddock is a prime example of a blend, albeit with Shiraz and Cabernet Franc as well. However utilised, the flavours are at the ripe end of the spectrum.

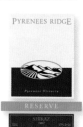

Wineries of the Pyrenees

Amherst Winery Est. 1991

Talbot–Avoca Rd, Amherst 3371

www.amherstwinery.com

Norman and Elizabeth Jones have planted 4 ha of vines on a property with an extraordinarily rich history, a shorthand reflection of which is the naming of Dunn's Paddock Shiraz. Dunn was a convict who arrived in Van Dieman's Land in 1838, enduring continuous punishment before fleeing to South Australia in 1846 and changing his name from Knowles to Dunn. When, at the end of 1851, he married 18-year-old Mary Therese Taaffe in Adelaide, they walked from Adelaide to Amherst pushing a wheelbarrow carrying their belongings. They had 14 children, and Samuel Dunn died in 1898, a highly respected citizen, his widow living until 1923.

Signature wine: Dunn's Paddock Pyrenees Shiraz

Berrys Bridge Est. 1990

633 Carapooee Rd, Carapooee 3478

www.berrysbridge.com.au

exports to US

Roger Milner purchased the property in 1975, intending to plant a vineyard, having worked for three years at Hardys Reynell winery in South Australia. In the mid 1980s he returned with Jane Holt, and together they began the construction of the stone house-cum-winery. Planting of the existing 7 ha of vineyard commenced in 1990, and between then and 2000 winemaker Jane completed two degrees at Charles Sturt University. Until 1997 the grapes were sold to others; since then a succession of deeply coloured, dense and rich Shirazs have appeared.

Signature wine: Shiraz

Blue Pyrenees Estate Est. 1963

Vinoca Rd, Avoca 3467

www.bluepyrenees.com.au

exports to UK, US

Very much the senior citizen, and still the largest winery in the region, now owned by a group of Sydney businessmen. It draws on 180 ha of estate plantings, with the Estate Reserve wines of The Richardson, Reserve Red and Reserve Chardonnay at the top, then estate-produced varietals, and non-regional Fiddlers Creek the much cheaper second label. The Blue Pyrenees sparkling wines are headed by the vintage Midnight Cuvee.

Signature wine: The Richardson

Dalwhinnie Est. 1976

448 Taltarni Rd, Moonambel 3478

www.dalwhinnie.com.au

exports to UK, US

Most (including the author) would rate Dalwhinnie as the best of the region's wineries. The tightly focussed production has a small quantity of surprisingly good Pinot Noir; the main strings are Moonambel Chardonnay, Shiraz and Cabernet Sauvignon, with Eagle Series Shiraz the micro-quantity leader. All of the wines are beautifully balanced, smooth and supple, the Chardonnay emphatically underlining the ability of the region to produce high-quality wine from this variety.

Signature wine: Eagle Series Shiraz

Mount Avoca Winery Est. 1970

Moates Lane, Avoca 3467

www.mountavoca.com

Has bounced out of and back into Barry family ownership, with Matthew Barry (son of the founders) firmly in the saddle. Once again, while Shiraz and Cabernet Sauvignon are the core products, Mount Avoca provides a twist with Semillon Sauvignon Blanc and Sauvignon Blanc which, when the vintage conditions are right, can be very good.

Signature wine: Shiraz

Pyrenees Ridge

Est. 1998

532 Caralulup Rd,

Lamplough via Avoca 3467

www.pyreneesridge.com.au

exports to US

A small but exciting newcomer: Graeme Jukes (together with wife Sally-Ann) began with an Australian version of the French garagiste winemaking approach. This belies Jukes's extensive winemaking experience (and formal training), which is reflected in the excellence of the rich and concentrated Shiraz and velvety Cabernet Sauvignon. The doubling of the estate plantings and winery will make the wines easier to find.

Signature wine: Reserve Shiraz

Redbank Winery Est. 1973

1 Sally's Lane, Redbank 3467

www.sallyspaddock.com.au

exports to US

Neill and Sally Robb are district veterans; Neill's father was the first winemaker at Chateau Remy, and Neill and Sally's children have now followed them into the business. Sally's Paddock (a fruit salad single-vineyard blend of all the major red varieties) has long been

justly regarded as a classic, with a lovely range of minty cassis, blackberry and chocolate fruit. While this is produced in micro quantities, big volume comes from labels such as Fighting Flat, Long Paddock and Billa Bridge, with south-east Australian appellations.

Signature wine: Sally's Paddock

Summerfield Est. 1979

Main Rd, Moonambel 3478

www.summerfieldwines.com

exports to UK, US

Founder Ian Summerfield has now handed over the winemaking reins to son Mark, who, with consulting advice, produces consistently outstanding and awesomely concentrated Shiraz and Cabernet Sauvignon, both in varietal and Reserve forms, with Sauvignon Blanc and Trebbiano lesser sidelines. The reds are built for the long haul, and richly repay cellaring.

Signature wine: Reserve Shiraz

Taltarni Est. 1972

339 Taltarni Rd, Moonambel 3478

www.taltarni.com.au

exports to UK, US

Owned since inception by French-American citizen of the world John Goelet, who has likewise owned Clos du Val in the Napa Valley since it was founded. Long-serving winemaker Dominique Portet has departed, setting up his own winery in the Yarra Valley, and significant changes have followed, in particular with the introduction of the flagship wine Cephas (Shiraz Cabernet), utilising both Heathcote-grown fruit and estate-grown material. The use of grapes from the Tasmanian Lalla Gully vineyard has also increased both the range and quality of the Taltarni wines.

Signature wine: Cephas

Warrenmang Vineyard & Resort Est. 1974

Mountain Creek Rd, Moonambel 3478

www.bazzani.com.au

exports to US

Luigi and Athelie Bazzani (originally with Melbourne wine merchant Russell Brampton) are the utterly charming owners of Warrenmang. Luigi had a long career as one of the state's most celebrated chefs until he transferred his culinary skills to Warrenmang. The business became briefly involved in a proposed public issue of shares in 2004, but is now once again a stand-alone business. Its specialties without question are the red wines under the Warrenmang Estate label (which stands above the Bazzani label), both in turn headed by the ultra-premium Black Puma Avoca Shiraz.

Signature wine: Black Puma Avoca Shiraz

WESTERN VICTORIA ZONE

Henty 🌿

Previously (unofficially) known as Drumborg or Far South-west Victoria, the name adopted at the time of GI registration honours Edward Henty, the first permanent settler in what was to become the colony of Victoria. He landed at Portland Bay on 19 November 1834, bringing merino sheep and vines from Tasmania. While he presumably planted the vines, they disappeared without trace, but the sheep flourished. Henty is ideal grazing country, gently undulating, the grass staying green for much of the year in normal seasons.

One hundred and thirty years were to elapse before Karl Seppelt identified what was then known as Keppoch (now Padthaway) and Drumborg as promising cool-climate viticulture sites. Grazier John Thompson was the next to plant vines, seeking to diversify (in 1975) his farming activities, doing so with great success. While the climate is one of the coolest on the Australian mainland, and

poses real challenges in cooler vintages, the region can produce wines of quite marvellous intensity, elegance and finesse.

When Seppelt planted the first 60 hectares of its 100 hectare vineyard, knowledge of cool-climate viticulture was minimal. Almost inevitably, wrong varieties and wrong vine training techniques were employed, and there were times when it seemed possible Seppelt would sell or abandon the vineyard. Times have changed; given the suitability of the various soils in the region, the generous amounts of high-quality water available, and the still-modest land prices, it would not surprise to see major new entrants in the coming decades.

[RIGHT] TARRINGTON VINEYARDS, HENTY.
[OPPOSITE LEFT] ROD BARRETT.
[OPPOSITE RIGHT] BERT TOMLINSON, GOOSE, TARRINGTON VINEYARDS.

HENTY

Latitude **38°21'S**
Altitude **15–100 m**
Heat degree days **1204**
Growing season rainfall **300 mm**
Mean January temp. **17.7°C**
Harvest **Mid March to mid May**
Chief viticultural hazard **Poor fruit set**

• Melbourne

The Region

CLIMATE

Bordered on the coast by the Southern Ocean, and in the north by the most south-eastern tip of the Great Dividing Range, the climate is unambiguously cool.

SOIL & TOPOGRAPHY

The most important soils stem from volcanic activity, with Drumborg and Hamilton benefiting from moderately fertile, well-drained red kraznozem soils, with equally suited red volcanic soils over a limestone base in the region of Branxholme.

PRINCIPAL GRAPE VARIETIES

Sixty per cent red, 40 per cent white.
In descending order:

PINOT NOIR

CHARDONNAY

PINOT MEUNIER

RIESLING

SHIRAZ

CABERNET SAUVIGNON

SAUVIGNON BLANC

SEMILLON.

WHITE WINE STYLES

Riesling challenges Pinot Noir in terms of absolute quality, sharing the same characteristics of finesse, persistence of flavour and great varietal expression.

Chardonnay is in very much the same category as Pinot Noir and Riesling: fine, minerally and elegant.

Sauvignon Blanc and Semillon offer yet more of the same: wines with elegance and length.

RED WINE STYLES

Pinot Noir is the dominant red table wine, albeit produced in small quantities, its depth of colour, intensity and length of flavour simply outstanding.

Cabernet Sauvignon and Merlot need careful site selection, low crop levels and a dry, warm season to deliver their best, which is super-stylish and Bordeaux-like.

Wineries of Henty

Barretts Wines Est. 1983

Portland–Nelson Hwy, Portland 3305
barrettswines@hotkey.net.au

Has a low profile, selling its wines locally, but deserves a far wider audience. The initial releases were made at Best's, but since 1992 all wines have been made with increasing skill on the property by Rod Barrett, emulating John Thomson at Crawford River Wines. The 5.5 ha vineyard is planted to Riesling, Pinot Noir and Cabernet Sauvignon.

Signature wine: Riesling

Bochara Wines Est. 1998

Glenelg Hwy, Bochara 3300
www.bocharawine.com.au

This is the husband-and-wife business of experienced winemaker Martin Slocombe and former Yalumba viticulturist Kylie McIntyre. Their small estate plantings of 2.5 ha are supplemented by grapes purchased from local grapegrowers. The Chardonnay, Sauvignon Blanc, Pinot Noir and Shiraz Cabernet all reflect the quality and style of the region at its best.

Signature wine: Pinot Noir

Crawford River Wines
Est. 1975

Hotspur Upper Rd, Condah 3303
crawfordriver@h140.aone.net.au

 exports to UK

John Thomson rightly wishes to be regarded as a winemaker rather than a grazier. His is one of the very best small wineries in Australia, producing an exceptionally consistent array of flowery, piercing Riesling, fragrant Semillon Sauvignon Blanc, the eagerly sought Nektar (late-harvested Riesling in understated Germanic Auslese style), and elegantly proportioned and finely chiselled Cabernet Merlot.

Signature wine: Reserve Riesling

Seppelt Drumborg Est. 1865

Princes Hwy, Drumborg 3305
www.seppelt.com.au

 exports to UK

With 100 ha under vine, this is by far the largest vineyard in the region. The climatic challenges occasionally tempted Seppelt/Southcorp to sell the vineyard, and all too few wines are released under the Drumborg label. Drumborg Riesling is made in the majority of years, as superb when it is young as it is at 20 years or more of age. The occasional Drumborg Pinot Noir strongly suggests it should join Riesling more often.

Signature wine: Drumborg Riesling

Tarrington Vineyards Est. 1993

Hamilton Hwy, Tarrington 3301
www.seppelt.com.au

 exports to UK

Tamara Irish has established high-density plantings, up to 8170 vines per ha, of clonally selected Chardonnay and Pinot Noir. Strongly influenced by all of the Burgundian viticultural and winemaking practices, she produces incredibly long and intense unwooded Chardonnay (in the Chablis mould) and complex, spicy, fine Pinot Noir of the highest quality, albeit in microscopic quantities.

Signature wine: Cuvee Emilie Pinot Noir

Gippsland ❧

Gippsland is at once a zone and a co-extensive region, for, despite its large size and distinct climates, it is not yet possible to divide it into regions under the GI legislation. Were such a step able to be taken, there is every likelihood there would be three regions: South Gippsland, West Gippsland and East Gippsland. Even at that point winegrowers such as Phillip Jones (of Bass Phillip) would be suggesting subregions, for he asserts there are six climatic areas. At least, to make sense of the zone, it is necessary to adopt a de facto East, West and South division.

East Gippsland was the focus of winemaking in the area in the nineteenth century, with a number of vineyards. The most important were those of the Costellos and Louis Wuillemin in the Maffra–Bairnsdale region. The remains of the Wuillemin cellars are still visible, although winemaking ceased prior to the First World War.

East Gippsland was also the area in which viticulture resumed when Pauline and Dacre Stubbs began planting Lulgra in 1970, followed by Robert and Anne Guy in 1971 with Golvinda. Both ventures resulted in wines being commercially sold in the 1970s, but the labels are no more. Pioneers whose vineyards and wineries have survived are Peter Edwards of McAlister Vineyards (1977) and Ken Eckersley at Nicholson River (1979).

The zone has complex weather patterns, some moving south from the New South Wales coast, others driven by the high and low pressure cells which sweep from Western Australia across to Victoria and thence to the Tasman Sea. At times these may block each other, and the region has highly unpredictable rainfall, summer drought and floods making grapegrowing difficult in some seasons.

West Gippsland is at roughly the same latitude as East Gippsland, but over 200 kilometres (as the crow flies) to the west, its western boundary abutting the south-eastern boundary of the Yarra Valley. Its climate is distinctly less Mediterranean, being up to 100 kilometres from the coast, and is warmer than East Gippsland.

Coolest of all – though only by comparison – is South Gippsland, where the influence of the Bass Strait (and onshore winds) is marked. Rainfall, too, is higher, and the dark loam soils around Leongatha make this first-class dairy country. All in all, an unlikely environment for one of Australia's foremost Pinot Noir producers, Bass Phillip.

West Gippsland is by a small margin the coolest part, with overall climate slightly more predictable. Notwithstanding the large distances involved and the number of wineries spread across hundreds of kilometres, total production is minuscule, one per cent (under 200 tonnes) of that of the Yarra Valley. It is this which prevents the Zone seeking to legitimise the de facto division into South, West and East.

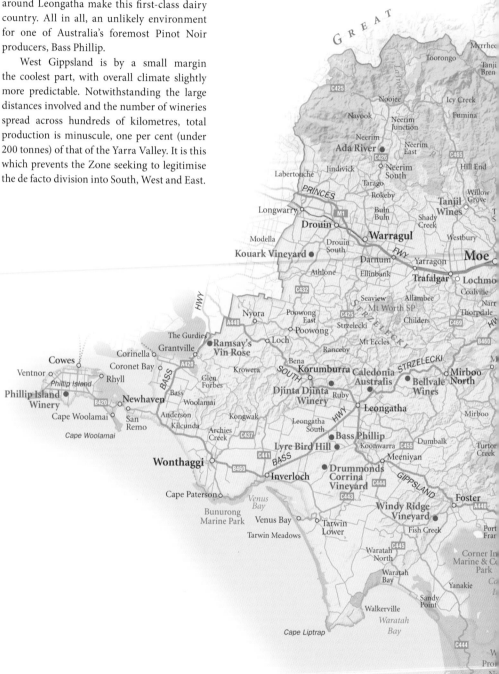

GIPPSLAND

Latitude **37°30'S–38°29'S**

Altitude **20–50 m**

Heat degree days **1300–1470**

Growing season rainfall **420–530 mm**

Mean January temp. **18.1–19°C**

Harvest **Early March to end April**

Chief viticultural hazards **Drought; flood**

RANGE

DIDING

Dargo

Waterford

Tambo Crossing

Castleburn

Tabberabbera

Aberfeldy

Licola

Deptford

B500

C608

Cobbannah

Mitchell
River
National
Park

Bullumwaal

R

Lake
Thomson

RANGE

C486

Glenaladale

C601

Wiseleigh

Bruthen

Mount
Taylor

Sarsfield

Sarsfield
Estate

Nowa
Nowa

Wairewa

Park

Walhalla
Historical
Area
Walhalla

Briagolong
Estate

Valencia
Creek

Wuk Wuk

Lindenow

Sarsfield

B500

Tambo
Upper

Nicholson River Winery

Tostaree

A1

Lake
Tyers
State
Park

Thomson

Lake Glenmaggie

Coongulla

Briagolong

Coongulmerang

Bairnsdale

Lucknow

Johnsonville

Nicholson

Wyanga
Park

Moondarra

Glenmaggie

Seaton

Boisdale

Providence
Ponds NR

Fernbank

A1

HIGHWAY

Swan
Reach

Kalimna

Lakes
Entrance

Lake King

Eagle
Point

Heyfield

Newry

Mourn
rth

Tinamba

Maffra

PRINCES

C106

Forge
Creek

Paynesville

Metung

Lake Tyers

Cowwarr

Stratford

Goon Nure

gh

Denison

River

C492

Perry
Bridge

Bengworden

Victoria

C481

Toongabbie

Winnindoo

Bundalaguah

Airly

Meerlieu

Lake

Narkoojee

C105

C488

Nambrok

C106

Clydebank

The Lakes
Nat. Park

Tyers

Glengarry

Kilmany

HWY

Fulham

Cobains

Loch Sport

BEACH

Mourn
rth

PRINCES

LaTrobe

A1

Rosedale

Sale

The Heart

Lake Wellington

Traralgon

C485

Longford

Seacombe

Morwell

HYLAND

Holey Plains
State Park

Dutson

C485

PARK

Churchill

Traralgon
South

Willung

Holley Hill

Paradise Beach

Jeeralang
North

Callignee
North

Gormandale

Golden Beach

C483

C482

Willung South

Stradbroke

C496

MILE

Coastal

STRAIT

Blackwarry

C484

Carrajung
South

Seaspray

Lakes

Jumbuk

Tarra-Bulga NP

Balook

A440

GIPPSLAND

Giffard

NINETY

Gippsland

Hiawatha

Won
Wron

C453

Darriman

Devon

Yarram

HWY

Woodside

Woodside Beach

rra

Alberton

Tarraville

McLoughlins Beach

HWY

Manns Beach

elshpool

Port Albert

Port Welshpool

BASS

Snake Island

rs Cove

rloo Bay

N

st Point

Melbourne

0   20 KM

ADA
RIVER

The Region

CLIMATE

The varied climate is described in the background on the previous page.

SOIL & TOPOGRAPHY

The soils are varied, from deep sandy clay loams, relatively rich in nutrients and of volcanic origin (South Gippsland) through to the gravelly, sandy loams of the coastal fringes of East Gippsland.

PRINCIPAL GRAPE VARIETIES

Sixty-six per cent red, 34 per cent white.
In descending order:

CHARDONNAY, PINOT NOIR, SHIRAZ AND CABERNET SAUVIGNON – ALL EQUAL

MERLOT

SAUVIGNON BLANC.

WHITE WINE STYLES

Chardonnay is successfully made in all parts of the zone, most strikingly in East Gippsland, where low yields produce wines of wholly exceptional flavour, structure and overall impact. Immaculate and more conventionally structured and balanced Chardonnay is made in West Gippsland, finer and more elegant versions in South Gippsland.

RED WINE STYLES

Pinot Noir varies somewhat throughout the zone, tending richer and somehow slightly more rustic in East and West Gippsland, but in South Gippsland Bass Phillip makes what most regard as Australia's greatest Pinot Noir, and certainly its most Burgundian – fine and elegant, but with a deceptive length and intensity.

Cabernet Sauvignon and Merlot are usually but not invariably blended, doing best in parts of West Gippsland, but also in the East. By and large medium-bodied, the wines do best in warmer vintages.

Wineries of Gippsland

Ada River Est. 1983

2330 Main Rd, Neerim South 3831
adariver@dcsi.net.au

The Kelliher family first planted vines on their dairy farm at Neerim South in 1983, extending the original vineyard (Millstream) in 1989 and increasing plantings further by establishing the nearby Manilla Vineyard in 1994, lifting the total to 6 ha. Ada River also has a long-term arrangement to buy 4 ha of Heathcote Shiraz and Cabernet Sauvignon. The wines are of excellent quality, made by Peter and Chris Kelliher.

Signature wine: Gippsland Chardonnay

Bass Phillip Est. 1979

Tosch's Rd, Leongatha South 3953
(03) 5664 3341

Phillip Jones makes tiny quantities of Pinot Noir in three categories: standard, Premium and an occasional barrel of Reserve. Painstaking site selection, ultra-close vine spacing, and the cool climate of South Gippsland are the keys to his superlative Pinot Noir which, at its best, has no equal in Australia. A hatful of Chardonnay is also made, plus Pinot Rose and a few bottles of Gamay.

Signature wine: Reserve Pinot Noir

[OPPOSITE] ADA RIVER, GIPPSLAND.

Caledonia Australis Est. 1995

75 Yarragon Rd, Leongatha North 3953
www.caledoniaaustralis.com

The somewhat reclusive but intensely ambitious Caledonia Australis is a Pinot Noir and Chardonnay specialist, with a total 18 ha planted to Chardonnay and Pinot Noir in three separate vineyard locations in the Leongatha area, the slopes east- to north-east-facing. Small batch winemaking by MasterWineMakers has resulted in consistently high-quality wines, the Chardonnay powerful, but with exceptional texture and balance, barrel fermentation, malolactic and wild yeast all contributing to the wine.

Signature wine: Chardonnay

Narkoojee Est. 1981

170 Francis Rd, Glengarry 3854
www.narkoojee.com
exports to UK

Narkoojee Vineyard is close to the old gold-mining town of Walhalla and looks out over the Strzelecki Ranges. The wines are produced from a little over 10 ha of estate vineyards, with Chardonnay accounting for half the total. Co-owner Harry Friend was an amateur winemaker of note before turning to commercial wine-making with Narkoojee, his skills showing through with all the wines, none more so than the Chardonnay. Cabernet Sauvignon and The Athelstan Merlot can also impress.

Signature wine: Reserve Chardonnay

Nicholson River Est. 1978

Liddells Rd, Nicholson 3882
www.nicholsonriverwinery.com.au
exports to UK, US

Ken Eckersley's fierce commitment to quality in the face of the temperamental Gippsland climate and the frustratingly small production has been repaid by some massive Chardonnays and quixotic red wines (from 9 ha of estate plantings). He does not refer to his Chardonnays as white wines but as gold wines, and lists them accordingly in his newsletter. However, in recent times his Merlot and The Nicholson (a blend of Merlot and Shiraz) have supplanted the Chardonnay at the top of the tree.

Signature wine: The Nicholson

Phillip Island Vineyard

Est. 1993
Berrys Beach Rd, Phillip Island
www.phillipislandwines.com.au

Phillip Island is one of the outstanding tourist attractions of Victoria, famous for sights as diverse as penguins emerging from the sea and Grand Prix motorbike races. When the Lance family (of Diamond Valley fame) began to establish the 2.5 ha vineyard in 1993, father David and son James Lance were not entirely prepared for the dual assault of wind and birds. The outcome is a vineyard totally enclosed in permanent net. To make the venture economically viable, grapes are also purchased from other Gippsland growers and from the Yarra Valley. Regardless of provenance, the wines are immaculately made, none more so than the beautifully silky, fine Pinot Noir.

Signature wine: Gippsland Pinot Noir

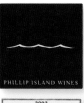

NORTH WEST VICTORIA ZONE
Murray Darling ❧

The story of the establishment of the Murray Darling region has all the elements of a Hollywood Wild West epic, full of visionary dreams, political intrigue, fortunes won and lost. It began with lawyer-turned-politician (and future Prime Minister) Alfred Deakin, who has been credited as the first person to envisage the possibilities of large-scale irrigation to transform the endless desert stretching along the Murray River. The inspiration came from a visit he had made to California in the 1880s, seeing at first hand the work done by irrigation engineers and brothers, George and William Chaffey.

Deakin successfully lured them to Victoria, and they immediately recognised the virtually unlimited potential of the Murray River and the red soil. Their prior experience also made them aware of the necessity of obtaining permanent land and water rights for the scheme. Bureaucratic delays in granting the rights so frustrated them that in 1887 they moved to Renmark, with the unconditional support of the South Australian government.

With formidable energy they quickly laid out plans for that town, with the wide streets and parklands which remain a feature of Renmark to this day. Stung by jealousy and having unsuccessfully sought tenders from others, the Victorian government then invited the Chaffeys to return, on the precise terms they had failed to obtain the first time around.

The return of the Chaffeys saw the town of Mildura's population rise from a handful to 3000 people by 1890, many taking up 4 hectare lots already supplied with water. The town, too, was laid out in much the same way as Renmark, with substantial parklands and public places held in perpetual trust.

In 1892 the Chaffeys built Chateau Mildura, but were brought down by events outside their control: the great bank crash of 1893 which affected every state, and a prolonged drought which halted all river traffic on the Murray. There was simply no way for the varied produce of the region to get to the Melbourne (or any other) market, and in 1897 William Chaffey was declared bankrupt.

The railway finally arrived in 1903, and the region slowly rebuilt its economic fortunes. In the meantime, most of the vineyards had been grafted from wine to table/drying grapes, and the unsold wine at Chateau Mildura had been distilled into brandy, leading to the closure of the winery in 1908.

In the ensuing years there were two further bankruptcies and two reconstructions, all with the Mildura name and all with the continued involvement of the exceptionally resilient William Chaffey, until his death in 1925. Fortified wine and brandy production were the business drivers, but the arrival of a youthful Ron Haselgrove (appointed technical director in 1935) saw the dawn of the new era, and the registration of the Mildara trademark in 1937. The Mildara Wine Company had arrived, and was to continue as an important production centre until Beringer Blass closed it in 2004.

In the meantime McWilliam's opened its Robinvale Winery in 1952 and Lindemans Karadoc in 1974; Stanley Buronga (on the New South Wales side of the border) was acquired by Stanley in 1984 (now part of Hardys), the same year as Buronga Hill Winery (now owned by McGuigan Simeon Wines, and one of the five largest wineries in Australia) was built.

In terms of volume of production, this is one of the three most important regions of Australia, the other two being the Riverland and the Riverina. Mildura is also home to one of Australia's finest restaurants, Stefano's, presided over by Stefano de Pieri. Its wine list, too, is outstanding.

MURRAY DARLING COLLECTION, MURRAY DARLING.

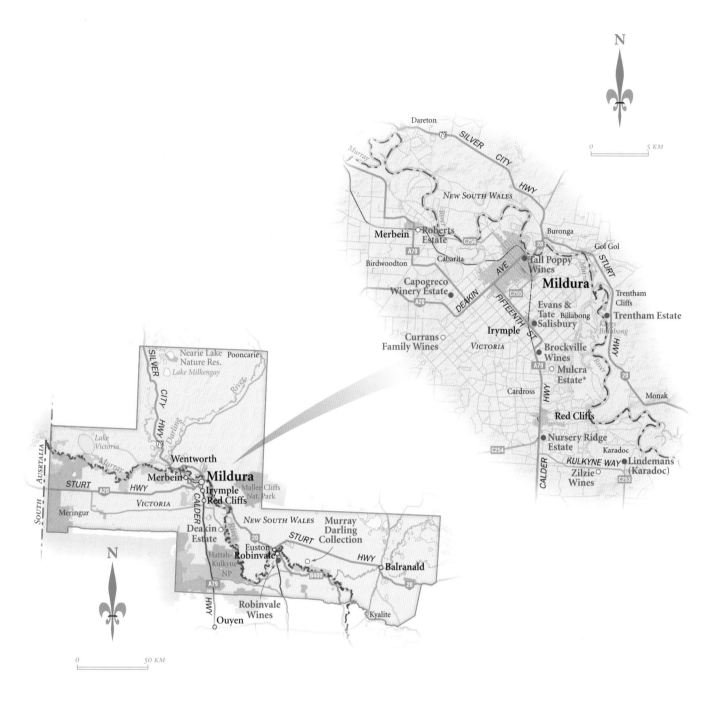

MURRAY DARLING

Latitude **34°10'S**

Altitude **55–70 m**

Heat degree days **2150–2240**

Growing season rainfall **130–150 mm**

Mean January temp. **23.7°C**

Harvest **Early February to mid March**

Chief viticultural hazard **Hail**

Cellar Door
* Mulcra Estate Wines
  at The Enjoywine Cafe, Mildura.

The Region

CLIMATE

Although the distance between the eastern and western extremity of the region is great (over 350 kilometres), the climate is similar. It is hot, with long sunshine hours, low humidity and negligible growing season rainfall all contributing to make irrigation absolutely essential. The continental influence is strong, with consequent high shifts in diurnal temperature ranges, but not sufficiently so to make spring frosts a problem. Fungal disease pressures are low, spray requirements minimal other than for control of eutypa (die-back disease).

SOIL & TOPOGRAPHY

The soil is unique to the Murray River system, but spreads along its entire length. It is technically known as calcareous earth, ranging from brown to red-brown loamy sand, sandy loam or loam. The surface soils are permeable, but perched watertables (partly due to soil properties and topography, partly due to management practices associated with salinity build up) can create problems in some areas.

PRINCIPAL GRAPE VARIETIES

Fifty-eight per cent white, 42 per cent red.
In descending order:

CHARDONNAY

SHIRAZ

SULTANA

CABERNET SAUVIGNON

MERLOT

COLOMBARD

MUSCAT GORDO BLANCO

RUBY CABERNET

PETIT VERDOT.

WHITE WINE STYLES

Chardonnay is the dominant variety, white or red, and is nigh on certain to remain so. Value for money is the key; the wines have a fruity softness and generosity which Australian consumers tend to take for granted, but export markets value highly. Lindemans Bin 65 Chardonnay is, of course, a brand of worldwide stature.

Other White Table Wines. The acid retention ability of Colombard stands it in good stead, although it is usually used in varietal or inter-regional blends.

RED WINE STYLES

Shiraz. While there are serious misgivings about the long-term viability of Cabernet Sauvignon as a major variety for the region, those concerns do not extend to Shiraz. The region's wineries have shown time and again that they are able to produce red wine which comfortably competes in its price bracket in the wine markets of the world.

Cabernet Sauvignon. This noble variety struggles in the hot climate, a struggle exacerbated by the high yield expectations for it. Freak vintages (such as 2002) to one side, demand for and belief in the variety is declining.

Petit Verdot and Sangiovese. Petit Verdot (strangely rather than Durif) performs exceptionally well, giving wines of far greater colour and fruit depth than all of the other red varieties (Shiraz included). Sangiovese does not fall quite into the same boat, but is another variety which seems to perform above expectations.

Wineries of the Murray Darling

Deakin Estate Est. 1980

Kulkyne Way, via Red Cliffs 3496
www.deakinestate.com.au

exports to UK, US

A particularly good example of the ability of the region to produce Sauvignon Blanc, Chardonnay, Merlot, Shiraz and Cabernet Sauvignon with positive varietal character and all the structure expected in the fighting varietal arena, which both domestically and internationally offer real value for money. It was no doubt this which drew the Spanish sparkling wine producer Freixinet to acquire 60 per cent of the business, and its big brother in Coonawarra, Katnook Estate.

Signature wine: Select Shiraz

Evans & Tate Salisbury

Est. 1977
Campbell Ave, Irymple 3498
(03) 5024 6800

exports to UK, US

The volume end of the publicly listed Evans & Tate Wine Group, and which produces both the Salisbury Estate and Milburn Park labels, the latter primarily for export. Like the other major producers in the region, there is a full range of table wines based on the traditional varieties, priced at or under the magic $10 barrier. No one wine stands out above its fellows.

Signature wine: Shiraz Cabernet

Lindemans (Karadoc)

Est. 1974
Edey Rd, Karadoc via Red Cliffs 3496
www.lindemans.com

exports to UK, US

In 2004 Southcorp rationalised all of its wine production facilities, placing even greater emphasis on Penfolds Nuriootpa and Lindemans (Karadoc) processing facilities: this already enormous winery complex seemed destined to grow even bigger, but it remains to be seen where it will fit into the long-term plans of Fosters Wine Estates. It is the nerve centre for the Lindemans Bin series varietals, which have long been recognised as leaders at their price point. The technical quality of these and the other brands made at Karadoc cannot be questioned.

Signature wine: Bin 65 Chardonnay

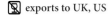

[OPPOSITE LEFT] BRUCE CHALMERS, MURRAY DARLING COLLECTION. [OPPOSITE RIGHT] ZILZIE WINES, MURRAY DARLING.

Mulcra Estate Wines Est. 2002

13 Newton Avenue, Irymple 3498 (postal)
www.mulcraestate.com.au

(at The Enjoywine Cafe, Mildura)

Samuel and Anna Andriske were part of a wave of Germans who left their homeland in the 1840s; the majority settled in the Barossa Valley, but one group was brought to Geelong. Grapegrowing was part of a mixed farming business for Andriskes, but in the wake of phylloxera the third generation (Charles Andriske) moved to Mildura. His sons established Mulcra Estate in 1933, selling grapes to the Mildara winery. Finally, the fifth generation, Marlene Andriske and son Mark, have taken the move from grapegrowing to winemaking, with 3 ha of Chardonnay, supplemented by grapes purchased from a local grower.

Signature wine: Windmill Reserve Petit Verdot

Murray Darling Collection

Est. 1989
PO Box 84, Euston 2737
www.murraydarlingcollection.com

This is the project of Bruce and Jenny Chalmers, who run the largest vine nursery propagation business in Australia, and Stefano de Pieri. As well as supplying rootlings to vignerons all over Australia, the Chalmers have established substantial plantings of a range of varietals, running from mainstream to rare. By using fine, misty, water sprays in the vineyard, the Chalmers are able to radically reduce the canopy temperatures in summer, thus achieving unexpected results with varieties which theoretically require a far cooler climate. The grapes are taken to the Mornington Peninsula, where the wines are made by Sandro Mosele.

Signature wine: Piano Del Bacino Lagrein

Robinvale Wines Est. 1976

Sea Lake Rd, Robinvale 3549
www.organicwines.com.au

exports to UK, US

Robinvale was one of the first Australian wineries to be fully accredited with the Biodynamic Agricultural Association of Australia. Most, but not all, of the wines are produced from organically grown grapes, with certain of the wines made preservative-free. Production has grown, no doubt reflecting the interest in organic and biodynamic viticulture and winemaking.

Signature wine:
Demeter No Preservatives Cabernets

Trentham Estate Est. 1988

Sturt Hwy, Trentham Cliffs 2738
www.trenthamestate.com.au

exports to UK, US

Consistent tasting notes across all wine styles since 1989 attest to the expertise of winemaker Tony Murphy, making the Trentham wines from his family vineyards. All of the wines, whether at the bottom or top end of the price range, offer great value for money. A feature of the winery is the eclectic nature of the varietals on offer, ranging from the traditional through to Viognier, Petit Verdot, Pinot Noir (the latter against all the odds) and the CSIRO-bred Taminga. The winery restaurant is also recommended.

Signature wine: Chardonnay

Zilzie Wines Est. 1999

Lot 66 Kulkyne Way,
Karadoc via Red Cliffs 3496
www.zilziewines.com

exports to UK, US

The Forbes family has been farming Zilzie Estate since 1911; a diverse range of farming activities now includes grapegrowing, with 250 ha of vineyards. Having established a position as a dominant supplier of grapes to Southcorp, Zilzie built a 16 000 tonne winery in 2000. It makes a wide range of varietal wines under three banners: Buloke Reserve at the bottom, then Zilzie Estate, and, at the top, Zilzie Show Reserve. The consistent quality of the wines (seasoned with varieties such as Tempranillo, Sangiovese and Petit Verdot) has underpinned the rapid growth of the brand.

Signature wine: Show Reserve Shiraz

NORTH WEST VICTORIA ZONE
Swan Hill ❧

Formerly known as the Mid-Murray region, Swan Hill straddles the Murray River, and is thus partly within New South Wales and partly within Victoria. Swan Hill was so named by the explorer Major Thomas Mitchell in 1836 because of the abundance of swans and other waterfowl.

Irrigated crops were established as early as 1880, but salinity and other problems caused the pioneer schemes to fail, and it was not until the 1930s that the present-day framework was established. Best's Wines is recognised as the pioneer winery; Frederick Thompson established Best's Lake Boga Vineyard and winery in 1930, then named St Andrews.

R. L. Buller of Rutherglen began purchasing grapes from the region in the 1930s, and (after the interruption of the Second World War) bought its vineyard at Beverford, 14 kilometres north of Swan Hill.

As is the case in the Murray Darling region, the number of small wineries is growing, with no obvious end in sight. Most are primarily grapegrowers, venturing into wine (via contract making) with a small portion of their total grape production. On the other side of the equation, Brown Brothers has established its 194 hectare Mystic Park vineyard, planted mainly to white varietals, using the production in its generic Victorian range of wines.

[RIGHT] WINTER MORNING, BULLERS BEVERFORD, SWAN HILL.

SWAN HILL

Latitude **35°20'S**

Altitude **60–85 m**

Heat degree days **2138**

Growing season rainfall **178 mm**

Mean January temp. **23.6°C**

Harvest **Early February to mid March**

Chief viticultural hazard **Hail**

• Melbourne

The Region

CLIMATE

Unambiguously hot and dry, the low humidity keeping the threat of downy mildew and botrytis to an absolute minimum, adding up to a low-risk environment for grapegrowing. While of little practical importance, the heat degree day summation is slightly lower than the Murray Darling, the rainfall slightly higher, with a slightly longer and slower ripening period. Harvest runs from February to mid March, with no clear break between variety maturity dates, placing maximum pressure on the wineries.

SOIL & TOPOGRAPHY

The soils are a mix of lacustrine (lake), fluviatile (river) and aeolian (wind) derived sands and clays up to 90 metres deep. It hardly needs to be said that irrigation from the Murray River is absolutely essential through the dry summer months; however, modern methods involve precise application through dripper lines. While superficially dead flat, subtle rises and falls in elevation are of significance.

PRINCIPAL GRAPE VARIETIES

Fifty-five per cent white, 45 per cent red.
In descending order:

CHARDONNAY

SHIRAZ

CABERNET SAUVIGNON

MERLOT

COLOMBARD

MUSCAT GORDO BLANCO

PETIT VERDOT

DURIF.

Wineries of Swan Hill

Andrew Peace Wines Est. 1980

Murray Valley Hwy, Piangil 3597
www.apwines.com

 exports to UK, US

The Peace family has been a major Swan Hill grapegrower since 1980, with almost 90 ha of vineyards, and moved into winemaking with the opening of a 2000 tonne, $3 million winery in 1996, producing 300 000 cases of wine a year. Andrew Peace is a Roseworthy graduate, and worked as a winemaker for 11 years in Coonawarra and elsewhere before returning to build the winery. The modestly priced wines are aimed at supermarket-type outlets in Australia and around the world.

Signature wine: Masterpeace Chardonnay

 WHITE WINE STYLES

Chardonnay. Soft, ripe peach and stonefruit flavours do not require much (if any) oak, and the wines are relatively quick-developing, both advantages in the lower-priced market sectors.

Chenin Blanc and Colombard. Specialist wine grapes such as these are progressively replacing multi-purpose (Sultana) and lesser-quality wine grapes (Gordo) in casks and generic, low-priced 750 ml bottles, lifting quality but not price.

 RED WINE STYLES

Shiraz. Even prior to the explosion in the red wine market and the international demand for Shiraz, this was the dominant premium variety. Its quality is proportional to yield, and this in turn determines whether it is sold as cask wine or in 750 ml bottle. The flavour profile is soft and fruit-sweet; the judicious use of inner staves or oak chips can produce satisfying wine at an internationally competitive price.

Cabernet Sauvignon. As is the case with the Murray Darling region, the once meteoric rise in popularity of Cabernet Sauvignon has now halted, its share of production destined to decrease in the coming decades.

Brumby Wines Est. 2001

Sandyanna, 24 Cannon Lane,
Wood Wood 3596
www.brumbywines.com.au

The owners are Stuart and Liz Brumby, who decided to plant grapes for supply to others before moving to having an increasing portion of their production from the 15 ha of Chardonnay, Cabernet Sauvignon, Shiraz and Durif vinified under their own label. The Brumbys use various contract winemakers, usually with an off-setting grape supply arrangement. Here, as elsewhere, the Durif performs heroically.

Signature wine: Durif

Bullers Beverford

Est. 1951
Murray Valley Hwy, Beverford 3590
www.buller.com.au

exports to UK

This is a parallel operation to the Calliope winery at Rutherglen, similarly owned and operated by third-generation Richard and Andrew Buller, offering table wines which in the final analysis reflect both their Riverland origin and a fairly low-key approach to style in the winery.

Signature wine: Sails Durif

Dos Rios Est. 2003

PO Box 353, Nyah 3594
www.dosrios.com.au

Bruce Hall entered the wine business as a small vineyard contract grower for McGuigan Simeon Wines. From this point on, the story goes in reverse: instead of McGuigan Simeon saying it no longer required the grapes, it purchased the vineyard outright in 2003. In the meantime Hall had hand-picked the grapes left at the end of the rows after the mechanical harvester had passed through, and had the wines (mainly Chardonnay) skilfully made by Alan Cooper of Cobaw Ridge. In 2004 he purchased a small property north-west of Swan Hill with plantings of 20-year-old Shiraz, which is to be extended by planting small areas of Viognier, Tempranillo, Durif and Merlot.

Signature wine: Chardonnay

Renewan Murray Gold Wines Est. 1989

Murray Valley Hwy, Piangil 3597
renewan@iinet.net.au

In 1990 former senior executive at Nylex Corporation in Melbourne, Jim Lewis, and artist wife Marg, retired to what is now Renewan Vineyard, set on the banks of the Murray River. It is a small business, based on 2.5 ha of estate plantings. The wines are very competently contract-made by John Ellis, who takes part of the grape production.

Signature wine: Shiraz

New South Wales

QUEENSLAND

WESTERN   PLAINS

NORTHERN

Lismore

Armidale

SLOPES

Coffs Harbour

Tamworth

SOUTH AUSTRALIA

Nyngan

Broken Hill

Port Macquarie

HASTINGS RIVER

UPPER HUNTER

Dubbo

Taree

NORTHERN RIVERS

HUNTER VALLEY

Forster-Tuncurry

MUDGEE

LOWER HUNTER

Parkes

CENTRAL

Cessnock

ORANGE

Newcastle

Orange

Bathurst

BIG   RIVERS

RANGES

SYDNEY

RIVERINA

Cowra

Griffith

HILLTOPS

Southern Highlands

COAST

Wollongong

GUNDAGAI

Goulburn

Wagga Wagga

CANBERRA DISTRICT

Nowra

J.B.T.

Canberra

SHOALHAVEN COAST

TUMBARUMBA

SOUTHERN

PERRICOOTA

VICTORIA

A.C.T

NSW

Albury

SOUTH

| | Wine Zone |
| | Wine Region |

N

PERRICOOTA

0   200 KM

Introduction ❧

The most populous state contributes little more than 27 per cent of Australia's wine, and more than three-quarters of that contribution comes from the Big Rivers Zone, for which one can in practical terms read the Riverina region.

But New South Wales was first out of the blocks. Grapevines came with the First Fleet in 1788, and were planted on the foreshores of Sydney Cove where the InterContinental Hotel now stands, producing a few bunches of grapes the following year, but then fading from history when attacked by what was called black spot.

Other pioneers were Macarthur and Blaxland. Captain John Macarthur assembled a large collection of cuttings during an 18-month trip to Europe in 1815 and 1816; not many survived, those which did formed the basis of a substantial vineyard and winery which the Macarthur family established at Camden Park. Gregory Blaxland produced the first commercial wine at Brush Farm on the banks of the Parramatta River, near the present-day suburb of Ermington. He was the first to export wine to England, in 1823, and again in 1828.

However, the father of viticulture in New South Wales was James Busby, who in the last three months of 1831 travelled across Spain and France collecting 547 'varieties of vines', including six cuttings of Shiraz from the Hill of Hermitage in the northern Rhône Valley. When DNA analysis is refined to the point of being able to identify clones of vines (it is already able to identify the parents of a given variety) it is very likely his Shiraz cuttings will be found to be the mother vines of much of Australia's best Shiraz.

Between 1815 and 1912 a viticultural map of the state had been drawn, encompassing the (present-day) Sydney metropolitan area, the Hunter Valley, Mudgee and the Riverina. That map was to remain largely unchanged until 1973, when the first vines were planted at Cowra. So it is that ten of the 14 New South Wales wine regions of today have come into existence since 1973, the majority on the western side of the Great Dividing Range but two on the coast.

The most promising candidate for the fifteenth spot is New England, in the Northern Slopes zone, highly likely to appear during the life of this book.

[PREVIOUS] KAMBERRA, CANBERRA DISTRICT.
[RIGHT] McWILLIAM'S BARWANG VINEYARD, HILLTOPS.

Zone	Page	Region	Page
HUNTER	Page 174	Lower Hunter Valley	Page 176
		Upper Hunter Valley	Page 184
CENTRAL RANGES	Page 186	Mudgee	Page 188
		Orange	Page 192
		Cowra	Page 196
SOUTHERN NEW SOUTH WALES	Page 198	Canberra District	Page 200
		Gundagai	Page 206
		Hilltops	Page 208
		Tumbarumba	Page 210
BIG RIVERS	Page 212	Riverina	Page 212
		Perricoota	Page 216
SOUTH COAST	Page 218	Shoalhaven Coast	Page 218
		Southern Highlands	Page 220
NORTHERN RIVERS	Page 222	Hastings River	Page 222
NORTHERN SLOPES	Page 224		
WESTERN PLAINS	Page 226		

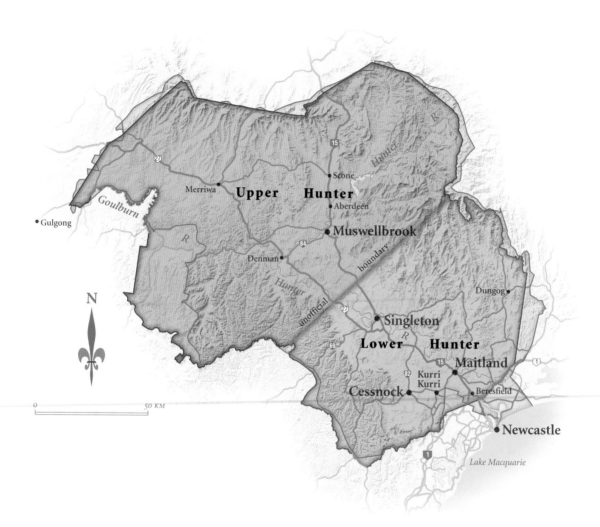

Hunter Zone ❧

Old habits die hard, as does half a century of experience. I have never been able to equate the Lower (or traditional) Hunter with the Upper Hunter. The somewhat Irish decision under the Geographical Indications legislation to call the zone the Hunter Valley, the region the Hunter, followed by a rag-bag of largely irrelevant (and yet to be finally registered) subregions has never made sense to me. So, with all due respect, I have adopted the unofficial Lower Hunter/Upper Hunter division.

It is appropriate – indeed, nigh-on inevitable – that the vinous history of the Hunter Valley should commence with James Busby, who in 1825 acquired a property halfway between Branxton and Singleton, which he named 'Kirkton' and where he installed his brother-in-law, William Kelman, as manager. The first vines were planted in 1830, but expanded to 4 hectares in 1834, no doubt with some of the vines Busby had brought from Europe the preceding year.

George Wyndham was the next to arrive in the area, and in 1830 planted 600 cuttings supplied by James Busby. Most failed to take, but when he tried again the following year the success rate soared. By 1832 there were ten small vineyards in existence, and the Hunter Valley was on its way.

In 1847 the Hunter Valley Viticultural Society was formed, and during that decade plantings increased from 80 to 200 hectares spread over 50 vineyards. Between 1866 and 1876 the Hunter Valley wine industry grew at a rate as spectacular as the boom which followed almost exactly a hundred years later. The number of wine presses increased from 116 to 339; production from 756 000 litres to 3.75 million litres; and the area under vines rose from 860 hectares to 1800 hectares. The peak appears to have been 1876, as by 1882 plantings had declined to 1630 hectares, although by and large the industry remained fairly prosperous until the economic woes of the 1890s. In the nineteenth century both Victoria and New South Wales had placed prohibitive duties on wines from other states, effectively locking out South Australia; Federation, and Section 92 of the Constitution, changed all that; and the first 50 years of the twentieth century saw the Hunter drawing in on itself.

In 1956 the Hunter Valley had only 466 hectares of vines in production, but the cycle of boom and bust was far from over. From the end of the 1960s plantings increased at a furious rate, reaching 4137 hectares by 1976. The wrong choice of soil and variety, coupled with over-production, saw the figure fall to 3169 hectares in 1983, but from the mid 1990s through the first five years of the new century the figure rose again, to 4651 hectares.

[OPPOSITE] EVANS FAMILY WINES, LOWER HUNTER VALLEY. [BELOW] McWILLIAM'S MOUNT PLEASANT, LOWER HUNTER VALLEY.

HUNTER ZONE
Lower Hunter Valley ❧

For those born and bred in Sydney, the Lower Hunter Valley is not only the greatest and the most important wine region in Australia, it is tantamount to the only region. If you come from overseas and have an interest in wine, it is a fair bet it is one of the two wine districts (the Barossa Valley being the other) you will have heard of prior to your arrival and which you propose to visit. For South Australians, it is an object of derision (with a generous dash of jealousy); for Victorians it is an area which arouses a mixture of curiosity and respect.

To a disinterested observer (if there is such a person) the most obvious characteristic is the peculiarly Australian beauty of the Valley. In no small measure this comes from the smoky blue of the Brokenback Range, rising threateningly above the nearest vineyards along Broke Road, and distantly though clearly etched as you look back from Allandale and Wilderness Roads – but wherever you are, a significant part of the landscape. Apart from the Brokenback Range, the Valley has only the most gentle undulations; the vineyards are concentrated on the southern side, and the Barrington Tops, on the northern side, are out of sight.

So there is that feeling of open, endless, timeless space so special to Australia. Under the pale blue summer sky, the dark, glistening green of the vines is a stark contrast to the patterns of straw, yellow and golden grass and the more olive tones of the gum trees. Attesting to the modest rainfall, which in any event tends to come in erratic, heavy bursts, the grass is brown through much of the year, tenuously greening in autumn and spring.

The brown landscape hints at what the statistics say loud and clear: the Hunter Valley is an unlikely place in which to grow grapes. But when vineyards were trialled across the state in the nineteenth century the situation was different. The coastal fringe (around Sydney) was too wet and too humid, and if one moved too far west, spring frosts could pose threats, even though some distinguished wines were made at Rooty Hill and Smithfield until the 1950s and 1960s. More importantly, overall soil fertility on the previously unfarmed Hunter Valley was high, and the modern diseases of downy and powdery mildew were unknown.

So it was that the Hunter Valley came to dominate viticulture in New South Wales extremely rapidly, although once again there are curious historical quirks. All the early vineyards were established well to the northeast of where they are located nowadays; it was not until the 1860s that the first vignerons came into the Rothbury and Pokolbin subregions, where many of the Lower Hunter vineyards of today are to be found.

History also reveals that at the Paris Exhibition of 1855 (which led to the 1855 classification of the great Bordeaux wines that stands to this day) James King of Irrawang Vineyard had his sparkling wine – said by the judges to have 'a bouquet, body and flavour equal to the finest champagnes' – served at the table of Napoleon III during the closing ceremony. Another fascinating snippet is that although most of the wines at the Exhibition were named by variety and vintage, H. J. Lindeman (the founder of Lindemans) produced what one can but guess to be Australia's only Lachryma Christi, far from the slopes of Mount Vesuvius.

The Hunter Valley wine industry of today is inextricably bound up with tourism. It was the wineries that brought the tourists in the first place – starting in the mid 1960s – but today more dollars are spent on tourism (meals, accommodation and so on) than on wine: the Lower Hunter Valley has no equal in Australia for the abundance of first-class accommodation, restaurants, golf courses and general tourist facilities.

It is this ready-made market that sees the cellar-door sales outlets of the wineries full from daybreak to dusk, and which provides that all-important cash flow for the small winery in particular. From the outside looking in, it is an ideal lifestyle (the reality is a little less perfect), and we will see more, rather than fewer, wineries in the future. So there is a mix of the big and the small, the new and the old, the professional and the amateur; all are geared to make the visitor welcome, and almost all succeed.

For all that, it has to be said that from a viticultural viewpoint the Hunter Valley is a difficult and often capricious place in which to grow grapes. There are larger areas of unsuitable soil (hard, acidic clay) than there are good soils, and the climate can only be described as perverse. Winter droughts are common, as is the propensity for such rain as there is to fall shortly prior to or during vintage. All things considered, it is truly remarkable that so many excellent wines (notably Semillon and Shiraz) are produced in the Hunter Valley with such regularity.

[OPPOSITE & BELOW] McWILLIAM'S MOUNT PLEASANT, LOWER HUNTER VALLEY.

Beaumont Estate

Cockfighter's Ghost*

Fordwich

CHARLTON

RD

Artillery

Firing Range

(Prohibited Ar

Wattlebrook
Vineyard

Wollombi

MILBRODALE

RD

BROKE

Catherine Vale
Vineyard

Broke Estate/
Ryan Family Wines

Brook

The Little Wine Company*

Hollyclare

ROAD

ROAD

YENGO

Broke CESSNOCK

NATIONAL

PARK

ROAD

Mount Broke Wines

WOLLOMBI

Krinklewood

DE IULIIS
1998 Semillon
HUNTER VALLEY

Sydney

Barrington Tops
National Park

Mt Royal
N.P.

Salisbury

boundary

Glendonbrook

Canyr Allyn
Wines

Dungog

Gresford

Allyn River
Wines

unofficial

Singleton

Yengo

Paterson

Clarence Town

Branxton

Seaham

Nat.

Broke

Lochinvar

Maitland

Morpeth

Pokolbin

N

Park

Cessnock

Kurri
Kurri

Beresfield

Raymond Terrac

Newcastle

0   50 KM

LOWER HUNTER VALLEY

Latitude **32°50'S**

Altitude **75 m**

Heat degree days **2070**

Growing season rainfall **530 mm**

Mean January temp. **22.7°C**

Harvest **Mid-January to early March**

Chief viticultural hazard **Heavy vintage rain**

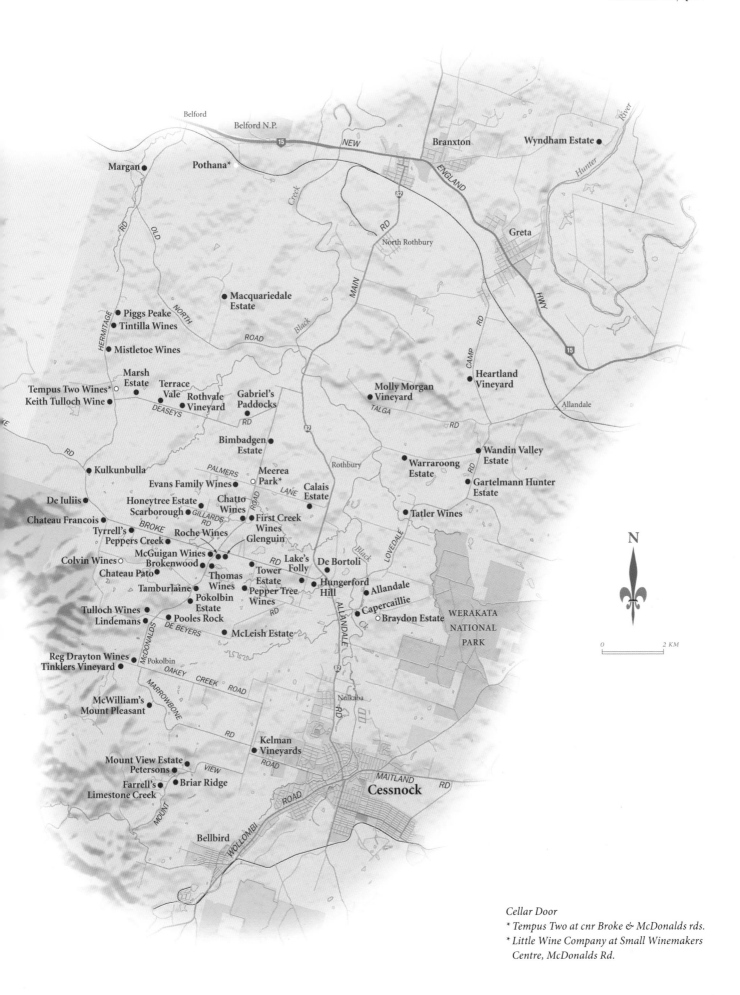

Belford

Belford N.P.

NEW

Branxton

Wyndham Estate ●

Margan ●

Pothana *

ENGLAND

Hunter River

Greta

North Rothbury

Macquariedale
Estate

Piggs Peake ●
● Tintilla Wines

Allandale

Heartland
Vineyard

● Mistletoe Wines

Molly Morgan
Vineyard

Marsh
Estate

Tempus Two Wines * ○
Keith Tulloch Wine ●

Terrace
Vale
Rothvale
Vineyard

Gabriel's
Paddocks

TALGA

Wandin Valley
Estate

DEASEYS

RD

Warraroong
Estate

Gartelmann Hunter
Estate

Bimbadgen
Estate

Kulkunbulla ●

PALMERS

Rothbury

Meerea
Park *

Evans Family Wines ●

Calais
Estate

● Tatler Wines

De Iuliis ●

Honeytree Estate ●
Scarborough ●

Chatto
Wines

First Creek
Wines
Glenguin

Chateau Francois ●

GILLARDS RD

BROKE

Roche Wines

Tyrrell's ●
Peppers Creek ●

De Bortoli

Colvin Wines ○

McGuigan Wines ●

Lake's
Folly

Brokenwood ●

Tower
Estate

Hungerford
Hill

Chateau Pato ●

Thomas
Wines

Pepper Tree
Wines

Allandale ●

Tamburlaine ●

Capercaillie ●

Pokolbin
Estate

Braydon Estate ○

WERAKATA
NATIONAL
PARK

Tulloch Wines ●
Lindemans ●

Pooles Rock ●

DE BEYERS

McLeish Estate ●

Reg Drayton Wines ●
Tinklers Vineyard ●

Pokolbin

OAKEY CREEK ROAD

Nulkaba

McWilliam's
Mount Pleasant ●

MARROWBONE

RD

Kelman
Vineyards

MAITLAND RD

Mount View Estate ●
Petersons ●

VIEW

Farrell's ●
Limestone Creek

● Briar Ridge

ROAD

Cessnock

MOUNT

WOLLOMBI

Bellbird

ROAD

N

0   2 KM

Cellar Door

* Tempus Two at cnr Broke & McDonalds rds.

* Little Wine Company at Small Winemakers
Centre, McDonalds Rd.

The Region

CLIMATE

One of the warmest, most humid and wettest climates in Australia. Of the 750 millimetres annual rainfall, 530 millimetres occurs between October and April, affecting most vintages. However, the rain, the humidity, the afternoon cloud cover and weak sea breezes all operate to reduce the impact of the heat that would otherwise seriously hamper the production of quality table wine.

SOIL & TOPOGRAPHY

The soils vary widely, from friable red duplex soils to deep friable loam soils (the Shiraz soils) to sandy alluvial flats (the Semillon soils).

PRINCIPAL GRAPE VARIETIES

Overall, 60 per cent white, 40 per cent red.
In descending order:

CHARDONNAY

SHIRAZ

SEMILLON

CABERNET SAUVIGNON

MERLOT

VERDELHO

SAUVIGNON BLANC.

[OPPOSITE & BELOW] McWILLIAM'S MOUNT PLEASANT, LOWER HUNTER VALLEY.

 WHITE WINE STYLES

Semillon is for many the great wine of the Lower Hunter. It demands time in bottle to build from a thin and vaguely grassy youth to a honeyed, nutty, buttery/toasty mouthfilling richness at 10–20 years of age.

Chardonnay started its Australia-wide reign when the late Murray Tyrrell produced the 1971 Vat 47 Pinot Chardonnay. Most Lower Hunter wineries today produce a Chardonnay; some are richer, more oaky than others, but all with a peaches-and-cream cast to their make up. By and large, they develop quickly.

Verdelho is a compliant, generously yielding variety which produces an inoffensive, medium-bodied white wine, often with a dash of sweetness, and is at its best within months of being bottled.

RED WINE STYLES

Shiraz is to Cabernet Sauvignon what Semillon is to Chardonnay. The Hunter Valley imposes its regional stamp on both red wines, and the varietal character of Shiraz bends more compliantly than does Cabernet Sauvignon to that stamp. Moreover, Shiraz makes the same transformation in bottle as Semillon, moving from an astringent, angular and spiky youth into a velvety, almost luminous maturity at 20 or even 30 years of age.

Cabernet Sauvignon. You would never confuse an old Hunter Cabernet Sauvignon with an old Bordeaux. You might well think it was an old Hunter Shiraz, however. After a hiatus of over 30 years, Cabernet Sauvignon was re-introduced to the Hunter Valley by Dr Max Lake at Lake's Folly in 1963 (along with Petit Verdot and Malbec it was relatively common in the golden years of the nineteenth century), and since that time has been planted at almost every vineyard in the valley. It produces an idiosyncratic style; some fine wines are made from it, but other (cooler) regions of Australia are more suited to the variety.

Wineries of the Lower Hunter Valley

Brokenwood Est. 1970
McDonalds Rd, Pokolbin 2321
www.brokenwood.com.au
⌷ exports to UK, US

A deservedly fashionable winery producing consistently excellent wines. The Graveyard Shiraz is one of the best Hunter reds, the unwooded Semillon a modern classic. Since 1978 it has progressively turned its attention to regions elsewhere – Beechworth, Orange, Cowra, McLaren Vale, to name a few – for varieties or styles unavailable in the Hunter Valley, but has always been careful to precisely label these wines to show their varietal and regional origins. In the interests of full disclosure, the author was one of the three founders.
Signature wine: Graveyard Shiraz

Capercaillie Est. 1995
Londons Rd, Lovedale 2325
www.capercailliewine.com.au
⌷ exports to UK

The former Dawson Estate, now owned and run by Hunter Valley veteran Alasdair Sutherland. The Capercaillie wines are very well made, with generous flavour, velvety mouthfeel and perfect balance. Following the example of Brokenwood, its fruit sources are spread across South Eastern Australia, including Orange and the Clare Valley, although the lion's share comes from the 7 ha of estate plantings in the Hunter Valley.
Signature wine: The Ghillie Shiraz

Chateau Pato Est. 1980
Thompsons Rd, Pokolbin 2321
hunterwinecountry@bigpond.com
⌷

Nicholas Paterson took over responsibility for this tiny winery following the death of father David Paterson during the 1993 vintage. The estate plantings comprise 2.5 ha of Shiraz, 1 ha of Chardonnay and 0.5 ha of Pinot Noir; most of the grapes are sold, with 300 cases of Shiraz being made into a marvellous wine. David Paterson's legacy is being handsomely guarded.
Signature wine: Shiraz

Chatto Wines Est. 2000
McDonalds Rd, Pokolbin 2325
www.chattowines.com.au
⌷

Jim Chatto spent several years in Tasmania as the first winemaker at Rosevears Estate; he then moved to the Hunter Valley to work for Monarch Winemaking Services, but has used his Tasmanian contacts to buy small parcels of Riesling and Pinot Noir, complemented by Hunter Valley Semillon and Shiraz. Possessed of a particularly good palate, he has made wines of excellent quality under the Chatto label. He was a star Len Evans Tutorial scholar and is an up-and-coming wine show judge.
Signature wine: Hunter Valley Shiraz

De Iuliis Est. 1990
21 Broke Rd, Pokolbin 2320
www.dewine.com.au
⌷ ⁌

Three generations of the De Iuliis family have been involved in the establishment of their 45 ha vineyard at Keinbah in the Lower Hunter Valley. The family acquired the property in 1986 and planted the first vines in 1990, selling the grapes from the first few vintages to Tyrrell's but thereafter retaining increasing amounts of grapes for release under the De Iuliis label. Roseworthy graduate and Len Evans Tutorial scholar, Michael De Iuliis, makes Semillon, Shiraz and Chardonnay of impressive quality.
Signature wine: Limited Release Shiraz

Keith Tulloch Wine Est. 1997
Hunter Ridge Winery,
Hermitage Rd, Pokolbin 2320
www.keithtullochwine.com.au
⌷ exports to UK, US

Keith Tulloch is a member of the Tulloch family which has played such a leading role in the Hunter Valley for over a century. Formerly with Lindemans and then Rothbury Estate, he is responsible for the production of Evans Family Wines as well as developing his own label. The only problem is the small scale of their production, like that of Jeffrey Grosset in his early days. There is the same almost obsessive attention to detail, the same almost ascetic intellectual approach, and the same refusal to accept anything but the best.
Signature wine: Semillon

Lake's Folly Est. 1963
Broke Rd, Pokolbin 2320
www.lakesfolly.com.au
⌷

Dr Max Lake founded the first of the weekend wineries to produce wines for commercial sale; it has been long revered for its Cabernet Sauvignon and thereafter its Chardonnay. Very properly, terroir and climate produce a distinct regional influence and thereby a distinctive wine style. Some find this attractive, others are less tolerant. The winery continues to enjoy an incredibly loyal clientele, with much of each year's wine selling out quickly by mail order. Only two wines are made, Chardonnay and Cabernets, the former challenging Tyrrell's Vat 47 as the region's best.
Signature wine: Chardonnay

McWilliam's Mount Pleasant
Est. 1921
Marrowbone Rd, Pokolbin 2320
www.mcwilliams.com.au
⌷ ⁌ exports to UK, US

McWilliam's Elizabeth Semillon and the glorious Lovedale Semillon are generally commercially available with four and six years of bottle age respectively and are undervalued treasures with a consistently superb show record. The three individual vineyard red wines, all based on Shiraz, together with the Maurice O'Shea memorial wines, add to the lustre of this proud name, and richly repay extended cellaring, as they come from vines ranging between 50 and 120 years old.

Signature wine: Lovedale Semillon

Margan Family Est. 1997

1238 Milbrodale Rd, Broke 2330
www.margan.com.au

⬚ ⬚ exports to UK, US

Andrew Margan entered the wine industry over 20 years ago and has covered a great deal of territory since, working as a Flying Winemaker in Europe, then for Tyrrell's. His wife Lisa, too, has had many years of experience in restaurants and marketing. They now have 46 ha of vines at their Ceres Hill homestead property at Broke, and the first stage of a 700 tonne on-site winery was completed in 1998. Wine quality is consistently good. Café Beltree is open for light meals and coffee.

Signature wine: Beltree Semillon

Petersons Est. 1971

Mount View Rd, Mount View 2325
www.petersonswines.com.au

⬚

Newcastle pharmacist Ian Peterson (and wife Shirley) was among the early followers in the footsteps of Max Lake, contributing to the Hunter Valley renaissance of the time. Grapegrowers since 1971 and winemakers since 1981, the second generation of the family, headed by Colin Peterson, now manages the business. It has been significantly expanded to include 16 ha at Mount View, a 42 ha vineyard in Mudgee (Glenesk), and an 8 ha vineyard near Armidale (Palmerston).

Signature wine: Glenesk Mudgee Cabernet Sauvignon

Thomas Wines Est. 1997

c/o The Small Winemakers Centre,
McDonalds Rd, Pokolbin 2321
www.thomaswines.com.au

⬚

Andrew Thomas came to the Hunter Valley from McLaren Vale, to join the winemaking team at Tyrrell's. After 13 years with Tyrrell's, he left to undertake contract work and to continue the development of his own winery label, a family

affair run by himself and his wife, Jo. The classic Semillon is sourced from a single vineyard owned by local grower Ken Bray, renowned for its quality, while the Shiraz is a blend of Hunter Valley and McLaren Vale.

Signature wine: Braemore Semillon

Tower Estate Est. 1999

Cnr Broke & Hall Rds, Pokolbin 2320
www.towerestatewines.com.au

⬚ ⬚ exports to UK

Tower Estate is a joint venture headed by Len Evans, featuring a luxury conference centre and accommodation. It draws upon varieties and regions which have a particular synergy, coupled with the enormous knowledge of Len Evans and the winemaking skills of Dan Dineen. The portfolio typically includes a Clare Valley Riesling, Adelaide Hills Sauvignon Blanc, Hunter Valley Semillon, Hunter Valley Chardonnay, Coonawarra Cabernet Sauvignon, Hunter Valley Shiraz, Barossa Valley Shiraz, Yarra Valley Pinot Noir, Orange Merlot and Orange Sangiovese.

Signature wine: Hunter Valley Semillon

Tyrrell's Est. 1858

Broke Rd, Pokolbin 2321
www.tyrrells.com.au

⬚ exports to UK, US

Driven first by the late Murray Tyrrell and now son Bruce, Tyrrell's has grown out of all recognition over the past 35 years. In 2003 it cleared the decks by selling its Long Flat range of wines for over $10 million, allowing it to focus on its premium, super-premium and ultra-premium wines. It has an awesome portfolio of single-vineyard Semillons released when 5–6 years old, and has long since ventured far afield from the Hunter Valley for red blend components or single varietals, with vineyards in Heathcote and McLaren Vale.

Signature wine: Vat 1 Semillon

Wyndham Estate Est. 1828

Dalwood Rd, Dalwood 2335
www.wyndhamestate.com.au

⬚ ⬚ exports to UK, US

Despite the one million-case production and Wyndham's 177-year connection with the Hunter Valley, its historic Dalwood winery is simply a cellar door, all winemaking in New South Wales having ceased. Its grape sources, too, come from here, there and everywhere, although its Show Reserve Range of Semillon, Chardonnay, Shiraz and Cabernet Merlot (which can be excellent) are principally derived from Hunter Valley and Central Ranges grapes.

Signature wine: Show Reserve Semillon

[OPPOSITE LEFT] CEILIDH. [OPPOSITE MIDDLE] JIM CHATTO. [OPPOSITE RIGHT] KEITH TULLOCH. [THIS PAGE LEFT] ANDREW THOMAS.

HUNTER ZONE
Upper Hunter Valley ❧

With the wisdom of hindsight, the 1958 decision by Penfolds to sell its Dalwood winery in the Lower Hunter Valley and establish Wybong in the Upper Hunter Valley can be seen as correct, even if some of the subsequent decisions were not. Notwithstanding that a young German settler named Carl Brecht had planted vines in 1860 at the junction of Wybong Creek and the Goulburn River, and had gone on to make wines that won gold medals at international shows throughout the 1870s, viticulture ceased in the region around 1900 to 1910, so there was effectively no viticultural experience for Penfolds to draw on. It took much trial and error by Penfolds to establish that this was white wine country first and foremost, and more particularly that the

staple red variety of the Lower Hunter – Shiraz – is basically unsuited to the area. It also became apparent that irrigation was absolutely essential, and that site (and soil) selection was as critical as it is in the Lower Hunter.

With appropriate management, site and varietal selection, grapegrowing in the Upper Hunter is economically viable – more so, indeed, than in many Lower Hunter locations. Thus, Lower Hunter wineries have become important stakeholders, either owning vineyards or as grape purchasers. But neither approach has given the Upper Hunter much focus or personality, something underlined by the continued dearth of small wineries and also by the decision not to seek recognition as a region under the Geographical Indications

legislation. The Upper Hunter seems to lie at the end of a vinous road that heads nowhere, and is thus rarely travelled. Arguably, this pretty area deserves better.

UPPER HUNTER VALLEY

Latitude **32°15'S**

Altitude **150–250 m**

Heat degree days **2170**

Growing season rainfall **400 mm**

Mean January temp. **22.3°C**

Harvest **Mid-January to early March**

Chief viticultural hazards **Vintage rain; mildew**

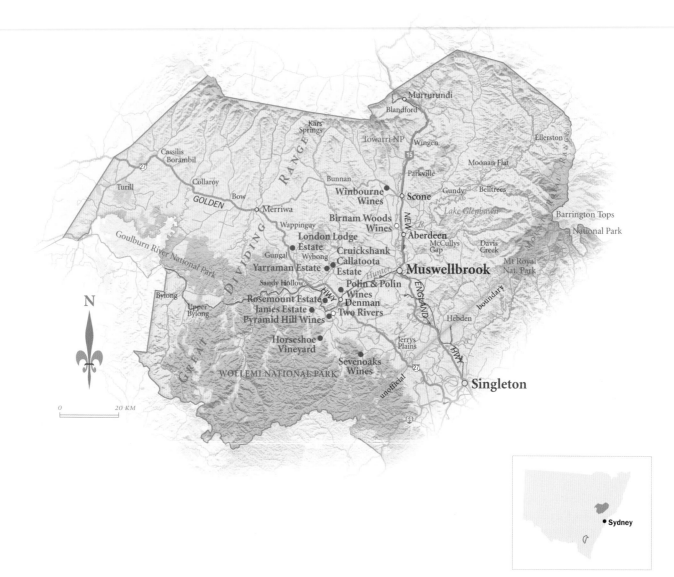

The Region

CLIMATE

The all-important difference from the Lower Hunter is the lower rainfall: 620 millimetres compared with 750 millimetres. As in the Lower Hunter, January and February are the two wettest months, with rain ever likely to interfere with vintage. The heat summation (at Muswellbrook) is even greater than that of the Lower Hunter, reflecting the lack of the afternoon sea breezes which slightly temper the latter district.

SOIL & TOPOGRAPHY

Well-drained and moderately fertile black silty loams, overlying alkaline dark clay loam, are the key to the success of the region from a viticultural standpoint.

PRINCIPAL GRAPE VARIETIES

Seventy per cent white, 30 per cent red.
In descending order:

CHARDONNAY

SEMILLON

SHIRAZ

CABERNET SAUVIGNON

VERDELHO

MERLOT

SAUVIGNON BLANC

TRAMINER.

Wineries of the Upper Hunter Valley

James Estate Est. 1971

951 Bylong Valley Way,
Baerami via Denman 2333
www.jamesestatewines.com.au

exports to UK, US

David James (chief executive and principal shareholder of James Estate) laid the base for what is now a substantial wine business with the acquisition of the former Serenella Estate in 1997. The wine portfolio is headed by Reserve Chardonnay and Reserve Shiraz; next a range of Estate varietals; and at the bottom, the Sundara range.

Signature wine: Reserve Chardonnay

WHITE WINE STYLES

Chardonnay develops relatively quickly, reaching full maturity at around three years; full bodied, soft and with honey/peach/butter flavours. Semillon Chardonnay blends exist, but Chardonnay has to be regarded as the outstanding wine of the region, Rosemount Roxburgh the icon.

Semillon is typically fleshy and soft; the wines develop more quickly than those of the Lower Hunter, peaking at 2–4 years of age, with soft, buttery fruit. Almost all wineries in the region produce a Semillon, some adding a Semillon Chardonnay blend for good measure.

RED WINE STYLES

Shiraz and Cabernet Sauvignon. Here, even more than with the white wines, cross-regional blending is commonplace. Mudgee is a major source, the Central Tablelands (Orange) potentially so, but the net is cast even wider by the larger companies, reaching all the way to South Australia.

Pyramid Hill Wines Est. 2002

194 Martindale Rd, Denman 2328
www.pyramidhillwines.com

exports to UK

A partnership between veteran viticulturist Richard Hilder, and Nicholas Adler and Caroline Sherwood, who made their mark in the international film industry before moving to Pyramid Hill in 1997. Seventy-two ha of Chardonnay, Semillon, Verdelho, Shiraz, Merlot, Cabernet Sauvignon and Ruby Cabernet have been established. Most of the grapes are sold to leading makers, but part has been very competently contract-made at Monarch Winemaking Services by Jim Chatto.

Signature wine: Semillon

Rosemount Estate Est. 1969

Rosemount Rd, Denman 2328
www.rosemountestate.com

exports to UK, US

Rosemount Estate achieved a miraculous balancing act, maintaining wine quality while presiding over an ever-expanding empire and dramatically increasing production, covering all the main and some secondary varietals, either South East Australian blends or special single-region wines. The wines were consistently of excellent value; all had real character and individuality; not a few were startlingly good. The outcome was the merger with Southcorp in March 2001; what seemed to be a powerful and synergistic move turned out to be little short of a disaster, and directly led to the acquisition of Southcorp by Fosters/Beringer Blass in 2005.

Signature wine: Roxburgh Chardonnay

Yarraman Estate Est. 1958

Yarraman Rd, Wybong 2333
www.yarramanestate.com

exports to UK, US

This is the oldest winery and vineyard in the Upper Hunter, established in 1958 as Penfolds Wybong Estate; it was acquired by Rosemount in 1974 and retained until 1994. During 1999–2001 a new winery and storage area was built; after hitting financial turbulence, Yarraman was acquired by a small group of Sydney businessmen. Management has been stabilised, and a wide spread of varietal wines are released under three labels, first Sensus, next the cheaper Black Cypress range, thirdly the higher-priced Classic Hunter range.

Signature wine: Classic Hunter Merlot

Central Ranges Zone

The three regions of the zone – Mudgee, Orange and Cowra – run from north to south along the western slopes of the Great Dividing Range. Orange is by far the coolest of the three, Cowra by far the warmest; elevation is the key to this apparent paradox. Mudgee is by far the oldest, with a continuous history of winemaking stretching back to the mid nineteenth century; Orange is the most recent, and arguably the most exciting.

There is a considerable tract of north to south land to the west of the regions, still with some elevation, and an equally large chunk east of Orange and Cowra, high in the Great Dividing Range. Zones being what they are, the wineries falling in these areas outside the regions are a rather untidy gaggle; one is tiny but very old (Chateau Champsaur), others newer, either in very warm or decidedly cool climates.

GEESE & GOSLINGS AT JARRETTS OF ORANGE.

Wineries of the Central Ranges Zone

Bell River Estate Est. 1974
Mitchell Hwy, Neurea 2820
www.bellriverestate.com.au

Situated 15 km south of Wellington, Bell River Estate was formerly known as Markeita Cellars, the name change due to its purchase by Michael and Sandra Banks. They have 2.5 ha of Grenache, Cabernet Sauvignon, Shiraz and Muscat and, as well as producing Bell River Estate wines, offer bottling, contract winemaking and viticultural services.
Signature wine: Shiraz

Bunnamagoo Estate Est. 1995
Bunnamagoo, Rockley 2795 (postal)
www.bunnamagoowines.com.au

Bunnamagoo Estate (on one of the first land grants in the region) is situated near the historic town of Rockley, itself equidistant to the south of Bathurst and the west of Oberon, in an unequivocally cool climate. Here a 7 ha vineyard planted to Chardonnay, Merlot and Cabernet Sauvignon has been established by Paspaley Pearls, a famous name in the pearl industry. The stylish wines are contract-made.
Signature wine: Chardonnay

Chateau Champsaur Est. 1866
Wandang Lane, Forbes 2871
(02) 6852 3908

No, the establishment date of 1866 is correct. In that year Frenchmen Joseph Bernard Raymond and Auguste Nicolas took up a 130 ha selection and erected a large wooden winery and cellar, with production ranging up to 360 000 litres a year in its heyday. They named it Champsaur after Raymond's native valley in France, and it is said to be the oldest French winery in the Southern Hemisphere. For some time it traded as Lachlan Valley Wines, but under the ownership of Pierre Dalle has reverted to its traditional name and French ownership.
Signature wine: Shiraz

Monument Vineyard Est. 1998
Cnr Escort Way & Manildra Rd, Cudal 2864
www.monumentvineyard.com.au

The joint venture of five mature-age students at Charles Sturt University, successful in their own professions, who decided to develop a substantial vineyard on a scale that they could not individually afford, but could collectively. After a lengthy search, a large property at Cudal was identified, with ideal terra rossa basalt-derived soil over a limestone base. The property now has 210 ha of 23 varieties in all, as a result of progressive planting since 1998.
Signature wine: Hospital Hill Shiraz Viognier

Mount Panorama Winery
Est. 1991
117 Mountain Straight,
Mount Panorama, Bathurst 2795
mountpanoramawinery@bigpond.com

For obvious marketing reasons, Mount Panorama Winery makes full use of its setting – on Mountain Straight after 'Hell Corner' on the inside of the famous motor racing circuit. All the winemaking is done on-site, from picking and using the hand-operated basket press through to bottling, labelling, etc. It is gradually extending both the size and scope of the cellar-door facilities to take advantage of the tourist opportunities of the site, in the meantime selling part of its Chardonnay crop to Brokenwood (in the Hunter Valley).
Signature wine: Unwooded Chardonnay

Winburndale Est. 1998
116 St Anthonys Creek Rd, Bathurst 2795
www.winburndalewines.com.au
exports to US

Michael Burleigh and family acquired the 200 ha Winburndale property in September 1998. One hundred and sixty ha is forest, to be kept as a nature reserve; three separate vineyards, each with its own site characteristics, have been planted under the direction of viticulturist Mark Renzaglia. The winery paddock has 2.5 ha of Shiraz facing due west at an altitude of 800–820 m; the south paddock, with north and north-west aspects, varying from 790–810 m, comprises Chardonnay (1.2 ha), Shiraz (1 ha) and Cabernet Sauvignon (3.5 ha). The home paddock is the most level, with a slight north aspect, and with 1.2 ha each of Merlot and Cabernet Franc. The wines are contract-made by David Lowe at Mudgee.
Signature wine: Solitary Shiraz

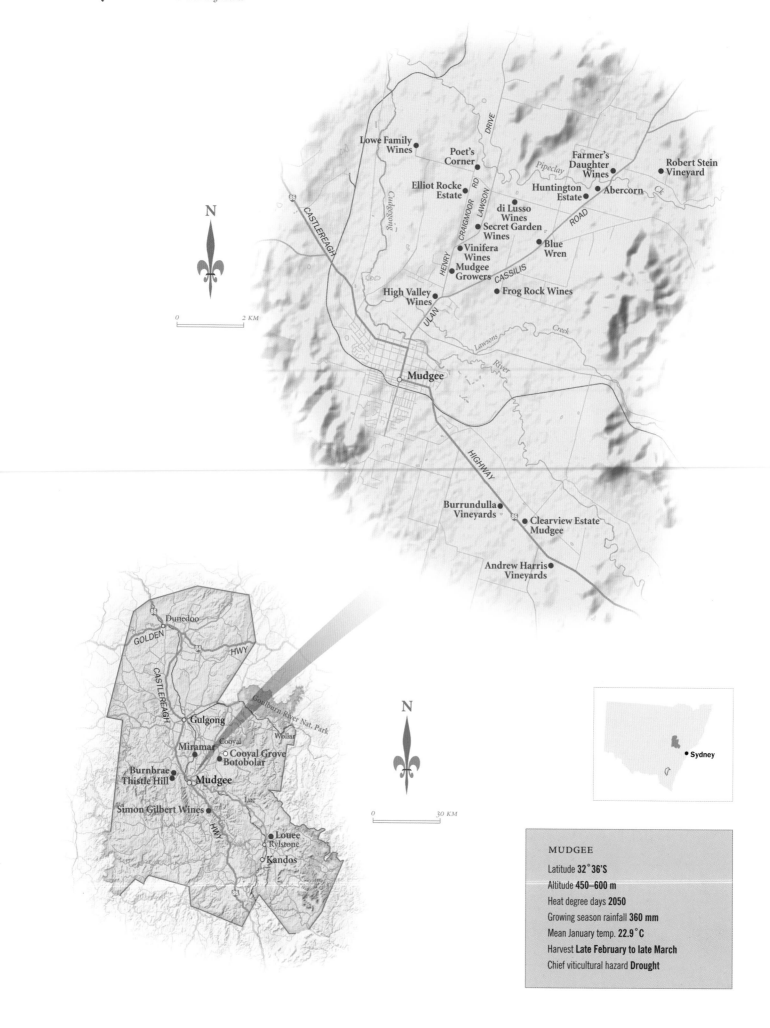

MUDGEE

Latitude **32°36'S**

Altitude **450–600 m**

Heat degree days **2050**

Growing season rainfall **360 mm**

Mean January temp. **22.9°C**

Harvest **Late February to late March**

Chief viticultural hazard **Drought**

CENTRAL RANGES ZONE
Mudgee ✿

Mudgee has its own particular history. Three German families – Roth, Kurtz and Buchholz – were instrumental in establishing vines from 1858, with the descendants of the first two carrying on viticulture for a century and keeping the tradition alive when all others had abandoned it. The next event of importance was the discovery of gold in 1872. This was nowhere near on the scale of Victoria's gold rush, but was enough to bring people and prosperity to the district until the great bank crash of 1893.

Then it was the turn of the Italian-born and -trained surgeon Dr Thomas Fiaschi, who not only served Australia well in war but became head of Sydney Hospital. Although his vineyard and winery continued in production until his death in 1927, and Craigmoor, founded by Adam Roth in 1858, survived until the renaissance of the 1960s, from the 1920s onwards the 55 vineyards which had existed in 1893 slowly dwindled. Even when the region's renaissance came, it was essentially driven by a few energetic enthusiasts.

Both through the circumstances of relatively small-scale winemaking and the softly beautiful and intimate nature of much of the scenery – the outer rim of hills providing a sense of security, and the smaller hills within the perimeter creating mini-vistas and valleys of their own – Mudgee has always seemed an especially friendly and welcoming place to visitors. Indeed, the Aboriginal people who lived there gave it the name Mudgee, meaning 'nest in the hills'.

There are two large wineries in the region. The first is Montrose, built in 1974, and acquired by Orlando Wyndham in the 1980s. In 1997 it closed its Hunter Valley winery, and centralised its regional winemaking at Montrose, which sends the wines to the Barossa Valley for bottling, packaging and distribution.

The second is the state-of-the-art $20 million Simon Gilbert winery, recently recapitalised and under the management of former Southcorp senior executives. This leaves the many small estate-based winemakers to get on with their business.

It is no-frills red wine country first and foremost, with the staples of Shiraz and Cabernet Sauvignon leading the way; Merlot, too, is a long-term resident, along with three Italian varieties – Sangiovese, Barbera and Nebbiolo.

If you live in Sydney, and want to get away from it all, Mudgee is the place to go.

FROG ROCK, MUDGEE.

The Region

CLIMATE

Situated as it is on the western slopes of the Great Dividing Range, Mudgee has a very different climate from its neighbour on the other (coastal) side, the Hunter Valley. Spring frosts and cold nights delay budburst; rainfall and humidity are lower; sunshine hours are greater; and irrigation is essential on all but the most favoured sites. The summer and autumn days are very warm; while harvest is four weeks behind the Hunter Valley, this is by no means a cool region.

SOIL & TOPOGRAPHY

The most common soils are similar or identical to those found in many – indeed, the majority of – Australian wine districts: slightly acidic loam or sandy loam topsoils over neutral clay subsoils. These brownish-coloured soils are quite friable and moderately fertile, and both surface and subsoils are relatively well drained.

PRINCIPAL GRAPE VARIETIES

Seventy-five per cent red, 25 per cent white. In descending order:

SHIRAZ

CABERNET SAUVIGNON

CHARDONNAY

MERLOT

SEMILLON.

🍇 WHITE WINE STYLES

Chardonnay is the best performer, consistently producing good wine. The flavours are usually in the peach/melon/fig spectrum, but sometimes citrus/grapefruit characters emerge, particularly where the maker employs barrel-ferment techniques. The wines do go on to develop into rich, regional, honeyed white burgundy styles.

Semillon is something of a dark horse, but can be eerily similar to young Hunter Valley Semillon at its best, and matures slowly but surely.

🍇 RED WINE STYLES

Cabernet Sauvignon makes some of Mudgee's best wines, usually as a 100 per cent varietal, but sometimes blended with Merlot or with Shiraz (Rosemount's superb Mountain Blue is an iconic Shiraz Cabernet blend). The wines have tremendous depth of colour, and hold their purple-red hues for longer than those of the Hunter, turning brick-red at seven to ten years of age. The generous flavours reflect the warm climate: a melange of tastes of red berry, dark chocolate and (sometimes) eucalypt/peppermint; the tannins balanced by the fruit generosity. Well-made wines demand five years' cellaring, and will usually profit from ten or more.

Shiraz. The style of Mudgee Shiraz has changed over the past 15 or so years; once distinctively leathery and earthy – rather like old-fashioned Hunter Valley Shiraz – it is now richer, riper and fuller, with an abundance of blackberry and plum fruit, and vies with Cabernet Sauvignon in producing the region's best grapes.

Sangiovese, Barbera and Nebbiolo. Some of the oldest plantings of these varieties in Australia (30 years plus) are to be found in the Montrose Vineyards, a tribute to Montrose's Italian-born founders.

Wineries of Mudgee

Abercorn Est.1996
Cassilis Rd, Mudgee 2850
www.abercornwine.com.au

 exports to UK

Former journalist Tim, and wife Connie, Stevens acquired the 25-year-old Abercorn Vineyard in 1996, admirably located next door to Huntington Estate, which they acquired in 2006. It was in a run-down condition when they took possession, and their hard work has paid big dividends. Tim Stevens also taught himself the art of fine winemaking, and Abercorn has consistently produced high-quality wines under the Stevens' ownership. The house specialties are Shiraz, Shiraz Cabernet and Cabernet Sauvignon, but it also produces fine Chardonnay.

Signature wine: A Reserve Shiraz

Andrew Harris Vineyards
Est.1991
Sydney Rd, Mudgee 2850
www.andrewharris.com.au

 exports to US

Andrew and Deb Harris moved quickly after purchasing a 300 ha sheep station south-east of Mudgee in 1991. The first 6 ha of vineyard were planted in that year and have since been expanded to 106 ha. A portion of the grape production is sold to others, but production of a core range of mainstream varietal wines under the Andrew Harris label has risen significantly in recent years to over 60 000 cases. There is now a spread of price and quality, so some care is needed in choosing the wines.

Signature wine: Shiraz

Botobolar Est.1971
89 Botobolar Rd, Mudgee 2850
www.botobolar.com

 exports to UK

One of the first organic vineyards in Australia, with present owner Kevin Karstrom continuing the practices established by founder Gil Wahlquist. Preservative Free Dry White and Dry Red extend the organic practice of the vineyard to the winery. Rain Goddess White, Rain Goddess Red, The King, The Saviour (both Cabernet Shiraz blends) give another insight into Kevin Karstrom's sense of humour in the face of prolonged drought; Marsanne is an estate-grown specialty.

Signature wine: Special Release Cabernet Sauvignon

[OPPOSITE LEFT] ED TURNER, FROG ROCK, MUDGEE.
[OPPOSITE RIGHT] POET'S CORNER, MUDGEE.

Elliot Rocke Estate Est.1999
Craigmoor Rd, Mudgee 2850
www.elliotrockeestate.com.au

Elliot Rocke Estate has 24 ha of vineyards dating back to 1987, when the property was known as Seldom Seen. Plantings comprise Semillon, Shiraz, Chardonnay, Merlot, Cabernet Sauvignon and Traminer, and contract winemaking by Jim Chatto and Greg Silkman at Monarch Winemaking Services in the Hunter Valley has produced a full range of well-balanced and structured varietal wines.

Signature wine: Mudgee Merlot

Frog Rock Est.1973
Edgell Lane, Mudgee 2850
www.frogrockwines.com

 exports to UK, US

Frog Rock was established over 30 years ago by leading Sydney chartered accountant Rick Turner. There are now 60 ha of vineyard, with 22 ha each of Shiraz and Cabernet Sauvignon, and much smaller plantings of Chardonnay, Semillon, Merlot, Petit Verdot and Chambourcin. The wines are competently contract-made by David Lowe, the Old Vine series ever reliable.

Signature wine: Old Vine Semillon

Huntington Estate Est.1969
Cassilis Rd, Mudgee 2850
www.huntingtonestate.com.au

The remarkable Roberts family members had a passion for wine which was equalled only by their passion for music, with the Huntington Music Festival a major bi-annual event. The wines are seldom exported; almost all are sold via cellar door and mailing list. Shiraz and Cabernet Sauvignon, deep in colour, rich in flavour and long of life are the principal refrain, made under various non-repeating Bin Numbers and Special Reserve labels. The Semillons, too, age with utmost conviction. Incoming owners Tim and Connie Stevens intend to keep its separate identity intact.

Signature wine: Special Reserve Shiraz

Lowe Family Wines Est.1987
Tinja Lane, Mudgee 2850
www.lowewine.com.au

 exports to UK

Former Rothbury winemaker David Lowe and Jane Wilson have consolidated their operations in Mudgee, moving back from the prior cellar door in the Hunter Valley. As if to make sure that life is not too simple, they have started a new Mudgee business, Mudgee Growers, situated at the historic Fairview winery.

Signature wine: Mudgee Reserve Shiraz

Poet's Corner Est.1858
Craigmoor Rd, Mudgee 2850
www.poetscornerwines.com

 exports to UK, US

The Poet's Corner cellar door is located in one of the oldest wineries in Australia to remain in more or less continuous production until the 1990s: Craigmoor (as it was previously known) was built by Adam Roth in 1858/1860; Adam's grandson Jack Roth ran the winery until the early 1960s. It is the public face for Poet's Corner, Montrose and Craigmoor wines, all of which are made at the Montrose winery, which does not have a cellar door facility of its own. The Montrose and Poet's Corner wines offer exceptional value for money; it is to be hoped they continue to do so.

Signature wine: Shiraz

Secret Garden Wines Est.2000
241 Henry Lawson Drive, Mudgee 2850
(02) 6373 3874

Owned by Ian and Carol McRae, and a sister operation to their main business, Miramar Wines. Estate plantings consist of 14 ha of Shiraz, Cabernet Sauvignon and Chardonnay. The wines are made at Miramar; the cellar door is open on-site at Secret Garden. The property is only 5 km from the town of Mudgee on Henry Lawson Drive and also fronts Craigmoor Road, giving it a prime position in the so-called 'golden triangle'.

Signature wine: Eljamar Shiraz

Simon Gilbert Wines Est.1993
1220 Sydney Rd, Mudgee 2850
www.simongilbertwines.com.au

 exports to UK

The late 2004 arrival of high-profile, ex-Southcorp senior executives David Coombe as chairman and Paul Pacino as chief executive has seen a complete restructuring of this $20 million, 5000 tonne winery. The wines, with new products being introduced, continue to be sourced from the Central Ranges regions of New South Wales, including Orange, Mudgee and Cowra. The winery will continue to act both as a contract maker for others, and, of course, on its own behalf.

Signature wine: Card Series Shiraz

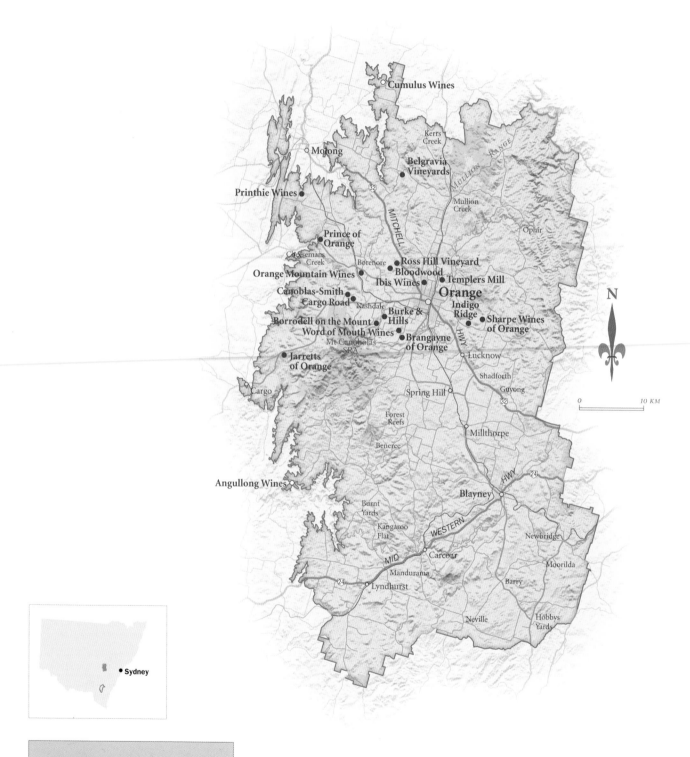

Cumulus Wines

Kerrs
Creek

Molong

Belgravia
Vineyards

MULLION RANGE

Mullion
Creek

MITCHELL

Printhie Wines

Ophir

Prince of
Orange

Cheesemans
Creek

Borenore   Ross Hill Vineyard
Orange Mountain Wines   Bloodwood
Ibis Wines   Templers Mill

Canoblas-Smith   Orange
Cargo Road   Nashdale   Indigo
Burke &   Ridge   Sharpe Wines
Borrodell on the Mount   Hills   of Orange
Word of Mouth Wines   Brangayne   HWY
Mt Canobolas   of Orange
SRA   Lucknow

Jarretts   Shadforth
of Orange   Guyong

Cargo   Spring Hill   32

Millthorpe

Forest
Reefs

Benerée

Angullong Wines   HWY   24

Blayney

Burnt
Yards

Kangaroo   WESTERN
Flat   Newbridge

MID   Moorilda
Carcoar
Mandurama   Barry
24   Lyndhurst

Neville   Hobbys
Yards

N

0   10 KM

● Sydney

ORANGE

Latitude **33°15'S**

Altitude **600–900 m**

Heat degree days **1200–1309**

Growing season rainfall **440 mm**

Mean January temp. **19.9°C**

Harvest **Mid-March to early May**

Chief viticultural hazards **Spring frost; birds**

CENTRAL RANGES ZONE

Orange ❧

Initially known as the Central Highlands, the Orange region has long been an important orchard area, producing apples, pears and cherries for both local and domestic markets. An experimental viticulture station was established at nearby Molong in the 1940s, but vines were first planted commercially in 1980 (at Bloodwood Estate). The region is one of few to have its boundaries dictated entirely by topography and altitude (Adelaide Hills is another), in this instance the 600 metres contour line. It is dominated by Mount Canobolas, which provides the high-altitude slopes and hence the cool climate; the volcanic basalt from which the soils have evolved; and the spectacular panoramic views which many of the vineyards enjoy.

Vineyard and winery development have gone along two quite different pathways. All but one of the estate wineries are small, mostly family-owned and run. These have come steadily in the footsteps of Bloodwood, although the pace quickened in the latter half of the 1990s and the first five or so years of the current century. The one slightly unusual winery in the small group is Templer's Mill, part of the University of Sydney's Orange campus.

The other, radically different, is the very large development previously known as Cabonne or Reynolds, and now called Cumulus. Reynolds was originally financed by a tax investment scheme, which saw the planting of over 500 hectares of vineyards and the erection of a 14 000 tonne capacity winery, involving the expenditure of tens of millions of dollars. The wines, made under the direction of Jon Reynolds, were of very good quality and excellent value, but the venture fell foul of the Commissioner of Taxation and (one suspects) overly ambitious export plans to the US.

In 2004 the assets of Reynolds were acquired by an international investment consortium, and Philip Shaw, ex-chief winemaker at Rosemount and Southcorp, was hired as chief winemaker and winery manager. In accepting the position, he was effectively putting his money where his mouth is, for he had already developed a personal vineyard in the region planted, inter alia, to Merlot.

There is now enough wine history to affirm that this is indeed a cool region, with a consistent elegance and fine-boned intensity across all styles. The one bugbear comes from the name: producers are increasingly putting the word 'region' after 'Orange', particularly where the wines are headed for the export market. The ambiguity is all too obvious.

[RIGHT] BRANGAYNE OF ORANGE.

The Region

CLIMATE

The climate is dependent on altitude: within 60 kilometres of the town of Orange, one can find viticultural climates varying from very hot (Cowra at just over 2000 heat degree days) to the cold 1200 heat degree day upper slopes of Mount Canobolas (which rises to 1396 metres). Overall, mild to warm midsummer temperatures, seldom rising above 32°C, are offset by cool to very cool nights during the growing season. The high ultra-violet light levels at low temperatures are also highly beneficial for ripening and flavour development. Wind is both friend and foe, helping reduce the major climatic threat of spring frosts, but interfering with fruit set on sensitive varieties such as Merlot.

SOIL & TOPOGRAPHY

The lovely, undulating hilly country is of fundamental importance in determining site selection. Reflecting the different geological ages of the parent rocks, the soils fall into four main groups: well-drained, friable, deep red-brown clays (derived from basalt) found on Mount Canobolas; deep-red-brown/yellow-brown clay loams of mixed origin, including volcanic ash; red-brown podzolic medium-vigour clay loam over a medium clay and shale base interspersed with gravel; and, finally, at lower elevation patches of terra rossa associated with visible limestone.

PRINCIPAL GRAPE VARIETIES

Seventy-five per cent red, 25 per cent white. In descending order:

SHIRAZ

CABERNET SAUVIGNON

CHARDONNAY

MERLOT

SAUVIGNON BLANC

RIESLING

PINOT NOIR

PINOT GRIS.

[ABOVE & RIGHT] PRINCE OF ORANGE.

🍷 WHITE WINE STYLES

Chardonnay has a neat balance between the fleshy, warm-climate wine and the ultra-fine, slow-developing citrus-and-cashew style of very cool climates. Melon, citrus and nectarine flavours are set in a wine of medium weight and pleasantly firm acidity, responding well to, but not relying on, the subtle use of oak and malolactic fermentation.

Sauvignon Blanc offers intense tropical fruit flavours that develop when grown at high elevation (above 750 metres). The more vigorous soils also produce grapes with a herbaceous character that complements the strong fruit flavours.

🍷 RED WINE STYLES

Shiraz produces wines with a near-perfect balance between red cherry and blackberry fruit on the one hand, and more spicy notes on the other. The style lends itself to the incorporation of a little Viognier, but regardless of this, the key word is elegance.

Cabernet Sauvignon and Merlot flavours run the gamut of the sappy/briary/herbaceous/earthy spectrum (though with some dark berry sweetness, of course); are of medium weight and body; and have fine tannins, all-in-all quite European in their structure. They can be effectively blended with wines from warmer parts of the Central Ranges.

Pinot Noir is produced in limited quantities, but given the right combination of site and vintage, can surprise.

Wineries of Orange

Belgravia Vineyards Est. 2003

Belgravia Rd, Orange 2800
www.belgravia.com.au

 exports to UK

Belgravia is an 1800 ha mixed farming property (sheep, cattle and vineyards), 20 km north of Orange. The first plantings took place in 1996, and there are now 180 ha contracted to Fosters Wine Estates, and 10 ha of Chardonnay, Viognier, Semillon, Shiraz, Merlot and Cabernet Sauvignon set aside for the Belgravia wine brand. The property also has a B&B cottage, and is presently restoring 300 ha of grassy whitebox woodland. The contract-made wine quality is exemplary.
Signature wine: Woodland Shiraz
Merlot Cabernet Sauvignon

Bloodwood Est. 1980

4 Griffin Rd, Orange 2800
www.bloodwood.com.au

exports to UK

Owners Rhonda and Stephen Doyle (winemaker at the on-site winery) are two of the pioneers of the Orange district. Bloodwood has done best with elegant but intense Chardonnay and the intermittent releases of super-late-harvest Ice Riesling, but seldom misses the mark with its other wines, notably Dry Riesling and the humorously named Big Men in Tights Rosé.
Signature wine: Chardonnay

Borrodell on the Mount

Est. 1998
Lake Canobolas Rd, Orange 2800
www.borrodell.com.au

Barry Gartrell and Gaye Stuart-Williams have planted 4 ha of Pinot Noir, Sauvignon Blanc, Pinot Meunier, Gewürztraminer and Chardonnay abutting their cherry, plum and heritage apple orchard and truffiere, ten minutes' drive from Orange, and adjacent to Lake Canobolas, at an altitude of 1000 m. The wines, contract made by French Flying Winemaker Chris Derrez, have been consistent medal winners, and are served in the two modern, self-contained three-bedroom homes on the property.
Signature wine: Winemaker's
Daughter Gewürztraminer

Brangayne of Orange Est. 1994

49 Pinnacle Rd, Orange 2800
www.brangayne.com

exports to UK

Orchardists Don and Pamela Hoskins diversified into grapegrowing in 1994 and now have 25 ha of vineyards. With viticultural consultancy advice from Dr Richard Smart and skilled contract winemaking, Brangayne made an extraordinarily auspicious debut, and the quality of subsequent vintages has fully lived up to early expectations for Chardonnay, Sauvignon Blanc, Pinot Noir and Cabernet Sauvignon. All the wines have the elegance this cool region can bestow, but without compromising intensity of flavour and complexity.
Signature wine: The Tristan (Cabernet blend)

Burke & Hills Est. 1999

Cargo Rd, Lidster 2800
doug@burkeandhills.com.au

A business built around the selection of a steeply sloping, frost-free, north-facing slope at 940 m on Mount Lidster; 10 ha of classic varieties, including a mix of the best clones of Pinot Noir; retaining former Gevrey Chambertin-cum-Flying Winemaker Christophe Derrez; the erection of a 200 tonne capacity winery to supplement cash flow by undertaking contract winemaking; and the running of the Lakeside Café at Lake Canobolas, 2 km from the winery … All point to a plan with the objective, in Doug Burke's words, 'Don't go broke.'
Signature wine: Orange Chardonnay

Canobolas-Smith Est. 1986

Boree Lane, off Cargo Rd,
Lidster via Orange 2800
canobolas.smith@netwit.net.au

 exports to US

Canobolas-Smith has established itself as one of the leading Orange district wineries with its distinctive blue wrap-around labels, and a decidedly eclectic range of wines, ranging from mainstream varietals through to a Chambourcin Cabernet blend, Shine Botrytis Chardonnay, and others. The two mainstays are outstanding Chardonnay and Alchemy (a Cabernet blend).
Signature wine: Chardonnay

Cargo Road Wines Est. 1983

Cargo Rd, Orange 2800
www.cargoroadwines.com.au

The original 2.5 ha vineyard was planted in 1983 by Roseworthy graduate John Swanson, which included Zinfandel 15 years ahead of its time. The property was acquired in 1997 by Charles Lane, James Sweetapple (the winemaker) and Brian Walters; since then they have rejuvenated the original vineyard, and made additional plantings of Zinfandel, Sauvignon Blanc and Cabernet.
Signature wine: Orange Sauvignon Blanc

Cumulus Wines Est. 1995

PO Box 41, Cudal 2864
www.cumuluswines.com.au

exports to UK, US

Cumulus Wines is the reborn Reynolds Wines, with Philip Shaw, previously head of winemaking for both Rosemount and Southcorp, as the Chief Executive Officer, and Philip Dowell as winemaker, returning to Australia after six years with Canada's largest wine group, Vincor/Iniskillin. This is an asset-rich business, with over 500 ha of vineyards planted to all the mainstream varieties. The quirky, striking labels will undoubtedly attract attention on the retail shelves of the world.
Signature wine: Climbing Chardonnay

Jarretts of Orange Est. 1995

Annangrove Park, Cargo Rd, Orange 2800
jarrettswines@colourcity.com

Justin and Pip Jarrett have established a 140 ha vineyard, planted to Chardonnay, Cabernet Sauvignon, Shiraz, Sauvignon Blanc, Merlot, Pinot Noir, Riesling, Marsanne, Cabernet Franc and Verdelho. As well as managing this vineyard, they provide management and development services to growers of another 120 ha in the region. Most of the grapes are sold, with a few thousand cases of modestly priced but stylish and fragrant wine made at Tamburlaine in the Hunter Valley.
Signature wine: Sauvignon Blanc

Prince of Orange Est. 1996

'Cimbria', The Escort Way, Borenore 2800
prince@netconnect.com.au

Harald and Coral Brodersen purchased the 40 ha Cimbria property in 1990, and planted 3 ha of Sauvignon Blanc and 2 ha of Cabernet Sauvignon in 1996, followed by more recent and smaller plantings of Merlot, Viognier, Shiraz and Semillon. The name was inspired by the link between Thomas Mitchell, Surveyor General of New South Wales, who served during the Peninsular Wars against Napoleon alongside Willem, Prince of Orange. It was Mitchell who named the town Orange in honour of his friend. The stylish wines are made by Monarch Winemaking Services in the Hunter Valley.
Signature wine: Sauvignon Blanc

CENTRAL RANGES ZONE

Cowra ❧

Given that Cowra is the southernmost region in the Central Ranges Zone, one might think it is the coolest, when in fact it is the warmest. The answer lies in its lower altitude, and its open front to warm winds that blow from central Australia.

Until 1973, when Cowra Estate planted the first vines in the region, Cowra was best known as the site of Australia's prisoner of war camp for Japanese soldiers and citizens in the Second World War. It was also the scene for a futile mass escape, and today has an attractive memorial garden and museum recording the events of those days.

To this day, the rolling hills with their sweeping vistas are predominantly given over to grazing. But since 1973, Cowra has grown enormously in importance as a wine region,

even if growth has come in sporadic bursts. The 1990s saw a major expansion, with larger companies (notably Rothbury and Orlando's Richmond Grove) and boutiques such as Brokenwood aggressively planting vineyards. It is primarily a white wine region able to produce generous yields with the aid of irrigation.

The vineyards are situated on gentle slopes within a broad valley cut into the western side of the Great Dividing Range by the head waters of the Lachlan and Belubula rivers, which converge into the Lachlan at Gooloogong, flowing into the Murrumbidgee River north of Balranald.

It would be idle to pretend that this is a premium region, or that it has more than one string to its bow. Chardonnay is its specialty;

it struggles with the remainder, none more so than its red wines, with only Shiraz holding the line. The official statistics show that growers would prefer to see a 75 per cent white, 25 per cent red split in lieu of the present representation. For all that, its production is substantial, even if most is sold to producers outside the region, and quietly blended away.

JOHN GEBER, COWRA ESTATE, COWRA.

COWRA

Latitude **33°57'S**

Altitude **300–380 m**

Heat degree days **2130**

Growing season rainfall **370 mm**

Mean January temp. **23.5°C**

Harvest **Early March to early Arpil**

Chief viticultural hazard **Spring frost**

Cellar Door
* Windowrie Estate at the Mill, Cowra.

The Region

CLIMATE

The climate is hot and dry, with the mean January temperature variously recorded between 23.5˚C and 24.4˚C, significantly above that of Cessnock (Hunter Valley) or Mudgee. Growing season rainfall is relatively high, but relative humidity is low, reflecting the continental nature of the climate. Spring frosts mean appropriate site selection is required.

SOIL & TOPOGRAPHY

The soils are those most commonly found throughout south-east Australia: brownish loamy sand to clay loam on the surface, with red clay subsoils. They are moderately acidic, and likewise moderately fertile.

PRINCIPAL GRAPE VARIETIES

Overall, 58 per cent white, 42 per cent red. In descending order:

CHARDONNAY

SHIRAZ

SEMILLON

CABERNET SAUVIGNON

VERDELHO

MERLOT

SAUVIGNON BLANC.

 WHITE WINE STYLES

Chardonnay. Invariably generously flavoured and, in most instances, relatively quick maturing. However, Petaluma Chardonnays from the late 1970s and the freak Rothbury Estate 1981 Cowra Chardonnay (in particular) demonstrated a largely unrecognised capacity to develop into ultra-rich, golden, honey and buttered-toast styles. In younger wines, yellow peach and ripe fig flavours tend to dominate; by the nature of things, a degree of American oak influence is commonplace.

Other White Wines. Semillon, Verdelho and Sauvignon Blanc are the most commonly encountered white wines, with both variety and region specified on the label. Verdelho shows the most promise.

 RED WINE STYLES

Shiraz, Cabernet Sauvignon and Merlot have been supported by the red wine boom, but plantings are unlikely to increase in the years ahead.

Wineries of Cowra

Cowra Estate Est. 1973

Boorowa Rd, Cowra 2794
cowraestate@ozemail.com.au

Region pioneer Cowra Estate was purchased from the family of founder Tony Gray by South African-born food and beverage entrepreneur (and cricket tragic) John Geber, in 1995. The Quarry Wine Cellars and Restaurant offer visitors a full range of all of Cowra Estate's wines but also wines from the other producers in the region. The Geber family, incidentally, also owns Chateau Tanunda in the Barossa Valley.
Signature wine: Eagle Rock Chardonnay

Hamiltons Bluff Est. 1995

Longs Corner Rd, Canowindra 2804
www.hamiltonsbluff.com.au

exports to US

Owned and operated by the Andrews family, which planted 45 ha of vines in 1995. 1998 produced the first crop, and three different contract-made Chardonnays had local show success. The major part of the grape production is sold, with a small portion retained for the Hamiltons Bluff label. Sangiovese and Shiraz tread outside the norm for the region.
Signature wine: Reserve Chardonnay

Mulyan Est. 1994

North Logan Rd, Cowra 2794
mulyan@westserv.net.au

Mulyan is a 1350 ha grazing property purchased by the Fagan family in 1886 from Dr William Redfern, a leading nineteenth-century figure in Australian history. In 1994 the current-generation owners Peter and Jenni Fagan began the establishment of 29 ha of Shiraz and 15 ha of Chardonnay, with an experimental plot of Sangiovese. In common with most producers in the region, the bulk of the grapes is sold to winemakers in other parts of Australia. Bushrangers Bounty is a second label. Several thousand cases of Chardonnay and Shiraz are contract-made each year.
Signature wine: Cowra Chardonnay

Wallington Wines Est. 1992

'Nyrang Creek', Eugowra Rd, Canowindra 2804
www.wallingtonwines.com.au

Anthony and Margaret Wallington commenced the development of their Nyrang Creek vineyard with 2 ha of Cabernet Sauvignon in 1992, followed by 7 ha of Chardonnay in 1994, Shiraz in 1995, Semillon and Cabernet Franc in 1997, thereafter a mix of Grenache, Mourvèdre, Tempranillo, Petit Verdot and Viognier. Most of the production is sold, but 20 tonnes are selected for winemaking on-site in the unusual straw bale winery.
Signature wine: Rockdell (Shiraz, Grenache and Mourvèdre blend)

Windowrie Estate Est. 1988

'Windowrie', Canowindra 2804
www.windowrie.com.au

(at The Mill, Cowra); exports to UK, US

Windowrie Estate is part of a substantial grazing property owned by the O'Dea family; some of the grapes from the 116 ha vineyard are sold to other makers, with increasing quantities being made at the substantial on-site winery for the Windowrie Estate and The Mill labels, making it the region's largest resident wine producer. Varietal wines made include Traminer, Sauvignon Blanc, Verdelho, Chardonnay, Shiraz, Petit Verdot, Sangiovese and Cabernet Merlot (mainly under The Mill label). The cellar door is situated in a flour mill built in 1861 from local granite, which ceased operations in 1905 and lay unoccupied for 91 years until restored.
Signature wine: Family Reserve Chardonnay

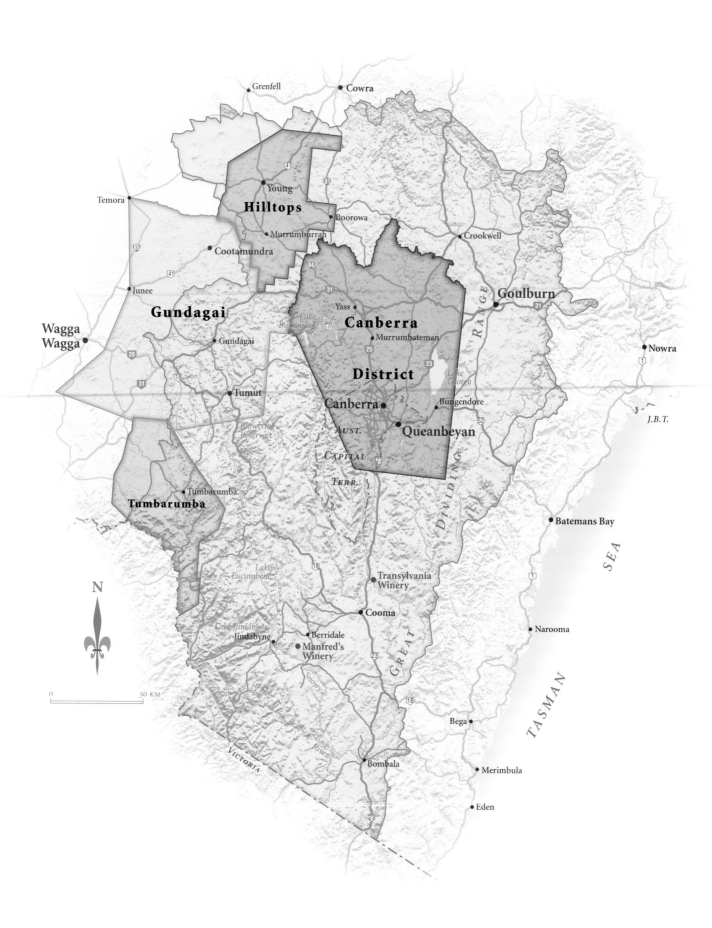

Southern New South Wales Zone ❧

As is the case in the Central Ranges Zone, the key to the four regions of this zone is altitude (rather than north–south orientation): Tumbarumba is the highest and coolest; then comes the Canberra District with vineyards at varying altitudes, the highest (over 800 metres) decidedly cool; next is the Hilltops, without so much variation around an average of 450 metres, and more temperate; and finally Gundagai, a hybrid region borne of necessity, but generally lower and warmer than the Hilltops (and, of course, the other two regions).

The link is once again the Great Dividing Range, albeit significantly eroded by the upper reaches of the Murrumbidgee River as it passes west through the Gundagai region. Overall, it is pastoral country, with sheep dominant; with the exception of the Canberra District, distances between vineyards are often substantial.

The scenery is on a grand, open scale, with long, rolling hills long since cleared of trees, sheep effectively preventing any regrowth.

Wineries of the Southern New South Wales Zone

Manfred's Winery Est. 1984
Rockwell Rd, Berridale 2628
(02) 6456 5041
🔲 🍴

An operation which relies entirely on the substantial tourist trade passing through or near Berridale on the way to the Snowy Mountains. The product range is, to put it mildly, eclectic; all the wines are said to be made on site, and the grapes for all of the white varietals are estate-grown.
Signature wine: Alpine Dry White

Transylvania Winery Est. 1989
Monaro Hwy, Cooma 2630
(02) 6452 4374
🔲 🍴

Peter Culici operates the Transylvania Vineyard and Winery, drawing in part on a 2.4 ha vineyard of Sauvignon Blanc, Gewürztraminer, Chardonnay, Pinot Noir, Cabernet Sauvignon, Merlot and Muscadelle. Both table and fortified wines are sold through the cellar door and on-site restaurant, which is 14 km north of Cooma.
Signature wine: Chardonnay

[ABOVE] RIPE SHIRAZ. [BELOW] MCWILLIAM'S BARWANG VINEYARD, HILLTOPS.

SOUTHERN NEW SOUTH WALES ZONE
Canberra District ❦

Apart from some long-forgotten and small vineyards established near Yass in the latter part of the nineteenth century, the Canberra District is a reflection of the Real Politik of the late twentieth century. It is a wry commentary on the unreality of the political hothouse of Canberra that only two of the Canberra District vignerons should actually have had a vineyard in Canberra, and even more appropriate that none is a politician. The reason for the territorial exclusion was essentially a pragmatic one, however much the concept might have pleased Lewis Carroll: freehold does not exist within the Australian Capital Territory, and land used for anything other than housing, commerce or industry is liable to be rezoned (and the lease terminated) at short notice.

In 1997 Hardys showed there was a solution to the problem: simply enter into an agreement with the Territory Government for the erection of a 2000 tonne winery and the establishment of a 250 hectare vineyard, an enterprise to dwarf all the others. But one has to have the clout of Australia's second-largest wine company to achieve an outcome such as this; the winery was duly opened in 2000.

So the remaining, much smaller, vignerons cluster just outside the Territory's borders in two groups: in the Yass Valley around Murrumbateman, and along the shores of Lake George. It was indeed within a few hundred metres of the edge of Lake George that Dr Edgar Riek planted the first vines in 1971, and others – mainly from the public service or scientific communities, many with Doctorates of Philosophy to their credit – quickly followed in his wake.

Overall, growth was steady rather than spectacular until the mid 1990s, and the general quality of the wines was equally modest. This was due to three main reasons: first, the virtual absence of qualified winemakers; second, initial lack of understanding of the particular problems posed by the Canberra climate and terroir; and third, the inherent difficulty of small-scale winemaking of white wines.

The lack of technical expertise was partially overcome by the use of consultants, partially by skills learned on the winery floor (for example at Lark Hill, Clonakilla and Kyeema Estate), although supplemented by external studies at Charles Sturt University, and partially by the acute intelligence and high scientific qualifications of many of the winemakers who – strictly speaking – are unqualified.

It hardly needs be said the arrival of Hardys has acted as a major catalyst for change in the early years of this century as wines from its development start to come on to the market. In the interim, it is an emphatic vote of confidence in the ability of the region to produce first-class table wine.

The climatic question has already been addressed: it took a long time for the vignerons to realise to what extent the summer drought made irrigation essential, and – having recognised the problem – to do something about it. The other learning curve was with respect to the danger of spring frost in sites with poor or non-existent air drainage. Taken together, these problems reduced yields to sub-economic levels without providing compensation in the form of increased quality. A more rigorous approach to viticulture has now addressed most of these problems.

Through the 1990s and early 2000s the growth rate increased and the quality of the wines rose significantly. In 2000 there were 19 wineries; by 2006 the number had run to 36, with more coming. Clonakilla's Shiraz Viognier is an icon wine, one of the best in Australia. Lark Hill has shown what can be achieved with Pinot Noir (amongst other varieties); Helm is a highly proactive champion of Riesling; Brindabella Hills makes excellent Sauvignon Blanc Semillon and Cabernet Merlot; while Kamberra and numerous others produce stylish Chardonnay.

The Canberra District has emphatically arrived on the scene.

[OPPOSITE] KAMBERRA, CANBERRA DISTRICT.
[BELOW] BRINDABELLA HILLS, CANBERRA DISTRICT.

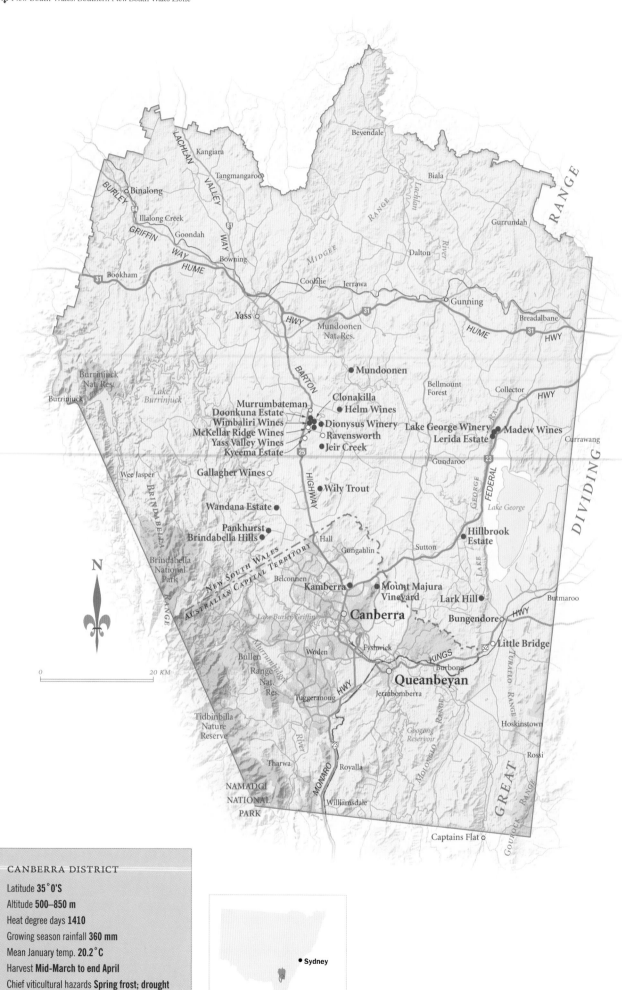

N

0   20 KM

CANBERRA DISTRICT

Latitude **35°0'S**

Altitude **500–850 m**

Heat degree days **1410**

Growing season rainfall **360 mm**

Mean January temp. **20.2°C**

Harvest **Mid-March to end April**

Chief viticultural hazards **Spring frost; drought**

● **Sydney**

The Region

CLIMATE

With its extremely continental climate, the Canberra District shows just how inadequate a single index of climate can be. It is a mix of warm and cool factors, compounded by different site climates. A very warm, dry summer (but with cold nights) gives way to a cool autumn, with harvest not infrequently interrupted by significant rain. The major viticultural limitation lies in the very dry spring and summer months.

SOIL & TOPOGRAPHY

The soils are principally in the hard red duplex group, with brownish clay loam surface soils which are usually shallow. The subsoils are not particularly water-retentive, adding to the need for irrigation.

PRINCIPAL GRAPE VARIETIES

Overall, 60 per cent red, 40 per cent white.
In descending order:

SHIRAZ

CABERNET SAUVIGNON

MERLOT

CHARDONNAY

SAUVIGNON BLANC

RIESLING

SEMILLON

PINOT NOIR.

[ABOVE] TASTING THE SOIL AT MOUNT MAJURA VINEYARD, CANBERRA DISTRICT.
[RIGHT] LARK HILL, CANBERRA DISTRICT.

WHITE WINE STYLES

Chardonnay does well enough in the region, producing wines of good quality and complexity. Achieving both physiological and technical ripeness is seldom a problem, and botrytis is fairly easily controlled. Soft fig and stonefruit flavours are achieved, which comfortably support reasonably generous use of new oak.

Sauvignon Blanc and Semillon produce attractive, moderately herbaceous wines, usually blended, but sometimes with Sauvignon Blanc appearing on its own. The wines have good structure, with the best flavours appearing in the cooler vintages.

Riesling vies with Chardonnay as the most important white wine, and arguably has more personality and typicity. The majority are made in a crisp, gently toasty, dry style; in the warmer years, more tropical characters can appear. Modest yields ensure that the wines age well in bottle for up to a decade.

RED WINE STYLES

Shiraz has left all others in its wake, the best examples redolent of spice, black cherry and liquorice. Clonakilla's Shiraz (with a touch of Viognier, Rhône-style) stands out like a beacon.

Cabernet Sauvignon and Merlot. Cabernet Sauvignon is sometimes made as a single varietal, but is being increasingly blended with Merlot; as with all the wines of the region, the varied climatic conditions which prevail from one vintage to the next (and differing approaches in the winery) make generalisations about style more than usually hazardous. Overall, the weight and extract varies from light, leafy and minty to rich, concentrated and chocolatey.

Pinot Noir shines unexpectedly well in the cooler vintages; site selection at higher altitudes is also a key; clear-cut varietal character can be achieved.

Wineries of the Canberra District

Brindabella Hills Est. 1986
Woodgrove Close, via Hall 2618
brindabellahills@bigpond.com

Distinguished research scientist Dr Roger Harris presides over Brindabella Hills, which increasingly relies on estate-produced grapes, from its 4 ha of Cabernet Sauvignon, Cabernet Franc, Merlot, Shiraz, Chardonnay, Sauvignon Blanc, Semillon and Riesling, complemented by grapes sourced from Tumbarumba and Hilltops. Wine quality across all varietal styles has been consistently impressive.
Signature wine: Shiraz

Clonakilla Est. 1971
Crisps Lane, Murrumbateman 2582
www.clonakilla.com.au
exports to UK, US

The fiercely committed Tim Kirk has taken over the management of Clonakilla from father and scientist Dr John Kirk. The quality of the wines is exceptional, none more so than the highly regarded Shiraz Viognier, which sells out so quickly every year that Kirk has introduced a second Shiraz from the Hilltops region. The range also extends to smaller amounts of Riesling, Viognier, Chardonnay, Semillon Sauvignon Blanc and Cabernet Merlot.
Signature wine: Shiraz Viognier

Doonkuna Estate Est. 1973
Barton Hwy, Murrumbateman 2582
www.doonkuna.com.au

Following the acquisition of Doonkuna by Barry and Maureen Moran in late 1996, the plantings have been increased from a little under 4 ha to 20 ha. The cellar-door prices remain modest, and increased production has followed in the wake of the new plantings. The range of wines made is substantial, covering all the mainstream varietals and blends in a fruit-forward but balanced style. The Rising Ground series is a cheaper, second-label range.
Signature wine: Chardonnay

Gallagher Wines Est. 1995
Dog Trap Rd, Murrumbateman 2582
www.gallagherwines.com.au

Greg Gallagher was senior winemaker at Taltarni for 20 years, where he worked with Dominique Portet. He began the establishment of a small vineyard at Murrumbateman in 1995, planting a little over 1 ha each of Chardonnay and Shiraz. He has now moved to the region with his family, where he provides contract winemaking and consultancy services to others, as well as making 2500 cases a year of his own label wines.
Signature wine: Chardonnay

Helm Est. 1973
Butts Rd, Murrumbateman 2582
www.helmwines.com.au

Ken Helm has for long been known as one of the more stormy petrels of the wine industry and is an energetic promoter of his wines and of the Canberra District generally. His wines have been consistent bronze medal winners, with silvers and the occasional gold trophy dotted here and there. Riesling has been the most consistent performer, sometimes outstanding, variously made in early and late harvest styles. The Reserve Merlot, Cabernet Merlot and Helm Reserve Blend can also impress.
Signature wine: Riesling

Kamberra Est. 2000
Cnr Northbourne Ave & Flemington Rd, Lyneham 2602
www.kamberra.com.au
exports to UK, US

Kamberra is part of Hardys, established in 2000 with the planting of 40 ha of vines and a new winery within the Australian Capital Territory, only a few hundred metres from the showground facilities where the National Wine Show is held every year. The wines come in two ranges: the Meeting Place range of mainstream

white and red varietals from various New South Wales regions, and under the predominantly estate-grown Kamberra range Riesling, Chardonnay, Shiraz, Cabernet Sauvignon and a Sparkling Pinot Noir Chardonnay.
Signature wine: Kamberra Chardonnay

Lark Hill Est. 1978
521 Bungendore Rd, Bungendore 2621
www.larkhillwine.com.au
exports to UK, US

The Lark Hill vineyard is situated at an altitude of 860 m, level with the observation deck on Black Mountain Tower, and offers splendid views of the Lake George Escarpment. Right from the outset, Dr David and Sue Carpenter have made wines of real style and elegance but have defied all the odds (and conventional thinking) with the quality of their Pinot Noirs, the high standard of the other wines coming as no surprise. The Exaltation Pinot Noir, Merlot and Cabernet are the icon wines.
Signature wine: Exaltation Pinot Noir

Little Bridge Est. 1996
PO Box 499, Bungendore 2621
www.littlebridgewines.com.au

Little Bridge Vineyard is the venture of long-term friends John and Val Leyshon, and Rowland and Madeleine Clark. The establishment date of 1996 marked the formation of the business partnership; 4.5 ha of Chardonnay, Pinot Noir, Riesling and Merlot were planted between then and 2004. Greg Gallagher makes the white wines; the Pinot Noir is made at Lark Hill Winery, in each case with John Leyshon's active involvement. The quality has been very impressive.
Signature wine: Riesling

[LEFT] ROGER HARRIS. [MIDDLE] KEN HELM. [RIGHT] DAVID CARPENTER.

Mount Majura Vineyard
Est. 1988
RMB 314 Majura Rd, Majura 2609
www.mountmajura.com.au

The first vines were planted in 1988 on red soil of volcanic origin over limestone, the reasonably steep east and north-east slopes providing some frost protection. The 1 ha vineyard was planted to Pinot Noir, Chardonnay and Merlot in equal quantities. The syndicate which purchased the property in 1999 has extended the plantings, and Dr Frank van de Loo makes the stylish wines in leased space at Brindabella Hills; an on-site winery and expanded cellar door are to follow.

Signature wine: Chardonnay

Mundoonen Est. 2003
1457 Yass River Rd, Yass 2582
www.mundoonen.com.au

Jenny and Terry O'Donnell built the estate winery beside the Yass River behind one of the oldest settler's cottages in the Yass River Valley, dating back to 1858. Six ha of estate plantings of Shiraz and Viognier are supplemented by contract-grown Riesling, Sauvignon Blanc and Cabernet Sauvignon. The quality of the initial releases has been exemplary, particularly given that the wines are made on-site by Terry O'Donnell.

Signature wine: Canberra District Riesling

Pankhurst Est. 1986
Old Woodgrove, Woodgrove Rd, Hall 2618
www.pankhurstwines.com.au

Agricultural scientist and consultant Allan Pankhurst and wife Christine (with a degree in pharmaceutical science) planted 5.7 ha of split-canopy Sauvignon Blanc, Semillon, Chardonnay, Pinot Noir, Merlot and Cabernet Sauvignon. Tastings of the first wines produced showed considerable promise; in more recent years Pankhurst has shared success with Lark Hill in the production of surprisingly good Pinot Noir – surprising given the climatic limitations. Says Christine Pankhurst, 'the result of good viticulture here and great winemaking at Lark Hill', and she may well be right. The Chardonnay, too, is excellent.

Signature wine: Pinot Noir

Ravensworth Est. 2000
Rosehill Vineyard, PO Box 116, Mawson 2607
www.ravensworthwines.com.au

Winemaker, vineyard manager and partner Bryan Martin (with dual wine science and winegrowing degrees from Charles Sturt University) has a background of wine retail, food and beverage in the hospitality industry, and teaches part-time in that field. He is also assistant winemaker to Tim Kirk at Clonakilla, after seven years at Jeir Creek. Judging at wine shows is another string to his bow. Ravensworth has 7 ha of vineyards spread over two sites: Rosehill, planted in 1998, to Cabernet Sauvignon, Merlot and Sauvignon Blanc, and Martin Block, planted 2000/2001, to Shiraz, Viognier, Marsanne and Sangiovese.

Signature wine: Canberra District Shiraz

[ABOVE] TERRY O'DONNELL.
[RIGHT] BRYAN MARTIN.

SOUTHERN NEW SOUTH WALES ZONE

Gundagai 🌿

Gundagai is a thoroughly schizophrenic region, but one created with a good deal of common-sense. Its north-eastern corner is Temora; it and Cootamundra have warm to hot climates at relatively low elevations to the west of the Great Dividing Range. The region's south-eastern corner is Tumut at the northern end of the Snowy Mountains, with a cool to cold climate, and abutting the Tumbarumba region to the south. Had the boundaries not extended to take in Tumut and the area around it, there would have been a significant regional no man's land.

The first vines were planted at Kyeamba, south-east of Wagga Wagga, in the late 1840s. The most significant nineteenth-century development was that of John James McWilliam, who established Mark View near Junee in 1877 before moving to the Riverina in 1912. The vineyard continued in production until the 1950s; in the 1970s the New South Wales Wine and Food Society had bottles of McWilliam's Junee red wine made by the legendary Maurice O'Shea which I tasted on a number of occasions.

Significant vineyards have been established around Gundagai (including a 240 hectare red grape vineyard by Southcorp), Ladysmith, Borambola, Jugiong and Tumut. When site climate is factored in, the region will be able to produce as diverse a range of wine styles as any other region in Australia.

GUNDAGAI

Latitude **35°07'S (Junee), 35°17'S (Tumut), 34°38'S (Cootamundra)**

Altitude **210 m (Junee), 267 m (Tumut), 320 m (Cootamundra)**

Heat degree days **2110 (Junee), 1500 (Tumut), 2050 (Cootamundra)**

Growing season rainfall **240 mm (Junee), 420 mm (Tumut), 270 mm (Cootamundra)**

Mean January temp. **24°C (Junee), 21.2°C (Tumut), 23.7°C (Cootamundra)**

Harvest **Late February to mid March (Tumut much later)**

Chief viticultural hazard **Spring frost**

Cellar Door
* Bidgeebong Wines at 352 Byrnes Rd, Bomen, Wagga Wagga.

The Region

CLIMATE

Tumut is the odd man out in terms of climate, as it has a much lower HDD index and significantly higher rainfall than the rest of the region. The remainder has a climate which falls between the cooler Hilltops region and the distinctly warmer Griffith region. The climate is strongly continental, with cool nights and warm days, and a conspicuously high mean January temperature sandwiched between much cooler spring and autumn weather.

SOIL & TOPOGRAPHY

Geologists list five specific geological formations in the region, all with highly technical names, but unified by the soil types they give rise to, which are predominantly red earths and red podzolics, and lesser areas of red brown earths.

PRINCIPAL GRAPE VARIETIES

In descending order:

CHARDONNAY

SHIRAZ

CABERNET SAUVIGNON.

CHARDONNAY.

WHITE WINE STYLES

Chardonnay from the warmer parts of the region is soft, rich and peachy; that from the area around Tumut is much more vibrant and citrussy.

RED WINE STYLES

Shiraz. All three wineries produce opulently rich and deep wine flooded with blackberry, black cherry, liquorice and dark chocolate, with ripe tannins.

Cabernet Sauvignon, again made in a rich style, with a mix of blackcurrant, earth and bitter chocolate.

Wineries of Gundagai

Bidgeebong Wines Est. 2000

352 Byrnes Rd, Bomen 2650
www.bidgeebong.com

(at Byrnes Rd, Bomen, Wagga Wagga)
exports to UK, US

Bidgeebong (a made-up name) covers the area bounded by Young, Wagga Wagga, Tumbarumba and Gundagai, which provides grapes for the business. Two of the partners are Andrew Birks, with a 30-year career as a lecturer at Charles Sturt University, and Simon Robertson, who studied viticulture and wine science at Charles Sturt University, and after working in Europe and the Barwang Vineyard established by his father Peter in 1969, built a substantial viticultural management business in the area. A winery was completed for the 2002 vintage for Bidgeebong's own needs, and those of other local growers and larger producers.
Signature wine: Gundagai Shiraz

Borambola Wines Est. 1995

Sturt Hwy, Wagga Wagga 2650
www.borambola.com

Borambola Homestead was built in the 1880s, and in the latter part of that century was the centre of a pastoral empire of 1.4 million ha situated in rolling foothills 25 km east of Wagga Wagga. In 1992 ownership passed to the McMullen family. Just under 10 ha of vines surround the homestead (4 ha Shiraz, 3.5 ha Cabernet Sauvignon, 2.2. ha Chardonnay) and the wines are made for Borambola at Bidgeebong.
Signature wine: Premium Gundagai Shiraz

Paterson's Gundagai Vineyard Est. 1997

474 Old Hume Hwy Rd, Tumblong 2729
stuartlpaterson@ozemail.com.au

The Patersons began the planting of their 12 ha vineyard in 1996. It is a powerful team: Robert Paterson (M.Ec – Sydney; PMD – Harvard) was a Senior Vice President of Coca-Cola and his wife Rhondda was a teacher, before both turned to cattle farming in the early 1980s and grapegrowing in the mid 1990s. Son Stuart Paterson has a Ph.D. in Chemical Engineering from the University of New South Wales, and a wine science degree from Charles Sturt University in Wagga. The wines are made by the talented Celine Rousseau at Chalkers Crossing in the nearby Hilltops region.
Signature wine: Gundagai Shiraz

SOUTHERN NEW SOUTH WALES ZONE
Hilltops ❧

Australia may not have been a melting pot to challenge the United States in the nineteenth century, but it was most certainly multicultural, thanks in part to the gold rush decades. Gold brought Nichole Jasprizza from his native Croatia in 1860, but he prospered by selling the gold miners their daily needs and planted vines in the area. In 1880 he sponsored three nephews to come to Australia to join the business, and by the early years of the twentieth century they had won prizes at the Sydney Wine Show, and extended the vineyards to 240 hectares.

Grapegrowing and winemaking continued in the area until the Second World War, when labour shortages curtailed activities; by 1960 the vineyards were so neglected they were removed and cherries planted in their place.

Only nine years were to pass before the late Peter Robertson, together with sundry members of his family, commenced the establishment of his Barwang vineyard in 1969. It was a substantial farming property, with grapegrowing and winemaking a minor diversification from the core grazing activities. When McWilliam's acquired the 400 hectare property in 1989, only 13 hectares were planted to vines – although even then it was by far the largest vineyard in the region. McWilliam's has since increased the plantings to over 100 hectares, while Grove Estate Vineyard has 55 hectares. There are now over 400 hectares in bearing throughout the region.

McWILLIAM'S BARWANG VINEYARD, HILLTOPS.

HILLTOPS

Latitude **34°19'S**

Altitude **450 m**

Heat degree days **1880**

Growing season rainfall **310 mm**

Mean January temp. **22.5°C**

Harvest **Late March to May**

Chief viticultural hazard **Spring frost**

The Region

CLIMATE

While the climate is unequivocally continental, with substantial diurnal temperature variation during the growing season, the altitude at which most of the vineyards are established ensures a long and even ripening period. Heavy snowfalls in winter are quite common, but pose no threat to viticulture; spring frosts, however, do and necessitate careful site selection along ridge tops and upper, well air-drained slopes. While substantial rainfall occurs in the growing season, most falls in spring; the dry summer and autumn provide excellent ripening conditions, but make irrigation essential.

SOIL & TOPOGRAPHY

The soils are rich and deep, typically dark red granitic clays impregnated with basalt. While capable of holding water at depth, they are free draining and support strong vine growth. These soils persist along the ridge tops and hillsides, which provide the greatest degree of protection against frost.

PRINCIPAL GRAPE VARIETIES

Overall, 80 per cent red, 20 per cent white.
In descending order:

SHIRAZ

CABERNET SAUVIGNON

CHARDONNAY

MERLOT

SEMILLON.

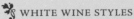

WHITE WINE STYLES

Chardonnay is typically lean and elegant, with citrus and melon flavours merging into more stony/minerally characters. The wines lend themselves to subtle oak handling, and will age with grace for five years or more.

Semillon. Barwang founder Peter Robertson produced several memorable late-harvest Semillons, but these days the accent is on dry table styles. They are powerful, with excellent mid-palate weight, and (increasingly with mature vines) good length.

RED WINE STYLES

Shiraz is arguably the variety best suited to the region, even though the plantings point to Cabernet Sauvignon. The aromas and flavours are complex, moderately spicy, with a range of chocolate, mint, black cherry and more briary characters. Acidity is good, the tannins supple.

Cabernet Sauvignon produces a powerful wine, yet neither aggressive nor heavy. The flavours are predominantly cassis/blackcurrant, balanced by more earthy/chocolatey undertones, the tannins quite strong.

Merlot produces wines of appropriate elegance and fine tannin texture.

Wineries of Hilltops

Barwang Vineyard Est. 1969

Barwang Rd, Young 2594 (postal)
www.mcwilliams.com.au
 exports to UK, US

Peter Robertson pioneered viticulture in the Young region when he began planting of 13 ha of vines in 1969 as part of a diversification program for his 400 ha grazing property. Under McWilliam's ownership the Barwang vineyards have been increased to over 100 ha of Semillon, Chardonnay, Shiraz, Merlot and Cabernet Sauvignon. Wine quality has been exemplary from the word go, always elegant, restrained and deliberately understated, repaying extended cellaring.
Signature wine: Chardonnay

Chalkers Crossing Est. 2000

387 Grenfell Rd, Young 2594
www.chalkerscrossing.com.au
exports to UK

Owned and operated by Ted and Wendy Ambler, who planted the first vines at the Rockleigh vineyard in late 1997, with follow-up plantings in 1998 lifting the total to 10 ha. They also purchase grapes from Tumbarumba and Gundagai to supplement the intake. A winery was opened for the 2000 vintage, with Celine Rousseau as winemaker. Born in France's Loire Valley and trained in Bordeaux, this French Flying Winemaker (now an Australian citizen) has exceptional skills and dedication, making both white and red wines of the highest quality.
Signature wine: Tumbarumba Chardonnay

Freeman Vineyards Est. 2000

RMB 101, Prunevale 2587 (postal)
www.brianfreeman.com.au

Dr Brian Freeman has spent much of his long life in both research and education, in the latter role as head of Charles Sturt University's viticulture and oenology campus. In 2004 he purchased the 30-year-old vineyard and winery previously known as Demondrille. He has also established a new vineyard, and in all has 14 varieties totalling 40.5 ha; these range from staples such as Shiraz, Cabernet Sauvignon, Semillon and Riesling through to the more exotic, trendy varieties such as Tempranillo, and on to Corvina and Rondinella.
Signature wine: Rondinella Corvina

Grove Estate Est. 1989

Murringo Rd, Young 2594
www.groveestate.com.au
exports to UK

A partnership of Brian Mullany, John Kirkwood and Mark Flanders has established a 30 ha vineyard planted to Semillon, Chardonnay, Merlot, Shiraz, Cabernet Sauvignon and Zinfandel. Some of the grapes are sold (principally to Southcorp), but an increasing amount of very good and interesting wine is contract-made by Monarch Winemaking Services for the Grove Estate label. The now mature vines result in wines of arresting richness and complexity.
Signature wine: The Partners Reserve Cabernet Sauvignon

SOUTHERN NEW SOUTH WALES ZONE
Tumbarumba ❧

Tumbarumba is one of the most remote wine regions in Australia – unless you are a fly fisherman (I am) or a skier (I was once). I have a special affection for this alpine high country, so perfectly captured on screen in the film *The Man from Snowy River*; the Tumbarumba region vineyards may be a little lower (ranging as they do from 300 to 800 metres) but are unequivocally part of the Snowy Mountains.

The first vines were established by Ian Cowell at Tumbarumba and by Frank Minutello at Tooma in the Maragle Valley, 18 kilometres south-east of Tumbarumba, in 1982 and 1983. The first harvest from Ian Cowell's vineyard was sold to Rosemount Estate for sparkling wine, and to this day the majority of the Pinot Noir and Chardonnay grown in the region is put to the same (sparkling wine) use. What is more, these two varieties account for 75 per cent of the total plantings, a double testament to the cool climate.

Between 1983 and 1992 the pace of development was slow. As at the end of that period, there were eight vineyards established with 78 hectares in total. By 1997 there were over 25 vineyards with a total of 309 hectares, thanks to a massive planting program in 1994, and continuing plantings thereafter.

Southcorp, Hardys, Hungerford Hill, Chalkers Crossing and McWilliam's purchase a large part of the annual production, but only Southcorp owns a vineyard here, understanding only too well the marginal nature of grapegrowing.

The ability of the region to produce table wine (as opposed to sparkling wine) is dependent on two things: seasonal conditions and site altitude. The margin for error is small, the need for first-class viticultural management high. But when all goes right, the region can produce excellent table wine, even if its main business will be firmly linked to the production of high-quality sparkling wine.

TUMBARUMBA

Latitude **34°36'S**

Altitude **300–800 m**

Heat degree days **1010**

Growing season rainfall **375 mm**

Mean January temp. **19.3°C**

Harvest **Early March to early May**

Chief viticultural hazard **Frost**

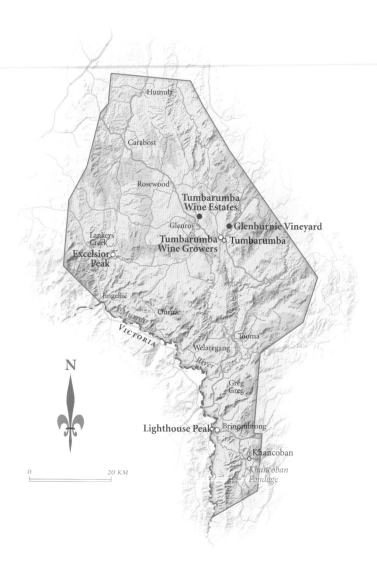

The Region

CLIMATE

With a mean January temperature of 19.3°C, Tumbarumba's climate may not seem so cool. But there are also a number of other mutually counterbalancing factors: high sunshine hours with brilliant light, cold summer nights, and a late start to the growing season. Frost is the chief viticultural threat, and dictates careful site selection and management. Night-time temperature inversion – the propensity of cold air to sink and warm air to rise – can play tricks, but elevation is significant in determining varietal choice.

SOIL & TOPOGRAPHY

These are typical high mountain soils, derived from decomposed granite and basalt, with a gritty/grainy texture. The choice of viticultural site is chiefly determined by aspect (north- and north-east-facing preferred, south-facing nigh on impossible) and slope (sufficiently steep to promote good air drainage at night and thus minimise the risk of frost).

PRINCIPAL GRAPE VARIETIES

Chardonnay and Pinot Noir together make up almost 80 per cent of the total plantings. In descending order:

CHARDONNAY

PINOT NOIR

SAUVIGNON BLANC

PINOT MEUNIER.

 WHITE WINE STYLES

Sparkling. The essence of Champagne (French, that is) lies in the blending of 50 or more different base wine components drawn from areas scattered across the length and breadth of the region. The best Australian sparkling wines use the same approach, employing the classic blend of Chardonnay, Pinot Noir and Pinot Meunier but also utilising multiple regional sources. Tumbarumba is always high on the shopping list.

Sauvignon Blanc is often a surprisingly bold style, showing abundant varietal character with rich gooseberry flavours neatly cut by underlying herbal notes that prevent the wine from cloying.

Chardonnay makes a classic cool-climate wine, graceful and willowy, but with great cellaring potential, and the ability to soak up a surprising quantity of new French oak.

 RED WINE STYLES

Pinot Noir. There is no doubt Tumbarumba has the capacity to produce very stylish Pinot Noir with clear varietal character, and none of the hot, boiled-fruit characters of Pinot Noir from some other high-altitude regions.

Wineries of Tumbarumba

Excelsior Peak Est. 1980

PO Box 269, Tumbarumba 2653

julietc@dragnet.com.au

Excelsior Peak proprietor Juliet Cullen planted the first vineyard in Tumbarumba in 1980. That vineyard was thereafter sold to Southcorp, and she subsequently established another vineyard, now releasing contract-made wines under the Excelsior Peak label. Plantings of Chardonnay and Pinot Noir total over 10 ha, with most of the grapes sold. Sales by mail order only.

Signature wine: Chardonnay

Glenburnie Vineyard Est.1992

Black Range Rd, Tumbarumba 2653

(02) 6948 2570

Robert Parkes has established 12 ha of vineyard planted to Riesling, Sauvignon Blanc, Chardonnay and Pinot Noir; the production is marketed under the Black Range Wines label. These are contract-made for Glenburnie by Cofield Wines in Rutherglen. The cellar door offers barbecue facilities, and accommodation is also available.

Signature wine: Sauvignon Blanc

Tumbarumba Wine Estates Est.1989

Glenroy Hills Rd, Tumbarumba 2653

mannus.wines@bigpond.com.au

Frank Minutello heads a group of grapegrowers who have 25 ha planted to Chardonnay, Pinot Noir, Shiraz, Merlot and Cabernet Sauvignon. Up to 300 tonnes of grapes are grown each year, and around 20 tonnes are contract-made (by Roger Harris at Brindabella Hills) into wines under the Tumbarumba Wine Estates label.

Signature wine: Mannus Reserve Pinot Noir

Tumbarumba Wine Growers Est. 1996

'Sunnyside', Albury Close, Tumbarumba 2653

(02) 6948 3055

Tumbarumba Wine Growers has taken over the former George Martin Winery (itself established in 1990) to provide an outlet for wines made from their joint plantings of 25 ha. It is essentially a co-operative venture, involving four local growers and businessmen, and with modest aspirations to growth; only a small amount is vinified under the Black Range label.

Signature wine: Black Range Chardonnay

WINTER VINES.

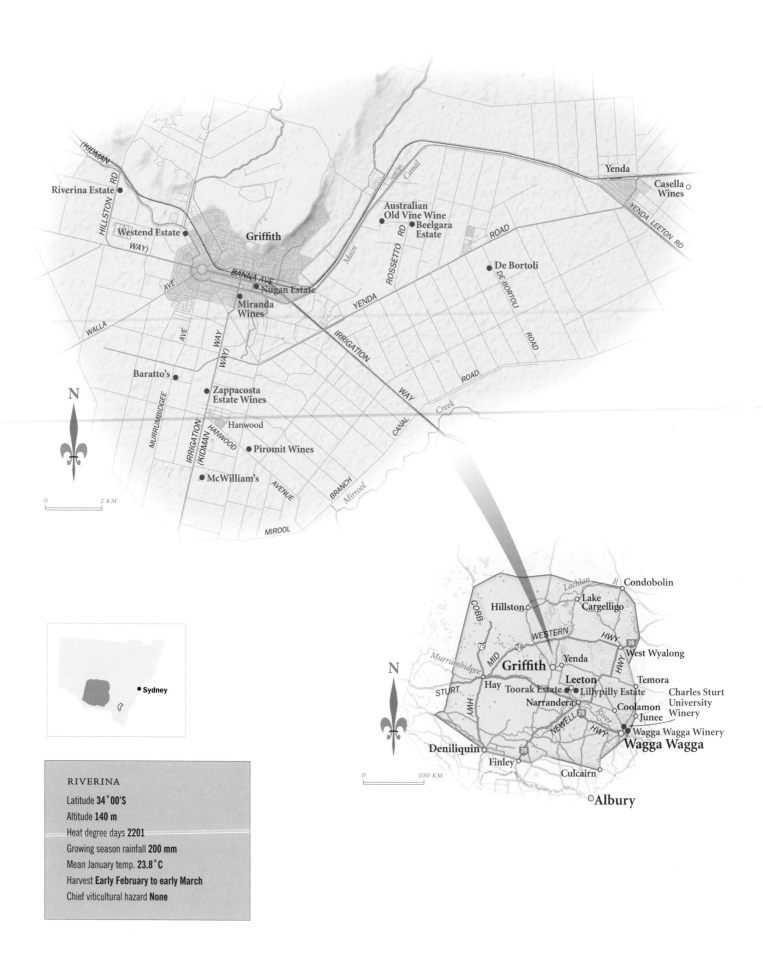

Big Rivers Zone
Riverina ✿

The birth of the Murrumbidgee Irrigation Scheme Area between 1906 and 1912 stands as a lasting testament to the skills and the vision of a group of dedicated Australians, all inspired by the imagination of Sir Samuel McCaughey. In securing the passage of legislation for the immense scheme through the New South Wales Parliament he said, 'In my opinion the waters of the rivers of the Commonwealth, if placed on the surface of the ground so that they could be utilised for irrigation, together with a supply for stock and household purposes, would be of more value to Australia than the discovery of gold; for gold will eventually become exhausted while water will continue as long as the world lasts.'

The subsequent development of the Riverina as a major wine-producing area was primarily due to the remarkable McWilliam family, even if two successive waves of Italian immigrants (after the First and Second World Wars) built on the opportunities created by the McWilliams.

Until the second half of the 1950s production in the area was almost entirely of fortified wine. Just as John James McWilliam had led the way in 1912, so Glen McWilliam thereafter pioneered the move to table wine. Not only was he responsible for the trial of premium varieties previously unknown in the district, but he was also responsible for leading the way in developing the winery technology necessary to produce modern table wine in a fiercely hot summer climate. He embraced the technology pioneered by Orlando and Yalumba in the mid 1950s for the handling of white grapes, adapting it to the particular requirements of the region.

De Bortoli, too, has been a major and successful innovator, growing to become another one of Australia's leading family wineries. It led the way in developing Botrytis Semillon in this most unlikely climate, picking the grapes as late as June, four months after normal maturity for table wine. The style is a benchmark for many producers.

Riverina's real strength lies in its agricultural efficiency, described by the notable American wine critic Robert Parker as industrial viticulture. This, and the industry of the Italian families – originally headed by the De Bortolis, and more recently the Casellas, with their multi-million case [yellow tail] brand phenomenon – has directly led to enormous export sales to the United States.

Another face of Riverina is the home for what started life as the Riverina College for Advanced Education and is now Charles Sturt University, Wagga Campus, the next most important wine school in Australia after the University of Adelaide.

Finally, it is here that A & G Industries was founded by Ron Potter, inventor of the eponymous fermenter; the company is now the largest stainless steel wine fabricator in the Southern Hemisphere.

Consistent with this penchant for efficiency and mega-sized businesses, the Riverina is a scenically barren area: the vineyards are laser-flat, the wineries functional, and the cellar-door sales areas a rococo blend of Australian–Italian do-it-yourself architecture. As a final deterrent to visitors, Griffith is a long way from anywhere.

Summer vines, Griffith.

The Region

CLIMATE

The climate is hot and dry, although slightly cooler than South Australia's Riverland and Victoria's Sunraysia. All forms of perennial agriculture here depend on irrigation from the Murrumbidgee River. Grapegrowing is reliable and yields are high with a minimal disease load. With a low requirement for sprays, growers have adopted low-impact vineyard management systems. Autumn rainfall, which usually commences in April, is essential for the development of botrytis in Semillon.

SOIL & TOPOGRAPHY

The soils are generally sandy loam overlying a sandy clay loam or clay subsoil: however, as they were deposited by ancient streams they are highly variable. They range from red sandy earths through to red and brown massive earths. While free draining near the surface, subsoil waterlogging has been a major problem, particularly with associated salinity build-up.

PRINCIPAL GRAPE VARIETIES

Overall, equally split between white and red. In descending order:

SHIRAZ

SEMILLON

CHARDONNAY

CABERNET SAUVIGNON

MERLOT

COLOMBARD

RUBY CABERNET.

 WHITE WINE STYLES

Semillon, picked at normal maturity, provides a pleasant wine (which may be blended with other varieties) and is used in the making of generic styles once having names such as chablis and white burgundy. When left on the vine for a full two months after normal maturity (and if the weather conditions are favourable) *Botrytis cinerea*, 'noble rot', may attack the grapes, concentrating both sugar and acid, and producing the luscious Sauternes-style dessert wine pioneered by De Bortoli in 1982 but with an increasing number of sincere flatterers. The best of these wines (especially De Bortoli) is of world class; intriguingly, no other part of Australia is able to work the same magic with such regularity.

Chardonnay is of major importance, and with the judicious use of oak (whether as oak chips or barrels) it can produce a wine of fair varietal flavour, weight and style. And, as [yellow tail] has proved, a little bit of sweetness goes a long way.

Other White Wines. The still-substantial plantings of Trebbiano, Muscat Gordo Blanco and Colombard are principally used as blend components in major wine company casks and flagons, with Orlando and McWilliam's the major users. How long these grapes (particularly Trebbiano and Muscat Gordo Blanco) will remain in demand given the increasing amounts of Chardonnay, Semillon and Colombard remains to be seen.

❧ RED WINE STYLES

Until the advent of [yellow tail], McWilliam's was the market leader with Riverina-based red wines. A few producers established premium brands in lesser quantities, but most of the local wine disappeared into the anonymity of casks and bulk wine for the export markets. The arrival of [yellow tail] has changed all that; the only question is whether the brand will wane as quickly as it waxed, or act as an ice-breaker for others to follow.

Fortified. The region is also a major producer of fortified wines. While most are cheap (and of modest reputation and quality), McWilliam's in particular has some superb aged material which it uses in its much-gold medal-winning Show Reserve series.

Wineries of Riverina

Beelgara Estate Est. 2001

Farm 576, Beelbangera 2686
www.beelgara.com.au

exports to UK, US

Beelgara Estate was formed in 2001 after the purchase of the 60-year-old Rossetto family winery in the Riverina district of NSW by a group consisting of growers, distributors and investors. The name Beelgara is a contraction of the Beelbangera town district, where the group is headquartered. The new management is placing far greater emphasis on bottled table wine (albeit at low prices), but continues to supply bulk, cleanskin and fully packaged product for both domestic and export markets. It is also spreading its wings to premium regions, while maintaining excellent value for money.

Signature wine: Rascals Prayer Sauvignon Blanc

Casella Wines Est. 1969

Wakely Rd, Yenda 2681
www.casellawines.com.au

exports to UK, US

One of the modern-day fairy-tale success stories, transformed overnight from a substantial, successful but non-charismatic business shown as making 650 000 cases in 2000. Its opportunity came when the American distribution of Lindemans Bin 65 Chardonnay was taken away from W.J. Deutsch & Sons, leaving a massive gap in the Deutsch portfolio, but filled by [yellow tail]. It has built its US presence at a faster rate than any other wine or brand in history, soaring to over six million cases by 2006.

Signature wine: The Reserve [yellow tail] Cabernet Sauvignon

De Bortoli Est. 1928

De Bortoli Rd, Bilbul 2680
www.debortoli.com.au

exports to UK, US

Famous among the cognoscenti for its superb Noble One Botrytis Semillon, which in fact accounts for only a minute part of its total production, this winery produces three million cases annually of low-priced varietal and generic wines which are invariably competently made and equally invariably provide value for money. These come in part from 250 ha of estate vineyards, but mostly from contract-grown grapes. The death of founder Deen De Bortoli in 2003 was mourned by the whole industry.

Signature wine: Noble One

[OPPOSITE LEFT] BARRELS, DE BORTOLI, RIVERINA.
[OPPOSITE RIGHT] BOTRYTISED GRAPES (NOBLE ROT), DE BORTOLI, RIVERINA.

Lillypilly Estate Est. 1982

Lillypilly Rd, Leeton 2705
www.lillypilly.com

exports to UK, US

The best Lillypilly wines by far are the botrytised white wines, with the Noble Muscat of Alexandria unique to the winery; these wines have both style and intensity of flavour and can age well. The table wines made by family owner Robert Fiumara are always sound, particularly the Tramillon – a neat blend of Traminer and Semillon.

Signature wine: Noble Muscat of Alexandria

McWilliam's Est. 1916

Jack McWilliam Rd, Hanwood 2680
www.mcwilliams.com.au

exports to UK, US

A proudly family-owned and thriving business which now has vineyards in the Hilltops, NSW (Barwang); Hunter Valley, NSW (Mount Pleasant); Riverina, NSW; Yarra Valley, VIC (Lillydale Estate); and Coonawarra, SA (Brand's). It also buys grapes from all manner of regions, ranging through the Riverland to premium areas including Orange, Eden Valley and Margaret River. These grapes are either used to make single-region wines under the Collection Series label, or to form blend components for the big-volume Hanwood brand, which offers outstanding value. It exports to many countries via a major distribution joint venture with Gallo, which also has quietly obtained a strategic 10 per cent shareholding in McWilliam's.

Signature wine: Hanwood range

Miranda Wines Est. 1939

57 Jondaryan Ave, Griffith 2680
www.mirandawines.com.au

exports to UK, US

In 2003 this previously family-owned, multi-million case producer was purchased by the McGuigan/Simeon group which has kept the brand portfolio largely intact, perhaps investing more in the most successful brands and markets. The wines are well made, with ever higher standards for the grapes – both estate-grown and purchased – underwriting increases in quality.

Signature wine: Golden Botrytis (white)

Nugan Estate Est. 1999

60 Banna Ave, Griffith 2680
enquiries@nuganestate.com.au

exports to UK, US

Nugan Estate is an offshoot of the Nugan Group, a family company established over 60 years ago in Griffith as a broad-based agricultural business. Over a decade ago the company began developing vineyards, and is now a veritable giant, with 310 ha at Darlington Point, 52 ha at Hanwood and 120 ha at Hillston (all in NSW), 100 ha in the King Valley, VIC, and 10 ha in McLaren Vale, SA. It sells part of the production as grapes, part as bulk wine and 400 000 cases under the Cookoothama, Manuka Grove, Nugan Estate, Frascas Lane and several other labels. Unlike some, it has built its business on quality rather than low prices.

Signature wine: Manuka Grove Durif

Riverina Estate Est. 1969

700 Kidman Way, Griffith 2680
www.riverinaestate.com

exports to US

One of the many large producers of the region, drawing upon 1100 ha of estate plantings, and production of 750 000 cases. While part of the wine is sold in bulk to other producers, selected parcels of the best of the grapes are made into table wines, under various versions of the Warburn Estate label at the top, followed by Ballingal Estate, Lizard Ridge, Kanga's Leap, Bushman's Gully, and so on and so forth. Labels such as these are either directed at specific export markets, or are destined to be cycled at relatively short intervals.

Signature wine: Warburn Estate Show Reserve Shiraz

BIG RIVERS ZONE
Perricoota ❧

The name of the region comes from Perricoota Station, established in the 1850s and purchased by the Watson brothers in 1911, whose descendants still own and farm the property. At first blush, one might assume the region was created to fill in the gap between the Murray River and Riverina. In fact it is but a pinhead in size compared to Riverina, and there is a large gap between the two regions, doubtless without available water. So it is that the Murray River constitutes the southern boundary of Perricoota, thus dividing the twin towns of Moama (on the New South Wales side) and Echuca (on the Victorian side).

While viticulture has been a significant part of the agricultural scene on the southern side of the Murray River, it was not until 1995 that vineyards were planted on the northern side, and two years later the first commercial vintage was harvested in the Perricoota region. (Sporadic attempts had been made in the middle of the nineteenth century, but were unsuccessful.)

In 1999 the 500-tonne production level required for registration as a region under the GI legislation was achieved, and has been since comfortably exceeded. With the best will in the world it is difficult to describe the wines of the region as anything other than relatively unimportant in terms of quality or character, but reasonably significant quantities of grapes are grown, headed towards a variety of end uses.

PERRICOOTA

Latitude **36°5'S**
Altitude **100 m**
Heat degree days **2100**
Growing season rainfall **224 mm**
Mean January temp. **22.8°C**
Harvest **Early February to mid-March**
Chief viticultural hazard **Spring frost**

● Sydney

Cellar Door
* Stevens Brook Estate at 620 High St,
Echuca, Victoria.

The Region

CLIMATE

The climate is typical of the Murray River area, with hot, dry summers making irrigation essential.

SOIL & TOPOGRAPHY

The soils are typically alluvial due to the meandering of the Murray River over the millennia. The most suitable to viticulture are red, sandy loams to fine clay loams over blocky clays which provide drainage to a depth of 2 metres or more. Soil pH ranges from 6.5 to 8.0, ideal for viticulture.

PRINCIPAL GRAPE VARIETIES

In descending order:

CHARDONNAY

SHIRAZ

CABERNET SAUVIGNON

MERLOT

SEMILLON.

❧ WHITE WINE STYLES

Chardonnay, ever-adaptive, produces wines with peach and light tropical fruit overtones.

Sauvignon Blanc. In cooler vintages, and with imaginative viticultural practices, fair quality wine can be made, notwithstanding the climate.

❧ RED WINE STYLES

Shiraz and Cabernet Sauvignon. While the very short history of the region, coupled with the swing from white wine to red, makes generalisations difficult, soft, ripe red wines will be the mainstay of the region for the foreseeable future. Other parts of the Big River Zone have shown that with appropriate irrigation techniques, yield can be limited and red wines with deeper colour, richer flavour and better tannin structure can be made. Shiraz will continue to prosper, Cabernet Sauvignon less so.

SUMMER VINES, BIG RIVERS ZONE.

Wineries of Perricoota

Morrisons Riverview Winery

Est. 1996
Lot 2, Merool Lane, Moama 2731
www.riverviewestate.com.au

Alistair and Leslie Morrison purchased this historic property in 1995. Plantings began the following year, with Shiraz and Cabernet Sauvignon, then in 1997 Sauvignon Blanc, with Frontignac and Grenache in 1998, totalling 6 ha. The cellar door and restaurant opened in spring 2000, serving light lunches, platters, picnic baskets, coffee and gourmet cakes; wines are sold by the glass, bottle or box and tastings are free of charge. The wines are made by John Ellis at Hanging Rock.
Signature wine: Sauvignon Blanc

St Anne's Vineyards Est. 1972

Cnr Perricoota Rd & 24 Lane, Moama 2731
mclean@blueskyinternet.com.au

Owner Richard McLean has established 80 ha of estate vineyards, with another 120 ha of grower vineyards to draw upon. Shiraz, Cabernet Sauvignon, Grenache and Mourvèdre account for over 75 per cent of the plantings, but there is a spread of the usual white wines and few red exotics. The heart of the business is bulk wine production for other large producers, and a certain amount of contract winemaking. Most of the 20 000 cases of St Anne's wines are sold through the two cellar-door operations, and in particular the one at Myrniong (near Ballarat, VIC), which is surrounded by a somewhat scrappy vineyard (planted in 1972), but which attracts considerable passing trade and wedding receptions.
Signature wine: Shiraz

Stevens Brook Estate Est. 1995

620 High St, Echuca 3564
stevensbrookestate@kitene.com.au
(at 620 High St, Echuca)

The 15 ha Stevens Brook Estate vineyard was established by Bill and Jacqui Stevens in 1995, with the first commercial production in 1999. Initially the grapes were sold to others, but are now being diverted to the Stevens Brook Estate label. The yield is restricted to 10–12 tonnes per hectare, roughly half the regional average. The winery was built in 1999 on a separate 40 ha property on the Echuca side of the Murray River, which will be fully planted. Just to complicate the picture a little further, Bill Stevens has established his cellar-door operation in the Port of Echuca district, the philosophy being to take the cellar door to the customer, rather than try to draw the customer to the vineyard.
Signature wine: Chardonnay

SOUTH COAST ZONE
Shoalhaven Coast ❧

Wineries stretch along the south coast of New South Wales from Nowra and the Shoalhaven River at the northern end to Bega at the southern end. Most have been established since the early 1970s, and all rely heavily on cellar-door sales to the tourist trade.

The principal threat to viticulture lies with unpredictable but sometimes substantial summer rainfall, a problem which diminishes as you move south. It is a situation with which the Hunter Valley and New South Wales' north coast wineries are thoroughly familiar, and fortunately it is far from insuperable. Nonetheless, it seems almost certain that vineyard holdings along the coast – and winery size – will remain small, and that the major vineyard developments of the future will continue to take place on the interior (or western) side of the Great Dividing Range.

What is more, it is notable that the two most successful wineries – Cambewarra Estate and Coolangatta Estate, both in the Shoalhaven Coast region – rely on contract making by experienced wineries in the Hunter Valley. Making small quantities of wine in isolated regions has never been easy unless the winemaker has both experience and technical qualifications. Yet here, more than any other region, the key to success rests with the tourist trade. It is not that the central and southern coasts of New South Wales are especially desirable or suitable places in which to grow grapes – quite simply, they are not – but they are desirable places in which to market wine.

It is generally accepted that the overall quality of wine made by the small winery of today is significantly better than that of 20 years ago. What is not so clear is just how discerning the average tourist is about wine style and quality. Good may be good enough for these wineries, but there is no question that Cambewarra Estate and Coolangatta Estate have lifted the height of the bar for the others in the region to jump over.

COOLANGATTA ESTATE, SHOALHAVEN COAST.

SHOALHAVEN COAST

Latitude **36°40'S**

Altitude **10–70 m**

Heat degree days **1900**

Growing season rainfall **324 mm**

Mean January temp. **22.1°C**

Harvest **Mid-February to mid-March**

Chief viticultural hazards **Vintage rainfall; mildew**

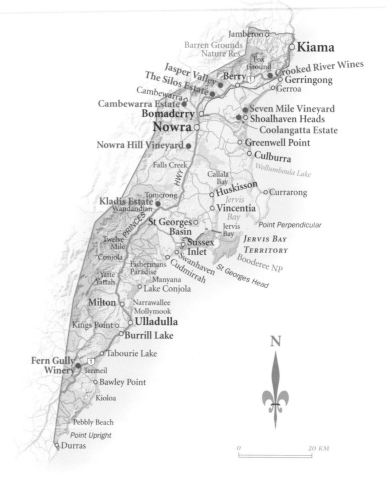

The Region

CLIMATE

Growing season temperatures are especially moderate, with extremely high summer temperatures uncommon due to the strong maritime influence of the Pacific Ocean. High humidity also diminishes stress on the vines and aids growth, but – together with heavy summer rainfall – significantly increases the risk of mildew (both downy and powdery) and of botrytis.

SOIL & TOPOGRAPHY

The soil varies in depth and consistency from the alluvial valleys to the hillsides, but most are red and brown earths which are well suited to viticulture and which promote good yields. Well-exposed, well-drained and ventilated slopes are best.

PRINCIPAL GRAPE VARIETIES

Overall, 55 per cent white, 45 per cent red. In descending order:

CHARDONNAY

CABERNET SAUVIGNON

SHIRAZ

CHAMBOURCIN

VERDELHO

SAUVIGNON BLANC.

 WHITE WINE STYLES

Chardonnay, ubiquitous and ever-flexible, is the most important grape, planted up and down the length of the coast. It produces a pleasant, mid-weight wine with gently peachy fruit flavours and a soft finish. Contract winemaking by Tyrrell's for Coolangatta Estate (a confusing name which sounds as if it should come from the north coast near Queensland) shows the variety to best advantage: clean, easy in the mouth, and not impaired by excessive or inferior oak and/or oak chips.

 RED WINE STYLES

Shiraz and Cabernet Sauvignon. Paired together because they are in fact often blended, and also because either as single varietal wines or as blends they produce soft, faintly earthy wines without especially distinctive varietal character. With appropriate winery techniques, these are fresh, well-balanced, light- to medium-bodied wines best consumed while young.

Chambourcin, a French hybrid, is planted for precisely the same reasons as it is in the Hastings River far to the north: it is highly resistant to mildew and rot, and performs well in even the wettest summers. The vibrant colour and fresh plum fruit aroma and flavour of the wine are best enjoyed while it is young; sometimes a touch of new oak is introduced in an endeavour to fill in the obvious hole in the mid-to-back palate structure.

Wineries of the Shoalhaven Coast

Cambewarra Estate Est. 1991

520 Illaroo Rd, Cambewarra 2540
www.cambewarraestate.com.au

Geoffrey and Louise Cole founded the 5 ha Cambewarra Estate near the Shoalhaven River on the central southern coast of New South Wales, with contract winemaking competently carried out (a considerable distance away) at Tamburlaine Winery in the Hunter Valley. This is not a tourist trap: these are most attractive wines which have had significant success in wine shows, the focus of attention being Chardonnay, Verdelho, Chambourcin and Cabernet Sauvignon.

Signature wine: John Chardonnay

Coolangatta Estate Est. 1988

1335 Bolong Rd, Shoalhaven Heads 2535
www.coolangattaestate.com.au

Coolangatta Estate is part of a 150 ha resort with accommodation, restaurants, golf course, etc., with some of the oldest buildings convict-built in 1822. It might be thought that the wines are tailored purely for the tourist market, but in fact the standard of viticulture is exceptionally high (immaculate Scott-Henry trellising), and the contract winemaking by Tyrrell's is wholly professional. The range includes Semillon, Verdelho, Chardonnay, Chambourcin and Cabernet Sauvignon, the Semillon ageing every bit as well as it does in the Hunter Valley.

Signature wine: Alexander Berry Chardonnay

Seven Mile Vineyard Est. 1998

84 Coolangatta Rd, Shoalhaven Heads 2535
www.sevenmilevineyard.com.au

The 1.8 ha Seven Mile Vineyard situated east of the town of Berry was established by Joan and Eric Swarbrick in 1997; the vineyard overlooks Coomonderry Swamp, one of the largest coastal wetlands in New South Wales. The first three vintages used Chambourcin, Verdelho and Cabernet Sauvignon from the estate, the Petit Verdot came on-stream in 2004. Chardonnay is purchased from the adjacent Southern Highlands region, and is made and released in unoaked form.

Signature wine: Chardonnay

Yarrawa Estate Est. 1998

PO Box 6018, Kangaroo Valley 2577
www.yarrawaestate.com

Susan and Mark Francis Foster established Yarrawa Estate in 1998 with the planting of a wide variety of trees, table grapes and 2.5 ha of Verdelho, Chardonnay, Chambourcin, Merlot and Cabernet Sauvignon. The hillside vineyard has views across the Kangaroo Valley, with the Kangaroo River directly below. Fingerboard directions up the hill point the way for the first-time visitor.

Signature wine: Chambourcin

SOUTH COAST ZONE
Southern Highlands 🌿

The government records for 1886 show a wine-grape harvest of 950 gallons (4275 litres) for the Berrima district, suggesting the first vineyards were planted in the 1870s. (Table grapes had been established earlier in that decade.) German vineyard workers from the Vogt family came from vineyards at Camden to establish plantings on Joadja Road in the 1890s, which remained in cultivation for a considerable time thereafter. Yet further vineyards were planted around the turn of the century, leading to exports to Europe.

It was not until the 1950s that all commercial grapegrowing ceased; in 1983 it resumed with the establishment of Joadja Vineyards and Winery. It and Eling Forest Winery began wine sales in 1990, and development accelerated thereafter. By 2005 there were 40 vineyards, most still coming into bearing, and 13 wineries.

When successfully seeking registration as a Geographic Indication region, it was decided to adopt the boundaries of the Shire of Wingecarribee for that of the region, thus taking in the towns of Mittagong, Bowral, Moss Vale and Berrima. Southern Highlands sits astride the Hume and Illawarra highways, along the spine of the Great Dividing Range, west to the Wollondilly River and east to the escarpment overlooking Wollongong on the coast.

It is rolling hill country, with abundant tree and vegetation cover, both native and exotic, which remains green for much of the year, and it is not surprising it should be a favoured country retreat for wealthy Sydney-siders. After an uncertain start, and notwithstanding some climatic challenges, its professionally run vineyards and wineries are providing some very impressive wines.

BLUE METAL VINEYARD, SOUTHERN HIGHLANDS.

SOUTHERN HIGHLANDS

Latitude **36°27'S**

Altitude **600–750 m**

Heat degree days **1330**

Growing season rainfall **596 mm**

Mean January temp. **18.9°C**

Harvest **Late March to early May**

Chief viticultural hazards **Vintage rain; hail**

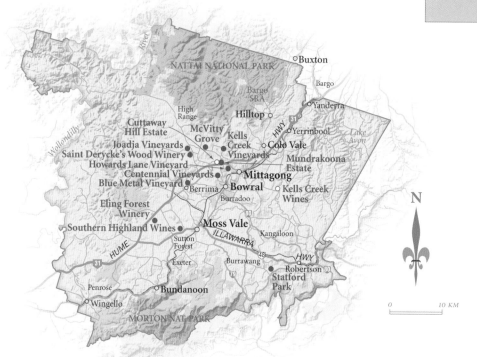

The Region

CLIMATE

The overall climate is cool sub-temperate, with mild summers and cool foggy, frosty winters. Rainfall is evenly distributed throughout the year; summer rainfall tends to occur during violent electrical storms, often accompanied by heavy hail.

SOIL & TOPOGRAPHY

The altitude varies from 550 metres to a few high spots at 880 metres; most of the vineyards are within the 600–750 metres range. The main soil types are those derived from basalt (red and brown kraznozems and red earths) and shale (red and brown podzolics and brown earths). They are relatively free draining, but acidic clay increases at depth.

PRINCIPAL GRAPE VARIETIES

Overall, 60 per cent red, 40 per cent white. In descending order:

CHARDONNAY

CABERNET SAUVIGNON

PINOT NOIR

SAUVIGNON BLANC

SHIRAZ

MERLOT

RIESLING.

Wineries of the Southern Highlands

Blue Metal Vineyard Est. 2002

Lot 18, Compton Park Rd, Berrima 2025

www.bluemetalvineyard.com

 exports to UK

The 10.5 ha Blue Metal Vineyard has been established at an elevation of 790 m; the name comes from the rich red soil that overlies the cap of basalt rock and is commonly called blue metal. Varieties planted include Sauvignon Blanc, Pinot Gris, Merlot, Cabernet Sauvignon, Sangiovese and Petit Verdot; the wines have been very competently contract-made, with Kim Moginie's long experience in the region (dating back to 1983), and assistant winemaker Joe Duncan's international cool-climate wine-making in Alsace and Chablis.

Signature wine: Southern Highlands Pinot Gris

 WHITE WINE STYLES

Chardonnay is fragrant and elegant, with citrus overtones to apple and melon fruit; it handles malolactic fermentation well.

Sauvignon Blanc has pungent and aromatic varietal character, with a mix of gooseberry, passionfruit and asparagus-accented fruit.

 RED WINE STYLES

Cabernet Sauvignon offers a convincing mix of blackcurrant, mint and cassis, moderately herbaceous, and with fine-grained tannins. Stands up to vintage rainfall.

Merlot is elegant, light to medium-bodied; quite aromatic and floral; fine savoury tannins.

Pinot Noir has made a recent debut, holding considerable promise for the future.

Shiraz can be impressively spicy and intense, with deep colour.

Centennial Vineyards Est. 2002

'Woodside', Centennial Rd, Bowral 2576

www.centennial.net.au

⚲ ⊞ exports to UK

Centennial Vineyards, owned by wine professional John Large and investor Mark Dowling, covers 133 ha of beautiful grazing land, with over 30 ha planted to Sauvignon Blanc, Riesling, Verdelho, Chardonnay, Merlot, Pinot Noir, Cabernet Sauvignon and Tempranillo. Production from the estate vineyards is supplemented by purchases of grapes from other regions, including Orange. The on-site winery has a 120 tonne capacity and is under the direction of winemaker Tony Cosgriff. Wine quality is consistently impressive.

Signature wine: Reserve Chardonnay

Cuttaway Hill Estate Est. 1998

PO Box 2034, Bowral 2576

www.cuttawayhillwines.com.au

⌧

Owned by the O'Neil family, Cuttaway Hill Estate is the second-largest vineyard property in the Southern Highlands, with 38 ha on three sites, covering all the major varieties and with varying soil types and mesoclimates. Both the standard of viticulture and of contract winemaking – under Jim Chatto at Monarch Winemaking Services – are evident in the high quality of the wines.

Signature wine: Southern Highlands Chardonnay

McVitty Grove Est. 1998

Wombeyan Caves Rd, Mittagong 2575

www.mcvittygrove.com.au

Mark Phillips had a 20-year career in finance and six years of tertiary qualifications in horticulture when he and wife Jane began the search for a Southern Highlands site suited to premium grapegrowing and olive cultivation,

culminating in the acquisition of 42 ha of farmland where they have established 5.5 ha of Pinot Noir and Pinot Gris on deep, fertile soils at the front of the property. A 1.5 ha olive grove surrounds the cellar door and café.

Signature wine: Pinot Noir

Mundrakoona Estate Est. 1997

Sir Charles Moses Lane,

Old Hume Hwy, Mittagong 2575

www.mundrakoona.com.au

⚲

During 1998 and 1999 Anton Balog progressively planted 3.2 ha of Pinot Noir, Sauvignon Blanc and Tempranillo at an altitude of 680 m. He is using wild yeast ferments, hand-plunging and other 'natural' winemaking techniques, with the aim of producing Burgundian-style Pinot and Chardonnay and Bordeaux-style Sauvignon Blanc and Cabernet Sauvignon, and having success. For the foreseeable future, estate production will be supplemented by grapes grown from local vineyards.

Signature wine: Artemis Pinot Noir

Southern Highland Wines Est. 2003

Oldbury Rd, Sutton Forest 2577

www.southernhighlandwines.com

⚲

The venture is owned by its five directors, with 50 years of cumulative experience in the wine industry and in commerce. Forty-one ha of vines have been established, a veritable fruit salad of Pinot Gris, Riesling, Gewürztraminer, Sauvignon Blanc, Chardonnay, Viognier, Nebbiolo, Sangiovese, Pinot Noir, Shiraz and Cabernet Sauvignon. The wines are made at the estate winery by Eddy Rossi, one of the directors.

Signature wine: Chardonnay

Northern Rivers Zone
Hastings River 🌿

Viticulture and winemaking in the Hastings River region date back to 1837, when the first vineyard was planted by Henry Fancourt White, a colonial surveyor; by the 1860s there were 33 vineyards in the area. Following Federation and the shift to fortified wine production, along with many other wine regions production declined and ultimately ceased in the Hastings Valley in the early years of the twentieth century.

In 1980, after 60 years of non-productivity, the French-descended Cassegrain family decided to expand into real estate and associated viticulture and winery interests. As a result they significantly – if improbably – expanded the modern viticultural map of Australia. In the process they pioneered (with considerable help from Dr Richard Smart) new varieties and new ways of managing vineyards to meet the unique climatic challenges of the region, and have indirectly encouraged the development of other vineyards and wineries along the Northern Rivers Zone and adjacent Northern Slopes Zone.

The best vintages are those in which the late summer rains are below average, but even in these circumstances the successful outcome of the vintage is dependent on split-second timing of the harvest and upon very careful management of the canopy. The only assured answer has been the propagation of the French hybrid Chambourcin, which is resistant to the mildews that otherwise pose a constant threat. Much the same applies to the other vineyards dotted along the coast.

DISEASE-FREE GRAPES.

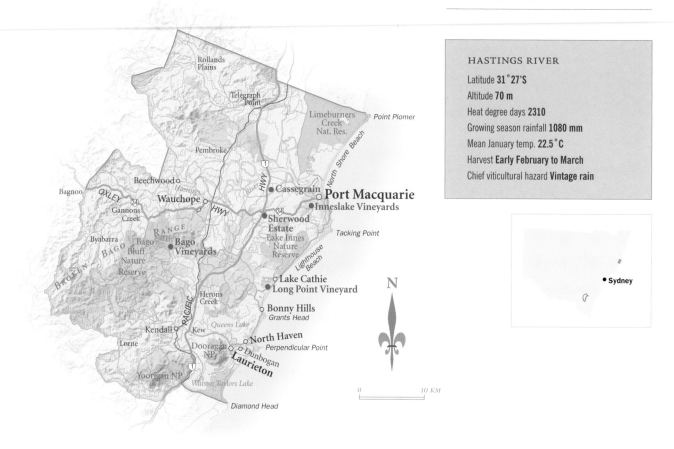

HASTINGS RIVER

Latitude **31°27'S**

Altitude **70 m**

Heat degree days **2310**

Growing season rainfall **1080 mm**

Mean January temp. **22.5°C**

Harvest **Early February to March**

Chief viticultural hazard **Vintage rain**

The Region

CLIMATE

The vineyards of the Hastings Valley, so claims Dr Richard Smart, are the only significant new plantings to have been established in Australia over the past 25 years which have not been supplied with irrigation – simply because they have no need of it. For this is a region with higher than normal summer humidity and high rainfall, as well as being uncompromisingly warm. It is much affected by the tail end of tropical cyclones moving down the coast from Queensland, and by its proximity to the warm waters of the Pacific Ocean.

SOIL & TOPOGRAPHY

The gently hilly terrain offers a wide choice of aspect and hence response to (and use of) prevailing winds, useful in assisting disease control. The soils vary greatly in fertility, depth and structure, spanning rich alluvial soils and volcanic free-draining soils, and running from sandy through to heavy clay. Some are deep, some overlie gravel, others overlie limestone.

PRINCIPAL GRAPE VARIETIES

Overall, evenly split between white and red. In descending order:

SEMILLON

CHAMBOURCIN

SHIRAZ

CHARDONNAY

CABERNET SAUVIGNON.

Wineries of the Hastings River

Bago Vineyards Est. 1985

Millingans Rd, off Bago Rd, Wauchope 2446

www.bagovineyards.com.au

Jim and Kay Mobs commenced planting the Broken Bago Vineyards in 1985 with 1 ha of Chardonnay and have now increased the total plantings to 12.5 ha and production to 6000 cases, with a kaleidoscopic array of styles made from Chardonnay, Verdelho, Chambourcin, Merlot and Pinot Noir, with sparkling versions and a Tawny Port firmly and successfully created for the general tourist trade. John Cassegrain is consultant winemaker.

Signature wine: Chambourcin

 WHITE WINE STYLES

Semillon. The thin skins and large berries of Semillon make it especially vulnerable to the effects of vintage rain. The saving grace is Semillon's unusual ability to produce excellent wine at lower than usual sugar (and hence alcohol) levels of around 10° baume. Thus early picking is the response, and the wines show many of the characters of, and develop in much the same way as, those of the Hunter Valley.

Chardonnay is not unlike a pumped-up version of that of the Hunter Valley – rich, generous and fruitily sweet in a peach/tropical fruit spectrum. It lends itself to manipulation in the winery, and to the use of oak. It matures quickly, but the wines from better (drier) vintages can hold their peak for several years.

 RED WINE STYLES

Chambourcin. This hybrid (bred in the nineteenth century) is strongly resistant to mildew, and for this reason has been planted in the Hastings Valley. The intense purple colour gives the wine a second use as a blend component where colour is thought to be needed. The flavour is pronounced, falling in the black cherry/plum range in its youth, sometimes with a slight spicy/gamey overlay. Its Achilles heel is a lack of structure, particularly on the back palate.

Shiraz is carried along by its overall popularity rather than any particular merit or suitability to the climate. Does best in the rare dry vintages.

Cassegrain Est. 1980

Hastings River Winery, Fernbank Creek Rd, Port Macquarie 2444

www.cassegrainwines.com.au

 exports to UK, US

The Cassegrain family pioneered grapegrowing in the region, with significant input from Dr Richard Smart, who for many years ran his consultancy business from an office at Cassegrain. It encouraged other growers to come into this challenging region, and has given them support (in some instance grape purchase contracts). It draws fruit from many parts of Australia but also has 12 ha of estate plantings which offer 14 varieties, including the mildew-resistant Chambourcin, a French-bred cross.

Signature wine: Fromenteau Reserve Chardonnay

Inneslake Vineyards Est. 1988

The Ruins Way, Inneslake, Port Macquarie 2444

www.inneslake.com.au

The property upon which the Inneslake (formerly Charley Brothers) vineyard is established has been in the family's ownership since the turn of the century, but in fact had been planted to vines (long gone) by a Major Innes in the 1840s. After carrying on logging and fruitgrowing at various times, the Charley family planted vines in 1988 with the encouragement of contract winemaker John Cassegrain. Around 7.5 ha of vines have been established, planted to Semillon, Chardonnay, Pinot Noir, Shiraz, Merlot and Cabernet Sauvignon.

Signature wine: Chardonnay

Long Point Vineyard Est. 1995

6 Cooinda Place, Lake Cathie 2445

longpointvineyard@tsn.cc

In turning their dream into reality, educational psychologist Graeme and chartered accountant Helen Davies took no chances. After becoming interested through wine appreciation courses the Davies moved from Brisbane so that 36-year-old Graeme could work at Cassegrain full time and begin his part-time study for a postgraduate diploma in wine from Roseworthy. Late in 1993 they purchased a 5 ha property near Lake Cathie, progressively establishing 2 ha of Chardonnay, Shiraz, Chambourcin, Cabernet Sauvignon and Frontignac. As well as having his job at Cassegrain and establishing the vineyard, Graeme Davies self-built the house, designed by Helen with a pyramid-shaped roof and an underground cellar. All of the wines are made on-site.

Signature wine: Chambourcin

Northern Slopes Zone

A large zone, but unified by the fact that much of the country is on the western slopes of the Great Dividing Range, most with significant altitude. As at 2005 there were signs that a New England region, with its northern boundary the New South Wales/Queensland border, was soon to seek registration. The number of wineries coming on-stream would clearly support such a move.

The Northern Slopes Zone had a significant pioneer in the nineteenth century, when George Wyndham, who had founded Dalwood Estate in the Hunter Valley in 1830, took vine cuttings to a large property he had acquired at Bukkulla near Inverell. In 1870 the vineyard was producing 50000 litres of rich, dark,

full-bodied red wine which was blended with the lighter-bodied Dalwood Estate wine to produce a much-esteemed Burgundy. Bukkulla remained in production until 1890, ended by the depression which led to the great bank crash of 1893. The modern-day pioneer was Inverell medical practitioner Dr Keith Whish, who founded Gilgai Wines in 1968, planting Malbec and Pinot Noir, quietly selling the tiny production through cellar door.

The core of the zone is, without question, the New England district. The soil map of the district is exceptionally complex, derived from six parent rocks: paleozoic (sometimes called greywacke, and the oldest in the district), granites (and associated volcanics), serpentine,

mesozoics, basalt, and (by derivation) alluvial deposits. This means there is a wide range of choice of suitable soils for viticulture, with grey-wacke, basalt and alluvial deposits to the fore.

The district lies in the zone of transition from the dominantly summer rainfall of northern Australia to the dominantly winter rainfall of the south. Thus subtropical summer rainfall contrasts with the cold winters and the risk of spring frosts. In this it shares many things in common with Queensland's Granite Belt to its immediate north. Careful site selection and a high level of canopy management during the summer are necessary prerequisites for success.

NORTHERN SLOPES ZONE

Latitude **30°31'S**

Altitude **980 m**

Heat degree days **1516**

Growing season rainfall **538 mm**

Mean January temp. **20.4°C**

Harvest **End February to end March**

Chief viticultural hazard **Spring frost**

The Region 🌹

CLIMATE

Dr John Gladstones, in his book *Viticulture and Environment*, describes the climate thus:

'Both Armidale and Glen Innes offer excellent potential temperatures, sunshine hours and relative humidities during ripening for making medium-bodied table wines. The highest maxima during ripening, and indeed, through the whole growing season, are remarkably moderate: the result of a firmly established summer monsoon influence in this high-altitude subtropical climate. Such equability during ripening is found in few other places in Australia. At the same time, sunshine hours and afternoon relative humidities are both very favourable. Growing season rainfall is just about optimal. Its summer dominance increases to the north, but at both Armidale and Glen Innes the average rainfall diminishes quite rapidly through the ripening period, leading into a mild, sunny, fairly dry autumn. Midseason to late grape varieties from Bordeaux, the Rhone and Northern Italy should be the best adapted to this ripening environment.'

KURRAJONG DOWNS.

Wineries of Northern Slopes Zone

Kurrajong Downs Est. 2000

Casino Rd, via Tenterfield 2372
www.kurrajongdownswines.com

Jonus Rhodes arrived at Tenterfield in 1858, lured by the gold he mined for the next 40 years until his death in 1898. He was evidently successful, for the family now runs a 2800 ha cattle-grazing property on which Lynton and Sue Rhodes have planted a little over 4 ha of vineyard at an altitude of 850 m. Development of the vineyard started in the spring of 1996, and encouraged further planting the following year. A substantial cellar door, restaurant and function centre has been established.
Signature wine: Louisa Mary Semillon

Richfield Estate Est. 1997

Bonshaw Rd, Tenterfield 2372
www.richfieldvineyard.com.au

Singapore resident Bernard Forey is the chairman and majority shareholder of Richfield Estate. The 500 ha property, at an altitude of 720 m, was selected after an intensive survey by soil specialists. Just under 30 ha of Shiraz, Cabernet Sauvignon, Merlot, Ruby Cabernet, Semillon, Chardonnay and Verdelho have been planted, the first vintage being made in 2000. Winemaker John Cassegrain is also a shareholder in the venture, and it is expected that the bulk of the sales will come from the export markets of south-east Asia and Japan.
Signature wine: Tenterfield Semillon

Tangaratta Estate Est. 1999

RMB 637 Old Winton Rd, Tamworth 2340
(02) 6761 5660
exports to US

Another major entry into the Northern Slopes Zone, with a substantial 29 ha vineyard planted to Verdelho, Cabernet Sauvignon, Merlot and Shiraz, and a 23 000 case production, contract-made by John Hordern in the Hunter Valley. The wines are widely exported, and are also available by mail order and through the cellar door, which has light meals and barbecue facilities when open.
Signature wine: Cabernet Sauvignon

Warrina Wines Est. 1989

Back Rd, Kootingal 2352
(02) 6760 3985

David and Susan Nicholls began the establishment of their 2.5 ha vineyard way back in 1989, and were content to sell the grapes to other producers, making occasional forays into winemaking, until deciding to commence winemaking on a micro-commercial basis in 2001. They produce Sauvignon Blanc, Chardonnay, Shiraz and Cabernet Sauvignon.
Signature wine: Cabernet Sauvignon

Wellington Vale Wines

Est. 1997
'Wellington Vale', Deepwater 2371 (postal)
(02) 6734 5226

David and Dierdri Robertson-Cuninghame trace their ancestry (via David) back to the Duke of Wellington, with an ancestor of David being an ADC to the Duke, and his son, Arthur Wellesley Robertson, the Duke's godson. Arthur Robertson migrated to Australia and took up the land upon which Wellington Vale is situated in 1839. Planting began in 1997 with 0.7 ha of Semillon, continuing with 1 ha of Pinot Noir and 0.3 ha of Riesling.
Signature wine: Deepwater Red Pinot Noir

Willowvale Wines Est. 1994

Black Swamp Rd, Tenterfield 2372
www.willowvalewines.com.au

John and Lyn Morley commenced planting 1.8 ha of vineyard of equal portions of Chardonnay, Merlot and Cabernet Sauvignon in 1994, with further plantings in 1999 and 2000 lifting the total to 3 ha. The vineyard is at an altitude of 940 m and was the first in the growing Tenterfield subregion. Advanced vineyard climatic monitoring systems have been installed, and a new winery building was constructed and equipped in time for the 2000 vintage.
Signature wine: Chardonnay

Western Plains Zone 🌿

It may be that the Western Plains Zone was created by the necessity of filling up the state map; it may be that the majority of the producers have moved into viticulture as a means of diversifying their farming activities; and it may be that not all the areas chosen will prove to be viable. The fact remains that a growing number of vignerons are active in the zone, and that more will follow.

In the 1870s and 1880s Dubbo supported a significant winemaking industry, with Eumalga Estate (owned and run by French-born J.E. Serisier) said (by the local newspaper of the time) to have the second-largest winery in Australia (which I doubt). Another highly successful winery was established by German-born Friederich Kurtz: his Mount Olive wines won a number of awards in international exhibitions in the 1880s.

Most of the wineries in the zone huddle together in its south-eastern corner around Dubbo, close to the border of the Central Ranges Zone, providing a climate warmer than Mudgee, mainly due to the lower altitude. Spring frost is not an issue, but the risk of late summer rainfall is. While vineyards are scattered further throughout the zone, summer heat (and humidity) progressively increases to the west, and lack of water availability circumscribes choice both in the west and south-west.

CANONBAH BRIDGE, WESTERN PLAINS.

Wineries of Western Plains Zone

Boora Estate Est. 1984

'Boora', Warrie Rd, Dubbo 2830
www.boora-estate.com

Frank Ramsay has established approximately 0.5 ha each of Chardonnay, Semillon, Cabernet Franc, Cabernet Sauvignon, Merlot, Tempranillo and Shiraz. Boora Estate won a silver medal at the Brisbane Wine Show with its 2000 Shiraz, matching the success of Mount Olive 120 years earlier.

Signature wine: Shiraz

Canonbah Bridge Est. 1999

Merryanbone Station, Warren 2824 (postal)
www.canonbahbridge.com

exports to UK, US

The 29 ha vineyard has been established by Shane McLaughlin on the very large Merryanbone Station, a Merino sheep stud which has been in the family for four generations. The wines are contract-made by John Hordern, and in some instances incorporate grapes grown in McLaren Vale and elsewhere; these are typically released under the Ram's Leap second label.

Signature wine: Semillon Sauvignon Blanc

Lazy River Estate Est. 1997

29R Old Dubbo Rd, Dubbo 2830
www.lazyriverestate.com.au

The Scott family have planted 3 ha each of Chardonnay and Semillon, 1 ha of Merlot, and 1.5 ha each of Petit Verdot and Cabernet Sauvignon. The vineyard is situated a little under 3 km from the end of the main street of Dubbo, and a cellar door opened in 2003. The wines are made at Briar Ridge.

Signature wine: Squatters Chair Chardonnay

Red Earth Estate Vineyard Est. 2000

18L Camp Rd, Dubbo 2830
www.redearthestate.com.au

Ken and Christine Borchardt look set to be the focal point of grapegrowing and winemaking in the future Macquarie Valley region of the Western Plains Zone. They have planted 1.3 ha each of Riesling, Verdelho, Frontignac, Grenache, Shiraz and Cabernet Sauvignon at the winery, with a further planting each of Shiraz, Cabernet Franc and Cabernet Sauvignon on another site. The winery has a maximum capacity of 14 000 cases (presently producing 5000 cases), and the Borchardts are offering contract winemaking facilities in addition to making and marketing their own brand.

Signature wine: Cabernet Sauvignon

Tombstone Estate Est. 1997

5R Basalt Rd, Dubbo 2830
robboatbourke@optusnet.com.au

The ominously named Tombstone Estate has been established by Rob and Patty Tilling, who have planted 5 ha of Chardonnay, Pinot Noir, Shiraz, Cabernet Sauvignon, Sangiovese, Barbera and Muscat. Rob Tilling makes the wine on-site, with sales through local outlets, mail order and cellar door, the last with barbecue and picnic facilities.

Signature wine: Chardonnay

RED EARTH ESTATE.

Western Australia

Introduction ❧

Two things are immediately obvious from a glance at the state map: first, the sheer immensity of Western Australia (it is a four hours' plus drive from Perth to Mount Barker, closer to five hours to Albany); second, how the need to cover the state – all states – with wine zones comes up with the result that all the regions so far registered are situated in two of the five zones, and that only nine out of 316 wineries are situated in the remaining three zones.

The Eastern Plains, Inland and North of Western Australia Zone is a massive blank page, roughly comparable to the land mass of New South Wales, Victoria and South Australia combined. Only two wineries have ventured into this vast area, adjacent to Lake Grace.

The Central Western Australia Zone stretches over 600 kilometres in a north–south irregular sausage, with Perth (away to the west) slightly closer to the northern than the southern end. Much is wheatbelt country, and the existence of the handful of vineyards show that viticulture is feasible in a strongly continental climate, with hot days and cold nights. The wines do not make their way out of the nearby towns.

The West Australian South East Coastal Zone stretches along the southern coast of the state from west of Bremer Bay to well east of Esperance. It has one winery: Dalyup River at Esperance.

This leaves the Greater Perth Zone and South West Australia Zone with all the action: nine regions and five subregions.

[PREVIOUS] WILLOW BRIDGE ESTATE, GEOGRAPHE.

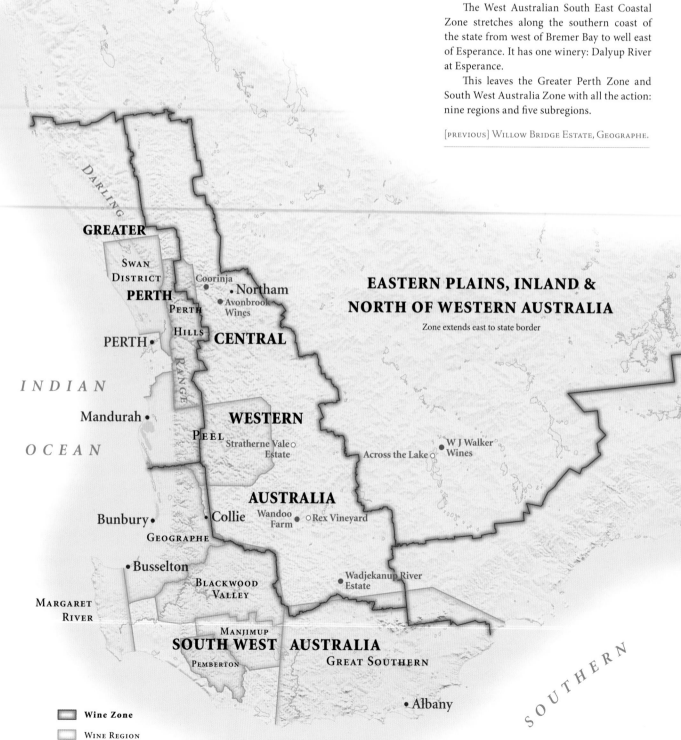

Eastern Plains, Inland & North of Western Australia Zone

Across the Lake Est. 1999

Box 66, Lake Grace 6353

ptaylor@treko.net.au

The Taylor family has been farming (wheat and sheep) for over 40 years at Lake Grace, and a small diversification into grapegrowing started as a hobby, but has developed into a little more than that with 1.6 ha of Shiraz. The Taylors were also motivated to support their friend Bill (W. J.) Walker, who had commenced growing Shiraz three years previously, and has since produced a gold medal-winning wine. Having learnt the hard way which soils are suitable, and which are not, the Taylors intend to increase their plantings.

Signature wine: Shiraz

W. J. Walker Wines Est. 1998

Burns Rd, Lake Grace 6353

(08) 9865 1969

Lake Grace is 300 km east of Bunbury, one of those isolated viticultural outposts which are appearing in many parts of Australia these days. There are 1.5 ha of Shiraz and 0.5 ha of Chardonnay, and the wines are sold through local outlets. The climate and terroir provide an ideal environment for Shiraz in a fragrant, gently peppery, medium-bodied mould.

Signature wine: Shiraz

Central Western Australia Zone

Coorinja Est. 1870

Toodyay Rd, Toodyay 6566

(08) 9574 2280

An evocative and historic winery owned by Michael Wood and family, nestling in a small gully which seems to be in a time warp, begging to be used as a set for a film. There are 15 ha of estate plantings, and a revamp of the packaging has accompanied a more than respectable Shiraz, with lots of dark chocolate and sweet berry flavour, finishing with soft tannins.

Signature wine: Shiraz

Wandoo Farm Est. 1997

'Glencraig', Duranillin 6393

dlctriplep@hotmail.com

Wandoo Farm lies outside any of the existing wine regions, north-east of the Blackwood Valley, its nearest regional neighbour. Donald Cochrane owns a 650 ha sheep, cattle and grain farm near Duranillin, with a 575 mm rainfall and abundant underground water. His maternal grandfather came to Australia from Kaiser Stuhl in Germany, later settling near Kojonup, where he planted a vineyard and made the community wine. Cochrane has planted 7 ha of Cabernet Sauvignon, Shiraz, Zinfandel, Verdelho, Viognier and Marsanne. When he planted the vineyard, he says he had no intention of ever having any wine made, intending simply to sell the grapes. Now he says he does not intend to build a winery, but acknowledges that intentions change.

Signature wine: Shiraz

West Australian South East Coastal Zone

Dalyup River Estate Est. 1987

Murrays Rd, Esperance 6450

dalyup@wn.com.au

Arguably the most remote winery in Australia, with 2.5 ha of estate vineyards. The quantities are as small as the cellar-door prices are modest; this apart, the light but fragrant wines show the cool climate of this ocean-side vineyard. Dalyup River came from out of the clouds to win the trophy for Best Wine of Show at the Qantas Wine Show of Western Australia in 1999 with its Shiraz, but hasn't repeated that success.

Signature wine: Shiraz

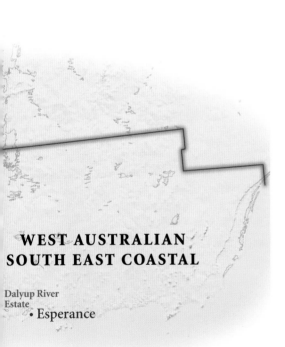

WEST AUSTRALIAN SOUTH EAST COASTAL

Dalyup River Estate
• Esperance

OCEAN

N

0   100 KM

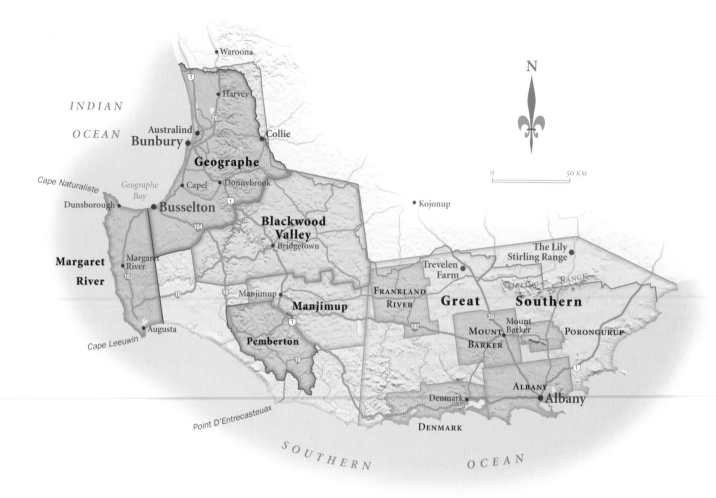

South West Australia Zone 🌿

By the standards of Western Australia, this zone is both densely populated viticulturally – indeed, it has six of the state's nine regions (or proposed regions) and over 85 per cent of its wineries – and the most logical. However, there are a few chinks in the regional armour plating, and wineries will likely work their way into these in due course.

On one view all the regions have links to the coast; certainly none of the more inland regions' winemakers and viticulturists would think twice about a day trip to the coast for surfing, boating or fishing, all of which are excellent. Equally, sea breezes can work their way inland from the two adjacent oceans, the Indian and the Southern.

On the other hand, Margaret River has the ultimate maritime Mediterranean climate, while thanks in part to altitude and in part to distance, the more north-easterly parts of the Great Southern have a much greater continental component in their climate. If Chardonnay, Sauvignon Blanc Semillon and Cabernet Merlot rule the roost in Margaret River, it is Riesling, Shiraz and Cabernet Sauvignon in the Great Southern.

Pemberton, Manjimup, Blackwood Valley and Geographe work their way from south to north, west to east, interlocking like pieces of a jigsaw puzzle, and becoming steadily more maritime in their climate as they do so. Like men in the middle, they are still to work out their destiny. The long stand-off between Manjimup and Pemberton was headed to the law courts in 2006.

Winery of South West Australia Zone

Trevelen Farm Est. 1993

Weir Rd, Cranbrook 6321
www.trevelenfarmwines.com.au

🍷 exports to UK

John and Katie Sprigg operate a 1300 ha wool, meat and grain-producing farm, with sustainable agriculture at its heart. As a minor but highly successful diversification, they have established 6.5 ha of Sauvignon Blanc, Riesling, Chardonnay, Cabernet Sauvignon, Merlot and Shiraz. Vines, it seems, are in the genes, for John Sprigg's great-great-grandparents established 20 ha of vines at Happy Valley, South Australia, in the 1870s. The quality of the wines is as consistent as the prices are modest, and visitors to the cellar door have the added attraction of both garden and forest walks, the latter among 130 ha of remnant bush, which harbours many different orchids that flower from May to December. The stylish wines are made by James Kellie at Harewood Estate, Denmark.

Signature wine: Riesling

[OPPOSITE] THE BEACH, MARGARET RIVER. [ABOVE] DEVIL'S LAIR, MARGARET RIVER.

South West Australia Zone
Margaret River ❧

Unlike the Great Southern region, Margaret River does have a nineteenth-century winemaking heritage, albeit on a small scale. The grandfather of the late Dr Kevin Cullen (founder of Cullen Wines) established a vineyard at Bunbury in 1890. Ephraim Clarke continued to grow and make wine until his death in 1921; the vineyard was ultimately swallowed up in Bunbury's urban sprawl.

Again unlike Great Southern, Margaret River owes less to Californian viticulturalist Professor Harold Olmo than to Dr John Gladstones, who published a paper in 1965 in which he (inter alia) wrote, 'Being virtually frost-free, and having a much lower ripening period, cloudiness, rainfall and hail risk than Manjimup and Mount Barker, it has distinct advantages over both those areas, and indeed over all other Australian vine districts with comparable temperature summations.' His report led Dr Tom Cullity to establish Vasse Felix in 1967, to be quickly followed by others.

Whether it is in part due to the subliminal suggestion of the name I do not know, but I have always felt there is a feminine quality to the soft beauty of the Margaret River region. Yet at one and the same time it is uncompromisingly Australian: Western Australia is home to many of our most striking native plants, and they grow in profusion in the Margaret River area. Stately eucalypts, gnarled banksias and ancient blackboys, their trunks blackened by centuries of bushfires, stand above carpets of flowering kangaroo paws, desert peas and countless other wildflowers.

The doctors-cum-winemakers who, for some strange reason, dominated the early development of viticulture in the region and whose families still have a strong presence, were unusually sensitive to the environment, and the Margaret River wineries tend to merge into the countryside rather than stand superimposed on it. Stone or rammed-earth walls and skilful use of local timber are commonplace, with subtle bush landscaping adding to the overall effect. (The Palandri winery is a notable – and some would say regrettable – exception.)

When the first Margaret River reds came on to the market in the eastern states in the mid 1970s they made a huge impression. There was a clarity and a delicacy to their red fruit flavours and an elegance in their structure which immediately set them apart. In retrospect it seems likely that part of this 'difference' was due to the absence of naturally occurring malolactic fermentation in the bacterially sterile confines typical of new wineries in a new wine region.

Almost overnight Margaret River became the most fashionable address in Australia, its future assured, its potential unlimited. But in the latter part of the 1980s it unexpectedly lost direction and momentum. However, the sheer quality of the region and its wines, not to mention the determination of its leading producers, meant that the pause was only temporary. Indeed, Margaret River began its surge forward while the rest of Australia was headed towards deep recession. The 1997

acquisition of Devil's Lair by Southcorp, Brookland Valley by Hardys, and the arrival of Palandri Wines, coupled with a veritable explosion of syndicate- and winery-funded broadacre plantings, caused further optimism. However, the large 2004 and 2005 grape crush came as a cold shower: Xanadu Wines was sold (under pressure from creditors) to the Rathbone family group (of Yering Station et al.), and Evans & Tate forced to make large-scale writedowns in stock and goodwill.

A wide array of restaurants, many operated by wineries, is liberally scattered through the region and in the township of Margaret River. There are many places to stay, ranging from the luxury of Caves House through conventional motels and hotels to vineyard cottages and bed and breakfast accommodation. There is a vibrant local craft community, focussing on Western Australian hardwoods and to a lesser degree on pottery. Then there are the surfing beaches, populated year-round thanks to the balmy temperatures, even in winter.

There are no official Margaret River subregions, but in 1999 Dr John Gladstones presented a detailed and very compelling paper suggesting there should be six subregions based on climate and soil differences: Yallingup, Carbunup, Wilyabrup, Treeton, Wallcliffe and Karridale.

Finally, there are the winemakers, a feisty lot if ever there was one, and the wines as distinctive as they are good.

[OPPOSITE] VOYAGER ESTATE, MARGARET RIVER.
[BELOW] CAPE MENTELLE, MARGARET RIVER.

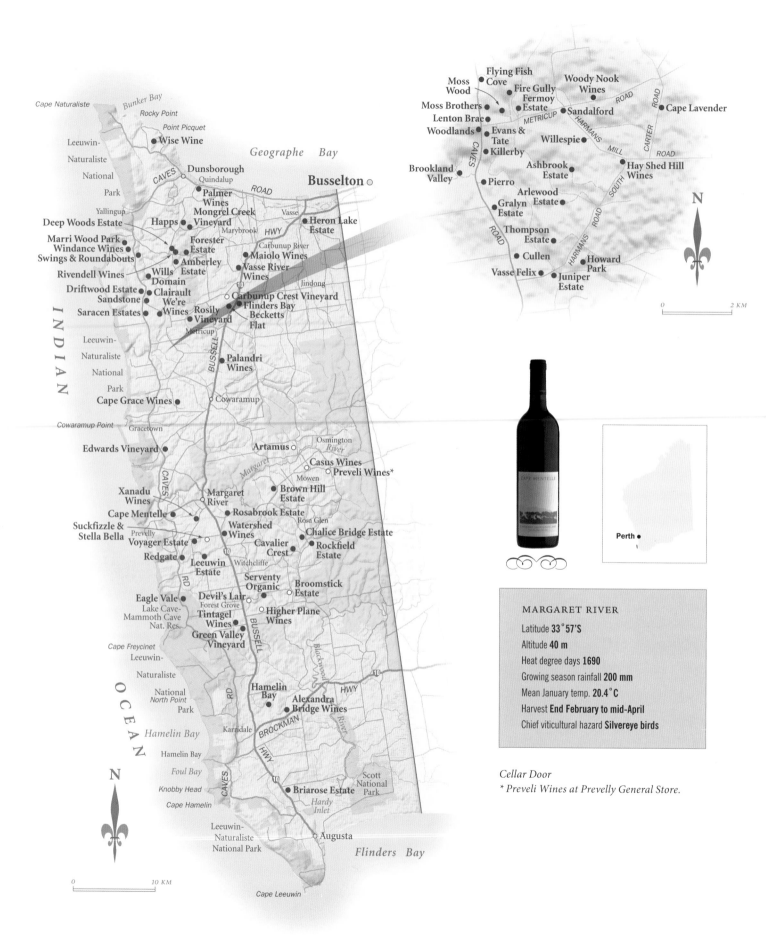

Cape Naturaliste

Bunker Bay

Rocky Point

Point Picquet

Leeuwin-
Naturaliste

National

Park

Yallingup

Geographe Bay

Dunsborough
Quindalup

CAVES ROAD

Busselton

Wise Wine

**Palmer
Wines**
**Mongrel Creek
Vineyard**

Happs

Vasse

HWY

Marybrook

Carbunup River

**Heron Lake
Estate**

Deep Woods Estate

**Forester
Estate**

Marri Wood Park
Windance Wines
Swings & Roundabouts

**Amberley
Estate**

Maiolo Wines
**Vasse River
Wines**

Rivendell Wines

**Wills
Domain**

Driftwood Estate
Sandstone
Saracen Estates

Clairault
**We're
Wines**

**Rosily
Vineyard**

Carbunup Crest Vineyard
Flinders Bay
Becketts
Flat

Jindong

Metricup

INDIAN

BUSSEL

**Palandri
Wines**

Leeuwin-
Naturaliste

National

Park

Cape Grace Wines

Cowaramup

Cowaramup Point

Gracetown

Edwards Vineyard

Margaret

River

Osmington
River

Artamus

Mowen

Casus Wines
Preveli Wines*

**Xanadu
Wines**

CAVES

**Margaret
River**

**Brown Hill
Estate**

Cape Mentelle

Rosabrook Estate

Rosa Glen

**Suckfizzle &
Stella Bella**

Prevelly

**Watershed
Wines**

Chalice Bridge Estate

Voyager Estate

**Cavalier
Crest**

**Rockfield
Estate**

Redgate

RD

**Leeuwin
Estate**

Witchcliffe

**Serventy
Organic**

**Broomstick
Estate**

Eagle Vale

Forest Grove

Devil's Lair

BUSSEL

**Higher Plane
Wines**

Lake Cave-
Mammoth Cave
Nat. Res.

**Tintagel
Wines**

**Green Valley
Vineyard**

Cape Freycinet

Leeuwin-

Naturaliste

National
North Point
Park

Blackwood

HWY

**Hamelin
Bay**

**Alexandra
Bridge Wines**

OCEAN

Hamelin Bay

Hamelin Bay

Foul Bay

Knobby Head

Cape Hamelin

Karridale

BROCKMAN

River

Scott
National
Park

CAVES
HWY

Briarose Estate

*Hardy
Inlet*

N

Leeuwin-
Naturaliste
National Park

Augusta

Flinders Bay

Cape Leeuwin

0   10 KM

Moss
Wood

Flying Fish
Cove

Woody Nook
Wines

Moss Brothers

Fire Gully
Fermoy
Estate

ROAD

ROAD

Sandalford

Cape Lavender

Lenton Brae

METRICUP

HARMANS

CARTER

Woodlands

**Evans &
Tate**

Willespie

MILL

ROAD

Killerby

CAVES

**Brookland
Valley**

**Ashbrook
Estate**

**Hay Shed Hill
Wines**

Pierro

**Arlewood
Estate**

SOUTH

**Gralyn
Estate**

ROAD

**Thompson
Estate**

HARMANS ROAD

N

Cullen

**Howard
Park**

Vasse Felix

**Juniper
Estate**

0   2 KM

Perth

MARGARET RIVER

Latitude **33°57'S**

Altitude **40 m**

Heat degree days **1690**

Growing season rainfall **200 mm**

Mean January temp. **20.4°C**

Harvest **End February to mid-April**

Chief viticultural hazard **Silvereye birds**

Cellar Door
* Preveli Wines at Prevelly General Store.

The Region ❧

CLIMATE

The climate of Margaret River is more strongly maritime-influenced than any other major Australian region. It has the lowest mean annual temperature range, of only 7.6°C, and for good measure has the most marked Mediterranean climate in terms of rainfall, with only 200 millimetres of the annual 1160 millimetres falling between October and April. The low diurnal and seasonal temperature range means an unusually even accumulation of warmth. Overall the climate is similar (in terms of warmth) to that of Bordeaux in a dry vintage.

SOIL & TOPOGRAPHY

The landscape constantly varies, given character by the abundance of small creeks and gentle valleys, as well as by the profusion of native trees, shrubs and flowers. In physical terms a degree of protection from sea wind is the most important factor. The principal soil type is that of the ridge which runs from Cape Naturaliste to Cape Leeuwin: it is predominantly gravelly or gritty sandy loam formed directly from the underlying granite and gneissic rock. The soils are highly permeable when moist, but quickly shed moisture from sloping sites, and overall water-holding capacities are low.

PRINCIPAL GRAPE VARIETIES

Overall, 53 per cent red, 47 per cent white. In descending order:

CABERNET SAUVIGNON

CHARDONNAY

SAUVIGNON BLANC

SEMILLON

SHIRAZ

MERLOT

CHENIN BLANC

VERDELHO.

🌿 WHITE WINE STYLES

Chardonnay. Leeuwin Estate was one of the pioneers of Chardonnay in the region, and makes Australia's greatest example of the breed. But it is by no means the only producer of outstanding Chardonnay, which seems to acquire an extra dimension unique to the Margaret River. It is more concentrated, more complex, more viscous, more tangy, yet does not cloy nor become heavy. The voluptuous fruit lends itself to the full range of winemaking techniques, and the region's winemakers do not shrink from using them.

Sauvignon Blanc and Semillon. The permutations of these two varieties – used either as single varietals, or as blends with one or other component dominant, or supplemented by Chenin Blanc to produce a regional specialty often called Classic Dry White – seem endless. But in most vintages the region welds the two varieties together in a way which no other area does: the Semillon (and even Chenin Blanc) acquires a pleasantly herbal/grassy cut which imperceptibly shades into Sauvignon Blanc.

🌿 RED WINE STYLES

Cabernet Sauvignon is the wine upon which Margaret River's reputation was founded, and in no small measure upon which it rests today. Virtually every winery produces a Cabernet, although Merlot is an increasingly common blend component. The style has evolved over the decades; common threads are physiologically ripe grapes that provide a sweet core to all the wines, which are never leafy or herbal, but can have slightly earthy/gravelly tannins that need to be controlled.

Shiraz is a relatively new arrival on the scene, still awaiting a final verdict, but with much promise; the wines are medium-bodied, usually with a generous pinch of spice and black pepper.

A FLOCK OF GUINEA FOWL, CAPE MENTELLE, MARGARET RIVER.

Wineries of Margaret River

Ashbrook Estate Est. 1975
Harmans Rd South, Wilyabrup
via Cowaramup 6284
ashbrook@netserv.net.au
exports to UK

Owned and run by the Devitt family (brothers Brian and Tony oversee the winemaking, Tony on a part-time basis as he is also state viticulturist for Western Australia) to the most exacting standards. By choice, it keeps a low profile, selling much of its wine through the cellar door and to an understandably very loyal mailing list clientele. All of the white wines, headed by Chardonnay, Sauvignon Blanc and Semillon, are of the highest quality, year in, year out.
Signature wine: Chardonnay

Brookland Valley Est. 1984
Caves Rd, Wilyabrup 6284
www.brooklandvalley.com.au
exports to UK

Hardys' showpiece in the Margaret River, Brookland Valley has an idyllic setting, with Flutes Café one of the best winery restaurants in the region, and its Gallery of Wine Arts housing an eclectic collection of wine and food-related art and wine accessories. The Brookland Valley wines have a stamp of understated elegance across the varietal span, from Semillon Sauvignon Blanc to Chardonnay and Merlot.
Signature wine: Reserve Chardonnay

Cape Mentelle Est. 1970
Off Wallcliffe Rd, Margaret River 6285
www.capementelle.com.au
exports to UK, US

One of the first movers in the Margaret River, and long regarded as one of its pre-eminent wineries. The Chardonnay and Semillon Sauvignon Blanc are among Australia's best, the potent Shiraz usually superb, and the berry/spicy Zinfandel makes one wonder why this grape is not as widespread in Australia as it is in California. Cape Mentelle is part of the LVMH (Louis Vuitton Moët Hennessy) group, and since the advent of Dr Tony Jordan as Australasian CEO there has been a concerted and successful campaign to rid the winery of the brettanomyces infection which affected the Cabernet Sauvignon.
Signature wine: Chardonnay

Cullen Est. 1971
Caves Rd, Cowaramup 6284
www.cullenwines.com.au
exports to UK, US

Cullen has always produced long-lived wines of highly individual style from the substantial and mature vineyards. These are managed as fully certified biodynamic plantings, using the Steiner formulations and procedures. Winemaking (and viticulture) is now in the hands of Vanya Cullen, daughter of the founders; she is possessed of an extraordinarily good palate. The Chardonnay is superb, while the Cabernet Merlot goes from strength to strength; indeed, I would rate it Australia's best.
Signature wine: Diana Madeline Cabernet Merlot

Devil's Lair Est. 1985
Rocky Rd, Forest Grove via
Margaret River 6285
www.devils-lair.com
exports to UK, US

Having rapidly carved out a high reputation through a combination of clever packaging and marketing allied with impressive wine quality under the ownership of the remarkable wine and beer man Phil Sexton, Devil's Lair was acquired by Southcorp in December 1996. It has 89 ha of estate plantings up to 20 years old, releasing its second label duo under the Fifth Leg White and Fifth Leg Red labels, using white and red Bordeaux blends respectively. Its top two wines in a commendably tight range are Chardonnay and Margaret River (a Cabernet-dominant blend).
Signature wine: Margaret River (Red)

Evans & Tate Est. 1970
Metricup Rd, Wilyabrup 6280
www.evansandtate.com.au
exports to UK, US

From humble beginnings in the Swan Valley, the rise and rise of Evans & Tate seemed unstoppable. It severed its ties with the Swan Valley, and built up its Margaret River vineyards and long-term grape supply contracts until it was one of the largest producers in the region.

It listed on the Stock Exchange, thereafter acquiring Oakridge Estate in the Yarra Valley and Cranswick/Barramundi Wines in 2003. However, the company was caught in the wine over-supply whirlpool of 2004–05, facing a challenging future.
Signature wine: Margaret River Merlot

Howard Park Est. 1986
Miamup Rd, Cowaramup 6284
www.howardparkwines.com.au
exports to UK, US

One of the two separate arms of the Jeff and Amy Burch-owned Howard Park business. Each has its own top-of-the-range labels (Leston for Margaret River and Scotsdale for Denmark) using grapes predominantly sourced from within the respective regions; the style is different, but the quality is not. Howard Park makes impeccable wines from the bottom-of-the-range MadFish (with no particular regional base) through to the top. In Margaret River it is a toss up between the Chardonnay and Leston Cabernet Sauvignon Merlot for top spot.
Signature wine: Leston Cabernet Sauvignon Merlot

Leeuwin Estate Est. 1974
Stevens Rd, Margaret River 6285
www.leeuwinestate.com.au
exports to UK, US

Since Leeuwin Estate released its first vintage (1980) of Art Series Chardonnay, it has never released its grip on the mantle of Australia's greatest maker of this variety, simply because of the consistency – random bottle oxidation excepted – of both style and quality. The second label Prelude Chardonnay, the Sauvignon Blanc, and Siblings Sauvignon Blanc Semillon provide powerful support at lesser price points.
Signature wine: Art Series Chardonnay

Moss Wood Est. 1969
Metricup Rd, Wilyabrup 6280
www.mosswood.com.au
exports to UK, US

Widely regarded as one of the best estates in the region, capable of producing richly robed Semillon, unctuous Chardonnay and elegant, gently herbaceous, superfine Cabernet Sauvignon (with a dash of Merlot) which lives for many years. In 2002 Moss Wood acquired the Ribbon Vale Estate, which is now merged within its own business, the Ribbon Vale wines being treated as vineyard-designated within the Moss Wood umbrella.

Signature wine: Cabernet Sauvignon

Suckfizzle & Stella Bella

Est. 1997
PO Box 536, Margaret River 6285
www.stellabella.com.au

⬚ exports to UK, US

First things first. The back label explains: 'the name Suckfizzle has been snaffled from the sixteenth-century monk and medico-turned-writer Rabelais and his infamous character the great Lord Suckfizzle'. Suckfizzle was founded by Janice McDonald and Stuart Pym (both Margaret River winemakers), with investor support. McDonald now runs the highly successful business, which makes high-quality wines with all the colour, character and seductive flamboyance the labels evoke. Production has increased dramatically in the wake of deserved market success.

Signature wine: Chardonnay

Vasse Felix Est. 1967

Cnr Caves Rd & Harmans Rd South,
Wilyabrup 6284
www.vassefelix.com.au

⬚ ⬚ exports to UK, US

Owned by leading Australian businesswoman Janet Holmes à Court, which partly explains its self-evident discipline and success. A relatively new 140 ha vineyard at Jindong in the north of the Margaret River region supplies a large part of the increased fruit intake. The wines are made in three ranges: at the bottom Classic Dry White and Dry Red; then varietal offerings of Semillon, Chardonnay, Noble Riesling, Shiraz, Cabernet Merlot and Cabernet Sauvignon; and at the top Heytesbury Chardonnay and Heytesbury (a Cabernet-dominant blend).

Signature wine: Heytesbury (Cabernet blend)

Voyager Estate Est. 1978

Lot 1, Stevens Rd, Margaret River 6285
www.voyagerestate.com.au

⬚ ⬚ exports to UK, US

Voyager Estate has come a long way since it was acquired by Michael Wright (of the mining family) in May 1991. It now has an important, high-quality 103 ha vineyard which puts Voyager Estate in the position of being able to select only the best parcels of fruit for its own label, and to supply surplus (but high-quality) wine to others. The Cape Dutch-style tasting room and vast rose garden are major tourist attractions,

and the winery has been upgraded. It is hard to choose between the Sauvignon Blanc Semillon, Chardonnay and Cabernet Sauvignon Merlot; all have exceptional complexity, presence and quality, vintage conditions the final determinant. Watch, too, for the intermittent Tom Price releases.

Signature wine: Chardonnay

Wise Wine Est. 1986

Lot 4, Eagle Bay Rd, Dunsborough 6281
cellar@wisewine.com.au

⬚ ⬚

Wise Wine, headed by Perth entrepreneur Ron Wise, is going from strength to strength, with 18 ha at the Meelup Vineyard in Margaret River, 10 ha at the Donnybrook Vineyard in Geographe, and leases over the Bramley and Bunkers Bay vineyards, with a total of almost 40 ha. Wine quality, too, has taken a leap forward, with a number of excellent wines.

Signature wine: Single Vineyard Chardonnay

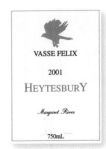

South West Australia Zone
Great Southern ❧

Even by the standards of Australia, Great Southern is a large region: a rectangle 150 kilometres from north to south, and 100 kilometres from east to west. It embraces climates which range from strongly maritime-influenced to moderately continental, and an ever-changing topography: there are the immense eucalypts of the south coast near Denmark and Albany which surround tiny vineyards like Tingle-Wood (taking its name from the Tingle Forest from which it was hewn), the striking round boulders and sweeping vistas of Porongurup, the harder blackboy country of Alkoomi (near Frankland), and the softer rolling hills of Mount Barker, where habitation seems to have somehow softened the remote savagery of many of the other subregions.

Two of the earlier prophets of the Great Southern area were Maurice O'Shea and Jack Mann, an unlikely pair in that not only did they never meet each other, but Maurice O'Shea did not even visit the region – his enthusiasm came from an armchair view of its climate. He is said to have expressed the opinion that if he had his time again, it was there that he would establish his vineyards. Jack Mann formed his favourable view of the Great Southern area as a result of

regularly playing cricket in the region between the two World Wars.

Almost as unlikely was the first serious consideration given to the region by a wine company. In the early years of this century, a large area of leasehold land was cleared at Pardelup, just to the west of Mount Barker. Regeneration problems with the scrub saw the land revert to the Crown, and the Government sought to interest Penfolds in the project. When Penfolds declined, the area became the Pardelup prison school. It was left to the distinguished Californian viticulturist Professor Harold Olmo, who was retained by the Western Australian Government in 1955 to report on the status of the industry, to recognise the potential of the area for the production of high-quality, light table wines.

Even then it took another ten years for the first vineyard sites to be selected. The selection was prompted by the Western Australian Department of Agriculture, which set up a joint venture with the Pearses at Forest Hill. This led to the progressive establishment of vineyards in the region: most were small, and some suffered from isolation (both from markets and technical expertise). Only one large vineyard

was established, Frankland River Wines with 100 hectares of vines, which was leased by Houghton in 1981 and ultimately purchased by it. The smaller Plantagenet, however, dominated proceedings, making wine not only for itself but for a number of other well-known labels, and only Goundrey ran an operation of any real size in competition with Plantagenet. Under the ownership of entrepreneur Jack Bendat, Goundrey grew mightily before the largest Canadian wine group, Vincor, acquired it in 2002. This, presumably, will underwrite continuing growth for Goundrey and the region as a whole.

Howard Park has dual residence, in both the Great Southern and Margaret River, and is a leader in wine quality, as well as being significant in terms of size. The other, even larger, venture is Ferngrove Vineyards, which came on-stream in 1997.

As if in recognition of its vast size, the Great Southern has created five subregions. While these encompass the majority of the wineries, they leave at least 50 per cent of the region untouched. Down the track, yet more subregions may be created.

[OPPOSITE] PRUNING. [BELOW] FOREST HILL VINEYARD, MOUNT BARKER.

GREAT SOUTHERN
Albany 🌿

It was not until Christmas Day 1826 that the western part of the Australian continent was formally claimed for Great Britain. The claim was not made at Perth or the Swan Valley (settled three years later) but here at Albany, 35 years after it had first been discovered and mapped in 1791.

While the surrounding country to the north, east and west was used for grazing and wheat farming, Albany became famous for whaling, which continued until 1978. Its convoluted bays and granite outcrops make this beautiful region (and in parts atmospheric town) seem like a mini Seattle, or perhaps Vancouver – itself named by Captain George Vancouver, the 1791 explorer of Albany and thereafter of British Columbia. Albany's whaling museum is the largest in the world and is a justifiably major tourist attraction.

The first vines were planted by the Sippe family at Redmond Vineyard in 1975, using cuttings of Riesling supplied by Forest Hills Vineyard. (Cabernet Sauvignon was also planted.) The first two crops of grapes were sold, but in 1981 a Riesling and a Cabernet Sauvignon were made at Plantagenet; for some time thereafter the vineyard was neglected, but now forms the core of Phillips Brooke Estate. However, the emphasis these days is more on Chardonnay and Pinot Noir than on Riesling and Cabernet Sauvignon.

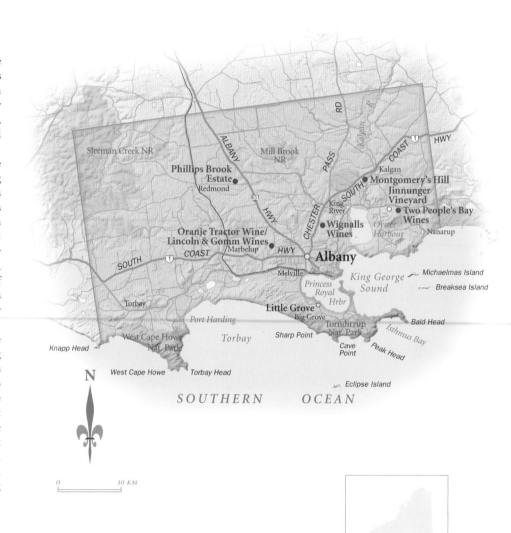

The Region 🌸

CLIMATE

Self-evidently, Albany's climate is strongly shaped and moderated by the Southern Ocean; the standard description is that it is Mediterranean, with moist, cool winters and warm, dry summers. Diurnal temperature range is minimal, and moderate humidity in summer assists ripening by reducing stress on the vines.

SOIL & TOPOGRAPHY

The hills and valleys make the area attractive enough, but when ocean views are added, and huge marri or karri eucalypts soar skywards, it takes on another dimension. These trees are an infallible guide to the best soils for grapevines: lateritic gravelly sandy loams or sandy loams derived directly from granite and gneissic rocks.

PRINCIPAL GRAPE VARIETIES

The total Great Southern region grape crush is 60 per cent red and 40 per cent white. In Albany, Riesling is rare, except for the northern part. In descending order:

CHARDONNAY

PINOT NOIR

SAUVIGNON BLANC

SHIRAZ

CABERNET SAUVIGNON

MERLOT.

ALBANY

Latitude **35°02'S**

Altitude **75 m**

Heat degree days **1495**

Growing season rainfall **303 mm**

Mean January temp. **19°C**

Harvest **Mid-March to end April**

Chief viticultural hazard **Birds**

Wineries of Albany

Jinnunger Vineyard Est. 1996

588 Nanarup Rd, Lower Kalgan, Albany 6330
www.jinnunger.com.au

Jinnunger Vineyard is situated 18 km east of Albany, the name taken from the local Aboriginal (Nyungah) language meaning 'good views': the property looks out over the Porongurup and Stirling Ranges. It is owned by research scientist Colin Sanderson. There is 1 ha each of Chardonnay and Pinot Noir, and while he expects to increase the plantings, it will always be a small, hand-tended vineyard, ideally situated on a north-facing slope of Mount Mason close to the Southern Ocean.
Signature wine: Chardonnay

Montgomery's Hill Est. 1996

South Coast Hwy, Upper Kalgan, Albany 6330
montwine@iinet.net.au

Montgomery's Hill is 16 km north-east of Albany on a north-facing slope on the banks of the Kalgan River. The vineyard is situated on an area which was previously an apple orchard and is a diversification for the third generation of the Montgomery family, which owns the property. Chardonnay, Cabernet Sauvignon and Cabernet Franc were planted in 1996, followed by Sauvignon Blanc, Shiraz and Merlot in 1997. Since 1999 Montgomery's Hill has been made at the new Porongurup Winery; Albany Chardonnay and Albany Shiraz are both of high quality and exemplary varietal character.
Signature wine: Chardonnay

Oranje Tractor Wine/Lincoln & Gomm Wines Est. 1998

198 Link Rd, Albany 6330
www.oranjetractor.com

The complicated name tells part of the story of the vineyard. Murray Gomm was born next door, but moved to Perth to work in physical education and health promotion. Here he met nutritionist Pamela Lincoln, who had completed the wine science degree at Charles Sturt University in 2000, before being awarded a Churchill Fellowship to study organic grape and wine production in the US and Europe. When the partners began the establishment of their 3 ha vineyard, they went down the organic path with the aid of an ancient 1964 vintage Fiat tractor, which is orange.
Signature wine: Sauvignon Blanc

 WHITE WINE STYLES

Chardonnay excels; its high-toned aromatic bouquet and intense though not heavy palate results in good unwooded styles, but the best are barrel fermented and taken through malolactic fermentation.

Sauvignon Blanc is also highly suited, and widely grown. Fragrant gooseberry and herb aromas, and a lively, lemony, tangy gooseberry palate is par for the course.

 RED WINE STYLES

Pinot Noir. Wignalls was one of the Australian pacesetters with the variety, but the bar has been lifted much higher. If the vintage conditions are right, and the crop restrained, perfumed, light-bodied wines, with the all-important length of palate, can be made.

Shiraz is a relative newcomer to this subregion (though not so new further north). It can make a very complex and compelling cool-grown style, with spicy blackberry and plum fruit, good texture, line and length, and fine tannins.

Phillips Brook Estate Est. 1975

Lot 2, Redmond–Hay River Rd,
Redmond 6332
newbury@albanyis.com.au

Bronwen and David Newbury purchased the long-established Redmond Vineyard, renaming it Phillips Brooke after the adjoining Phillips Brook Nature Reserve and its permanent creek running through their property. In 1975, 2.2 ha of Riesling and 2.4 ha of Cabernet Sauvignon had been planted but were thoroughly neglected in the intervening years. The Newburys have rehabilitated the old plantings, and have added 4.9 ha of Chardonnay, 1.15 ha of Merlot, 0.83 ha of Cabernet Franc and 0.71 ha of Sauvignon Blanc (complementing a single row of old vines).
Signature wine: Riesling

Two People's Bay Wines

Est. 1998
RMB 8700, Nanarup Rd, Lower Kalgan 6331
twopeoplesbay@westnet.com.au

The name comes from the Two People's Bay Nature Reserve to the east, which can be seen from the vineyard; it also has spectacular views to the Porongurups and Stirling Ranges 60 km north. The Saunders family (Phil and Wendy Saunders, with sons Warren and Mark) began planting Sauvignon Blanc, Riesling, Semillon, Shiraz, Cabernet Sauvignon, Cabernet Franc and Pinot Noir in 1998, and continued the plantings in 1999. The minerally backbone and lemony acidity of the Riesling is typical of the region at its best.
Signature wine: Great Southern Riesling

Wignalls Wines Est. 1982

Chester Pass Rd (Hwy 1), Albany 6330
info@wignallswines.com.au

 exports to UK, US

Wignalls was one of the early pacesetters for Pinot Noir, both in the Great Southern and Australia generally, but the wine does age fairly quickly. The white wines are elegant, and show the cool climate to good advantage. A winery was constructed and opened for the 1998 vintage, utilising the production from the 16 ha of estate plantings.
Signature wine: Reserve Pinot Noir

GREAT SOUTHERN
Denmark ❧

Mount Barker was the first subregion in Great Southern to be registered as a GI; adjoining Denmark has been one of the last to make the move. Denmark is wetter and cooler than Albany, but the differences are not of any significant magnitude. As one moves north away from the coast, the ocean influence lessens; there is also a series of steep hills and valleys before you emerge onto the rolling slopes of the Great Southern Region proper.

The pretty town of Denmark is a magnet for visitors, and some of the more remote wineries from other subregions have set up cellar doors in the town.

DENMARK

Latitude **31°56'S**

Altitude **50–150 m**

Heat degree days **1471**

Growing season rainfall **354 mm**

Mean January temp. **18.7°C**

Harvest **Early March to late April**

Chief viticultural hazard **Birds**

N

Perth ●

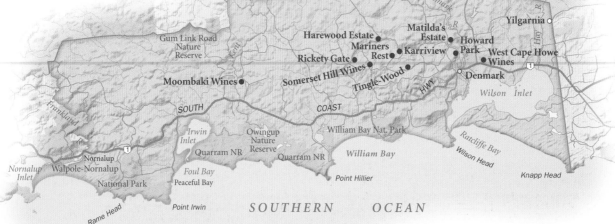

Cellar Door
John Wade Wines at Denmark.

The Region ❧

CLIMATE

While there is some north–south variation, the climate is broadly similar to Albany, the varieties being grown and the wines styles are also similar.

SOIL & TOPOGRAPHY

Once again, the soils are similar to Albany, the native eucalypts the equivalent of a water diviner for finding the best.

PRINCIPAL GRAPE VARIETIES

In descending order:

CHARDONNAY

SAUVIGNON BLANC

CABERNET SAUVIGNON

MERLOT

SHIRAZ

RIESLING

PINOT NOIR.

WHITE WINE STYLES

Chardonnay is the dominant variety, chiefly made as table wine, but also teamed with Pinot Noir to make sparkling wine (as it is, incidentally, in the other Great Southern subregions). The flavours are in the melon, nectarine, citrus spectrum, the structure fine and elegant, the palate long.

Sauvignon Blanc typically provides a dazzling array of passionfruit, gooseberry and tropical fruits, tied with a bow of minerally acidity.

Riesling has lime-blossom aromas, long lime/lemon/citrus flavour and, at times, piercing acidity. Often blended with Riesling grown further north in the Great Southern.

RED WINE STYLES

Cabernet Sauvignon at its best has intense, powerful, focussed blackcurrant, herb and olive aromas and flavours, plus excellent length. Once again, subregional blending needs to be taken into account.

Merlot is often blended with Cabernet to great effect.

Shiraz, as in Albany, is a relative newcomer, but of exciting character and style. It also marries well with Cabernet Sauvignon.

Wineries of Denmark

Harewood Estate Est. 1988

Scotsdale Rd, Denmark 6333
www.harewoodestate.com.au

In July 2003 James Kellie, who for many years was a winemaker with Howard Park and who had been responsible for the contract making of Harewood Wines since 1998, purchased the estate with his father and sister as partners in the business. Events moved quickly thereafter, with the construction of a 300 tonne winery, offering both contract winemaking services for the Great Southern region, and the ability to expand the Harewood range to include subregional wines that showcase both variety and region. Quality across the range is all one could wish for.

Signature wine: Denmark Sauvignon Blanc Semillon

Howard Park Est. 1986

Scotsdale Rd, Denmark 6333
www.howardparkwines.com.au

exports to UK, US

All of the Howard Park wines are made here at the new, large winery with a 100 000 case production. However, there are three groups of wines: those sourced from either Great Southern or Margaret River; the icon Howard Park multi-regional Riesling and Cabernet Sauvignon Merlot; and the multi-regional MadFish range. Thus the Leston wines come from Margaret River, the Scotsdale from Great Southern. All are very impressive, MadFish rising well above its price point.

Signature wine: Riesling

John Wade Wines Est. 2000

PO Box 23, Denmark 6333
johnwade@omninet.net.au

The impish, if at times reclusive, John Wade is arguably the most experienced winemaker in Western Australia, with over 20 years' experience following his role as chief winemaker at Wynns Coonawarra Estate. He is best known for his involvement with Plantagenet and then Howard Park, and, having sold his interest in Howard Park, has become a consultant winemaker to a substantial number of producers; his own label is a relatively small part of his total wine business. The wines are chiefly sold through premium retail outlets and restaurants; they include Riesling, Chardonnay, Merlot Cabernet Franc, and Cabernet Merlot Franc.

Signature wine: Chardonnay

Matilda's Estate Est. 1990

RMB 654 Hamilton Rd, Denmark 6333
www.matildasestate.com

In 2002 Matilda's Meadow (as it was then known) was acquired by former citizen of the world, Steve Hall. It is a thriving business based on 6 ha of estate plantings, with a restaurant offering morning and afternoon tea, lunch Tuesday to Sunday and dinner Thursday to Saturday. A kaleidoscopic range of wines is sold, some strictly for the tourist trade (Autumn Amethyst, Tawny Port Muscat) but most are more serious, and are competently contract-made.

Signature wine: Cabernet Merlot

Moombaki Wines

Est. 1997
RMB 1277 Parker Rd, Kentdale
via Denmark 6333
www.moombaki.com

David Britten and Melissa Boughey have established 2 ha of vines on a north-facing gravel hillside with a picturesque Kent River frontage. They have also put in significant mixed tree plantings to increase wildlife habitats and have fenced off wetlands and river from stock grazing and degradation. It is against this background that they chose Moombaki as their vineyard name, a local Aboriginal word meaning 'where the river meets the sky'. After a few disappointments with early contract winemaking, the quality of the grapes is now coming through in the wines, with Robert Diletti making the excellent 2003 vintage, and James Kellie (his winery is closer) the 2004 and subsequent vintages. Intense Shiraz and finely structured Cabernet Sauvignon lead.

Signature wine: Shiraz

West Cape Howe Wines

Est. 1997
Lot 42, South Coast Hwy, Denmark 6333
wchowe@denmarkwa.net.au

exports to US

After a highly successful seven years, West Cape Howe founders Brenden and Kylie Smith have moved on, selling the business to a partnership including Gavin Berry (until May 2004, senior winemaker at Plantagenet) and viticulturist Rob Quenby. As well as existing fruit sources, West Cape Howe now has the 80 ha Lansdale Vineyard, planted in 1989, as its primary fruit source. Overall the focus has shifted from contract winemaking to continued building of the strong West Cape Howe brand, which takes in all the mainstream wines styles.

Signature wine: Chardonnay

Yilgarnia Est. 1997

6634 Redmond West Rd, Redmond 6327
www.yilgarnia.com.au

Forty years ago Melbourne-educated Peter Buxton settled on a bush block of 135 ha on the Hay River, 6 km north of Wilson Inlet. For the first ten years Buxton worked for the Western Australian Department of Agriculture in Albany; in this role he surveyed several of the early vineyards in Western Australia, and recognised the potential of his family's property to produce high-quality wine. Today there are 16 ha of vines in bearing. All the vines (eight varieties in all) are on north-facing blocks, the geological history of which stretches back two billion years. The contract-made wines are modestly priced and of consistently high quality.

Signature wine: Reserve Sauvignon Blanc

UPRIGHT OAK VATS ARE COMING BACK INTO VOGUE.

GREAT SOUTHERN
Frankland River 🌿

The first vineyard in the Frankland River region was planted in 1968 on a property owned by the wealthy Roche family of Perth. Originally called Westfield, it is now owned by Houghton and known as Netley Brook Vineyard (a locality name). It is a major and important vineyard, giving Houghton some ultra-premium grapes. Then, in 1971, Merv and Judy Lange began the development of the now highly rated and substantial Alkoomi Vineyard and Winery.

This is open, and at times sparse, country, without the forests which populate the south, although the controversial Tasmanian blue gum plantings are to be found here as elsewhere (headed to wood pulp, but with no one certain about the recovery or future use of the land).

FRANKLAND RIVER

Latitude **34˚39'S**

Altitude **200–300 m**

Heat degree days **1441**

Growing season rainfall **310 mm**

Mean January temp. **19˚C**

Harvest **Mid-March to mid-April**

Chief viticultural hazards **Drought; birds**

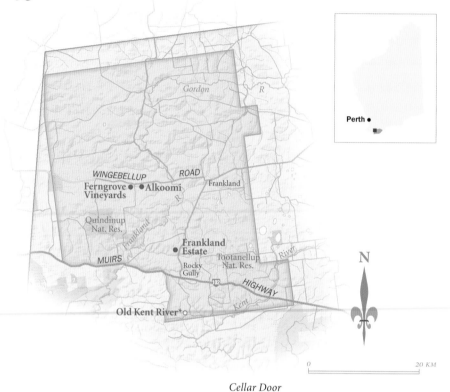

Perth ●

FERNGROVE VINEYARDS, FRANKLAND RIVER.

Cellar Door
* Old Kent River at the Kent River, South Coast Hwy, Denmark; see p. 244 for map.

The Region

CLIMATE

The most northerly, inland subregion of Great Southern, still Mediterranean in terms of dominant winter–spring rainfall, but with greater continentality, thus favouring Riesling (in particular), Shiraz and Cabernet Sauvignon. A unique feature is a sea breeze which finds its way inland and cools the late afternoon temperature by about 2˚C. Total rainfall decreases from west to east, and salinity in the soil and surface water makes irrigation very difficult. The answer is a complex and extensive system of very long collection channels and drains on slopes, holding dams, and long-distance pumping.

SOIL & TOPOGRAPHY

The generally open, gently rolling hill country is catchment for the Frankland, Gordon, Kent and Tone rivers. The soils are chiefly derived from granite or gneiss outcrops, typically rich, red in colour, and of uniform depth.

PRINCIPAL GRAPE VARIETIES

In descending order:

SHIRAZ

RIESLING

CHARDONNAY

CABERNET SAUVIGNON

SAUVIGNON BLANC

SEMILLON

MERLOT

PINOT NOIR.

Wineries of Frankland River

Alkoomi Est. 1971

Wingebellup Rd, Frankland 6396
www.alkoomiwines.com.au

⚲ exports to UK, US

Former graziers Merv and Judy Lange have patiently created one of the Great Southern's (and, indeed, Western Australia's) most success-ful estate-based wineries through sheer, unre-lenting hard work and attention to detail. The 80 000 case production covers all the mainstream varieties and three price ranges, the common denominators being consistency of quality and value for money.
Signature wine: Blackbutt (Cabernet Malbec Merlot blend)

WHITE WINE STYLES

Riesling is, in terms of character, quality and style (if not in area planted) the premier white variety. It has fragrant and diamond-clear lime and mineral aromas and flavours, with a remarkable delicacy and finesse.

Chardonnay is tightly framed and structured, with stone-fruit flavours and good acidity.

Sauvignon Blanc either on its own, or blended with Semillon, produces a wine of considerable class and surprising longevity.

RED WINE STYLES

Shiraz does as well here as elsewhere in the region; medium-bodied, with intense black fruits, liquorice and spice plus fine tannins.

Cabernet Sauvignon stands firmly alongside Shiraz in terms of quality; a little firmer in structure and body, perhaps. Merlot often provides a blend component, Malbec less frequently.

Ferngrove Vineyards Est. 1997

Ferngrove Rd, Frankland 6396
www.ferngrove.com.au

⚲ exports to UK, US

After 90 years of family beef and dairy farming heritage, Murray Burton decided to venture into premium grapegrowing and winemaking in 1997. With investor support, Ferngrove established over 400 ha on three vineyards in the Frankland River subregion, and a fourth at Mount Barker. The operation centres around the Ferngrove Vineyard, where a large rammed-earth winery and tourist complex was built in time for the 2000 vintage. Part of the production is sold as grapes; part sold as juice or must, part sold as finished wine; and part under the highly rated Ferngrove Vineyards label. One suspects the high quality of the wines has exceeded Ferngrove's expectations, with multiple trophy and gold medal awards.
Signature wine: Cossack Riesling

Frankland Estate Est. 1988

Frankland Rd, Frankland 6396
info@franklandestate.com.au

⚲ exports to UK, US

The 29 ha vineyard has been established progres-sively since 1988 on a large sheep property owned by Barrie Smith and Judi Cullam, and a winery was built on the site for the 1993 vintage. The recent introduction of an array of single-vineyard Rieslings has been a highlight. All the wines are energetically promoted and marketed by Judi Cullam, especially the Riesling, by important International Riesling tastings and seminars.
Signature wine: Isolation Ridge Riesling

Old Kent River Est. 1985

Turpin Rd, Rocky Gully 6397
www.valleyofthegiants.com.au/oldkentriver

⚲ (at Kent River, South Coast Highway)
exports to UK

Mark and Debbie Noack have done it tough all of their lives but have earned respect from their neighbours and from the other producers to whom they sell more than half the production from the 16.5 ha vineyard established on their sheep property. More importantly still, the quality of their wines goes from strength to strength, thanks in part to contract-winemaking at Alkoomi, and in part to increasingly mature vines.
Signature wine: Reserve Pinot Noir

GREAT SOUTHERN
Mount Barker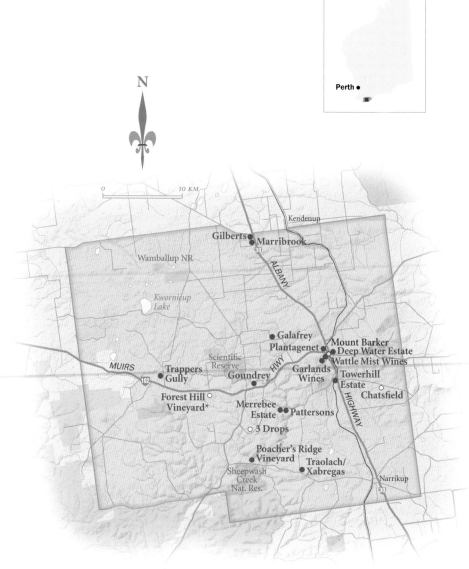

Mount Barker is not only the senior subregion of the Great Southern, but was the first to be declared in Australia. If this were not enough, it was also here that the first vines in the Great Southern region were planted. It is large-scale, gently undulating, largely open grazing country, with widely scattered vineyards separated by large distances. But there is a feeling of 'oneness' akin to that of a micro-terroir of France, a hundredth of the size of Mount Barker.

MOUNT BARKER

Latitude **34°36'S**

Altitude **180–250 m**

Heat degree days **1488**

Growing season rainfall **287 mm**

Mean January temp. **19°C**

Harvest **Early March to mid-April**

Chief viticultural hazards **Spring frost; late vintage rain**

The Region

CLIMATE

Situated in the very heart of the Great Southern region, the continental aspects of the climate make this quintessential country for Riesling and Shiraz. While, as with the rest of the region, rainfall is winter–spring dominant, late vintage rains can create problems. Mount Barker's continentality also means greater diurnal temperature fluctuations and the occasional spring frost.

SOIL & TOPOGRAPHY

The Plantagenet Plateau, with Mount Barker its centre-point, is marked by its relatively poor marri soils, lateritic gravelly/sandy loams coming directly from granite rock protrusions. Yields are generally low, in places very low.

PRINCIPAL GRAPE VARIETIES

In descending order:

RIESLING

SHIRAZ

CABERNET SAUVIGNON

CHARDONNAY

SAUVIGNON BLANC

MERLOT

CABERNET FRANC.

Cellar Door
* Forest Hill Vineyard at South Coast Hwy, Denmark; see p. 244 for map.

WHITE WINE STYLES

Riesling has an extra degree of power and focus; ripe apple and lime flavour flows strongly and evenly across the palate, finishing with perfect acidity.

Chardonnay is often successfully made unwooded, but the best is barrel fermented, the nectarine fruit depth and power absorbing the oak.

RED WINE STYLES

Shiraz is medium- to full-bodied, responding to vintage variation (the amount of spice) and winemaking (the degree of extract). Blackberry, herb, leaf, spice and liquorice are supported by persistent, fine tannins.

Cabernet Sauvignon has excellent colour, texture and mouthfeel, with classic cassis, blackcurrant and cedar notes, developing earth and olive nuances with bottle development over a 20-year span.

Wineries of Mount Barker

Chatsfield Est. 1976
O'Neil Rd, Mount Barker 6324
www.chatsfield.com.au
🈲 exports to UK, US

Irish-born doctor Ken Lynch has 17 ha of mature estate vineyards which underpin the impressive range of Chatsfield wines. Unoaked, early bottled Cabernet Franc was an initial, somewhat eclectic, success. These days vigorously spicy, black cherry and liquorice Reserve Shiraz, piercing nectarine Chardonnay and mineral and lime blossom Riesling lead the way.
Signature wine: Reserve Shiraz

Forest Hill Vineyard Est. 1966
Muirs Hwy, Mount Barker 6324
www.foresthillwines.com.au
🍷 (at South Coast Hwy, Denmark)

This is one of the oldest 'new' winemaking operations in Western Australia. It was the site for the first experimental grape plantings in the Great Southern region, in 1966, on a farming property owned by the Pearse family. The Forest Hill brand became well known, aided by the fact that a 1975 Riesling made by Sandalford from Forest Hill grapes won nine trophies in national wine shows. In 1997 the property was acquired by interests associated with Perth stockbroker Tim Lyons, and a program of renovation and expansion of the vineyards commenced. A winery near Denmark was completed in time for the 2003 vintage, and a new cellar door opened in September 2004.
Signature wine: Chardonnay

Garlands Est. 1996
Marmion St off Mount Barker Hill Rd,
Mount Barker 6324
www.garlandswines.com.au
🍷 exports to UK

Garlands is a partnership between Michael and Julie Garland and their vigneron-cum-medico neighbours, Craig and Caroline Drummond. Michael Garland came to grapegrowing and winemaking with a varied background in biological research, computer sales, retail clothing, and a degree in oenology. A tiny but highly functional winery was erected prior to the 2000 vintage, the earlier wines being made elsewhere. The winery has a capacity of 150 tonnes, and will continue contract-making for other small producers in the region as well as making the wine from the 9 ha of estate vineyards planted to Cabernet Franc, Merlot, Sauvignon Blanc, Chardonnay, Riesling, Shiraz and Cabernet Sauvignon.
Signature wine: Shiraz

Gilberts Est. 1980
RMB 438 Albany Hwy, Kendenup
via Mount Barker 6323
gilberts@rainbow.agn.net.au
🍷 🍴 exports to UK, US

One of the foremost producers of Riesling (intense, flowery, lime, apple and spice) in Western Australia, having won the trophy for Best Wine of Show at the Qantas Wine Show of Western Australia on several occasions for Best Riesling. It is a part-time occupation for graziers Jim and Beverly Gilbert; the wines sell out quickly each year, particularly since a restaurant and function area opened in April 2003.
Signature wine: Riesling

Goundrey Est. 1976
Muir Hwy, Mount Barker 6324
www.goundreywines.com.au
🍷 exports to UK, US

Jack Bendat acquired Goundrey when it was on its knees; through significant expenditure on land, vineyards and winery capacity, it became the House that Jack Built. In late 2002 it was acquired by Vincor, Canada's largest wine producer, for a price widely said to be more than $30 million, a sum that would have provided Bendat with a very satisfactory return on his investment. Vincor followed up with the acquisition of Amberley Estate in the Margaret River region, then Kim Crawford in Marlborough, New Zealand.
Signature wine: Reserve Cabernet Sauvignon

Pattersons Est. 1982
St Werburghs Rd, Mount Barker 6324
patwine@omninet.net.au
🍷

Schoolteachers Sue and Arthur Patterson have grown Chardonnay, Shiraz and Pinot Noir and grazed cattle as a weekend relaxation for two decades. The cellar door is in a very beautiful rammed-earth house, and a number of vintages are on sale at any one time. Good Chardonnay and Shiraz have been complemented by the occasional spectacular Pinot Noir, all contract-made at Plantagenet.
Signature wine: Shiraz

Plantagenet Est. 1974
Albany Hwy, Mount Barker 6324
www.plantagenetwines.com
🍷 exports to UK, US

The senior winery (130 000 cases) in the Mount Barker region, which is making superb wines across the full spectrum of variety and style – highly aromatic Riesling, tangy citrus-tinged Chardonnay, glorious Rhône-style Shiraz and ultra-stylish Cabernet Sauvignon. It played a very important role in the development of the region with its contract winemaking services for small businesses scattered across the open landscape, and has gained lasting respect (and affection) for doing so.
Signature wine: Riesling

Poacher's Ridge Vineyard
Est. 2000
Lot 2, Spencer Rd, Narrikup 6326
www.prv.com.au
🍷

Alex and Janet Taylor purchased the Poacher's Ridge property in 1999, prior to which time it had been used for cattle grazing. Seven ha of vineyard (in descending order, Shiraz, Cabernet Sauvignon, Merlot, Riesling, Marsanne and Viognier) were planted in 2000, the first small crop appeared in 2003, a larger one in 2004, together making an auspicious debut. A cellar door and café were constructed in 2005; the wines are made by Robert Diletti at Castle Rock.
Signature wine: Late Harvest Riesling

GREAT SOUTHERN
Porongurup 🌿

While this subregion locks into that of Mount Barker on its west, and covers the same latitude range, the feel of Porongurup is quite different. Great stands of lowering eucalypt forest and a massive series of rounded granite knobs in one part give way to sweeping views out over the Stirlings towards Esperance in another.

It was the scene of relatively early viticultural activity after the Olmo and Gladstones reports; two hectares of Cabernet Sauvignon were planted at the Bolyanup Vineyard in 1974; others followed in the 1970s, more in the 1980s (Castle Rock in 1983), and yet more in the 1990s.

PORONGURUP

Latitude **34°10'S**

Altitude **250–300 m**

Heat degree days **1441**

Growing season rainfall **310 mm**

Mean January temp. **19°C**

Harvest **Mid-March to early May**

Chief viticultural hazard **Birds**

MOUNT TRIO VINEYARD, PORONGURUP.

The Region

CLIMATE

A feature of the climate is a night-time thermal zone, created by a layer of warm air which rises above the denser cold air sliding down the projecting hillsides of the subregion and settling on the lower valley floor. It is on these slopes that most of the vineyards are planted. The excellent air drainage further diminishes the risk of frost.

SOIL & TOPOGRAPHY

Throughout the region, soil types are often named after the dominant eucalypt species of the location. Thus the soils are deep karri loams derived from weathered granite (as opposed to the marri soils of Mount Barker, which nonetheless have a similar parent source).

PRINCIPAL GRAPE VARIETIES

In descending order:

RIESLING

SHIRAZ

CABERNET SAUVIGNON

CHARDONNAY

MERLOT

CABERNET FRANC

VERDELHO

PINOT NOIR.

WHITE WINE STYLES

Riesling is deceptively light, indeed delicate when young, but develops superbly in bottle; mineral, apple, herb and lime/citrus flavours emerge with time.

Chardonnay shows abundant depth and richness, with stone fruit, fig, melon and citrus combining.

RED WINE STYLES

Cabernet Sauvignon is elegant, medium-bodied, with savoury edges to black fruits, especially when blended with Merlot.

Shiraz, like Cabernet Sauvignon, is elegant, offering briar, spice, blackberry and cherry.

Pinot Noir tends to be slightly light, with dark plum and spice flavours.

Wineries of Porongurup

Castle Rock Estate Est. 1983

Porongurup Rd, Porongurup 6324
www.castlerockestate.com.au

An exceptionally beautifully sited and immaculately maintained vineyard, winery and cellar-door sales area on a 55 ha property with sweeping vistas from the Porongurups, operated by the Diletti family. The two-level winery, set on the natural slope, was completed in time for the 2001 vintage and maximises gravity flow, in particular for crushed must feeding into the press. The Rieslings have always been elegant and handsomely repay a long time in bottle. In more recent times some fragrant, light-bodied Pinot Noirs have been made, easily the best from the subregion.

Signature wine: Riesling

Gibraltar Rock Est. 1979

Woodlands Road,
Porongurup 6324
(08) 9481 2856

Prior to the 2001 vintage Perth orthopaedic surgeon Dr Peter Honey acquired this former Riesling specialist vineyard, which had started life as Narang before being forced to change its name by Lindemans because of the latter's (now defunct) Nyrang Shiraz brand. The vineyard has 25 ha of Riesling, Sauvignon Blanc, Chardonnay, Pinot Noir, Merlot, Shiraz and Cabernet Franc. The lion's share of the grapes is sold under a long-term contract to Houghton, the remainder vinified for Gibraltar Rock with the utmost skill, Riesling and Chardonnay to the fore.

Signature wine: Porongurup Riesling

Mount Trio Vineyard Est. 1989

Cnr Castle Rock & Porongurup Rds,
Porongurup 6324
mttrio@omninet.net.au
exports to UK

Mount Trio was established by Gavin Berry and Gill Graham shortly after they moved to the Mount Barker district in late 1988. Gavin Berry was assistant winemaker to John Wade, and Gill managed the cellar-door sales. Gavin became senior winemaker and managing director of Plantagenet, Gill the mother of two young children, before Berry left Plantagenet to focus entirely on the Mount Trio business, based in part upon estate plantings of 2 ha of Pinot Noir and 0.5 ha of Chardonnay, and in part on purchased grapes. An additional 6 ha were planted in the spring of 1999, bringing production of the finely crafted and balanced wines to the 6500-case level.

Signature wine: Cabernet Merlot

Zarephath Wines Est. 1994

Moorialup Rd, East Porongurup 6324
www.zarephathwines.com
exports to UK

The 9 ha Zarephath vineyard is owned and operated by Brothers and Sisters of The Christ Circle, a Benedictine community. They say the most outstanding feature of the location is the feeling of peace and tranquillity which permeates the site, something I can well believe on the basis of numerous visits to Porongurup. The wines made for Zarephath by Robert Diletti include Riesling, Unwooded Chardonnay, Chardonnay (complex and long), Pinot Noir, Shiraz and Cabernet Sauvignon.

Signature wine: Chardonnay

SOUTH WEST AUSTRALIA ZONE
Blackwood Valley ❧

The Blackwood Valley has long been a mixed farming region, with orchards and the odd patch of table grapes representing diversification from grazing. The first wine grapevines were planted by the Fairbrass family in 1976 at what is now called Blackwood Crest, inspired in part by the table grapes grown by Max Fairbrass's grandfather on the same property in the north-eastern corner of the region.

Subsequent expansion has seen the establishment of 50 vineyards supporting five wineries. The region's boundaries are in large part self-defining: in the south it abuts Pemberton, to the west and north Geographe, and on the south-east it meets the northern limits of Great Southern. There are no subregions, but there are three separate areas of vineyards: around Boyup Brook, Bridgetown and Nannup. Progress has been slow but steady, with the limited number of wineries largely choosing to have their wines contract-made outside the region. There are many more vineyards, mainly established by local farmers and graziers seeking diversification.

By far the largest single venture is the Blackwood Valley Wine Partnership, with 85 hectares of vines at Boyup Brook. Around 800 tonnes are produced by the partnership each year; slightly less than half is vinified at Ferngrove Winery. All sales are of grapes or bulk wine to the industry.

The major impediment to viticulture in the region has been and remains salination of the Blackwood River, forcing surface water collection via kilometres of hillside contour ditches feeding into dams.

BLACKWOOD VALLEY

Latitude **34°00'S**

Altitude **100–340 m**

Heat degree days **1578**

Growing season rainfall **219 mm**

Mean January temp. **20.7°C**

Harvest **Late February to early April**

Chief viticultural hazard **Spring frost**

The Region

CLIMATE

Blackwood Valley is on the same latitude as Margaret River, and shares many of the same basic climatic characters, most notably wet and relatively warm winters and relatively cool, dry summers. Typically, the variation between summer and winter daytime temperatures is little more than 10°C. The points of difference stem from the Blackwood Valley's more continental climate, with winter frosts sometimes extending into spring (and consequent crop losses) and a slightly higher summer temperature range than that of Margaret River.

SOIL & TOPOGRAPHY

The soils are part of the Darling Plateau system, with moderately incised valleys providing gravel and gravelly soils on the divides, and yellow soils and red earths on valley slopes. Overall, the result is well-drained gravelly loam soils perfectly suited to viticulture.

PRINCIPAL GRAPE VARIETIES

Overall, 69 per cent red and 31 per cent white.
In descending order:

CABERNET SAUVIGNON

SHIRAZ

CHARDONNAY

MERLOT

SAUVIGNON BLANC

SEMILLON.

Wineries of Blackwood Valley

Blackwood Crest Wines

Est. 1976
RMB 404A, Boyup Brook 6244
(08) 9767 3029

The senior winery in the region, with 8 ha of Chardonnay, Riesling, Semillon, Sauvignon Blanc, Cabernet Sauvignon, Shiraz and Pinot Noir. Of the 50 or so tonnes crushed each year, around 15 tonnes are used to make 1000-plus cases of Blackwood Crest wines.

Signature wine: Shiraz

 WHITE WINE STYLES

Chardonnay. A considerable part of the production is sold to wineries outside the region. As in Margaret River, the style is generous and rich, with ripe melon and peach fruit flavours.

 RED WINE STYLES

Cabernet Sauvignon is the most widely planted red grape. It regularly achieves full ripeness across the length and breadth of the region. Blackcurrant and dark chocolate flavours are supported by long, fine tannins, giving the wines excellent ageing potential.

Shiraz. Here, as everywhere else, plantings have increased rapidly and crops have produced wine with a mix of dark black fruits having touches of pepper, spice and game.

Hillbillé Est. 1998
Blackwood Valley Estate,
Balingup Rd, Nannup 6275
www.hillbille.com

Gary Bettridge began planting 19 ha of Shiraz, Cabernet Sauvignon, Merlot, Chardonnay and Semillon in 1998. Hillbillé is situated in the Blackwood Valley between Balingup and Nannup, which the RAC describes as 'the most scenic drive in the south-west of Western Australia'. A significant part of the grape production is sold to other winemakers, but as from the 2003 vintage part has been vinified by the Watsons at Woodlands Wines in Margaret River. Distinguished Merlot Shiraz, Reserve Shiraz, Merlot and Chardonnay make this the region's leading winery in terms of quality, seemingly with more to come.

Signature wine: Reserve Shiraz

Scotts Brook Est. 1987
Scotts Brook Rd, Boyup Brook 6244
goodwine@iinet.net.au

The Scotts Brook vineyard at Boyup Brook (equidistant between the Margaret River and Great Southern regions) has been developed by local schoolteachers Brian Walker and wife Kerry – hence the opening hours during school holidays. There are 17 ha of vineyards, but the majority of the production is sold to other winemakers, with limited quantities being skilfully contract-made.

Signature wine: Sauvignon Blanc

Wattle Ridge Vineyard Est. 1997
Lot 11950, Boyup–Greenbushes Rd,
Greenbushes 6254
wattleridgevineyard@bigpond.com

James and Vicky Henderson have established 6.5 ha of vines at their vineyard, planted to Riesling, Verdelho, Merlot and Cabernet Sauvignon. The contract-made wines are sold by mail order and through the cellar door, which offers light meals, crafts and local produce.

Signature wine: Two Tinsmith Greenbushes Cabernet Sauvignon

SOUTH WEST AUSTRALIA ZONE
Geographe ❧

Geographe was initially joined with Peel in an amorphous region called the South West Coastal Plain, but this grouping was abandoned before registration under the GI process was finalised, and the boundaries redrawn. Geographe's centre is Bunbury, its southern (or, more properly, south-eastern) corner is Busselton, while the Harvey River meanders through the northern boundary on its way to the coast. It is bisected by the Vasse, Capel, Fergusson, Collie and Brunswick rivers, which – as they descend from the hills in the east – create valleys with distinctive climates.

Indeed, while there are (as yet) no officially recognised subregions of Geographe, there are in truth three quite distinct areas. The first is the true coastal sector, stretching from Busselton to Bunbury, and with the lush, peaceful Capel River (and the town of Capel) at its centre. Wholly maritime-influenced by the warm Indian Ocean, its climate is similar to that of the northern part of the Margaret River, although the soil types vary considerably – the richer alluvial soils around Capel leading to exceptionally vigorous vine growth.

Next is the Donnybrook area, which has a distinctly different climate, as it is cut off from the maritime influence of the Indian Ocean by the intervention of the Darling and Whicher ranges. The net result is a climate which Dr John Gladstones describes as closely resembling that of Bendigo and Rutherglen in Victoria, with considerable diurnal temperature fluctuations.

The third area is the Ferguson Valley; here, early success with Sauvignon Blanc, Shiraz, Merlot and Cabernet Sauvignon has led to rapid expansion in plantings. The largest venture is Willow Bridge, with a 100 hectare vineyard and a 2000 tonne capacity winery.

The major winery is, and has been from the start, Capel Vale, driven by the energy and passion of Perth-based former radiologist Dr Peter Pratten, producing 100 000 cases a year. However, Hackersley, Harvey River Bridge Estate and Willow Bridge Estate are all important producers by any standards.

Geographe is an area of considerable beauty and even greater variation in its topography and scenery. The unifying force is the West Australian flora: magnificent gum trees, ranging from the tuarts of the coastal sands of the same name through to marri and karri further inland, and the spectacular, omnipresent native shrubs and flowers.

Perth ●

GEOGRAPHE

Latitude **33°18'S**

Altitude **5–70 m**

Heat degree days **1700**

Growing season rainfall **185–220 mm**

Mean January temp. **22°C**

Harvest **Early February to mid-March**

Chief viticultural hazard **Birds**

WILLOW BRIDGE ESTATE, GEOGRAPHE.

The Region

CLIMATE

The climate of the coastal region is warm, sunny and dry (in the growing season), with minimal diurnal temperature fluctuations. Geographe shares with the Bunbury Hills the tempering effect of sea breezes which take hold relatively early in the day, and high afternoon relative humidity which alleviates the stress the warm climate might otherwise induce. While frost presents no threat on the coast, site selection at Donnybrook is important if frosts are to be avoided.

SOIL & TOPOGRAPHY

The coastal tuart sands have limestone as their parent material, and overlie limestone; a permanent watertable at a depth of 3–15 metres is a further aid to viticulture. However, low natural fertility and ready leaching of nutrients mean care has to be taken to achieve the best results. The soils of the traditional farming and orchard land at Donnybrook are richer, being either gravelly sandy loams or heavier soils derived from the gneissic country rock in the valleys.

PRINCIPAL GRAPE VARIETIES

Overall, 62 per cent red, 38 per cent white. In descending order:

SHIRAZ

CABERNET SAUVIGNON

CHARDONNAY

MERLOT

SAUVIGNON BLANC

SEMILLON.

Wineries of Geographe

Barrecas Est. 1994

South Western Hwy, Donnybrook 6239
barreca@bigpond.com

Three generations of the Barreca family have been involved in grapegrowing and winemaking, first in Italy and ultimately in Donnybrook. Third-generation Tony Barreca sold his orchard in 1994, using the proceeds to buy the site upon which he has since established 33 ha planted to a Joseph's Coat of 26 different varieties. Most of the grapes are sold under contract, but a small, modern winery was erected on-site in 2002 for the production of a limited amount of wine.
Signature wine: Shiraz

 WHITE WINE STYLES

Chardonnay is propagated everywhere in the region, producing wines which reflect the varying site climate, the cooler sites with intense grapefruit characters, the warmer sites veering through melon to butter and cashew.

Semillon and Sauvignon Blanc are typically blended to good effect, producing a crisp, tangy wine with a mix of grassy/herbal overtones to a tropical fruit base; a light touch of oak is an optional extra.

RED WINE STYLES

Shiraz is the most important grape, usually presented as a varietal wine but also used in complex multi-blends. The weight and extract varies substantially, from elegant medium-bodied to the sumptuous, rich Kinnaird Shiraz (and other single-vineyard wines) of Capel Vale.

Cabernet Sauvignon tends to be finer and more elegant than that of either the Margaret River or Mount Barker regions, with soft, fine-grained tannins.

Merlot produces truly classy wines, with enticing raspberry and blackcurrant fruit supported by lingering, fine-grained tannins.

Capel Vale Est. 1979

Lot 5, Stirling Estate, Mallokup Rd, Capel 6271
www.capelvale.com
exports to UK, US

Single-mindedly driven by Dr Peter Pratten, Capel Vale has expanded its viticultural empire to the point where it is entirely an estate-run business, with 220 ha of vineyards spread through Mount Barker, Pemberton, Margaret River and Geographe. Its wines cross every price point and style, from fighting varietal to ultra-premium; always known for its Riesling, powerful red wines are now very much part of the portfolio. The icon reds are Kinnaird Shiraz and Howecroft Merlot, heading a four-tiered range encompassing all the mainstream varietal wines.
Signature wine: Kinnaird Shiraz

Hackersley Est. 1997

Ferguson Rd, Dardanup 6236
www.hackersley.com.au

Hackersley is a partnership between the Ovens, Stacey and Hewitt families, friends since their university days, and with (so they say) the misguided belief that growing and making their own wine would be cheaper than buying it. They found what they describe as a 'little piece of paradise in the Ferguson Valley just south of Dardanup', and in September 1998 they planted a little under 8 ha, extended in August 2000 to 9.5 ha of the mainstream varieties, but interestingly turning their back on Chardonnay. Most of the

crop is sold to Houghton; however, small quantities of immaculately packaged and beautifully made Semillon Sauvignon Blanc, Shiraz, Merlot and Cabernet have been made for release under the Hackersley label.
Signature wine: Sauvignon Blanc

Willow Bridge Estate Est. 1997

Gardin Court Drive, Dardanup 6236
www.willowbridgeestate.com
exports to UK, US

The Dewar family followed a fast track in developing Willow Bridge Estate since acquiring their spectacular 180 ha hillside property in the Ferguson Valley in 1996. Sixty ha of Chardonnay, Semillon, Sauvignon Blanc, Shiraz and Cabernet Sauvignon have already been planted, with Tempranillo added in the spring of 2000, and another 10 ha thereafter. A state-of-the-art winery was constructed, which is capable of handling the 1200–1500 tonnes from the estate plantings. Wine quality has been consistently good since day one.
Signature wine: Reserve Sauvignon Blanc

South West Australia
Manjimup

After a seemingly interminable time, the determination of the names for, and boundaries of, the Manjimup and Pemberton regions was finalised in August 2005. For the time being, at least, the regional jigsaw of Western Australia is complete. The Warren River (and Valley) runs through the centre of both regions; this, plus high annual rainfall and lack of salinity, removes the problems encountered further south.

There were no vineyard plantings prior to 1988, and there was considerable debate as to which varieties and wine styles the Warren Valley as a whole would be best suited. Dr John Gladstones had been in no doubt: pointing to the similarities in the sunlight hours, humidity and mean temperatures between Bordeaux and the Warren Valley, he wrote, 'the wines produced from the appropriate grape varieties should be very much in the mainstream of Bordeaux style'.

The Bordeaux versus Burgundy (Pinot Noir) argument has now been resolved with a resounding varietal vote for Bordeaux, and Merlot in particular.

MANJIMUP

Latitude **34°26'S**
Altitude **200–300 m**
Heat degree days **1422**
Growing season rainfall **288 mm**
Mean January temp. **19.9°C**
Harvest **Mid-March to mid-April**
Chief viticultural hazard **Late season rain**

Perth ●

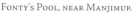

FONTY'S POOL, NEAR MANJIMUP.

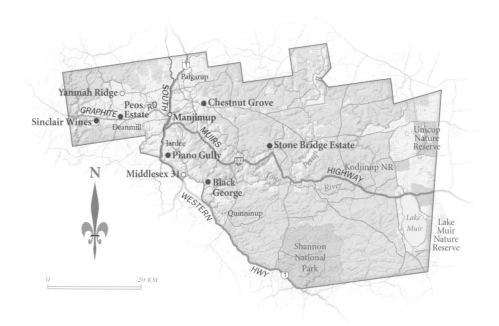

The Region

CLIMATE

Manjimup's climate is influenced by both the lower west coast of Australia and the adjacent south coast. It has some similarities to Margaret River, but is more continental and is at a higher altitude. Cold winters provide true vine dormancy, but plentiful spring rainfall promotes good budbreak and early growth. The relatively dry but stress-free summer/autumn conditions are no less favourable.

SOIL & TOPOGRAPHY

The best soils of the region belong to the Kennan-Queenup series of sandy, gravelly loams created over millions of years by the erosive effects of the Warren River and its tributaries. An ironstone laterite gravel layer several metres below the original horizon has been eroded so that the gravel has been mixed with red soil formed from the underlying granite to produce a red, gravelly loam.

PRINCIPAL GRAPE VARIETIES

Overall, 67 per cent red, 33 per cent white.
In descending order:

CHARDONNAY

CABERNET SAUVIGNON

MERLOT

SHIRAZ

PINOT NOIR

SAUVIGNON BLANC

VIOGNIER

VERDELHO.

Wineries of Manjimup

Chestnut Grove Est. 1988

Chestnut Grove Rd, Manjimup 6258
www.chestnutgrove.com.au

 exports to UK

The 16 ha vineyard was planted by the late Vic Kordic, and passed on to sons Paul and Mark. As the vines matured, so did the reputation of the winery, most notably for its trophy-winning Merlot. In 2002 the brand and business (though not the underlying real estate and vineyard) was sold to Australian Wine Holdings Ltd. This has led to the development of a well-priced second label (Tall Timbers), made from purchased grapes, and to new packaging across the line.

Signature wine: Merlot

 WHITE WINE STYLES

Chardonnay is light to medium-bodied, with elegant citrus and stone fruit flavours, and balanced acidity.

Sauvignon Blanc, often with a dash of Semillon, shows crisp mineral and passionfruit aromas and flavours.

Verdelho can surprise with its quality, particularly from Chestnut Grove.

Viognier, rare but very stylish, mouthfilling but not heavy.

🌿 RED WINE STYLES

Merlot, while less widely planted than Cabernet, consistently produces the region's best wines, with spice and olive overtones to a core of plush blackcurrant and plum fruit, velvety but not heavy.

Cabernet Sauvignon is medium-bodied and frequently blended to good effect with Merlot.

Shiraz abounds with dark berry, liquorice and spice fruit, with excellent texture and mouthfeel.

Peos Estate Est. 1996

Graphite Rd, Manjimup 6258
www.peosestate.com.au

🍷

The Peos family (with a background of grapegrowing in Macedonia before migrating to Australia) has farmed in the West Manjimup district for 50 years, the third generation – of four brothers – commencing the development of a substantial vineyard in 1996. It has a little over 33 ha of vines, with Shiraz (10 ha), Merlot (7 ha), Chardonnay (6.5 ha), Cabernet Sauvignon (4 ha) and Pinot Noir, Sauvignon Blanc and Verdelho (2 ha each). Most of the grapes are sold, but a useful amount is skilfully vinified under the Peos label.

Signature wine: Four Acres Shiraz

Sinclair Wines Est. 1994

Graphite Rd, Glenoran 6258
www.sinclairwines.com.au

🍷 exports to UK

Sinclair Wines is the child of Darelle Sinclair, a science teacher, wine educator and graduate viticulturist from Charles Sturt University, and John Healy, a lawyer, traditional jazz musician and wine marketing graduate of Adelaide University, Roseworthy Campus. Five ha of estate plantings underpin high-quality wines (made by Brenden Smith) at mouthwatering prices, ranging from spicy gooseberry Sauvignon Blanc to elegant stonefruit Chardonnay, to rich, supple and fleshy Cabernet Sauvignon.

Signature wine: Giovanni Manjimup Cabernet Sauvignon

Yanmah Ridge Est. 1987

Yanmah Road, Manjimup 6258
www.yanmahridge.com.au

🍷 exports to UK

What is now Yanmah Ridge was identified by Peter Nicholas in 1986 as 'the perfect location' in a study of grapegrowing regions in Western Australia, enabling him to complete his winemaking degree at Roseworthy Agricultural College. He and wife Sallyann purchased the property and planted 26 ha of Semillon, Sauvignon Blanc, Chardonnay, Pinot Noir, Sangiovese, Merlot, Cabernet Franc and Cabernet Sauvignon on its elevated, north-facing slopes. Their viticulture is environmentally friendly, with no residual herbicides or chemical pesticides. Although a new winery was built on-site in time for the 2001 vintage, the lion's share of the annual production is still sold (as grapes or wine) to other producers.

Signature wine: Chardonnay

SOUTH WEST AUSTRALIA ZONE

Pemberton 🌿

The history of viticulture at Pemberton is recent, the first vines being planted by the Western Australia Department of Agriculture in 1977 on an experimental block midway between the towns of Pemberton and Manjimup. Given the prolonged stand-off on regional boundaries and names between the two, the choice of site was ironically felicitous.

The region has a slightly cooler and wetter climate than Manjimup, although site climates can always move outside the norm. It has a far larger aggregation of wineries than Manjimup, and has achieved more in winemaking terms. It shares with Manjimup an at times disconcerting lushness and richness to its forests, fields and waterways, particularly in red soil country. Indeed, it is so heavily forested that only 15 per cent of the region is available for, and suited to, viticulture or horticulture.

With both the Warren and Donnelly rivers flowing through the region, the valleys and slopes, plus the lakes and streams, and the often vivid red soils all make this a region of great beauty.

The Region 🌹

CLIMATE

Pemberton is cooler than neighbouring Manjimup, with slightly lower temperatures, fewer sunshine hours, more rainfall (except in January and February) and greater relative humidity – although temperature variability remains about the same. The high annual rainfall means that a number of vineyards do not use irrigation, but the very pronounced winter/spring dominance can lead to stress late in the growing season if subsoil moisture diminishes.

SOIL & TOPOGRAPHY

Eighty-five per cent of the Pemberton region remains under native vegetation, with magnificent marri forests in the northern half, moving to karri in the south. There are two major soil types. The first are lateritic gravelly sands and gravelly loams overlying medium clay of moderate water-holding capacity. These moderately fertile soils are found on many of the higher slopes around Pemberton. The second soil is the more fertile karri loams, formed directly from the gneissic country rock, and which – together with the abundant winter and spring rainfall – leads to vigorous growth.

PRINCIPAL GRAPE VARIETIES

Overall, 53 per cent white and 47 per cent red. In descending order:

CHARDONNAY

SAUVIGNON BLANC

CABERNET SAUVIGNON

MERLOT

VERDELHO

SHIRAZ

SEMILLON.

PEMBERTON

Latitude **34°27'S**

Altitude **170 m**

Heat degree days **1394**

Growing season rainfall **361 mm**

Mean January temp. **19.2°C**

Harvest **Early March to mid-April**

Chief viticultural hazard **Silvereye birds**

Perth ●

Wineries of Pemberton

Bellarmine Wines Est. 2000

PO Box 1450, Manjimup 6258
www.bellarmine.com.au

Owned by German residents and long-term wine lovers, Dr Willi and Gudrun Schumacher. With a large personal wine cellar, the Schumachers decided to take the next step by establishing a vineyard and winery of their own. The venture is managed by Mike and Tam Bewsher, both with extensive knowledge of the wine industry. Twenty-five ha of Chardonnay, Riesling, Sauvignon Blanc, Pinot Noir, Shiraz, Merlot and Petit Verdot.

Signature wine: Pinot Noir

Channybearup Vineyard

Est. 1999

Lot 4, Channybearup Rd, Pemberton 6260
www.channybearup.com.au

 exports to US

Channybearup is owned by a small group of Perth businessmen, who have been responsible for the establishment of 62 ha of vineyards (the majority planted in 1999 and 2000). The principal varieties are Chardonnay (22 ha), Pinot Noir (10 ha), Merlot (10 ha), Shiraz (9 ha), Cabernet Sauvignon (7.5 ha) and Pinot Noir (7 ha), with lesser amounts of Verdelho and Sauvignon Blanc. While Channybearup is principally a grape supplier to other makers, a range of quality wines is being marketed under the Fly Brook and Wild Fly labels. Merlot, Cabernet Sauvignon and Shiraz lead the way.

Signature wine: Fly Brook Merlot

Fonty's Pool Est. 1998

Seven Day Rd, Manjimup 6258
www.fontyspoolwines.com.au

exports to UK

This is a joint venture between Cape Mentelle (which makes the wine) and Fonty's Pool Farm. The vineyards are part of the original farm owned by pioneer settler Archie Fontanini; in the early 1920s a large dam was created to provide water for intensive vegetable farming, and became known as Fonty's Pool. The first grapes were planted in 1989, and at 110 ha, the vineyard is now one of the region's largest, supplying grapes to a number of leading Western Australian wineries. An increasing amount of the production is used for Fonty's Pool, which has now established an on-site cellar door. Its Chardonnay, Sauvignon Blanc Semillon, Viognier, Merlot and Shiraz are all distinguished wines.

Signature wine: Viognier

Merum Est. 1996

Hillbrook Rd, Quinninup 6258
www.merum.com.au

exports to UK

Owned and managed by viticulturalist Mike Melsom and partner Julie Roberts; the 6.3 ha vineyard was planted in 1996, and the first wine made in 1999. The quality of the wines has been truly excellent since day one. The Semillon is particularly noteworthy for its mouthfilling complexity, which is achieved without compromising elegance.

Signature wine: Semillon

Picardy Est. 1993

Cnr Vasse Hwy & Eastbrook Rd,
Pemberton 6260
www.picardy.com.au

exports to UK, US

Picardy is owned by Dr Bill Pannell, his wife Sandra and son Daniel; Bill and Sandra were the founders of Moss Wood winery in the Margaret River region (in 1969). Picardy reflects Bill Pannell's view that the Pemberton area would prove to be one of the best regions in Australia for Pinot Noir and Chardonnay, but it is perhaps significant that the wines also include a Shiraz, and a Bordeaux-blend (called Merlimont). Time will tell whether Picardy has more Burgundy, Rhône or Bordeaux in its veins.

Signature wine: Chardonnay

Salitage Est. 1989

Vasse Hwy, Pemberton 6260
www.salitage.com.au

exports to UK, US

Salitage is the showpiece of Pemberton. If it had failed to live up to expectations, it is a fair bet the same fate would have befallen the whole of the Pemberton region. The 20 ha vineyard is planted to Chardonnay, Sauvignon Blanc, Pinot Noir, Cabernet Sauvignon, Merlot, Cabernet Franc and Petit Verdot. The quality and style of Salitage has varied substantially, partly in response to vintage conditions and yields, with premature development an issue from time to time. It may be that random bottle oxidation has been a problem here, as with so many other Australian wineries.

Signature wine: Chardonnay

Smithbrook Est. 1988

Smith Brook Rd, Middlesex
via Manjimup 6258
www.smithbrook.com.au

exports to UK

Smithbrook was the first major vineyard in the Pemberton region, with 60 ha of vines now in production. A majority interest was acquired by Petaluma in 1997 but Smithbrook has continued its principal role as a contract grower for other companies, as well as supplying Petaluma's needs and making wine under its own label. Perhaps the most significant change has been the removal of Pinot Noir from the range of products, and the introduction of Merlot.

Signature wine: Merlot

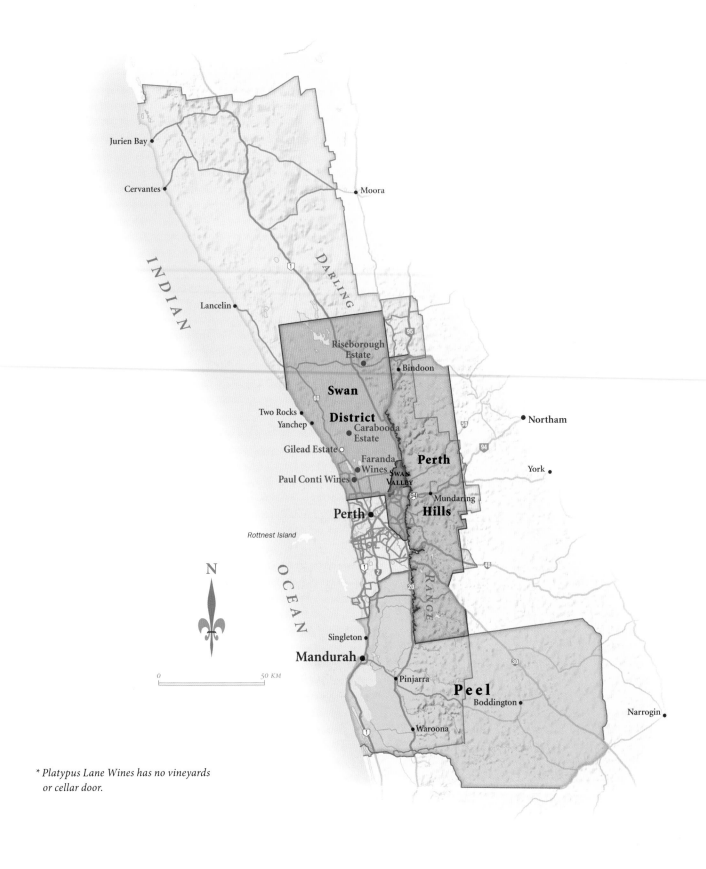

INDIAN

Jurien Bay •

Cervantes •

• Moora

DARLING

Lancelin •

Riseborough
Estate •

• Bindoon

Swan

Two Rocks •
Yanchep •   **District**
                    Carabooda
                    Estate •
Gilead Estate ○
        Faranda   **Perth**
        • Wines •
Paul Conti Wines • SWAN
                    VALLEY

• Northam

• York

Perth •
                    • Mundaring
                    Hills

Rottnest Island

OCEAN

RANGE

Singleton •

Mandurah •

Pinjarra •

Peel
        Boddington •

• Narrogin

Waroona •

0   50 KM

** Platypus Lane Wines has no vineyards
  or cellar door.*

Greater Perth Zone ❧

Quite why the boundary of the Greater Perth Zone extends so far north of Perth makes no more sense than the extreme southern end of the catch-all zone of the Eastern Plains, Inland and North of Western Australia. On the other hand, taking in Gingin and Bindoon (60 kilometres to the north of the Swan Valley proper) makes eminent sense.

The three regions (treating the Swan Valley as tantamount to a region) would seem to have very different climates: the Swan Valley a dry, hot oven; the Perth Hills cooled by altitude and slope; and the western third of Peel moderated by the immediately adjacent Indian Ocean. Yet there is more to bind them and their wine styles: the core of the summer heat remains the same. Exceptions come from site climate and/or winemaking techniques – and, of course, regional blending.

The western section of Peel and what is now Geographe were originally part of a proposed region called the South West Coastal Plain. Geographe divorced itself, and while it remains a logical region, Peel was in danger of becoming an orphan without the sufficient number of vineyards and tonnage of grape production. It was presumably for this reason that it was dramatically extended to the east, taking in country which has little in common either in terms of climate or soil with the coastal section. It is arguably the most extreme example of pragmatism by the Geographic Indications Committee, not far short of the type of ruling routinely given for American Viticultural Areas (AVAs).

Wineries of Greater Perth Zone

Carabooda Estate Est.1989
297 Carabooda Rd, Carabooda 6033
(Swan District)
www.caraboodaestatewines.com.au

1989 is the year of establishment given by Terry Ord, but it might as well have been 1979 (when he made his first wine) or 1981 (when he and wife Simonne planted their first vines). But it has been a slowly, slowly exercise, with production from the 3 ha of estate plantings now supplemented by purchased grapes, the first public release not being made until mid 1994. Since that time production has risen significantly.
Signature wine: Semillon Sauvignon Blanc

Gilead Estate Est.1995
1868 Wanneroo Rd, Neerabup 6031 (postal)
(Swan District)
(08) 9407 5076

A retirement – but nonetheless serious – venture for Judy and Gerry Gauntlett, who planted 1.2 ha on the tuart sands of Wanneroo in 1990. The name comes from the Balm of Gilead which, in Biblical times, was produced from trees on the hills north-east of Galilee; it had healing and purifying qualities. The tiny production is mainly sold by mail order, with occasional tasting days. The medium-bodied Shiraz, with spicy blackberry, black cherry and spice flavours, suggests finding the wines will be worth the effort.
Signature wine: Shiraz

Paul Conti Wines Est.1948
529 Wanneroo Rd, Woodvale 6026
(Swan District)
www.paulcontiwines.com.au
 exports to UK

Third-generation winemaker Jason Conti has now assumed day-to-day control of winemaking, although father Paul (who had succeeded his father in 1968) remains interested and involved in the business. Over the years Paul Conti challenged and redefined industry perceptions and standards; the challenge for Jason Conti (which he shows every sign of meeting) will be to achieve the same degree of success in a relentlessly and increasingly competitive market environment. This is the foremost winery in the zone, producing spotlessly clean and beautifully balanced wines.
Signature wine: Mariginiup Shiraz

Platypus Lane Wines Est.1996
PO Box 1140, Midland 6936
www.platypuswines.com.au
exports to UK

Platypus Lane, with a small core of 2.5 ha of old wine Shiraz, gained considerable publicity for owner Ian Gibson when its 1999 Shiraz won the inaugural John Gladstones Trophy at the 2000 Qantas Wine Show of Western Australian for the wine showing greatest regional and varietal typicity. The portfolio now includes Unwooded Chardonnay, Sauvignon Blanc Semillon and a Margaret River Cabernet Merlot.
Signature wine: Shiraz

Riseborough Estate Est.1998
Lot 21, Petersen Rise, off Mooliabeenee Rd, Gingin 6503
slamp@bigpond.net.au

Don Riseborough and Susan Lamp are near-neighbours of the Moondah Brook Vineyard, with 8.7 ha planted to Shiraz, Cabernet Sauvignon, Merlot, Cabernet Franc and Grenache. The estate-grown wines are contract-made in the Margaret River region (an unusual trip south). Chenin Blanc, Chardonnay and Verdelho are purchased from local growers, made for them in the Swan Valley. The purpose-built cellar door has expansive views across the Gingin Valley.
Signature wine: Cabernet Sauvignon

SWAN DISTRICT
Swan Valley 🌿

Two waves of immigration by Yugoslavs, the first in the early years of the twentieth century (principally from Dalmatia) and the second after the Second World War, gave the Swan Valley two claims to fame. The first is that, most surprisingly, for a time it had more wineries in operation than either New South Wales or Victoria; the second is that, more obviously, it joined the Barossa Valley (German) and the Riverland (Italian) as a significant ethnically-driven wine producing region.

It was not always so. Viticulture was started by English settlers, most notably Thomas Waters who dug the cellar at Olive Farm in 1830, thus giving this winery the distinction of being the oldest winemaking establishment in Australia to be in use at the start of the new millennium. Sadly, it has since been sold and decommissioned.

Another link with the past comes through the colonial surgeon Dr John Ferguson, who purchased part of a substantial land grant owned by three Indian Army officers, the most senior of whom was Colonel Richmond Houghton. Even though Houghton never came to Australia, the property was named after him – likewise the Houghton wines of today (Western Australia's largest wine company).

The Swan Valley (which is the core subregion of the Swan District, cowering in the south-eastern corner of the region) has always been a friendly place in which to grow vines and make wine. The completely flat, alluvial river plain provides soils which are immensely deep and well drained (or are so in the prime vineyard locations) and the hot, dry summer means that grapes ripen easily and quickly. This is an ideal climate for table grapes (huge quantities were produced for export markets in bygone years) and for fortified wines. It is likewise suited to the production of bulk table wine which was once sold to a large but uncritical local clientele, many of whom were of Yugoslavian origin, and they brought their own flagons, drums and sundry other containers to be filled up at their chosen winery.

The export market for table grapes has shrunk, the fortified wine market likewise, and third-generation Yugoslavs have entirely forgotten their cultural heritage and abandoned their parents' ways. Also, the big wine companies of the eastern states have put cask wine on supermarket shelves for less than it costs local Swan Valley wineries to produce, let alone sell. And it must be said that the big

company cask wine can be easier to live with the morning after.

Inevitably, the ethnic base of the Swan Valley winemaking has declined steadily through the years, while the dominance of Houghton Wines has grown. After years of uncertainty, Sandalford has been revived under new ownership and new management. But it is no accident that both Houghton and Sandalford draw the majority of their grapes from the Margaret River, Great Southern, Pemberton and Manjimup, or that at the other end of the scale, the self-effacing but brilliant John Kosovich has established a new vineyard at Pemberton.

The Swan Valley will continue to be an important part of the Western Australian industry, of course. Houghton White Burgundy – already renamed HWB for the export market – continues to be one of the largest selling white wine brands (in its semi-premium price category) in Australia. And just when it seemed that the smaller wineries would quietly fade away, the opposite has happened. New wineries have opened, older ones revived, accommodation upgraded and restaurants opened – all driven by wine, food and lifestyle tourism within an hour's drive of the Perth CBD.

[OPPOSITE & BELOW] SANDALFORD, SWAN VALLEY.

SWAN VALLEY

Latitude **31°50'S**

Altitude **45 m**

Heat degree days **2340**

Growing season rainfall **145 mm**

Mean January temp. **24.3°C**

Harvest **End January to end March**

Chief viticultural hazard **Excessive heat**

Perth

The Vines

Upper Swan

COPLEY ROAD

The Natural Wine Company

River

Belhus

Swan HWY

Brook

Ellenbrook

LedaSwan

Baskerville

Faber Vineyard

Swan Valley Wines

Upper Reach Vineyard

John Kosovich Wines

HADDRILL

ROAD

CAMPERSIC

Lamont's

Millendon

Susannah Brook Wines

NORTHERN

River

Henley Brook

Henley Brook

Talijancich

GREAT

Herne Hill

ROAD

Swan

Sittella Wines

BARRETT ST

Valley Wines

Whiteman

52

West Swan

Vino Italia

50

Oakover Estate

YUKICH CLOSE

DALE RD

JOHN FORREST NATIONAL PARK

Houghton; Moondah Brook

Jane Brook

ROAD

Garbin Estate Wines

Middle Swan

Jane Brook Estate

REID HWY

HWY

TOODYAY

ROE HWY

Sandalford

NTHN

RIVER

Midvale

Beechboro

BENARA ROAD

Viveash

Midland

Lilac Hill Estate

RiverBank Estate

GREAT

Caversham

52

Bellevue

EASTERN

Greenmount

SWAN

HWY

51

GREAT

Koongamia

Guildford

EASTERN

ROE HWY

N

Hazelmere

Bassendean

GREAT

Ashfield

EASTERN HIGHWAY BYPASS

0   2 KM

94

The Region

CLIMATE

Whichever yardstick is used, the Swan Valley proper has an unequivocally hot climate. It has the highest mean January temperature of any significant Australian district. It has the lowest summer rainfall of any Australian region, the lowest relative humidity (47 per cent) and the most hours of sunshine per day. Its heat summation (HDD) almost comes as an anticlimax at 2340. The Gin Gin/Moondah Brook area, well to the north of the Swan Valley, is somewhat cooler, and although still at the warm end of the climatic spectrum, has consistently demonstrated a surprising capacity to produce full-flavoured, full-bodied white wines.

SOIL & TOPOGRAPHY

The Swan Valley proper is a flat alluvial plain flanked by the Darling Range and permeated by the tributaries of the Swan River. The best soils are brown or yellow-brown loamy sand surface soils passing gradually through lighter-coloured (and slightly more clayey) subsurface soils, thence into porous sandy clay loam subsoils. This structure allows deep penetration by the vine roots to tap the reserves of the heavy winter rainfall.

PRINCIPAL GRAPE VARIETIES

Overall, 71 per cent white, 29 per cent red. In descending order:

CHENIN BLANC

CHARDONNAY

VERDELHO

SHIRAZ

GRENACHE

SEMILLON.

WHITE WINE STYLES

Chenin Blanc dominates plantings in the Swan Valley, contributing 25 per cent of the annual crush. Arguably, the Swan Valley is the one region in Australia in which this grape (and the wine it makes) rises above mediocrity, producing a wine with a certain luscious richness.

Chardonnay plantings have steadily increased; Houghton and Sandalford blend it with material from the south in their lower-priced wines to good effect.

Verdelho is a traditional variety which was appreciated well before the eastern states' vogue for it in the 1980s. Almost all of the best wineries produce a varietal wine from this grape, and are usually content to allow the honeyed/honeysuckle/fruit salad flavour free rein without introducing new oak.

Blended White Wines. The three principal white varieties coalesce to produce one of Australia's largest selling and eternally popular white wines, Houghton White Burgundy, known as HWB in export markets, and likely headed in the same direction domestically. In many ways, a freakish wine which, despite its modest price and large volume, has the capacity to age magnificently in bottle for five to ten years.

RED WINE STYLES

Shiraz is the most important red wine grape in what is essentially white wine country. It produces a warm, fleshy wine in the hands of most makers.

Fortified Wines, once an immensely important part of the Swan District's production, now actively promoted by only a few, notably Talijancich. Sandalford Sandalera and the tiny output from John Kosovich Wines are also jewels.

[RIGHT] SANDALFORD, SWAN VALLEY.

Wineries of the Swan Valley

Faber Vineyard Est.1997

233 Haddrill Rd, Baskerville 6056 (postal)
johngriffiths@iinet.net.au

Former Houghton winemaker and now university lecturer and consultant John Griffiths teamed with his wife Jane Micallef to found Faber Vineyard. Since 1997 they have established 3.5 ha of Shiraz, Chardonnay, Verdelho, Cabernet Sauvignon, Petit Verdot and Brown Muscat. Says Griffiths, 'It may be somewhat quixotic, but I'm a great fan of traditional warm area Australia wine styles … made in a relatively simple manner that reflects the concentrated ripe flavours one expects in these regions.' Possessed of an excellent palate, and with an impeccable winemaking background, John Griffiths' search has succeeded handsomely, although extending his skills to wines from the Margaret River and Great Southern.

Signature wine: Reserve Shiraz

Garbin Estate Est.1956

209 Toodyay Rd, Middle Swan 6056
binwine1@bigpond.com

Peter Garbin, winemaker by weekend and design draftsman by week, decided in 1990 that he would significantly upgrade the bulk fortified winemaking business commenced by his father in 1956. The 11 ha vineyards were replanted, 2 ha of Chardonnay planted at Gingin, the winery was re-equipped, and the first of the new generation wines was produced in 1994. Consistent quality across both white and red wines has seen production steadily increase since that time.

Signature wine: Basket Pressed Reserve Shiraz

Houghton Est.1836

Dale Rd, Middle Swan 6056
www.houghton-wines.com.au
exports to UK, US

The Houghton portfolio may start with modestly priced, large-volume white wines, and move through to elegant, barrel-fermented Chardonnay, but it certainly doesn't stop there. The Jack Mann red (a blend of Cabernet Sauvignon, Malbec and Shiraz from the Frankland River), Gladstones Shiraz, Houghton Reserve Shiraz, the Margaret River reds and Frankland Riesling are all of the highest quality, and simply serve to reinforce the rating. To borrow a phrase of the late Jack Mann, 'There are no bad wines here.'

Signature wine: Jack Mann

Jane Brook Estate Est.1972

229 Toodyay Rd, Middle Swan 6056
www.janebrook.com.au
exports to UK, US

An attractive winery which relies in part on substantial cellar-door trade and in part on varying export markets, with much work having been invested in the Japanese market. It has established a vineyard in the Margaret River and also is now sourcing fruit from Pemberton, Ferguson Valley and Arthur River. The appointment of Julie Smith (nee White) as chief winemaker led to a distinct improvement in wine quality and consistency.

Signature wine: Back Block Shiraz

John Kosovich Wines Est.1922

Cnr Memorial Ave & Great Northern Hwy, Baskerville 6056
www.johnkosovichwines.com.au

The name change from Westfield to John Kosovich Wines in 2003 did not signify any change in either philosophy or direction for this much-admired producer of a surprisingly elegant and complex Chardonnay. (The other wines are more variable, but from time to time it has made attractive Verdelho and excellent Cabernet Sauvignon.) 1998 saw the first release of wines partly or wholly coming from the family's new planting at Pemberton, those being Swan/Pemberton blends released under the Bronze Wing label. The cellar also houses some magnificent old fortified wines.

Signature wine: Westfield Chardonnay

Lamont's Est.1978

85 Bisdee Rd, Millendon 6056
www.lamonts.com.au

Corin Lamont is the daughter of the late Jack Mann and, with the recent involvement of Keith Mugford as consultant, oversees the making of wines in a style which would have pleased her father. Lamont's also boasts a superb restaurant run by granddaughter Kate Lamont, plus a gallery for the sale and promotion of local arts. The wines are going from strength to strength, utilising both estate-grown and contract-grown (from southern regions) grapes, including vibrantly fresh lime and citrus Frankland River Riesling, mineral and herb Margaret River Semillon Sauvignon Blanc and creamy stonefruit and fig Chardonnay.

Signature wine: Chardonnay

Lilac Hill Estate Est.1998

55 Benara Road, Caversham 6055
www.lilachillestate.com.au

Stephen Murfit, and his young family, are typical of the new arrivals on the scene contributing to the renaissance of the Swan Valley, even if the cellar door takes you back a pace through time. Consistently well-made wines come from the 4 ha of estate vineyards, and Murfit also has an active contract winemaking business.

Signature wine: Verdelho

Moondah Brook Est.1968

c/o Houghton, Dale Rd, Middle Swan 6056
www.moondahbrook.com.au
exports to UK, US

Part of the Hardys wine group, but which has its own special character as it draws part of its fruit from the large Gingin vineyard, 70 km north of the Swan Valley, and part from the Margaret River and Great Southern. In recent times Moondah Brook has excelled even its own reputation for reliability with some quite lovely wines, in particular honeyed, aged Chenin Blanc and finely structured Cabernet Sauvignon.

Signature wine: Cabernet Sauvignon

[LEFT] JOHN GRIFFITHS.
[OPPOSITE LEFT] PAUL BOULDEN.
[OPPOSITE RIGHT] SANDALFORD.

Oakover Estate Est. 1990

14 Yukich Close, Middle Swan 6056
www.oakoverwines.com.au
🍷 🍴 exports to UK

Owned by the Yukich family, part of the long-established Dalmatian Coast/Croatian cultural group in the Swan Valley, with its roots going back to the early 1900s. However, Oakover Estate is very much part of the new wave in the Swan Valley, with a large vineyard holding of 64 ha, planted predominantly to Chardonnay, Shiraz, Chenin Blanc and Verdelho. Part of the production is sold to others, but with increasing amounts sold through the cellar door and the large café/restaurant and function centre in the heart of the vineyard.

Signature wine: Chardonnay

RiverBank Estate Est. 1993

126 Hamersley Road, Caversham 6055
www.riverbankestate.com.au
🍷 🍴

Robert Bond had 20 years' experience as a viticulturist in the Swan Valley, and a degree from Charles Sturt University, when he established RiverBank Estate in 1993. He shares with John Griffiths of Faber Vineyard a belief in 'unashamedly full-bodied' wines 'produced from ripe grapes in what is recognised as a hot grapegrowing region'. In his spare time Bond conducts eight-week wine courses affiliated with the Wine Industry Association of Western Australia.

Signature wine: Padlock Paddock Cabernet

Sandalford Est. 1840

West Swan Rd, Caversham 6055
www.sandalford.com
🍷 🍴 exports to UK, US

Some years ago the upgrading of the winery and the appointment of Paul Boulden as chief winemaker resulted in far greater consistency in quality, and the proper utilisation of the excellent vineyard resources of Sandalford in Margaret River and Mount Barker. Things have continued on an even keel since, with 100 000 cases of excellent Riesling, Semillon Sauvignon Blanc, Semillon, Shiraz, Cabernet Sauvignon and Merlot leading the way.

Signature wine: Margaret River Cabernet Sauvignon

Sittella Wines Est. 1998

100 Barrett Rd, Herne Hill 6056
www.sittella.com.au
🍷 🍴

Perth couple Simon and Maaike Berns acquired a 7 ha block (with 5 ha of vines) at Herne Hill, making the first wine in February 1998 and opening the most attractive cellar-door facility later in the year. They also own the 10 ha Wildberry Springs Estate vineyard in the Margaret River region. The 5000 case annual production from the two vineyards is contract-made by John Griffiths, with consistently good outcomes for Cabernet Sauvignon, Shiraz, Verdelho and unoaked Chardonnay, all showing exemplary varietal character.

Signature wine: Margaret River Cabernet Sauvignon

Talijancich Est. 1932

26 Hyem Rd, Herne Hill 6056
talywine@wantree.com.au
🍷

James and Hilda Talijancich own and run this neat blend of old and new, the old represented by its 15-year-old Liqueur Muscat, the new by its Chenin Blanc, Verdelho (both varietal and Reserve) and Reserve Shiraz. On the third Saturday of August each year there is a tasting of fine three-year-old Verdelho table wines from Australia and overseas; they also run an active wine club and export to China, Japan and Hong Kong.

Signature wine: Liqueur Muscat

Upper Reach Vineyard Est. 1996

77 Memorial Avenue, Baskerville 6056
www.upperreach.com.au
🍷 🍴 exports to UK

Another milestone in the new Swan Valley, with a modern winery, tasting room and restaurant situated on the bank of the upper reaches of the Swan River. Laura Rowe and Derek Pearse purchased the property in 1996, at the time with 4 ha of 12-year-old Chardonnay. As well as erecting the winery and other buildings, they have planted 1.5 ha of Shiraz and 1 ha of Cabernet Sauvignon; importantly, they also own a 4 ha vineyard in the Margaret River region. The fish on the label is a black bream, which can be found in the pools of the Swan River during the summer months.

Signature wine: Verdelho

GREATER PERTH ZONE
Peel 🌿

The European settlement of Peel dates back to 1829 when a visionary Thomas Peel brought three ships of migrants from England for the Peel Settlement Scheme. Thomas Peel, who arrived with an entourage from England to take up his entitlement, was apparently totally unprepared for both the climate and the work required to put the country into shape for farming, and quickly retired to the beach to drink gin and tonic (or its equivalent) under the protection of umbrellas. The British government was understandably unimpressed and three-quarters of his grant was revoked. Nonetheless, Thomas Peel was left with one-quarter of a million acres (101 215 hectares); this founded what became known as the Peel Estate, from which the vineyard takes its name.

In 1846 the first mine (lead, silver and zinc) in Western Australia was opened; while short-lived, it presaged the large-scale mineral sands, gold and bauxite mining and processing operations that commenced in the 1970s.

A vineyard was established near Pinjarra in 1857, and remained in production for over 40 years, winning a gold medal at the 1878 Melbourne Centenary Exhibition, before being uprooted by the owner's widow in 1898. The first commercial vineyard in modern times was started by Will Nairn at Peel Estate in 1974 with a planting of Shiraz, and while most other varieties have since been established, Shiraz remains the flagship variety for the region, Peel Estate its flagship producer.

PEEL

Latitude **32°31'S**
Altitude **5–290 m**
Heat degree days **2300–2350**
Growing season rainfall **160–280 mm**
Mean January temp. **22–23°C**
Harvest **Mid-February to mid-March**
Chief viticultural hazard **Silvereye birds**

Perth ●

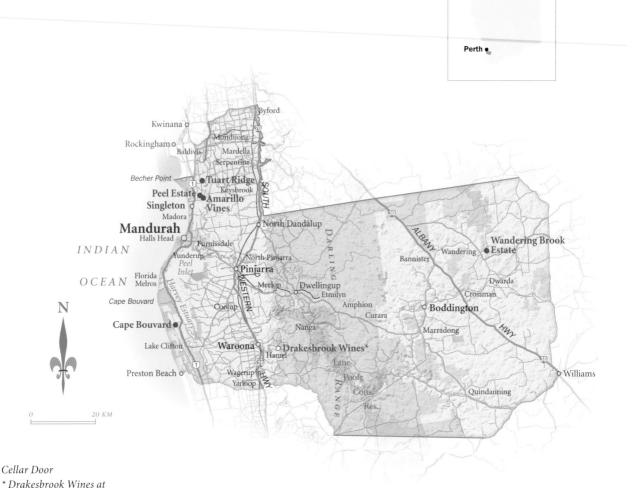

Cellar Door
* Drakesbrook Wines at
  Lake Navarino Forest Resort.

The Region

CLIMATE

The coastal region has a Mediterranean climate with cool, wet winters and dry summers, the sea breezes moderating extremes; inland and at higher altitudes land breezes are stronger, rainfall higher and temperatures slightly lower.

SOIL & TOPOGRAPHY

The eastern extension of the Peel region to incorporate the Darling Plateau around Boddington / Wandering / Mount Saddleback takes in very old granitic, gravel soils totally different to the limestone sands and fluvial sediments of the coastal area, which have significant groundwater reserves 3–15 metres below the surface.

PRINCIPAL GRAPE VARIETIES

Overall, 61 per cent white and 39 per cent red. In descending order:

CHENIN BLANC

CHARDONNAY

SHIRAZ

VERDELHO

CABERNET SAUVIGNON.

 WHITE WINE STYLES

Chenin Blanc is a popular variety throughout much of Western Australia's wine regions, and was the first white grape to be planted in Peel. Produced in both oaked and unoaked versions, it gains character and depth with short- to medium-term cellaring.

Chardonnay is planted in most of the localities throughout the region, attesting – as ever – to the versatility of the variety. Characters range from melon and stonefruit to rich and buttery.

 RED WINE STYLES

Shiraz is not only the longest established but arguably the most successful variety, particularly at Peel Estate. Overall, the style is medium-bodied with sweet, fine, ripe tannins.

Cabernet Sauvignon is planted in many parts, producing a medium-bodied wine, slightly firmer when grown in the inland, higher-altitude regions.

Wineries of Peel

Drakesbrook Wines

Est. 1998

PO Box 284, Waroona 6215

www.drakesbrookwines.com.au

 (at Lake Navarino Forest Resort)

Bernard (Bernie) Worthington, a Perth-based property specialist, developed a serious interest in wine more than ten years ago; all his interests coalesced when he found Drakesbrook, a 216 ha property taking its name from the Drakesbrook River which flows through it. At an altitude of 265 m, it has views out to the ocean and is adjacent to the Lake Navarino tourist resort. He subdivided the property, retaining 121 ha and selling the remainder. His 11.9 ha vineyard is planted to Semillon, Chardonnay, Shiraz, Merlot, Petit Verdot, Cabernet Franc and Cabernet Sauvignon.

Signature wine: Chardonnay

Peel Estate Est. 1974

Fletcher Rd, Baldivis 6171

www.peelwine.com.au

 exports to UK, US

Peel Estate's Shiraz is a wine of considerable finesse and a remarkably consistent track record. Every year Will Nairn holds a Great Shiraz Tasting for six-year-old Australian Shirazs, and pits Peel Estate (in a blind tasting attended by 60 or so people) against Australia's best. It is never disgraced. The white wines are workmanlike, the wood-matured Chenin Blanc another winery specialty, although not achieving the excellence of the Shiraz. At five years of age the Shiraz will typically show well, with black cherry and chocolate flavours, a strong dash of American oak, and surprising youth.

Signature wine: Shiraz

Tuart Ridge Est. 1996

344 Stakehill Rd, Baldivis 6171

www.tuartridgewines.com

Former Swan Valley resident Phil Franzone has established 5 ha of Chardonnay, Verdelho, Shiraz, Cabernet Sauvignon, Grenache and Merlot on the coastal tuart soils. 2001 was the first vintage, and production will peak at around 3000 cases. Franzone also acts as contract winemaker for several of the many new ventures springing up in the Peel region. The quality of the wines is every bit as good as one could expect.

Signature wine: Shiraz

Wandering Brook Estate

Est. 1989

North Wandering Rd, Wandering 6308

(08) 9884 1064

Laurie and Margaret White have planted 10 ha of Verdelho, Chardonnay and Cabernet Sauvignon on their 130-year-old family property in a move to diversify. Up to 1994 the wines were made at Goundrey, currently they are made at Jadran in the Perth Hills. The vineyard was renamed Wandering Brook Estate late in 1994; up till then it was known as Red Hill Estate. Over half the annual production of grapes is sold.

Signature wine: Chardonnay

GREATER PERTH ZONE
Perth Hills 🌿

Viticulture has been practised intermittently in the picturesque Perth Hills for over a century, but on a generally tiny scale. The first known winery was built in the 1880s, and continued production until it was burnt down in 1945. Thus while Despeissis was able to report in 1902 that grapes grown in the Mundaringa-Chidlow subregion ripened two to three weeks later than in the Swan Valley, the longest-established of the present-day wineries (Hainault) dates back to only 1980, and until the latter part of the 1990s none of the wineries crushed more than 50 tonnes a year. That has changed with the arrival of first Millbrook Winery and even more emphatically with the opening of Western Range Wines.

It is a pretty region, with constantly changing vistas. The exotic native plant vegetation grows in rich profusion: Western Australia was given far more than its fair share by nature, and this is shown to full advantage in the Perth Hills, with patches of introduced exotics from Europe and elsewhere adding an unexpected contrast near streams and in home gardens. Moreover, it is only 22 kilometres from Perth, making it easily accessible to daytrippers.

The Region 🍇

CLIMATE

The tempering influences which reduce the heat summation and delay ripening for 10–21 days (compared to the Swan Valley) are first, the altitude; second, the free air drainage; and third, exposure to afternoon sea breezes. Warm evenings, however, mean continuous ripening, and frosts pose no threat at any time of year. Overall, Dr John Gladstones likens its climate to that of the Douro Valley in Portugal.

SOIL & TOPOGRAPHY

Rivulets and (often dry) creek beds, ridges, hills and valleys criss-cross the region in every direction, offering an almost unlimited choice of aspect and slope, but those sites cut off from the sea breeze influence tend to be warmer rather than cooler. The valley slopes have ironstone and gravel sandy loams and gravelly loams which overlie clay, similar in type to many parts of Western Australia and which were once covered with marri. They are well suited to viticulture, being of moderate fertility, producing moderate yields.

PRINCIPAL GRAPE VARIETIES

Overall, 54 per cent red, 46 per cent white. In descending order:

SHIRAZ

CHARDONNAY

CABERNET SAUVIGNON

MERLOT

PINOT NOIR.

PERTH HILLS

Latitude **31°59'S**

Altitude **150–400 m**

Heat degree days **1770**

Growing season rainfall **220–250 mm**

Mean January temp. **23.3°C**

Harvest **Late February to mid-March**

Chief viticultural hazard **Birds**

Wineries of Perth Hills

Cosham Est. 1989

101 Union Rd, Carmel via Kalamunda 6076
www.coshamwines.com.au

Cosham has grown significantly over recent years, though admittedly from a small base. A complex Methode Champenoise and savoury/earthy Cabernet Merlot are both creditable wines, the restrained mineral and melon-accented Chardonnay even better. The vineyard is planted on an old orchard, and consists of 2 ha of Cabernet Sauvignon, Merlot, Shiraz, Pinot Noir, Cabernet Franc, Chardonnay and Petit Verdot, established between 1990 and 1995. They grow in gravelly loam with some clay, but overall in a well-drained soil with good rainfall.

Signature wine: Bickley Valley Chardonnay

Hainault Est. 1980

255 Walnut Rd, Bickley 6076
www.hainault.com.au

Lyn and Michael Sykes became the owners of Hainault in 2002, after Bill Mackey and wife Vicki headed off elsewhere. The 11 ha of close-planted vines are hand-pruned and hand-picked, and the Pinot Noir is very sensibly used to make a sparkling wine, rather than a table wine. The plans are to open a restaurant when the necessary bureaucratic regulations have been dealt with.

Signature wine: Talus (Sparkling)

Hartley Estate Est. 1999

260 Chittering Valley Rd,
Lower Chittering 6084
laura@highway1.biz

Bernie and Erin Stephens purchased the property now named Hartley Estate without any forethought. While driving the Chittering Valley one Sunday, Stephens saw a For Sale sign on a property, and later that day the contract for sale was signed. Planting of 17 ha of vines began, and Cabernet Sauvignon and Shiraz were made in commercial quantities in 2003. They form part of the Generations Series, recognising the involvement of three generations of the family: the founders, their children and the grandchildren. The major part of the crop goes to Western Range Wines, the remainder (made by Western Range) under the Hartley Estate label.

Signature wine: Cabernet Merlot

 WHITE WINE STYLES

Chardonnay The ubiquitous Chardonnay does not disappoint: the best white wines to have come from the Perth Hills have been made from this variety. One would expect the style to be generous, and it usually is, but some quite tight, minerally wines are also produced.

 RED WINE STYLES

Cabernet Sauvignon and Merlot. Frequently blended, sometimes released as straightforward varietal wines, and produced by the majority of the wineries in the region. Full-flavoured, with chocolatey/earthy/berry flavours, the wines are reliable and pleasant.

Shiraz. Mid-weight wines are the order of the day, with gentle cherry/earthy fruit flavours and – I suspect – with the ability to develop well in bottle for some years.

Jarrah Ridge Winery Est. 1998

Lot 11, Jenkins Rd, Bullsbrook 6084
www.jarrahridge.com.au

Syd and Julie Pond have established a 13.5 ha vineyard: 5 ha of Shiraz the most important grape, the remainder divided between Chenin Blanc, Chardonnay (3 ha each), Cabernet Sauvignon, Verdelho and Viognier (1 ha each) and Merlot (2 ha). Children Michael and Lisa are also involved in the business, with the experienced Rob Marshall as contract winemaker. Most of the wines have a degree of sweetness which will doubtless appeal to cellar-door and restaurant customers.

Signature wine: Balladonia Chenin Blanc

Millbrook Winery Est. 1996

Old Chestnut Lane, Jarrahdale 6124
www.millbrookwinery.com.au

 exports to UK, US

The strikingly situated Millbrook Winery, opened in December 2001, is owned by the highly successful, Perth-based entrepreneur Peter Fogarty and wife Lee. They also own Lake's Folly in the Hunter Valley, and Deep Woods in the Margaret River. Millbrook draws on 7.5 ha of vineyards in the Perth Hills, planted to Sauvignon Blanc, Semillon, Chardonnay, Viognier, Cabernet Sauvignon, Merlot, Shiraz and Petit Verdot. It also purchases grapes from the Perth Hills, Geographe and Margaret River regions. The wines under both the Millbrook label and the second label, Barking Owl, are of consistently high quality.

Signature wine: Chardonnay

Western Range Wines Est. 2001

Lot 88, Chittering Rd, Lower Chittering 6084
www.westernrangewines.com.au

exports to UK, US

Between the mid 1990s and 2001 several prominent Western Australians, including Marilyn Corderory, Malcolm McCusker, Terry and Kevin Prindiville and Tony Rechner, established approximately 125 ha of vines (under separate ownerships) in the Perth Hills, with a kaleidoscopic range of varietals. The next step was to join forces to build a substantial winery, which is a separate venture to the growers' individual vineyards, but which takes the grapes and then markets the wine under the Western Range brand. All in all, an impressive combination; this and Millbrook Winery are by some distance the best producers in the region.

Signature wine: Julimar Shiraz Viognier

Tasmania

King
Island

Flinders
Island

Cape Barren Island

BASS   STRAIT

Banks   Strait

• Smithton

Wynyard •
Somerset •   • Burnie   • Devonport   • Bridport

Ulverstone •   • George Town   • Scottsdale
    • Latrobe   • Beaconsfield

    • Sheffield

    • St Helens

Deloraine •   • Launceston
    • Westbury

Longford •

NORTHERN   • St Marys

• Rosebery   TASMANIA

• Zeehan   Great
    Lake

    • Bicheno

Queenstown •   Lake
• Strahan   Sorell   • Ross

    • Swansea

SOUTHERN
    • Triabunna
TASMANIA

Lake   Maria Island
Gordon

New Norfolk •   • Bridgewater
Lake Pedder   • Sorell

    • HOBART
    • Kingston

Huonville •   Tasman
    Peninsula

Bruny
Island

N

0   50 KM

▭ UNOFFICIAL WINE REGION

Introduction 🌿

Tasmania can claim to have founded both the Victorian and South Australian wine industries. Wine was being commercially made and sold in Tasmania several years before vines were planted in either of those states, and it was the source of the first vines for those states. When William Henty sailed from Launceston to Portland (in Victoria) on board the schooner *Thistle* in 1834, his personal effects included 'one cask of grape cuttings and one box of plants'. John Hack planted vines in South Australia (said by some authorities to be the first to do so, although the records are not conclusive) in 1837, followed by John Reynell in 1838; both men obtained their cuttings from Port Arthur in Southern Tasmania.

The state's first commercial vineyard was planted by Bartholomew Broughton in 1823, and in 1827 he advertised that he had 300 gallons (1365 litres) of 1826 vintage wine for sale. By 1827 commercial nurseries were offering vine cuttings, and by 1865 had 45 varieties available, including Pinot Noir, Cabernet Sauvignon, Shiraz, Malbec, Pinot Blanc and Sauvignon Blanc.

Ironically, that decade marked the sudden collapse of the industry, due in part to the gold stampede on the mainland draining Tasmania of labour. There was a brief flurry of activity in the 1880s when Diego Bernacchi obtained cuttings from St Huberts in the Yarra Valley, planting them on Maria Island, east of Hobart, and exhibited a wine at the Melbourne Centennial Exhibition of 1888–89. He subsequently sought investors, and is said to have attached artificial bunches to his vines and sailed past the island

at night with potential investors, pointing to the vines with the aid of a lamp. They were unimpressed, and Bernacchi faded away.

Tasmania's winemakers have so far taken no action to establish official regions, and until the new millennium may have been prevented from seeking registration by the 500 tonne requirement. However, it is no longer a bar to (taking a few examples) the Pipers River or Coal River/Richmond areas so doing. Declining official registration may well be an astute move: brand Tasmania has both domestic and international strength.

At some point, however, the wide spread of Tasmanian vineyards, and the marked differences in site climates and soils, may lead to a change of philosophy. For the flip side of the coin is that outside observers not only habitually exaggerate the extent of Tasmania's viticulture, but are oblivious to the diversity of terroir and climate in the island's extremely complex geography. There are sites which are both warmer and very much drier than southern Victoria (for example, the Coal River/Richmond area north-east of Hobart, and, in terms of warmth, the Tamar River valley south of Launceston). The one clear pattern is that Pinot Noir finds itself at home in all parts of the

state, with the qualified exception of parts of the Tamar River valley.

Zinfandel was once grown successfully at Coal River, while the colour and extract of the Tamar River red wines is extraordinary, hinting misleadingly at a warm to very warm climate. Instead, the island's major producers have hitched their future to such cool-climate varieties as Riesling, Pinot Gris, Chardonnay and Pinot Noir (the latter two for both table and sparkling wine use). However, the apparent effect of climate change – or at least, some warm vintages – has led recently to some impressive Merlot, Cabernet Sauvignon and Shiraz coming from the warmer sites of the Tamar River and the Coal River.

A high level of corporate takeover activity between 1994 and 2004 has seen the emergence of some well-resourced, medium-sized companies, and also investment by Hardys. Tasmania no longer has a doll's house-sized industry, although happily many tiny producers continue to populate the scene, relying entirely on the tourism which is such an important part of the economy of this island paradise.

[PREVIOUS] Jansz, Northern Tasmania.
[BELOW] Tamar Ridge, Northern Tasmania.

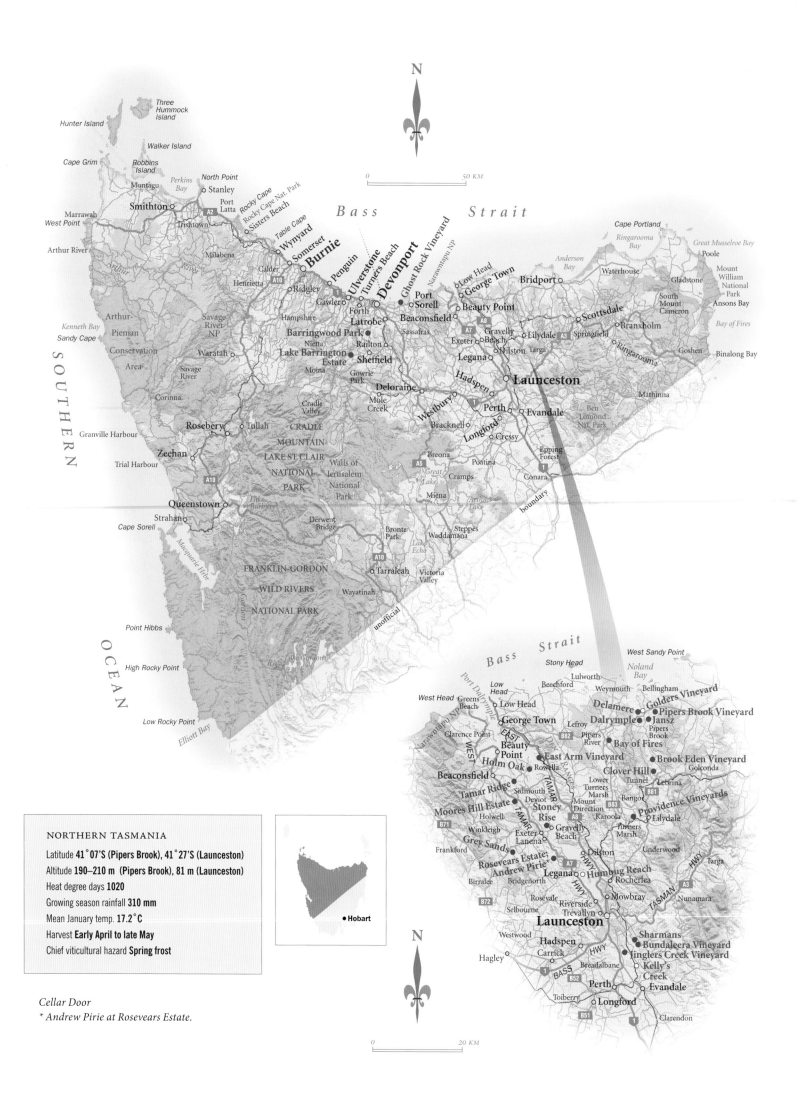

NORTHERN TASMANIA

Latitude 41°07'S (Pipers Brook), 41°27'S (Launceston)

Altitude 190–210 m (Pipers Brook), 81 m (Launceston)

Heat degree days **1020**

Growing season rainfall **310 mm**

Mean January temp. **17.2°C**

Harvest **Early April to late May**

Chief viticultural hazard **Spring frost**

Cellar Door

* *Andrew Pirie at Rosevears Estate.*

TASMANIA
Northern Tasmania 🌿

All of the recorded grapegrowing and winemaking activity in the nineteenth century took place in the south of the state. From the 1890s to the mid 1950s there was no activity in either north or south; it was the official view of the Tasmanian Department of Agriculture that the island was unsuited to commercial wine grapegrowing. A Frenchman, Jean Miguet, working with the Hydro Electric Commission, had other ideas and between 1956 and 1960 planted 1.3 hectares at his La Provence vineyard (he came from Provence) at Lalla, just to the north-east of Launceston. He returned to France in 1974, and died there. Another 20 years passed, and the ever-vigilant French authorities got wind of the name, forcing a change to Providence.

By 1984 the Pipers Brook area had six vineyards, the Tamar Valley had 11 and the East Coast three (out of a state total of 31). The entire state produced 240 tonnes of wine grapes that year; within another 20 years, the crush had risen to just under 6400 tonnes from about 100 wineries. The two major wineries in the north, Pipers Brook and Tamar Ridge, have 182 and 240 hectares of vines respectively, and Tamar Ridge in particular has aggressive plans for further expansion.

It hardly needs be said that the north of the state is indeed suited to viticulture and the production of fine wine. The east side of the Tamar River, the Pipers River area, the north-west coast and the north-east corner near Waterhouse (to be developed by Tamar Ridge) offer a range of terroir and climate as diverse as the southern half of Victoria, ripening every variety from Chardonnay and Pinot Noir to Shiraz and Cabernet Sauvignon.

Nor will anyone the least bit familiar with Tasmania be surprised by the ever-changing but always beautiful landscape; those vineyards facing the Tamar River offer breathtakingly beautiful vistas.

The atmosphere of the Pipers River area is very different, much being undulating and forested, the undergrowth lush and the roadside grass remaining green for most of the year. It was indeed Andrew Pirie's observation of the last feature which was one of the factors that led him to establish Pipers Brook Vineyards here. The green of bush and vineyards (in summer) then provides a compelling contrast with the vivid red basalt-derived soils.

PIPERS BROOK VINEYARD, NORTHERN TASMANIA.

The Region

CLIMATE

The climate of the Pipers River area is comparable to that of Champagne and the Rhine Valley; 40 per cent of the annual rainfall is recorded in the growing season, and the relatively high humidity also ameliorates stress, promoting vigorous growth. Take in the soil, and the reasons for the varietal choice become even more evident. Spring frosts are a serious problem, necessitating wind machines or overhead sprinklers in many sites. The figures for the Tamar Valley are superficially similar, but this area achieves physiological ripeness far earlier than the Pipers River, and allows late ripening varieties to do relatively well.

SOIL & TOPOGRAPHY

Almost all vineyards are on slopes facing north, north-east and east. The vivid red soils of the Pipers River area are very deep, free-draining, friable and fertile; those of the Tamar Valley are gravelly basalt on a clay and ironstone base.

PRINCIPAL GRAPE VARIETIES

Overall, 51 per cent white, 49 per cent red (Pinot Noir accounts for all but 10 per cent of the total red grape plantings across the state).
In descending order:

PINOT NOIR

CHARDONNAY

RIESLING

SAUVIGNON BLANC

CABERNET SAUVIGNON

MERLOT

PINOT GRIS

GEWÜRZTRAMINER.

WHITE WINE STYLES

Chardonnay. The high natural acidity of the grapes means total or partial malolactic fermentation is par for the course; coupled with barrel fermentation, the result is wines with an admirable combination of elegance and complexity, subtlety and intensity.

Riesling produces highly fragrant wines with a steely acidity and outstanding length and persistence of flavour, which repay ten years or more in bottle.

Gewürztraminer is more delicate, spice and rose petals coming in the warmer vintages.

Pinot Gris is on the march in a climate eminently suited to produce wine with real presence.

Sauvignon Blanc is sometimes deficient in clear varietal character, sometimes redolent with it.

Sparkling wines are Australia's best if Arras, Pirie (aka Kreglinger), Clover Hill, Jansz and the Hardy sparkling wines ranged under Arras, but still with a significant Tasmanian contribution, are any guide.

RED WINE STYLES

Pinot Noir flourishes both in the Pipers River and Tamar Valley areas, much destined for sparkling wine (along with Chardonnay). Pinot Noir from the Tamar Valley has greater weight and depth and is more likely to be used to make table wine of high quality.

Cabernet Sauvignon, Merlot and Shiraz are grown in small areas on the warmest sites facing the Tamar River, and in warm vintages can produce formidable wines deep in colour and flavour.

[OPPOSITE] BRUCE MCCORMACK, PIPERS BROOK VINEYARD, NORTHERN TASMANIA.
[ABOVE] KRASNOZEM SOIL, CLOVER HILL, NORTHERN TASMANIA. [RIGHT] PIPERS BROOK VINEYARD, NORTHERN TASMANIA.

Wineries of Northern Tasmania

Andrew Pirie Est. 2004

1a Waldhorn Drive, Rosevears 7277 (postal)
www.andrewpirie.com

🍷 (at Rosevears Estate); exports to UK

Following a relatively short break after leaving Pipers Brook, Andrew Pirie re-established his winemaking activities in Tasmania. He has leased the Rosevears Winery, where he produces the wines for the Rosevears Group; for his own brands (in two ranges, Pirie and Pirie South); and for others on a contract basis. For the foreseeable future he will rely on contract-grown fruit of the highest possible quality.

Signature wine: Pinot Noir

Bay of Fires Est. 2001

40 Baxters Rd, Pipers River 7252
www.bayoffireswines.com.au

🍷 exports to UK, US

First the home of Rochecombe Wines, next Ninth Island and, since its purchase by Hardys in 1994, Bay of Fires. Initially focussed on making the base wine for Arras (Hardys' ultra-premium sparkling wine), Bay of Fires now has two ranges of table wines – under the Bay of Fires and Tigress (second label) brands. All the wines live up to expectations.

Signature wine: Bay of Fires Pinot Noir

Clover Hill Est. 1986

Clover Hill Rd, Lebrina 7254
www.taltarni.com.au

🍷 exports to UK, US

Clover Hill was established by Taltarni in 1986 with the sole purpose of making a premium sparkling wine. Its 21 ha of vineyards, comprising 12 ha of Chardonnay, 6.5 of Pinot Noir and 1.5 of Pinot Meunier, are now all in bearing, although extensive re-trellising took place in 2002. The sparkling wine quality is excellent, combining finesse with power and length. Clover Hill now has a second role, providing part of the base wines for the Taltarni sparkling wines (much improved in consequence) and Chardonnay for Taltarni-group table wines.

Signature wine: Clover Hill Vintage

Dalrymple Est. 1987

1337 Pipers Brook Rd, Pipers Brook 7254
www.dalrymplevineyards.com.au

🍷

A partnership between former radio PR supremo Jill Mitchell and her sister and brother-in-law, Anne and Bertel Sundstrup, inspired by father Bill Mitchell's establishment of the Tamarway Vineyard in the late 1960s. The vineyards have increased to 11 ha of Chardonnay, Pinot Gris, Sauvignon Blanc and Pinot Noir. As production has grown (significantly), so has the wine quality across the board, often led by the Sauvignon Blanc, more recently joined by powerful but very stylish Pinot Noir.

Signature wine: Sauvignon Blanc

East Arm Vineyard Est. 1993

111 Archers Rd, Hillwood 7250
jwetten@bigpond.com

Established by Launceston gastroenterologist Dr John Wettenhall and partner Anita James, who completed the Charles Sturt University Diploma in Applied Science (winegrowing), on a 25 ha property sloping down to the Tamar River. It is a historic block, part of a grant to retired British soldiers of the Georgetown garrison in 1821. The 2 ha vineyard, which came into full production in 1998, is more or less equally divided between Riesling, Chardonnay and Pinot Noir. There are plans for further planting and, down the track, a winery.

Signature wine: Riesling

Grey Sands Est. 1989

Cnr Kerrisons Rd & Frankford Hwy,
Glengarry 7275
www.tassie.net.au/greysands

🍷

Bob and Rita Richter began the planting of the vineyard in 1988, gradually increasing the plantings over the ensuing ten years to the present total of 2.5 ha of Pinot Gris, Merlot and Shiraz. The ultra-high density of 8900 vines per hectare (3000 is normally considered high) reflects the experience gained by the Richters during a three-year stay in England, during which time they visited many vineyards across Europe, underpinned by Bob Richter's graduate diploma in wine from Roseworthy.

Signature wine: Pinot Gris

Holm Oak Est. 1983

RSD 256 Rowella, West Tamar 7270
www.holm-oak.com

The Butler family produces tremendously rich and strongly flavoured wines from the 6 ha of Riesling, Pinot Noir, Cabernet Sauvignon, Merlot and Cabernet Franc situated on the banks of the Tamar River. The vineyard takes its name from the grove of oak trees planted around the turn of the twentieth century and intended for the making of tennis racquets. It made its reputation with full-bodied red wines; its Riesling, too, is impressive. Winemaker Nicholas Butler also provides contract winemaking services for others.

Signature wine: Riesling

Jansz Est. 1985

1216b Pipers Brook Rd, Pipers Brook 7254
www.jansz.com.au

🍷 exports to UK, US

Jansz was one of the first sparkling wines from Tasmania, stemming from a short-lived relationship between Heemskerk and Louis Roederer. Now part of the Yalumba group, its 15 ha of Chardonnay, 12 ha of Pinot Noir and 3 ha of Pinot Meunier correspond almost exactly to the blend composition of the Jansz wines. It is the only Tasmanian winery entirely devoted to the production of sparkling wine, which is of very high quality. Vintage, non-vintage and late-disgorged versions are made.

Signature wine: Jansz Vintage

Pipers Brook Vineyard

Est. 1974
1216 Pipers Brook Rd, Pipers Brook 7254
www.pipersbrook.com

🍷 🍴 exports to UK, US

Still the highest-profile Tasmanian wine producer, and even if overtaken in size by Tamar Ridge or any other, will remain so in the wake of its acquisition by the Belgian-based Kreglinger group in 2001. The de Moor family has made Launceston its home, and Paul de Moor runs both Pipers Brook and Kreglinger's Norfolk Rise winery (Mount Benson, SA) from here, as well as the company's 100-year-old Australian wool business. The immaculately packaged wines are still made with the utmost care, and deserve their high reputation.

Signature wine: The Summit Chardonnay

Providence Vineyards

Est. 1956
236 Lalla Rd, Lalla 7267
www.providence-vineyards.com.au

🍷

Jean Miguet, a French technician raised in Provence, came to Tasmania to work for the Hydro Electric Commission, and in 1956 planted a 1.3 ha pioneer vineyard, which he called La Provence. He died in 1976 and the vineyard was sold to the Bryce family in 1980, but another decade was to pass before French authorities woke up and forced a name change to Providence. The original 1.3 ha vineyard has been expanded to a little over 3 ha, as well as unsuitable Grenache and Cabernet (left from the original plantings) being grafted over to Chardonnay, Pinot Noir and Riesling.

Signature wine: Miguet Reserve Pinot Noir

Rosevears Estate Est. 1999

1a Waldhorn Drive, Rosevears 7277
www.rosevearsestate.com.au

🍷 🍴

The multi-million-dollar Rosevears Estate winery and restaurant complex (opened in November 1999) is built on a steep hillside overlooking the Tamar River. It is owned by a group of investors headed by Notley Gorge founder Dr Mike Beamish and incorporates both the Notley Gorge and Ironpot Bay brands. Spacious, high-quality accommodation units with a splendid view over the Tamar River were opened in September 2003. In 2004, Dr Andrew Pirie leased the winery, and makes both his wines and the Rosevears, Notley Gorge and Ironpot Bay wines here.

Signature wine: Rosevears Merlot

GRAPE PICKERS UNDER STORM CLOUDS AT PIPERS BROOK VINEYARD.

Tamar Ridge Est. 1994

Auburn Rd, Kayena 7270
www.tamarridgewines.com.au

🍷 🍴 exports to UK, US

In April 2003 Gunns Limited, a large, publicly listed Tasmanian forestry and agricultural business entity, purchased Tamar Ridge. With the retention of Dr Richard Smart as viticultural advisor, an ambitious vineyard expansion is underway, lifting plantings in the region of the winery to 240 ha. The management team was significantly strengthened by the appointment of Dr Andrew Pirie as CEO in late 2005. Gunns' tax-effective investment schemes (across forestry and vineyards) have caused a certain amount of controversy, but the quality of the Tamar Ridge wines – especially its Riesling – cannot be faulted.

Signature wine: Riesling

Tasmania
Southern Tasmania 🌿

If Jean Miguet was the modern-day harbinger of viticulture in the north, Claudio Alcorso filled the role in the south when he planted vines on the banks of the Derwent River in 1958, thus founding Moorilla Estate. He did so not knowing Miguet had beaten him by two years, but shared with Miguet the scorn of the state Department of Agriculture, and the difficulty of self-taught winemaking with no one to turn to for advice in the early years. It was not until the second half of the 1970s that Moorilla Estate realised the potential it always had.

The other twentieth-century pioneer in the south was George Park who, like Miguet, worked for the Hydro Electric Commission. Together with wife Priscilla, he planted a half-hectare vineyard at Campania in the Coal River area in 1973. Into this small area they crammed Cabernet Sauvignon, Pinot Noir, Shiraz, Zinfandel, Riesling, Traminer, Sylvaner and four other varieties. Stoney Vineyard, as it was called, produced some lovely, long-lived wines (including a spicy, perfumed Zinfandel), and showed that the very dry Coal River/Richmond area could easily accommodate late-ripening varietals.

Today the vineyard is the kernel of a much-expanded Domaine A, where Swiss-born and trained Peter Althaus and wife Ruth produce Tasmania's most distinguished Cabernet Sauvignon. The arrival of water for irrigation transformed the previously precarious business of grapegrowing in this part of Tasmania, which is now growing at a pace close to that of the north, albeit from a much smaller base. The dry climate is also conducive to organic and biodynamic viticulture, led by Frogmore Creek's Tony Scherer.

To the north-east is a string of four coastal or near-coastal wineries around Bicheno, with the natural amphitheatre of Freycinet providing a local site climate which caused the eminent climate researcher Dr John Gladstones to shake his head in admiration when he visited it in the 1990s.

Vineyards stretch up along the banks of the Derwent River to Meadowbank Estate. But they also extend down to the D'Entrecasteaux Channel country and the Huon Valley 50 kilometres to the south of Hobart, and up into the nearby Hartz Mountains. Placenames such as Snug and Cygnet tell the tale of the usually placid and outrageously beautiful Channel Country, but not the wild and savage scenery up in and around the Hartz Mountains.

In viticultural and climate terms there are three distinct regions in the south – the Derwent Valley, the Huon Valley and Coal River/Richmond – and a fourth on the east coast in the Cranbrook/Bicheno area. They underline yet again the gross over-simplification of regarding Tasmania as a uniform 'region', but also point to the constantly changing backdrop, measured as much in the feel or atmosphere as in the more tangible scenic highlights.

Tasmania is an exquisitely drawn cameo, with travel times compressed from hours to minutes. The drive time from the southern end of the Mornington Peninsula to the Yarra Valley (over two hours) would get you more than halfway from Hobart to Launceston, and from the Huon Valley to Bicheno. With its wealth of stone buildings and houses, its towering forests, huge lakes and beautiful rivers, Tasmania is a tourist paradise.

[OPPOSITE] EARLY GROWTH. [BELOW] HARDY WINE COMPANY, COAL RIVER VALLEY, TASMANIA.

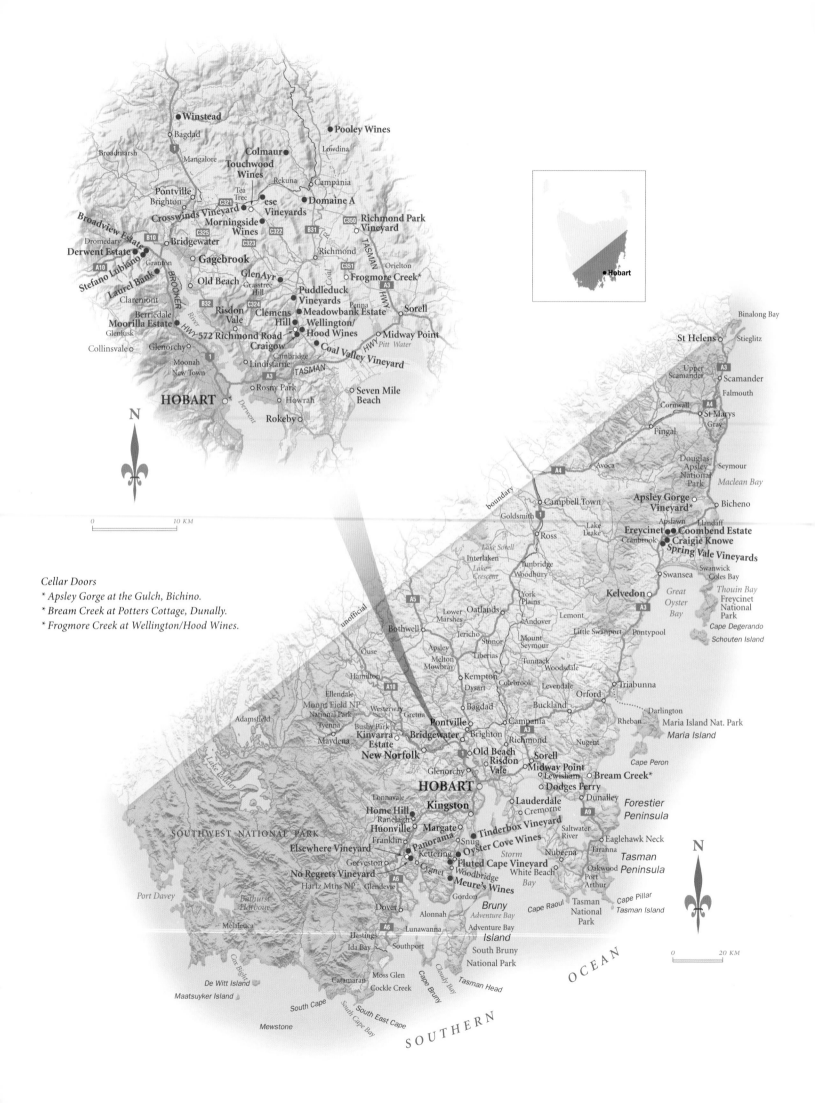

Winstead

Bagdad

Broadmarsh

Mangalore

Pooley Wines

Lowdina

Colmaur

Touchwood
Wines

Rekuna

Campania

Pontville

Brighton

Tea
Tree

...ese
Vineyards

Domaine A

Crosswinds Vineyard

Morningside
Wines

Richmond Park
Vineyard

Broadview Estate

Dromedary

Bridgewater

Richmond

Derwent Estate

Stefano Lubiana

Granton

Old Beach

GlenAyr

Grasstree
Hill

Frogmore Creek*

Laurel Bank

Claremont

Puddleduck
Vineyards

Penna

Orielton

Gagebrook

Berriedale

Risdon
Vale

Clemens
Hill

Meadowbank Estate

Sorell

Moorilla Estate

Glenlusk

Wellington/
Hood Wines

Richmond Road

Midway Point

Collinsvale

Glenorchy

HWY 572

Craigow

Pitt Water

Coal Valley Vineyard

Moonah
New Town

Cambridge

Lindisfarne

HOBART

Rosny Park

Howrah

Seven Mile
Beach

Rokeby

N

0   10 KM

Cellar Doors
* Apsley Gorge at the Gulch, Bichino.
* Bream Creek at Potters Cottage, Dunally.
* Frogmore Creek at Wellington/Hood Wines.

Hobart

St Helens

Binalong Bay

Stieglitz

Upper
Scamander

Scamander

Cornwall

Falmouth

St Marys

Fingal

Gray

Douglas-
Apsley
National
Park

Seymour

Maclean Bay

boundary

Campbell Town

Goldsmith

Avoca

Apsley Gorge
Vineyard*

Apslawn

Bicheno

Llandaff

Freycinet

Coombend Estate

Craigie Knowe

Cranbrook

Spring Vale Vineyards

Ross

Lake
Leake

Swansea

Swanwick

Coles Bay

Lake Sorell

Interlaken

Lake
Crescent

Tunbridge

Woodbury

Kelvedon

Great
Oyster
Bay

Thouin Bay

Freycinet
National
Park

unofficial

Bothwell

York
Plains

Oatlands

Lower
Marshes

Jericho

Stonor

Andover

Lemont

Little Swanport

Pontypool

Cape Degerando

Schouten Island

Ouse

Apsley
Melton
Mowbray

Kempton

Tiberias

Mount
Seymour

Tunnack

Woodsdale

A5

Hamilton

Ellendale

Mount Field NP
National Park

Westerway

Gretna

Dysart

Colebrook

Levendale

Triabunna

Adamsfield

Tyenna

Busby Park

A10

Bagdad

Buckland

Orford

Maydena

Kinvarra
Estate

Bridgewater

Brighton

Campania

Nugent

Darlington

Rheban

Maria Island Nat. Park

Pontville

Richmond

New Norfolk

Old Beach

Sorell

Maria Island

Glenorchy

Risdon
Vale

Midway Point

Cape Peron

Lewisham

Bream Creek*

HOBART

Dodges Ferry

Home Hill

Kingston

Lauderdale

Dunalley

Forestier
Peninsula

Lonnavale

Ranelagh

Cremorne

A9

Huonville

Margate

Saltwater
River

Franklin

Tinderbox Vineyard

Eaglehawk Neck

Panorama

Snug

Oyster Cove Wines

Taranna

Tasman
Peninsula

Elsewhere Vineyard

Kettering

Storm

Nubeena

Geeveston

Cygnet

Fluted Cape Vineyard

Bay

Oakwood

No Regrets Vineyard

Woodbridge

White Beach

Port
Arthur

Hartz Mtns NP

Glendevie

Meure's Wines

Tasman
National
Park

Cape Pillar

SOUTHWEST NATIONAL PARK

Dover

Gordon

Bruny

Cape Raoul

Tasman Island

Lake Pedder

Port Davey

Bathurst
Harbour

Hastings

Ida Bay

Southport

Alonnah

Lunawanna

Adventure Bay

Island

Adventure Bay

SOUTHERN

N

0   20 KM

Melaleuca

De Witt Island

Maatsuyker Island

Catamaran

Moss Glen

Cockle Creek

South Cape

South East Cape

South Cape Bay

Cape Bruny

Cloudy Bay

Tasman Head

South Bruny
National Park

OCEAN

Mewstone

The Region

CLIMATE

Given Southern Tasmania's latitude, and with nothing between it and the Antarctic, it is not surprising the statistics suggest the climate is colder than that of the north. In reality, some sites are, but others draw upon special local features (such as the much higher number of sunlight hours in the Coal River/Richmond area, or the Freycinet vineyard amphitheatre) to create notable exceptions to the rule.

SOIL & TOPOGRAPHY

The unifying feature of the topography is that there is none, so varied is it. The soils follow suit, from sandstone-based with some schist in the Derwent Valley, the Coal River offering similar weakly structured, sandy, low-humus soils in parts, and black peaty alluvial soils in others.

PRINCIPAL GRAPE VARIETIES

Overall, 54 per cent white, 46 per cent red (Pinot Noir accounts for all but 10 per cent of the total red grape plantings across the state). In descending order:

PINOT NOIR

CHARDONNAY

RIESLING

SAUVIGNON BLANC

PINOT GRIS

CABERNET SAUVIGNON

MERLOT.

SOUTHERN TASMANIA

Latitude **42°45'S (Hobart)**

Altitude **50–175 m**

Heat degree days **1013**

Growing season rainfall **360 mm**

Mean January temp. **16.8°C**

Harvest **April to early June**

Chief viticultural hazard **Spring frost**

WHITE WINE STYLES

Chardonnay responds well, in much the same way as it does in the north, although there are more unoaked wines from the south (or made there) which rely on their tangy citrus and apple flavours and crisp acidity to provide appeal.

Riesling performs much as it does in the north, making wines of great purity and length.

Sauvignon Blanc, Pinot Gris and Sparkling by and large are not significantly different to those of northern Tasmania, always elegant, fine and crisp.

RED WINE STYLES

Pinot Noir. While the south and east have fewer hectares planted to Pinot Noir (and all other varieties) they produce more high-quality Pinot table wine, with an important contribution from the East Coast wineries. The style is always complex and rich, yet with all the prerequisites of fine Pinot, including length and an expansion of flavour on the finish and aftertaste.

Cabernet Sauvignon and Merlot flourish only in the Coal River/Richmond and East Coast areas.

[RIGHT] FROGMORE CREEK, SOUTHERN TASMANIA.

Wineries of Southern Tasmania

Bream Creek Est. 1975

Marion Bay Rd, Bream Creek 7175
peacockf@mpx.com.au

🍷 (at Potters Croft, Dunally)

The two estate vineyards – one at Bream Creek, the other in the Tamar Valley – are owned and run by Fred Peacock, former long-serving viticulturist for Moorilla Estate, legendary for the meticulous care and attention he lavishes on the vines. The wines are competently made, the quality core coming – as ever – from the vineyards. Riesling, Chardonnay and Pinot Noir are the key wines, supplemented by Cabernet Sauvignon from the Tamar Valley vineyard.

Signature wine: Chardonnay

Coombend Estate Est. 1985

Coombend via Swansea 7190
coombendest@bigpond.com

🍷 exports to UK

John Fenn Smith originally planted 1.75 ha of Cabernet Sauvignon, 2.25 ha of Sauvignon Blanc, 0.5 ha of Pinot Noir and 0.3 ha of Riesling (together with a little Cabernet Franc) on his 2000 ha sheep station, choosing that part of his property which is immediately adjacent to Freycinet. The slightly quixotic choice of Cabernet Sauvignon has been justified by the success of the wine in limited show entries. In December 1998 Coombend opened a purpose-built cellar-door sales area and it has also expanded its plantings of Riesling and Sauvignon Blanc, lifting the total area under vine to 6 ha.

Signature wine: Cabernet Sauvignon

Domaine A Est. 1973

Tea Tree Rd, Campania 7026
www.domaine-a.com.au

🍷 exports to UK

Swiss-born and trained Peter and Ruth Althaus are unabashed perfectionists, and have not always found easy-going Australian attitudes to life compatible with their own values. But this hasn't deterred them; the wines are made without compromise, and reflect the low yields from the immaculately tended vineyards. The wines represent aspects of both Old World and New World philosophies, techniques and styles, and are of wholly admirable quality. Stoney Vineyard is the second label.

Signature wine: Cabernet Sauvignon

Elsewhere Vineyard Est. 1984

42 Dillons Hill Rd, Glaziers Bay 7109
www.elsewherevineyard.com

🚫

Evocatively named Elsewhere Vineyard was established by Eric and Jette Phillips as part of a business which also included a commercial flower farm. The latter added to the beauty of the gently sloping property, but such was the success of the wines that in 1993 flowers made way for additional Chardonnay and Riesling. The 10 ha vineyard, predominantly planted to Pinot Noir, is now owned by Kylie and Andrew Cameron; the powerful, long-lived Pinots are supported by Chardonnay and Riesling.

Signature wine: Pinot Noir

Freycinet Est. 1980

15919 Tasman Hwy via Bicheno 7215
www.freycinetvineyard.com.au

🍷 exports to UK

The Bull family, headed by abalone licence holder Geoff Bull and daughter Lindy Bull, with partner Claudio Radenti in charge of winemaking, planted the original 9 ha vineyard in a unique amphitheatre, which acts as a heat trap. The soils are podsol and decaying granite with a friable clay subsoil, and the combination of aspect, slope and heat summation produces stunning Pinot Noir of unusual depth of colour and ripe flavours, while also producing top-quality Riesling. The wines are made at the on-site winery, and are exported under the Spyglass Bay label.

Signature wine: Pinot Noir

Frogmore Creek Est. 1997

Brinktop Rd, Penna 7171
www.frogmorecreekvineyards.com

🍷 (at Wellington/Hood wines)

While still in its infancy, this is the only organically certified commercial vineyard in Tasmania, with plans to ultimately increase the area under vine to 80 ha from its present 28 ha, and with an on-site winery being constructed in three stages. When completed, Frogmore Creek will offer a visitor centre and cellar-door sales area; an environmental centre with walking trails and lakeside picnic areas; an organic garden; a restaurant, accommodation and event

facilities. It is the joint venture of Tony Scherer and Jack Kidwiler, with a long background of organic vegetable growing in California. Andrew Hood is winemaker, the Reserve Pinot Noir making its debut at the Tasmanian Wine Show, winning multiple trophies including Best Wine of Show.

Signature wine: Reserve Pinot Noir

Meadowbank Estate Est. 1974

699 Richmond Rd, Cambridge 7170
www.meadowbankwines.com.au

🍷 🍴 exports to UK

While always owned by the Ellis family, what was originally a diversification from farming (and opium poppy production) has now become the centre of the family business. Increased plantings are under contract to Hardys, and a most attractive new winery has replaced the originally converted shearing shed. There are extensive entertainment and function facilities capable of handling large numbers of visitors, and offering an ongoing arts and music program throughout the year; the restaurant is open seven days.

Signature wine: Grace Elizabeth Chardonnay

Moorilla Estate Est. 1958

655 Main Rd, Berriedale 7011
www.moorilla.com.au

🍷 🍴 exports to US

While founded two years after Providence, it was Moorilla Estate which first proved to a sceptical world that Tasmania was capable of producing wines of the highest quality. The property has long since passed from the ownership of the founding Alcorso family, although son Julian has a highly successful career as a contract winemaker. Wine quality continues to be unimpeachable, while the opening of the museum in the marvellous Alcorso house designed by Sir Roy Grounds adds even more attraction for visitors to the estate, a mere 15–20 minutes from Hobart. Five-star self-contained chalets are available, with a recently redesigned restaurant open for lunch seven days a week.

Signature wine: Claudio's Reserve Pinot Noir

No Regrets Vineyard Est. 2000

40 Dillons Hill Rd, Glaziers Bay 7109
(03) 6295 1509

Having sold Elsewhere Vineyard, Eric and Jette Phillips have planted a micro-vineyard almost next door, called No Regrets, an equally evocative name. They say this is their 'retirement' vineyard because they produce only one wine from the 1 ha of Pinot Noir. The first vintage came in 2003. The wines are also available most Saturdays at Hobart's Salamanca Market.

Signature wine: Pinot Noir

Spring Vale Vineyards Est. 1986

130 Spring Vale Rd, Cranbrook 7190
www.springvalewines.com

exports to UK

Rodney Lyne progressively established 1.5 ha each of Pinot Noir and Chardonnay and then added 0.5 ha each of Gewürztraminer and Pinot Gris; the latter produced a first crop in 1998. The portfolio of wines ranges through varietal wines from each planting to late-harvest Louisa and Salute (sparkling). Frost has caused havoc from time to time, not only financially destructive, but also frustrating, for Spring Vale can, and does, produce first-class wines when the frost stays away.

Signature wine: Pinot Noir

[OPPOSITE LEFT] PETER ALTHAUS.
[OPPOSITE RIGHT] ANDREW HOOD.
[BELOW] RICHMOND, COAL RIVER VALLEY.

Stefano Lubiana Est. 1990

60 Rowbottoms Rd, Granton 7030
www.slw.com.au

The charming, self-effacing Steve Lubiana moved from one climatic extreme to the other when he left Lubiana Wines at Moorook in the South Australian Riverland to relocate at Granton. In the first ten years, contract winemaking (especially sparkling) was a major part of the business, but has since been scaled back significantly. The estate-produced Stefano Lubiana wines come from 14 ha of beautifully located vineyards sloping down to the Derwent River; the wines are immaculately crafted.

Signature wine: NV Brut

Wellington/Hood Wines

Est. 1990
Cnr Richmond & Denholms Rds,
Cambridge 7170
wellington@hoodwines.com

In late 2003 Wellington was acquired by Tony Scherer and Jack Kidwiler of Frogmore Creek. The Wellington winery continues to operate as previously, making both its own label wines and those of its contract customers, while a new winery is constructed on the Frogmore Creek property – the latter will be exclusively devoted to organically grown wines. Andrew Hood remains in charge of winemaking both at Wellington and at the new Frogmore Creek operation, with able support from executive winemakers Jeremy Dineen and Alain Rousseau.

Signature wine: Riesling

Queensland

N

0   100 KM

• Bundaberg

• Childers

Mundubbera •   • Gayndah

• **Hervey Bay**

• **Maryborough**

Romavilla •• Roma

SOUTH BURNETT   • Murgon

• **Gympie**

• Noosa Heads

SUNSHINE COAST & HINTERLANDS

• Miles

• Kingaroy

• Chinchilla

Nambour •

• **Maroochydore**

• Kilcoy

• **Caloundra**

Dalby •

DARLING DOWNS

• Crows Nest

• **Caboolture**

BRISBANE & SCENIC RIM

• Oakey

Toowoomba •

• Gatton

○ **BRISBANE**

• St George

GOLD COAST & HINTERLANDS

Boonah •   • Beaudesert

• **Surfers Paradise**

Warwick •

• Coolangatta

• Goondiwindi

NEW SOUTH WALES

Smithfield •

GRANITE BELT   • Stanthorpe

▭ WINE REGION

⬭ UNOFFICIAL WINE REGION

Lilyvale Wines •

Introduction ❧

The Queensland wine industry was growing faster – in terms of the numbers of producers – as at 2005 than any other state, albeit from a low base. In 2001 there were 39 wineries; by the end of 2004 there were 143. The annual crush has risen from 500 tonnes in 1998 to over 5000 tonnes in 2005.

Nor has the spread been confined to the two formally recognised regions, the Granite Belt and the South Burnett, with 48 and 16 producers respectively. In the Queensland Wine Industry Strategy released in December 2004 by the Minister for Wine (yes, there is such a person) six other regions (unofficial) were identified. They were Darling Downs (12 wineries), Gold Coast and Hinterland (15), Central Queensland/North Burnett (11), Sunshine Coast and Hinterland (15), Brisbane and Scenic Rim (10), D'Aguilar Ranges (five), and Western Downs including Maranoa (four). However, the major part of the total 1300 hectares of vineyards falls within the Granite Belt (400 hectares), South Burnett (300 hectares) and Darling Downs (100 hectares).

In the foreseeable future, only the Darling Downs would seem likely to be able to pass the threshold requirement – at least five separate vineyards producing at least 500 tonnes of grapes a year – for registration as a new Geographic Indication. It also happens to be Queensland's next logical area in which to grow grapes on a commercial scale (after the Granite Belt and South Burnett).

As in so many parts of Australia, there were significant wine grape and table grape plantings in Queensland by the middle of the nineteenth century; table grape production has continued as a profitable industry through to the present time, but wine grapes withered on the economic vine as first Federation (and the removal of tariffs) and then the First World War shifted the dynamics.

Whether the rate of growth in the first half of this decade can be maintained to 2010 is very doubtful; indeed, the medium-term question may be whether the present level of activity can be sustained. A tropical climate, with summer the wet season, winter the dry season, presents formidable challenges for viticulture. The Granite Belt is clearly the best region in Queensland, and can produce wines of international standard; South Burnett can do so in some vintages by some growers. The list doesn't necessarily stop there, but lifestyle tourism will be the key to the wine industry's survival and growth.

[PREVIOUS] ROBERT CHANNON WINES, GRANITE BELT. [BELOW] SIRROMET WINES, BRISBANE & SCENIC RIM.

QUEENSLAND
Granite Belt ❦

In 1965 the first wine grapes were planted in the Granite Belt: one hectare of Shiraz. It was an appropriate choice because this variety outshone all others (with the possible exception of Semillon) over the next 25 years. It was not long before others followed suit. Toowoomba solicitor John Robinson and wife Heather established Robinsons Family Vineyards in 1969, while the following year third-generation farmer Angelo Puglisi commenced what was initially called Sundown Valley Vineyards but is now called Ballandean Estate.

The Granite Belt is an interesting region. It owes much to the late Sydney-based wine consultant John Stanford, who became involved in the early 1970s, and was something of a Messiah for its potential. Angelo Puglisi, too, gained recognition for the district when he was awarded a Churchill Fellowship in 1977 to study European winemaking techniques (an honour also accorded to his then winemaker, Rodney Hooper, a decade later).

But the Granite Belt's prosperity hinges to a large degree on the parochial Queensland market and on the steady flow of tourists passing up and down the New England Highway. For although many of the local vignerons would have it otherwise, the Granite Belt is no more a 'natural' grapegrowing region than is the Hunter Valley.

The principal drawbacks are spring frosts and vintage-time rainfall. True, these do not occur every year, and appropriate site selection can significantly reduce the risk of frost. But then there is the vexed question of the climate, and how one really assesses a high-altitude region with a continental climate. Finally, there are the variable soils, some far too sandy and granitic, others much better suited to viticulture – a distinction ignored in some of the plantings made in the 1970s.

It took a long time, but by the start of the new millennium the region had proved it was and is capable of producing grapes and wines of high quality, judged by any standards. Excuses and/or reliance on the tourist trade were no longer necessary; success in national wine shows against all comers, and national distribution, are objective proof of quality. Two small wineries (Boireann and Robert Channon) and two larger wineries (Ballandean Estate and Sirromet, the last situated on the coast but with its 100 hectares of estate vineyards in the Granite Belt) have been chiefly (though not exclusively) responsible for the transformation.

The Granite Belt is the northernmost extension of the New England Tableland – and is a massive granite protrusion approximately 200 million years old. The hardness of the rock has guaranteed that this landscape stands out above the surrounding country (600 to 1000 metres). The most spectacular scenery is in the southern end of the Granite Belt where streams have dissected the rock to produce dramatic boulder-strewn landscapes. It is certainly worth a detour; indeed, it is worth a single-purpose trip.

GRANITE BELT

Latitude **28°40'S**

Altitude **810 m**

Heat degree days **1602**

Growing season rainfall **519 mm**

Mean January temp. **20.6°C**

Harvest **End February to mid April**

Chief viticultural hazard **Spring frost**

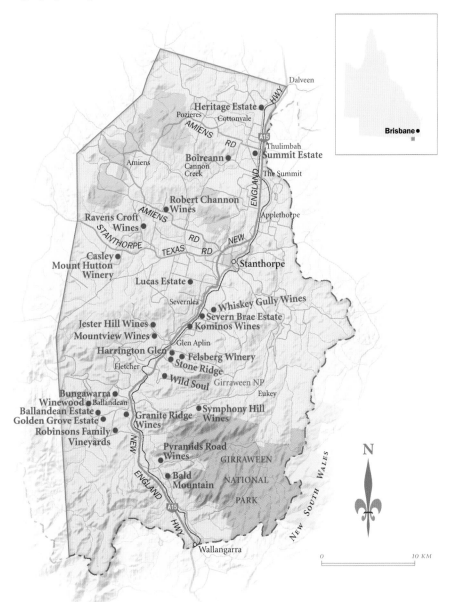

The Region

CLIMATE

The climate of a region such as the Granite Belt is not easy to pigeonhole. Because vintage is relatively late, and because it is fashionable to say so, there are those who categorise this as a cool-climate region. Location and altitude give it a continental climate, with a late budburst, and nights which are often cold. It is the only continental climate in Australia with dominant summer rainfall, over two-thirds of the total.

SOIL & TOPOGRAPHY

The two principal soil types are different from those encountered in most Australian wine regions. One is a highly permeable, speckled (from granite) sandy, grey-black soil, the other a light brownish-grey soil, also speckled; the subsoils are a bleached sand passing into clay at depth. Their drainage is good, but this increases the need for irrigation.

PRINCIPAL GRAPE VARIETIES

Overall, 55 per cent red and 45 per cent white. In descending order:

SHIRAZ

CABERNET SAUVIGNON

CHARDONNAY

SEMILLON

MERLOT

SAUVIGNON BLANC

VERDELHO.

WHITE WINE STYLES

Semillon. Echoes of the Hunter Valley appear in the Semillons of the region, wines which grow gracefully in bottle for five years or more. Early in its life, Semillon can exhibit striking tropical fruit characters (possibly botrytis-influenced) but with age, classic honeyed/toasty characters emerge.

Chardonnay performs well, as it usually does, adapting to techniques ranging from unwooded to fully barrel fermented and matured.

Verdelho in the hands of the best makers delivers all one could ask for, with abundant tropical fruit.

🌱 RED WINE STYLES

Shiraz is the one consistently distinctive wine style of the region: dark in colour; strong in body, flavour and tannins; and above all else, redolent of spice when young, but developing soft, sweet velvety fruit with time in bottle, reminiscent of Shiraz from the Hunter Valley.

Cabernet Sauvignon is full, dark and rich in flavour – at times perhaps rather too much so, but arguably too much is better than too little. Cassis/red berry/sweet fruit flavours predominate, attesting to the warm growing conditions, and the often warm vanillin oak. Increasing amounts of Merlot are adding interest.

[RIGHT] ANGELO PUGLISI, BALLANDEAN ESTATE, GRANITE BELT.

Wineries of Granite Belt

Bald Mountain Est. 1985

Hickling Lane, Wallangarra 4383
(07) 4684 3184

Former oil executive Denis Parsons is a self-taught but exceptionally competent vigneron who turned the 7 ha Bald Mountain vineyard into a viticultural showpiece in the early days of the Granite Belt. The two Sauvignon Blanc-based wines, Classic Queenslander and the occasional non-vintage Late Harvest Sauvignon Blanc, are interesting alternatives to the mainstream wines, all contract-made offsite. Increasing quantities of grapes are coming from new vineyards near Tenterfield just across the border in New South Wales.

Signature wine: Reserve Chardonnay

Ballandean Estate Est. 1970

Sundown Rd, Ballandean 4382
www.ballandeanestate.com

exports to UK

Churchill Fellowship winner Angelo Puglisi is the very friendly and boisterous godfather of the Queensland wine industry, and has steadily built a highly successful business, while over the years he has employed and trained some highly talented winemakers. The former Ballandean Estate now has two vineyards, both of 20 ha, one at Ballandean, and one at Bellevue. The white wines are of diverse but interesting styles, the red wines smooth and well made. The estate specialty is the Sylvaner Late Harvest, a wine of great character and flavour if given ten years' bottle age, but it isn't made every year.

Signature wine: Late Harvest Sylvaner

Boireann Est. 1998

Donnellys Castle Rd, The Summit 4377
(07) 4683 2194

Peter and Therese Stark have a 10 ha property set amongst the great granite boulders and trees which are so much part of the Granite Belt. They have established 0.6 ha of vines planted to no less than 11 varieties, including the four varieties which go to make a Bordeaux-blend; Grenache and Mourvèdre provide a Rhône blend, and there will also be a straight Merlot. Tannat (French) and Barbera and Nebbiolo (Italian) make up the viticultural League of Nations. Peter Stark is a winemaker of exceptional talent, producing cameo amounts of red wines which are quite beautifully made and of a quality equal to Australia's best.

Signature wine: Shiraz Viognier

Golden Grove Estate Est. 1946

Sundown Rd, Ballandean 4382
goldengrove@halenet.com.au

Golden Grove Estate was established by Mario and Sebastiana Costanzo in 1946, producing stonefruits and table grapes for the fresh fruit market. Shiraz was planted in 1972, but it was not until 1985, when ownership passed to son Sam Costanzo and wife Grace, that the primary focus of the property started to change. In 1993 Chardonnay and Merlot joined the Shiraz, followed by Cabernet Sauvignon, Sauvignon Blanc and Semillon. Wine quality has steadily improved, with medals in regional shows leading to national (though limited) retail distribution.

Signature wine: Cabernet Merlot

Heritage Estate Est. 1993

Granite Belt Drive, Cottonvale 4375
www.heritagewines.com.au

Bryce and Paddy Kassulke operate this very successful winery, with many awards in recent years. The estate plantings, established in 1993, comprise Chardonnay (2.5 ha), Merlot (1 ha), Shiraz (0.4 ha) and Cabernet Sauvignon (0.1 ha). Heritage Estate also showcases its wines through its cellar door at Mount Tambourine in an old church converted into a tasting and sales area, with views over the Gold Coast hinterland, also incorporating a restaurant, barbecue area and art gallery. The quality of the wines has been very reliable, in the top ten of the now numerous Queensland wineries.

Signature wine: Private Reserve Merlot

Kominos Wines Est. 1976

New England Hwy, Severnlea 4352
www.kominoswines.com

exports to US

Tony Comino is a dedicated viticulturist and winemaker, following his father by guarding all the things Kominos Wines stands for: estate-grown grapes and unostentatious winemaking techniques. He is particularly proud of the fact that all the grapes are hand-picked, and that all the wines are made and bottled at the estate winery. The portfolio is in fact wide, embracing Semillon, Sauvignon Blanc, Sauvignon Semillon, Chenin Blanc Semillon Sauvignon Blanc, Chardonnay, Vin Doux, Nouvelle, Shiraz, Shiraz Cabernet, Merlot, Cabernet Franc and Cabernet Sauvignon.

Signature wine: Merlot

Robert Channon Wines Est. 1998

Bradley Lane, Stanthorpe 4380
www.robertchannonwines.com

Peggy and Robert Channon (the latter an English-trained corporate lawyer) have established 1.6 ha each of Chardonnay, Merlot and Cabernet Sauvignon, 2.4 ha of Chardonnay and just under 1 ha of Shiraz, all under permanent bird protection netting. While primarily aimed at excluding birds, this also protects the grapes against hail damage. Finally, there is no pressure to pick the grapes before they are fully ripe. The strategy has provided ample rewards, with Verdelho of the highest quality and some very good Merlot and Shiraz Cabernet Sauvignon; these wines (made by South African-trained Mark Ravenscroft) have enjoyed exceptional show success.

Signature wine: Verdelho

Robinsons Family Vineyards
Est. 1969

Curtin Rd, Ballandean 4382
robinsonswines@halenet.com.au

One of the pioneers of the Granite Belt, with the second generation of the family Robinson (Craig as winemaker, Annie as viticulturist) now in control. One thing has not changed: the strongly held belief of the Robinsons that the Granite Belt should be regarded as a cool, rather than warm, climate. It is a tricky debate, because some climatic measurements point one way, others in the opposite direction. Embedded in all this are semantic arguments about the meaning of the words cool and warm. Suffice it to say that Chardonnay, Shiraz and Cabernet Sauvignon are the Robinsons' most successful wines.

Signature wine: Shiraz

Summit Estate Est. 1997

291 Granite Belt Drive, Thulimbah 4377
www.summitestate.com.au

Summit Estate is the public face of the Stanthorpe Wine Company, owned by a syndicate of ten professionals who work in Brisbane, but who share a love of wine. They operate the Stanthorpe Wine Centre, which offers wine education as well as selling wines from other makers in the region, and, of course, Summit Estate. The 17 ha vineyard is planted to Chardonnay, Marsanne, Pinot Noir, Shiraz, Merlot, Tempranillo, Petit Verdot and Cabernet Sauvignon, and they have set up a specialised winemaking facility, producing some of the better red wines from the Granite Belt.

Signature wine: Merlot Cabernet Shiraz

QUEENSLAND
South Burnett ✿

While the modern viticultural history of the South Burnett region dates back only to 1993, vines were first planted in the early 1900s, and wine for home consumption was made from some of these vines. Sue Crane's (of Crane Winery) great-grandfather planted Shiraz in 1898, the vineyard remaining in production until 1970. As in the Granite Belt, table grapes were used both for winemaking and eating, and a small table grape industry has continued in existence since that time.

The countryside is varied, with continually changing vistas overlooking valleys or up to mountains and hills. Rich, red soils in many places contrast with the vivid green of grapevines and native vegetation alike. This is sub-tropical Queensland, with rainfall spread throughout the year, in fact more falling in the growing season than in the mild winters.

The town of Kingaroy is the geographical centre of the region, which is basically defined by the Blackbutt, Brisbane and Coast Ranges in the east, the Great Divide to the south-west and west, and gently declines to the Central Burnett and Burnett River to the north. The Stuart and Booie Ranges run south to north through the centre of the South Burnett, with undulating, rolling landscape to the Stuart and Boyne river plain in the west and Barkers Creek in the east.

The majority of the wineries are clustered around Kingaroy (the most important town) or Murgon (to the north). So far the western half has no wineries. Vineyards compete with all manner of farms, from peanuts to orchards to pigs to grains and the remnants of once-dominant grazing. A feature of the region is the very large Bjelke-Peterson dam, used extensively for boating and fishing in the holiday seasons.

[OPPOSITE] BARAMBAH RIDGE, SOUTH BURNETT.

SOUTH BURNETT

Latitude **26˚00'S**

Altitude **300–600 m**

Heat degree days **2500**

Growing season rainfall **490 mm**

Mean January temp. **23.8˚C**

Harvest **End January to early March**

Chief viticultural hazard **Hail**

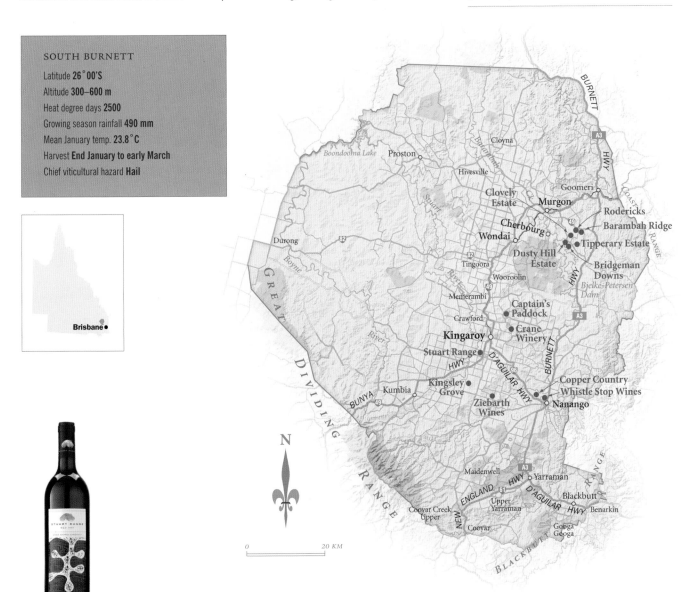

The Region

CLIMATE

The South Burnett is sub-tropical with long summers and mild winters. The hottest months are December and January. During an average year, there are only ten days where the temperature exceeds 32°C and one day when the temperature is over 38°C. So, while the area is hot, temperature variability is relatively low compared with other inland grape-growing regions. Temperatures are comparable throughout the region except for a minor effect of elevation.

SOIL & TOPOGRAPHY

The soils are principally basalt and granite-derived, with small areas of volcanic soils in northern parts of the region. At lower elevations sandy alluvial soils are common, and on slopes red soils of light clay, through to brown and black clay predominate. The red, brown and black soils are quite fertile, and controlling vine vigour becomes an issue.

PRINCIPAL GRAPE VARIETIES

Overall, 55 per cent red and 45 per cent white. In descending order:

SHIRAZ

CHARDONNAY

CABERNET SAUVIGNON

MERLOT

SEMILLON

VERDELHO.

 WHITE WINE STYLES

Chardonnay tends to be soft, but has pleasant and clear varietal character in a nectarine and melon spectrum; some highly competent winemaking has invested the better wines with good complexity and structure, but unwooded Chardonnay also works quite well.

Semillon style is better compared to that of the Upper Hunter Valley rather than the Lower. In other words, it mirrors some of the softness of the former region's Chardonnay, and is relatively quick developing. But it does provide distinctive varietal flavour, with some citrus and herb, and it is not surprising to find it in second place in the white wine plantings.

RED WINE STYLES

Shiraz produces wines which are smooth and supple, light- to medium-bodied, and with soft tannins. There are none of the spice and pepper notes sometimes evident in the Shiraz of the Granite Belt; instead there are ripe cherry, plum, mint and chocolate flavours present in varying degrees.

Cabernet Sauvignon and Merlot produce medium-bodied wines with soft, sweet berry flavours. As the vines age, more extract and structure can be expected when vintage conditions are favourable.

[RIGHT] END POST BUILT TO LAST.

Wineries of South Burnett

Barambah Ridge Est.1995
79 Goschnicks Rd, Redgate via Murgon 4605
www.barambahridge.com.au

Barambah Ridge, like Stuart Range, hit turbulent financial waters in 2004. Owned by an unlisted public company, it had an administrator appointed, and the 2005 vintage was made under the direction of leading wine consultancy business Winenet. Coupled with its high quality 7 ha vineyard (some regard it as the best in South Burnett) top-quality wines were made, but attempts to sell the business as a going concern failed, with a break up of the assets likely.
Signature wine: Chardonnay

Captain's Paddock Est.1995
18 Millers Rd, Kingaroy 4610
www.captainspaddock.com.au

Don and Judy McCallum planted the first hectare of vineyard in 1995, followed by a further 3 ha in 1996, focussing on Shiraz and Chardonnay. It was a family affair; the mudbrick cellar door building was made with bricks crafted by Don McCallum, and Judy's screen printing adorns the tables and chairs and printed linen for sale to the public. Their two children are both sculptors, with works on display at the winery. Meals are served either inside or alfresco in the courtyard, with its views over the Booie Ranges. It is business as usual under the new owners, Maryanne Pidock and Peter Eaton.
Signature wine: Double-Pruned Shiraz

Clovely Estate Est.1998
Steinhardts Rd, Moffatdale via Murgon 4605
www.clovely.com.au

exports to UK

Although a relative newcomer, Clovely Estate has the largest estate vineyards in Queensland, having established 174 ha of immaculately tended vines at two locations just to the east of Murgon in the Burnett Valley. There are 127 ha of red grapes (including 74 ha of Shiraz) and 47 ha of white grapes. The attractively packaged wines are sold in four tiers: Clovely Estate at the top end, and which will not be produced every year; Left Field, strongly fruity and designed to age; Fifth Row, for early drinking; and Queensland, primarily designed for the export market. A large winery has been established in an old but spacious dairy cooperative building in Murgon.
Signature wine: Estate Chardonnay

Crane Winery Est.1996
Haydens Rd, Kingaroy 4610
www.cranewines.com.au

Founded by John and Sue Crane, Crane Winery has 8 ha of estate plantings but also purchases grapes from 20 other growers in the region. Sue Crane's great-grandfather established a vineyard planted to shiraz 100 years ago (in 1898) and which remained in production until 1970. The vineyard was sold to Bernard and Judy Cooper on condition that John Crane made the 2005 vintage, and will be available to make the 2006 and 2007 wines.
Signature wine: Cabernet Sauvignon

Dusty Hill Estate Est.1996
Barambah Rd, Moffatdale via Murgon 4605
www.dustyhill.com.au

Joe Prendergast and family have established 6 ha of Shiraz, Cabernet Sauvignon, Verdelho, Semillon, Merlot and Black Muscat. The vines are crop-thinned to obtain maximum ripeness in the fruit and to maximise tannin extract, and wines such as Forbidden Shiraz show how beneficial the process can be. The winery's specialty is Dusty Rose, continuing a long tradition of rosé/Beaujolais-style wines from Queensland. The property also has a luxury B&B cottage with three queen-sized bedrooms which takes advantage of the 20 km of waterfront to Lake Barambah.
Signature wine: Dusty Rose

Stuart Range Est.1997
67 William St, Kingaroy 4610
www.stuartrange.com.au

Stuart Range has had a turbulent history since 1997, when a newly equipped winery was established in a large, old butter factory in Kingaroy. Seven growers with a total of 52 ha under vine were involved in the establishment of the business. Prior to the 2005 vintage an administrator was appointed, and ultimately the principal creditor, Graham Helmhold, purchased the business and assumed the role of winemaker. Part of the winery was also leased to Glastonbury Estate.
Signature wine: Goodger Shiraz

Ziebarth Wines Est.1998
Foleys Rd, Goodger 4610
www.ziebarthwines.com.au

The 4 ha vineyard (with 1 ha each of Semillon, Cabernet Sauvignon, Merlot and Chardonnay, together with 0.25 ha of Chambourcin) is a minor diversification on a substantial beef cattle property set on the edge of the Stuart Range, and which enjoys superb views. It is a small family operation with the aim of providing a wine experience for visitors, the wines being skilfully contract-made for owners Janet and Bernard Ziebarth.
Signature wine: Reserve Shiraz

QUEENSLAND

QUEENSLAND
Brisbane & Scenic Rim 🌿

Tourism, both general and lifestyle/food/ wine, is now and will remain the raison d'être for these (unofficial) regions and the vast majority of their wineries. But there are always exceptions to prove the rule, and so it is in the case of the Brisbane and Scenic Rim district.

Taking in, as it does, the Mount Cotton and Brisbane Valley areas, it encompasses Sirromet Wines at Mount Cotton and Warrego Wines at Marburg. Sirromet's location on the coast several hours drive distant from its 100 hectares of vineyards in the Granite

Belt, is neither accidental nor whimsical. This is Queensland's largest, most modern and best equipped winery, intent on making Queensland's best wines courtesy of a highly skilled and motivated winemaking team. But the wealthy owners, the Morris family, are very astute business people, and knew the high profile of the winery could not be achieved in the Granite Belt, so far from Brisbane, nor its restaurant be filled to capacity day in, day out.

If Sirromet has five bob each way, Warrego Wines at Marburg is primarily about the

business end of the industry. Also known as Marburg Custom Crush, it is the contract winemaking facility for scores of small Queensland wineries under the direction of Peter Scudamore-Smith MW. The reality is that the majority of wineries outside the Granite Belt and South Burnett are simply cellar-door facilities with token vineyards, the grapes coming from elsewhere (indeed, not necessarily from Queensland) and the wine made elsewhere.

Brisbane ●

Wineries of Brisbane & Scenic Rim

Sirromet Wines Est. 1998

850–938 Mount Cotton Rd,
Mount Cotton 4165
www.sirromet.com

🍷 🍴 exports to UK, US

This is an unambiguously ambitious venture, with the professed aim of creating Queensland's premier winery, and which has succeeded in doing just that. The Morris family retained a leading architect to design the striking state-of-the-art winery with an 80 000-case production capacity; the state's foremost viticultural consultant to plant the three major vineyards in the Granite Belt, which total 100 ha planted to 14 varieties; and the most skilled winemaker practising in Queensland, Adam Chapman, to head the winemaking team. Sirromet has a 200-seat restaurant and a wine club offering all sorts of benefits to its members; it is firmly

aimed at the domestic and international tourist market, taking advantage of its situation halfway between Brisbane and the Gold Coast. Both the consistency and quality of the wines are totally commendable.
Signature wine: Seven Scenes Shiraz

Warrego Wines Est. 2000

9 Seminary Rd, Marburg 4306
www.warregowines.com.au

🍷 🍴 exports to US

With a wine science degree from Charles Sturt University, Kevin Watson set about establishing the leading contract winemaking business in Queensland, attracting investment from the state government, local investors and China. Marburg Custom Crush, as that business is known, provides the winemaking facilities for all of the numerous local clients of Peter Scudamore-Smith

MW, who directs the winemaking activities. The 3000-case own-brand Warrego wines come from 0.5 ha of estate Chambourcin, the remainder from grapes purchased in various regions.
Signature wine: The Bacchae (Cabernet Shiraz)

Queensland
Sunshine Coast & Hinterland 🌿

The flavour of Queensland is encapsulated in the names of some of the 15 or so wineries in these localities, including the Little Morgue Winery at Yandina and Dingo Creek at South Gympie. Particularly in the hinterland, viticulture has proved viable, but the businesses are heavily dependent on tourists from the Sunshine Coast proper and from Brisbane. Both Glastonbury Estate and Settlers Rise, incidentally, employ the consulting winemaking services of Peter Scudamore-Smith MW.

Wineries of Sunshine Coast & Hinterland

Glastonbury Estate Wines

Est. 2001
Shop 4, 104 Memorial Drive, Eumundi 4562
www.glastonburyvineyard.com.au

Steve Davoren is building a combined real estate and vineyard development, with a strong tourism and lifestyle focus in the hills of Glastonbury, high up in the Sunshine Coast hinterland, 50 minutes from Noosa. Six and a half ha of Chardonnay, Merlot and Cabernet Sauvignon have been established on terraces cut into the hillsides, with further plantings underway.

Signature wine: Shiraz Cabernet

Settlers Rise Montville

Est. 1998
249 Western Ave, Montville 4560
www.settlersrise.com.au

Settlers Rise is located in the beautiful highlands of the Blackall Range, 75 minutes' drive north of Brisbane and 20 minutes from the Sunshine Coast. A little over 1 ha of Chardonnay, Verdelho, Shiraz and Cabernet Sauvignon has been planted at an elevation of 450 m on the deep basalt soils of the property. First settled in 1887, Montville has gradually become a tourist destination, with a substantial local arts and crafts industry and a flourishing bed and breakfast and lodge accommodation infrastructure.

Signature wine: Queensland Classic White

QUEENSLAND
Gold Coast & Hinterland

Arguably the most beautiful of the burgeoning areas, the Gold Coast and Hinterland takes in the rainforest beauty of Mount Tamborine, and the evergreen countryside of Albert River and Canungra. Mount Tamborine and Springbrook have slightly cooler climates, Albert River and Canungra Valley slightly warmer. As is the case with the other regions near Brisbane or the coast, winery restaurants and cafés abound, as do cheese platters, gourmet picnics and – above all else – distractions to keep children happily occupied while the business of wine tasting proceeds.

Wineries of Gold Coast & Hinterland

Albert River Wines Est. 1998

1–117 Mundoolun Connection Rd,
Tamborine 4270
www.albertriverwines.com.au

The proprietors are David and Janette Bladin, with a combined 30 years' experience in tourism and hospitality, who have acquired and relocated two of Queensland's most historic buildings, Tamborine House and Auchenflower House. The Bladins have established 10 ha of vineyards on the property, and have another 50 ha under contract. The perfectly restored buildings provide spacious and beautiful surroundings for the popular restaurant and cellar door, and much of the production is sold through these channels. The reliably good wines are made under the direction of Peter Scudamore-Smith MW.

Signature wine: Merlot

Canungra Valley Vineyards

Est. 1997
Lamington National Park Rd,
Canungra Valley 4275
www.canungravineyards.com.au

Situated in the hinterland of the Gold Coast, Canungra Valley Vineyards is clearly focussed on broad-based tourism. Eight ha of vines have been planted around the nineteenth-century homestead (relocated to the site from its original location in Warwick) but these provide only a small part of the wine offered for sale. In deference to the climate, 70 per cent of the estate plantings is Chambourcin, the rain- and mildew-resistant hybrid, the remainder being Semillon. Most of the wine sold is in fact made from purchased grapes.

Signature wine: Platypus Play
Unwooded Chardonnay

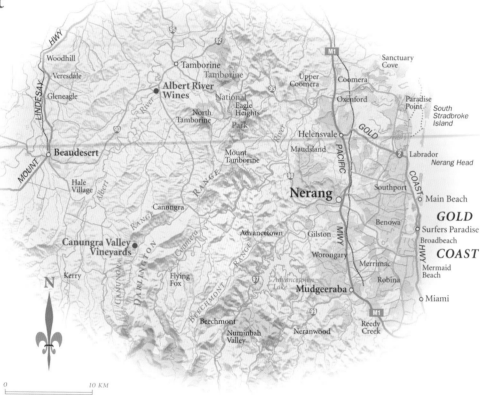

Roma

This exceptional outpost has been in continuous production since its only winery was established in 1863 under the grand name of 'The Romavilla Vineyards Ltd Wine Vaults', a reference to the fact that the cellars are at two underground levels, only the Madeira-style fortified wines being stored in the galvanised-iron building above ground. In its heyday it was a major undertaking, with 180 hectares of vineyards planted to varieties as rare as Solverino and Syrian.

Winery of Roma
Romavilla

Est. 1863
Northern Rd, Roma 4455
www.romavilla.com

A remote but historic relic, the winery largely untouched since its nineteenth-century prime, producing conventional table wines but still providing some extraordinary fortifieds, including a truly stylish Madeira made from Riesling and Syrian (the latter variety originating in Persia). David Wall has now been joined by son Richard in the business, which will hopefully ensure continuity for this important part of Australian wine history.

Signature wine: Rose Black Muscat

Queensland
Darling Downs 🌿

Centred around the town of Toowoomba, this has been a famous grazing and farming region for over 150 years. At the end of the nineteenth century wine production was a significant activity, but rapidly declined in the wake of Federation. Viticulture is arguably as well suited to this area as it is to the Granite Belt or South Burnett; this is reflected – perhaps – in the substantial size of the larger wine enterprises, although a number of smaller ventures happily co-exist. The absolute number of visitors may be less than that of either the Granite Belt or South Burnett, but the higher level of interest in wine is sufficient compensation.

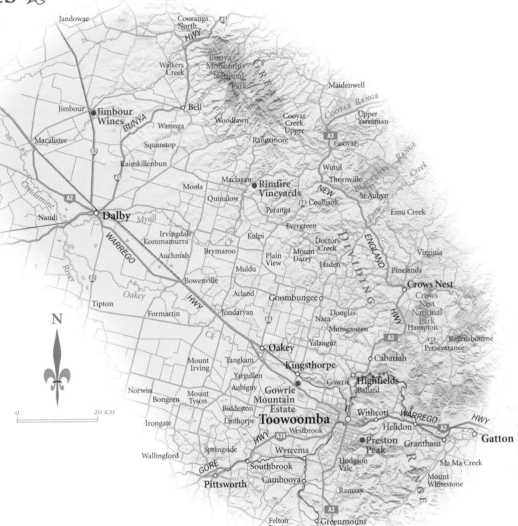

● Brisbane

Wineries of Darling Downs

Jimbour Wines Est. 2000

86 Jimbour Station, Jimbour 4406
www.jimbour.com

▣ exports to US

Jimbour Station was one of the first properties opened in the Darling Downs, the heritage-listed homestead having been built in 1876. The property has been owned by the Russell family since 1923, which has diversified by establishing a 22 ha vineyard and opening a cellar door on the property. Increasing production is an indication of its intention to become one of Queensland's major wine producers. Peter Scudamore-Smith MW is winemaker, but also provides marketing and financial advice to Jimbour, one of the state's most successful wine businesses.

Signature wine: Jimbour Station Shiraz

Preston Peak Est. 1994

31 Preston Peak Lane, Toowoomba 4352
www.prestonpeak.com

▣ ⑪

Dentist owners Ashley Smith and Kym Thumpkin had highly ambitious plans for Preston Peak when they established it in 1994. The reality of the marketplace, and in particular the rapid proliferation of competing wineries throughout Queensland, forced a major reappraisal. However, Preston Peak has a substantial tourism business, with a strong accent on functions. The property is situated less than ten minutes' drive from Toowoomba city centre, with views of Table Top Mountain, the Lockyer Valley and the Darling Downs. There is no charge for tastings, but bookings for groups of more than 20 people are appreciated.

Signature wine: Leaf Series
Cabernet Sauvignon Petit Verdot

Rimfire Vineyards Est. 1991

Bismarck St, Maclagan 4352
www.rimfirewinery.com.au

▣ ⑪

The Connellan family (parents Margaret and Tony and children Michelle, Peter and Louise) began planting the 12 ha, 14-variety Rimfire Vineyards in 1991 as a means of diversification of their large (1500 ha) cattle stud in the foothills of the Bunya Mountains, 45 minutes' drive north-west of Toowoomba. A kaleidoscopic array of wines, includes one simply called 1893, said to be made from a vine brought to the property by a German settler in about 1893. The original vineyard ceased production in the early 1900s, but a single vine remained, and DNA testing has established it does not correspond to any vine cultivar currently known in Australia. Rimfire propagated cuttings, and a small quantity is made each year.

Signature wine: Verdelho

Index

PHOTOGRAPHY CREDITS

James Halliday 61, 73, 82–3, 84, 86, 87, 93 (top left), 134, 142 (below), 147, 174, 209, 211, 245, 275, 288–9, 292, 296, 298.

Richard Humphrys ii, vi–vii, x–xi, xii, 7, 11 (right), 14, 15, 17, 18 (left), 22, 32, 33, 35 (left), 41, 42, 43, 60, 63 (above & right), 66, 68, 69, 74, 81, 96, 133, 170–1, 173, 175, 176, 177, 180, 181, 199 (below), 200, 207 (left), 208, 213, 240, 282, 292.

INTRODUCTORY PAGES
Trisha Garner v, 5; Sandalford 3; Shadowfax 6.

SOUTH AUSTRALIA
Nepenthe Vineyards 8–9, 11 (left), 26, 27, 29 (left & right), 30 (right); Penfolds Magill Estate 13 (left); Uleybury Wines/photographer Natalie Pipicella 13 (right); Penfolds 16, 20 (left), 21 (left); Yalumba 18 (right), 24 (left), 25 (left), 76 (right), 78 (below); Charles Melton/photographer Randy Larcombe 19 (top left); Dutschke Wines 19 (bottom right); Haan Wines 19 (top middle); Kaesler Wines 19 (bottom middle); Kalleske Wines/photographer Lorraine Kalleske 19 (right); Rockford/photographer Chris Goldspink 20 (middle); Seppelt 20 (right); Wolf Blass Visitor Centre 21 (right); Henschke 24 (right); Anvers/photographer Tony Lewis 30 (left); Geoff Weaver/photographer Milton Wordley 30 (middle); Shaw & Smith 31 (left); Setanta Wines 31 (right); Jim Barry Wines 34; Kilikanoon 35 (right), 36 (middle); Grosset 36 (left); Pikes 37; Hardy Wine Company 45 (left), 75, 76 (left), 78 (right), 79 (right); Foggo Wines/photographer Sandie Van Der Wiel 45 (right); d'Arenberg 46 (middle); Geoff Merrill Wines 46 (right); Rosemount Estate 47; Bremerton Wines 49, 50 (right); Ben Potts Wines 50 (left); Currency Creek Estate 53; The Islander Estate Vineyards/photographer Charmaine Grieger, 54, 55; Lindemans 59, 64 (right); Balnaves of Coonawarra/photographer Adam Bruzzone 64 (left); Zema Estate 65; Ralph Fowler Wines/photographer Adam Bruzzone 71; Angove's/photographer Kevin O'Daly, Aspect Photographics 79 (left).

VICTORIA
Coldstream Hills 85, 89, 91, 93 (right); Domaine Chandon 88; TarraWarra Estate/photographer John Gollings 92; Yering Station 93 (bottom left), 95; De Bortoli 94; Moorooduc Estate 97, 100 (top right/photographer Rebecca McIntyre); Ten Minutes by Tractor Wine Co. 98 (Skypics Peter Barker Photography), 101 (David Hannah Photography); Dromana Estate 100 (left); Port Phillip Estate/photographer Adrian Lander 100 (bottom right); Scotchmans Hill 102, 104; Shadowfax Vineyard and Winery 105; Curly Flat 107, 108 (bottom left); Hanging Rock Winery/photographer James Lauritz 108 (top left & right); Goona Warra Vineyard 110, 111; Maygars Hill 113 (top); BlackJack Vineyards 113 (bottom); Trisha Garner 115, 130, 131, 132, 139, 140 (above, left & right); Water Wheel 116 (left); Sandhurst Ridge/photographer Peter Wiseman 116 (right); Tallis Wines 119; Sugarloaf Creek Estate/photographer Andrew Deal 120; Redesdale Estate 123; Munari Wines 124; Elgo Estate/photographer David Hannah 127; Tallarook/photographer Robert Colvin 128; Cofield Wines 137 (left); Pizzini 141; Annapurna Estate 142 (above); North East Victoria Tourism 142 (below); Giaconda 145; Dalwhinnie 149, 155, 156 (right); Mount Langi Ghiran 151, 153 (right); Grampians Estate 152 (left & right); Taltarni/photographer Phil Weymouth 156 (left); Tarrington Vineyards/photographer Reimund Zunde Photography 158, 159 (right); Barretts Wines 159 (left); Ada River 162, 163; Murray Darling Collection 164, 166 (left); Zilzie Wines/photographer Evan Meads, Photo Media 166 (right); Bullers Beverford 168.
And a special thank you to Chrismont Wines v, 5, 115, 130, 131, 132, 139, 140 (above, left & right).

NEW SOUTH WALES
Capercaillie/photographer Paul Foley 182 (left) Chatto Wines 182 (top middle) De Iuliis 182 (below middle) Keith Tulloch Wine 182 (right) Thomas Wines 183 (left) Tyrrell's 183 (middle) James Estate 185 Jarretts of Orange 187 Frog Rock 189, 190 (left) Poet's Corner 190 (right) Brangayne of Orange 193 (top & bottom) Prince of Orange 194 (left & right) Cowra Estate 196 Trisha Garner 199 (above) Brindabella Hills 201, 204 (left) Mount Majura Vineyard 203 (left) Lark Hill 203 (right/photographer Sue Carpenter), 204 (right/photographer Ben MacMahon) Helm 204 (middle) Mundoonen 205 (left) Ravensworth 205 (right) Paterson's Gundagai Vineyard 207 (right) De Bortoli 214 (left & right), 217, 222 Coolangatta Estate 218/photographer Ross Pulsford Blue Metal Vineyard 220 De Bortoli 222 Kurrajong Downs 225 Canonbah Bridge 226 Red Earth Estate 227.

WESTERN AUSTRALIA
Willow Bridge Estate 228–9, 254; Voyager Estate/photographer Simon Westlake 232, 234, 239; Devil's Lair 233; Cape Mentelle 235, 237; Cullen/photographer Frances Andrijicho 238 (left); Leeuwin Estate 238 (right); Forest Hill Vineyard 241, 265 (left) (photographer Leon Bird); Ferngrove Vineyards 246; Mount Trio Vineyard 250; Hillbillé 253; Fonty's Pool 256; Sandalford 262, 263, 265, 267 (left & right); Faber Vineyard/photographer Melissa Ozich 266.

TASMANIA
Jansz 272–3; Pipers Brook Vineyard 277, 278, 279 (right), 281; Taltarni (Clover Hill)/photographer Emily White 279 (left); Hardy Wine Company 283, 287; Frogmore Creek 285, 286 (right); Domaine A 286 (left).

QUEENSLAND
Sirromet Wines 291; Ballandean Estate/photographer Paul Fuller, Malo Photographics 294.

University of California Press, one of the most distinguished university presses in the United States, enriches lives around the world by advancing scholarship in the humanities, social sciences, and natural sciences. Its activities are supported by the UC Press Foundation and by philanthropic contributions from individuals and institutions. For more information, visit www.ucpress.edu.

University of California Press
Berkeley and Los Angeles, California

First published in 2006 by Hardie Grant Books.

Hardie Grant Books
85 High Street
Prahran, Victoria 3181, Australia
www.hardiegrant.com.au

Cataloging-in-Publication Data for this title is on file with the Library of Congress.

ISBN-13: 978-0-520-25031-4 (cloth : alk. paper),
ISBN-10: 0-520-25031-1 (cloth : alk. paper)

Editor Clare Coney
Cover and text design Trisha Garner
Cartography Craig Molyneux, Cart Deco Cartographics and Bruce McGurty, Explore Australia Publishing Pty Ltd
Cover photography Trisha Garner at Chrismont Wines
Typography Set in Minion Pro and Adobe Jensen Pro
Printed and bound in China by SNP Leefung

The paper used in this publication meets the minimum requirements of ANSI/NISO Z39.48-1992 (1997) (*Permanence of Paper*).

Every effort has been made to incorporate up-to-date information, statistics and maps in this book. The publishers regret any errors or omissions and invite readers to contribute additional relevant information to University of California Press. Note that the representation of any road or track is not necessarily evidence of public right of way or safe travelling conditions.

15 14 13 12 11 10 09 08 07
10 9 8 7 6 5 4 3 2 1

ACKNOWLEDGEMENTS

There are many people without whose help and cooperation this *Atlas* could not have come into being. To name them all is impossible; Australia's winemakers have answered my questions for almost four decades, and continued to do so for the specific purposes of this *Atlas*. To all of them, my thanks.

The guardian of the gate is Ernie Sullivan, the Secretary of the Geographic Indications Committee. He has patiently dealt with queries and pleas for help from myself, the editorial team at Hardie Grant, and in particular its cartographic team. Thank you, Ernie.

Clare Coney has worked tirelessly for many months editing my manuscript. Her questions have saved me from myself on countless occasions, her corrections precise and to the point. Trisha Garner has done a superb job designing the book and dealing with text of constantly varying lengths, creating a seamless page-by-page flow. Jasmin Chua has coordinated many aspects of the book's production.

The maps have exceeded all my hopes and expectations. Here, too, painstaking double-checking of winery positions has paid handsome dividends, and not infrequently pointed out the error of my ways. Visually, the maps are wonderful. Here my thanks go to Craig Molyneux and Bruce McGurty.

Finally, and most importantly, is my heartfelt gratitude to Sandy Grant, whose immediate and continuing belief in this complex and expensive project allowed it to come to fruition.

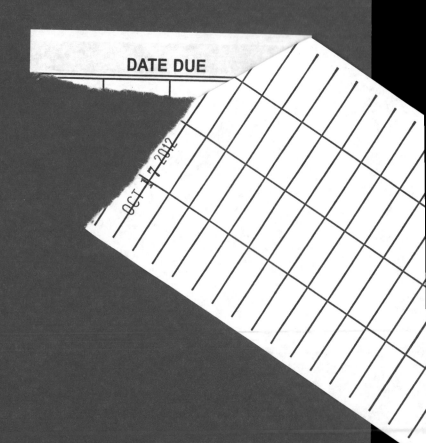